THE
DARKEST
SUMMER

PUSAN AND INCHON 1950:
THE BATTLES THAT SAVED SOUTH KOREA—
AND THE MARINES—FROM EXTINCTION

★ ★ ★

BILL SLOAN

SIMON & SCHUSTER

New York   London   Toronto   Sydney

Simon & Schuster
1230 Avenue of the Americas
New York, NY 10020

First Simon & Schuster hardcover edition November 2009

SIMON & SCHUSTER and colophon are registered trademarks of
Simon & Schuster, Inc.

For information about special discounts for bulk purchases,
please contact Simon & Schuster Special Sales at 1-866-506-1949 or
business@simonandschuster.com.

The Simon & Schuster Speakers Bureau can bring authors to your
live event. For more information or to book an event contact the
Simon & Schuster Speakers Bureau at 1-866-248-3049 or visit our
website at www.simonspeakers.com.

Designed by Dana Sloan
Maps by Jeff Ward
Illustration credits follow the Index.

Manufactured in the United States of America

10   9   8   7   6   5   4   3   2   1

Library of Congress Cataloging-in-Publication Data

Sloan, Bill.
   The darkest summer : Pusan and Inchon 1950 : the battles that saved
South Korea—and the Marines—from extinction / Bill Sloan. —
1st Simon & Schuster hardcover ed.
       p.   cm.
Includes bibliographical references and index.
   1. Korean War, 1950–1953—Campaigns—Korea (South)—Pusan
Region.   2. Inchon Landing, Inch'on, Korea, 1950.   3. United States.
Marine Corps—History—Korean War, 1950–1953.   4. Pusan Region
(Korea)—History, Military—20th century.   5. Inch'on (Korea)—History,
Military—20th century.   I. Title.
DS918.2.P87S56   2009
951.904'24—dc22   2009015329

ISBN 978-1-4165-7174-2
ISBN 978-1-4165-7593-1 (ebook)

To Alana Alyeene Henderson Sloan—
my anchor, my armor, my compass, and the love of my life.
Thanks for being there.

CONTENTS

THE
DARKEST
SUMMER

★ ★ ★

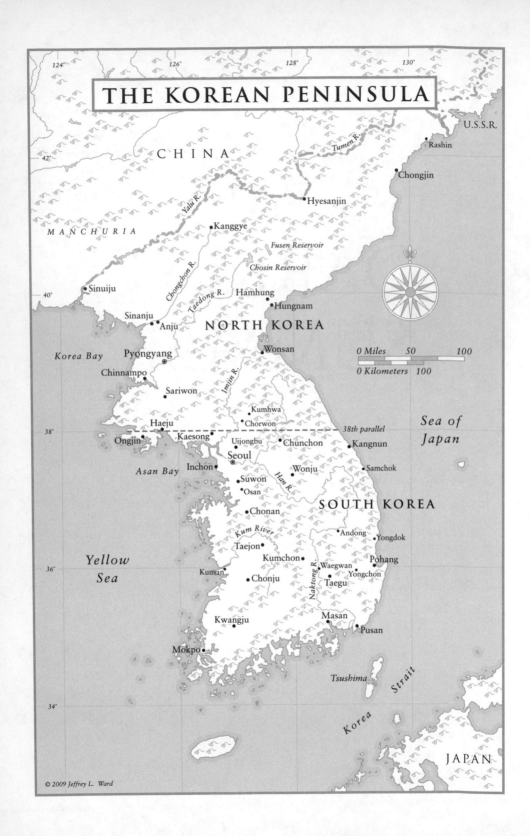

THE KOREAN PENINSULA

124° 126° 128° 130°

42°

Tumen R.

U.S.S.R.

CHINA

• Rashin

• Chongjin

• Hyesanjin

Yalu R.

• Kanggye

MANCHURIA

Fusen Reservoir

Chongchon R.

Chosin Reservoir

40°

• Sinuiju

Taedong R.

• Hamhung

Sinanju •

• Hungnam

• Anju

NORTH KOREA

Korea Bay

Pyongyang ⊛

• Wonsan

Imjin R.

Chinnampo •

• Sariwon

Kumhwa •

• Haeju

• Chorwon

38°

Ongjin •

Kaesong •

38th parallel

Uijongbu •

• Chunchon

• Kangnun

Sea of Japan

Seoul ⊛

Asan Bay

Inchon •

• Wonju

• Samchok

• Suwon

Han R.

• Osan

SOUTH KOREA

• Chonan

Kum River

• Andong

• Yongdok

Taejon •

Naktong R.

• Pohang

36°

• Kumchon

• Waegwan

• Yongchon

Yellow Sea

Kunsan •

• Chonju

• Taegu

• Kwangju

• Masan

Mokpo •

• Pusan

Tsushima

Korea Strait

34°

JAPAN

0 Miles   50   100

0 Kilometers   100

© 2009 Jeffrey L. Ward

CHAPTER 1

★ ★ ★

SUDDENLY, A NOT-SO-SUDDEN WAR

A s DARKNESS FELL on Saturday, June 24, 1950, it was "party time" in Seoul, capital of the fledgling Republic of South Korea. The afternoon had been oppressively hot and humid, but by dusk, storm clouds were gathering above the mountains to the north, and a celebratory mood, nurtured by hopes of rain, blossomed among the ancient city's 1.5 million residents.

A bountiful rice harvest depended on the torrential downpours of the summer monsoon season. Without them, famine would sweep like a plague across the Korean peninsula, one of the poorest and most primitive areas of Asia. The spring had been unseasonably dry, but now it appeared certain that the indispensable rains were on their way.

In anticipation, Republic of Korea Army headquarters had authorized fifteen-day leaves for thousands of enlisted men to allow them to help their families in the rice paddies. Many other troops in the ROK defensive force stationed at the 38th Parallel—the line, just over thirty-five miles north of Seoul, that divided South Korea and the Communist North—had been given the weekend off as a reward for serving through months of hostile

1

incidents and false alarms along the frontier. These were comforting, perhaps necessary, gestures toward the troops, but their effect was to leave fewer than a third of the 38,000-man ROK force assigned to border defense on duty at the parallel.

The Republic of Korea Army brass, meanwhile, were celebrating the opening of a new officers' club in Seoul, where they were joined by virtually all the American officers of the 500-member Korean Military Advisory Group (KMAG), charged with helping the ROKs achieve combat readiness. Later in the evening, the Americans would return the favor by hosting the South Koreans at the regular Saturday night dance at the lavish KMAG officers' open mess. Having completed his tour of duty, Brigadier General William L. Roberts, retiring commander of the KMAG, had sailed for the States that very afternoon. Otherwise, he doubtlessly would have been at the center of the festivities.

In embassy bars and other elite venues, the 2,000 members of the American diplomatic mission in Seoul also came out to play. Since the arrival of the first Americans in South Korea in 1945, the mission had grown into the largest such U.S. contingent in the world, but only a handful of the staff was involved in military matters. Most were there to support the struggling economic and political systems of a nation that, after generations of outside control, had virtually no experience in administering its own affairs.

The diplomats' cocktail conversations focused on the recent visit to Seoul and the 38th Parallel by John Foster Dulles, U.S. ambassador to the United Nations. They joked about Dulles's remarks on South Korea's progress toward "responsible representative government" and a "vitalized economy," both still distant goals. There was almost no mention of rice harvests or monsoons, much less the possibility of a North Korean invasion.

On the eve of his retirement as head of the KMAG, General Roberts had boasted in an interview with *Time* magazine of his group's success in molding the ROK military into a force capable of meeting any threat posed by the North Korean People's Army (NKPA). "The South Koreans have the best damn army outside the United States," Roberts had said flatly. He also maintained that tank warfare was impossible among the narrow roads and boggy rice paddies of Korea. His superiors in Washington and Tokyo took the general at his word, despite damning evidence to the contrary. He could not have been more wrong.

In terms of sheer numbers, the ROK Army was actually a bit larger than its northern counterpart, with total manpower of about 145,000—nearly 50 percent of whom would become casualties within the first six weeks of the war. It encompassed eight divisions, half of them clustered along the 38th Parallel or in the vicinity of Seoul, but most ROK infantry units were armed with nothing more formidable than M-1 rifles, light machine guns, and small-caliber mortars. Backing the infantry were five battalions of field artillery, but they were equipped only with obsolete, short-range 105-millimeter howitzers of a type the U.S. Army had scrapped several years earlier.

The ROKs didn't have a single tank or combat aircraft. They had no heavy artillery, large-bore 4.2-inch mortars, recoilless rifles for antitank warfare, or spare parts for their vehicles. Up-to-date weaponry had been withheld from the South Koreans on orders from Washington for fear that overzealous ROK officers might use it to attack North Korea. Nevertheless, U.S. Ambassador John Muccio's first secretary, Harold Noble, had confidently assured the powers at home that "The ROKs can not only stop an attack but move north and capture the Communist capital in two weeks."

Washington apparently took Noble at his word, and on this last night of peace on the Korean peninsula, almost no one in Washington was very interested in the ROK Army anyway. That was about to change with heart-stopping suddenness.

Steady rain began falling after midnight, saturating parched rice paddies across the countryside and gaining steadily in intensity until it was cascading down in endless sheets. Wet but happy workers sang in the early morning as they splashed across the bridge over the Han River, grateful for the reviving downpour. For American and ROK officers, soldiers on leave, and minor diplomats, the festive atmosphere began to fade. Last call came at the embassy bars and the KMAG officers' open mess, and weary or inebriated celebrants toddled off to their beds (or to someone else's).

What had been a fine night for a party became a fine predawn for a refreshing sleep. Soon, most of Seoul joined in, oblivious to what was happening just over thirty-five miles to the north.

Poised within a few dozen yards of the 38th Parallel on that rainy Sunday morning stood 90,000 North Korean troops—seven infantry divisions, plus another infantry regiment; an armored brigade; a motorcycle regiment; and a brigade of border guards. Despite their exceptionally large numbers, they were apparently unnoticed by the ROKs or the KMAG—possibly because the attention of the South Korean and American officers was focused elsewhere. The NKPA troops were supported by 150 Soviet T-34 medium tanks, 200 combat aircraft, numerous 122-millimeter howitzers, 76-millimeter self-propelled guns, and heavy mortars. They'd been standing by ever since Friday, June 23, awaiting final orders to invade South Korea at five key points along the frontier. Their officers were mostly young but experienced veterans of combat against the Japanese and the Chinese Nationalists, and now they were tense and eager as the moment neared to surge across the parallel. Three of the massed infantry divisions, led by tanks, would strike directly toward Seoul.

The smell of diesel fumes rose in the murky darkness as the Soviet T-34s began cranking their engines. They were heavily armored, battle-proven, and formidably armed, each mounting an 85-millimeter cannon and two heavy machine guns. These were the same kind of tanks that had halted the Nazi assault on Moscow, and they had been the standard of Soviet armored divisions ever since. There was nothing in the thinly manned, ill-equipped ROK lines to the south that could possibly slow them down, much less stop them.

Captain Joseph Darrigo, the only member of the Korean Military Advisory Group who hadn't joined the Saturday night revelry in Seoul—and therefore the lone remaining U.S. officer at the 38th Parallel on Sunday morning, June 25, 1950—awoke with a start at about 4:00 AM to the thunder of heavy artillery. Darrigo's housemate, Lieutenant William Hamilton, was spending the weekend in the capital city, along with the rest of the KMAG.

As Darrigo sat up in bed, listening intently, the young captain from Darien, Connecticut, felt very much alone.

At first, he thought the firing might be merely another in an ongoing series of border incidents involving rival patrols and gunners on opposite sides of the parallel; dozens of such incidents had flared along the frontier in recent weeks. But as the sounds intensified and the ground shuddered beneath the stone house where he and Hamilton were quartered, Darrigo realized he was witnessing something much larger—and ominously close.

Darrigo had been stationed at the parallel for six months, a near record for members of the high-turnover KMAG. During that time, he'd become increasingly convinced that the 135,000-man North Korean People's Army was planning a blatant attack on the South, aimed at reuniting the two Koreas by force. In Darrigo's mind, the only remaining question was *when* the NKPA would strike.

He bounded out of bed and grabbed his trousers, pulling them on as he raced outside for a better look and wondering, *Is this it? Is this the start of the war I've been expecting?*

The answer was soon obvious. Darrigo saw scores of artillery muzzle flashes reflecting off low-hanging clouds to the north. Even more alarming, he heard the distinctive clatter of automatic weapons fire nearby and getting closer. By the time he could run back to snatch up his shoes and shirt, jump into his jeep, and careen down a dusty road toward the town of Kaesong, a few hundred yards away, machine-gun and small-arms rounds were pinging off the stone walls of the house.

At a traffic circle in the center of the town, he jerked the jeep to a halt and stared in amazement as a train packed with a full regiment of North Korean infantry pulled into the railway station, and the soldiers poured off the cars and into the streets. They spotted Darrigo almost immediately, and it seemed to him as if every one of them began firing in his direction at once. With bullets whining past him, Darrigo floor-boarded the jeep and streaked south toward the headquarters compound of the ROK First Division to sound the alarm.

As far as can be documented today, Joe Darrigo had just become the only American military eyewitness to the invasion of South Korea by massive forces from the Communist North. He would always consider it a miracle that he survived to tell about it.

• • •

To Lieutenant Jin Hak Kim, a young officer of the ROK First Division, also stationed near Kaesong and a short distance from Captain Darrigo, the blitzkrieg-style attack by the NKPA seemed to come as abruptly as a flash of lightning. As he slept in a dugout carved into the side of a hill and topped with sandbags, the force of the first enemy shells knocked Jin out of his cot and sent dirt and debris pouring down on him.

"The war began with a sudden eruption of artillery fire," he recalled years later, "a barrage laid onto our lines all along our sector of the frontier. One minute there was rain and silence; the next, a hellish din and explosions all around us."

Jin struggled into his clothes and ran outside. The first thing he saw was one of his sergeants sprawled near the door of the dugout and groaning in agony. When the stunned lieutenant reached down and tried to move the wounded man out of his path, the sergeant's whole right arm fell off. "It had been severed near the shoulder," Jin said. "He groaned again and was dead."

Despite the shock felt by Jin and countless others, there was nothing sudden about the invasion. Storm clouds of war had been gathering over the Korean peninsula for well over a year, and Joe Darrigo was far from alone in expecting the Communist North to launch a full-scale assault against its southern neighbor.

Many other on-site observers had watched and listened uneasily for months as ominous warnings, bellicose threats, and border incursions by both sides inflamed relations between the two Koreas. In May 1949, ROK forces had been guilty of one of the most inflammatory border incidents when they crossed the parallel, advanced more than two miles into North Korea, and attacked several villages. By December 1949, the situation had deteriorated to the point that Major J. R. Ferguson, a British military attaché in Seoul, reported his grave concern to the Foreign Office in London.

"On the question of aggression by the North," Ferguson warned, "there can be no doubt whatever that their ultimate objective is to overrun the South; and I think in the long term there is no doubt that they will do so." He went on to add, however, that subversion by Communist sympathizers in the South seemed a likelier vehicle for a takeover than open aggression by the NKPA.

There were, in fact, many in the South who wished to unify Korea by embracing communism and joining the North, and they played a key role in laying the groundwork for the invasion through sabotage and harassing guerrilla actions. Simultaneously, the Soviet Union and the new Communist rulers of China, who had recently ousted Chiang Kai-shek's Nationalists from the Asian mainland, were also pouring military equipment and expertise into North Korea. The equipment was plainly offensive in nature, and 3,000 tough, seasoned Soviet officers were busily teaching the NKPA to use it to maximum advantage.

Only hours before the invasion, Captain Vyvyan Holt of the British Legation had advised British civilians to leave Seoul for safer areas to the south. For weeks, U.S. Intelligence had also heard, and duly reported, ongoing rumors of impending conflict, but Washington had paid little heed. High-ranking officials in the State Department—and the Truman administration in general—as well as top American military commanders in the Far East continued to turn blind eyes and deaf ears to increasingly volatile signals.

In his memoirs, published in 1956, Truman utilized the advantages of hindsight to excuse his administration's failure to heed those signals. He acknowledged receiving warnings from the Central Intelligence Agency throughout the spring of 1950 that North Korea might "attack at any time." But there was nothing in the information to provide any clue, Truman wrote, "as to whether an attack was certain or when it was likely to come." Furthermore, he added, Korea was merely one among "any number of other spots in the world" where the Soviets or their allies were capable of launching an attack.

Rather than reacting to increasingly obvious threats from the north by beefing up the ROK Army and U.S. combat forces in the region, Washington's major concern was that the South Korean military might itself resort to aggressive force. Published remarks such as those of the KMAG's General Roberts only added to this concern and reinforced the Pentagon's decision to withhold up-to-date weaponry from the ROK Army.

Hence, even if South Korea's border defense force had been at full strength, it would have been no match for the NKPA and its tanks. For the Soviets' part, they had scant reason to fear interference in Korea from the same U.S. government that had meekly stood by the previous year as Nationalist China, a principal American ally in World War II, was overrun by Mao Zedong's Communist armies.

The prevailing mood across the United States in the late spring of 1950 could be described as a mixture of smug indifference to tensions brewing in the Far East and determination not to allow any foreign disturbances to spoil the public's indulgence in peace, prosperity, and propagation. It had been five years since Americans had led the Allies to victory in World War II, the largest conflict in history; now, as citizens of the mightiest superpower ever created, they were intent on enjoying the fruits of peace.

The postwar "baby boom" was in full blossom. Young, growing families were tightly focused on obtaining new houses, new cars, new appliances, and other long-denied consumer goods. They were consumed with nest-building, child-raising, and "getting ahead." After a decade and a half of privation and sacrifice, America was experiencing its "best years." People in general had never felt freer or more optimistic about the future. The last thing on Earth they wanted to think about was another damn war.

The attitude on Capitol Hill closely mirrored the public mood. With the full approval of President Truman and much of Congress, Defense Secretary Louis Johnson was busily downsizing, and demoralizing, the U.S. military establishment with drastic budget cuts. Many political leaders—and even some generals and admirals—believed that America's clear superiority in nuclear weapons was enough to prevent any serious armed threat to U.S. power anywhere in the world.

America's vast conventional war machine and huge armies that had defeated the Nazis and Japanese in World War II were now considered obsolete relics of the past. The same military that had paid in blood for the Allied victory was now cast as a self-indulgent national villain, guilty of wanton waste and senseless duplication, and thus a deserving target of federal cost cutters.

In the transition to peace, significant reductions in military spending were, without question, amply justified. But Washington's budgetary axmen didn't stop with trimming the fat; they also hacked away dangerous amounts of muscle and bone. As a result, by June 1950, the nation's armed forces bore no resemblance to what they had been in September 1945. During that fifty-seven-month span, military manpower had shrunk to approximately 8.5 percent of its peak wartime strength, and most of what was left was minimally trained, poorly conditioned, and meagerly equipped for conventional warfare.

Meanwhile, although the Soviet bloc had yet to confront U.S. arms directly, it had blatantly pursued a Cold War aimed at worldwide Communist domination, repeatedly challenging American resolve around the globe. It had gobbled up Eastern Europe by force, tried to strangle West Berlin with a blockade, aided Communist rebels in Southeast Asia, and helped Mao's armies seize control of the Chinese mainland.

The official U.S. response to all this ranged from the nonconfrontational determination of the Berlin Airlift to the bland acceptance of Communist China. Dean Acheson, Truman's dovish secretary of state, insisted on a conciliatory policy toward the Red Chinese that included cutting off aid to Nationalist forces on Formosa. Members of the Senate's conservative "China lobby" were enraged, charging both Truman and Acheson with being "soft on communism," although they were unable to do anything of substance to toughen or alter the administration's position. They were less upset, however, in January 1950, when Acheson pointedly left Korea out of a projected American defense zone in the Far East.

The series of events that had led to the division of Korea at the close of World War II seemed at the time to occur haphazardly, almost by accident. But these events, which continue to impact international politics today, were actually products of a well-calculated land grab by an opportunistic Soviet Union and a marked lack of control or planning by an indifferent United States.

The shattering defeat of czarist Russia in its 1905 war with Japan had left a forty-year-old wound in Russian national pride that lingered long

after the czar had been overthrown and replaced by a Soviet Socialist regime. Among the territories lost in the Russo-Japanese War was the Korean peninsula, seized by Japan in 1910 and held until 1945 as a captive
nation in which every facet of Korean industry, agriculture, government,
and society had been ruled by the Japanese for the sole benefit of Japan.
Now the Soviets wanted those lands back, and Korea, lying at the center of
a "strategic triangle" bordered by China, Japan, and Russia, was the major
prize at stake.

Throughout its history, Korea (or Chosen, as it was known under Japanese rule) had never enjoyed true independence or self-rule because it was
always dominated by one of its powerful neighbors. China had held sway
on the peninsula from ancient times until 1895, when Japan wrested Korea
away. But the very next year, intervention by several European powers and
an alliance between Russia and China had forced the Japanese out and
given the Russians control of Korea through a long-term "lease." Less than
a decade later, however, Japan's victory in the Russo-Japanese War had nullified that arrangement.

In the late summer of 1945, the Soviets saw a golden opportunity to regain control of Korea—and this time they intended for the lease to be permanent.

Two days after an American atomic bomb incinerated Hiroshima, the Soviets knew the time was ripe to make a last-minute entry into the Pacific
conflict. By declaring war against Japan on August 8, 1945, the U.S.S.R.
tacitly fulfilled a pledge made months earlier by Joseph Stalin to President
Franklin Roosevelt at the Yalta Conference. At the same time, with a notable absence of forethought, the Americans had agreed that the Soviets
would be allowed to accept the surrender of Japanese troops in the northern part of Korea while U.S. forces did the same in the South. From the
seeds planted by this arrangement, massive armed conflict would erupt on
the Korean peninsula less than five years later.

If the Kremlin's declaration of war on Japan had come three or four
months earlier, when U.S. troops were caught up in the bloodbath at Okinawa, it might have materially hastened the end of hostilities. But as it was,

the Soviet declaration was of no military value to the United States. The "war" between the U.S.S.R. and Japan lasted exactly one week.

On August 11, a second U.S. atomic bomb devastated Nagasaki, and four days later, Emperor Hirohito told his countrymen by radio that Japan had accepted Allied surrender terms. At that point, thousands of Red Army troops were poised just across the Korean border in Manchuria and ready to claim whatever share of the victors' spoils might be available.

Until a few days before the Pacific war ended, the Pentagon had shown little or no long-range strategic interest in Korea, and few Americans knew—or cared—anything about the little-known land. During the Soviets' rapid, almost unopposed advance through Manchuria in the final days of the war, however, U.S. military leaders belatedly decided that America needed to retain a sizable stake in postwar Korea. Their reasoning was based less on any strategic value attached to the Korean peninsula than on a desire to test the intentions of the Soviets in the Far East. The Americans suggested that the 38th Parallel become the informal boundary line of the moment between the U.S. and Soviet occupation zones, despite the fact that the Red Army was clearly in a position to occupy all of Korea, if it chose, before U.S. occupation forces could reach the country in strength. To Washington's relief, Moscow accepted the line without hesitation. One key reason may have been that Stalin was aiming for bigger game—namely a Soviet-controlled sector of Japan proper, similar to the one held by the Red Army in Germany, but Truman refused even to discuss such an arrangement.

At any rate, by September 8, 1945, when the first token American military unit landed at the Korean port of Inchon, Soviet troops had been encamped at the 38th Parallel for several weeks. A few Red Army units had temporarily moved farther south, toward Seoul, but when they were informed of the approved demarcation line, they hastily—and quietly—withdrew.

In this period of preliminary sparring leading up to the Cold War, Washington was anxious to see how Moscow would react if some sort of permanent and binding limits were set on Soviet territorial claims. Consequently, on the night of November 10, 1945, a coordinating committee composed of representatives from the State, War, and Navy departments hastily designated the 38th Parallel as the formal dividing line between the Soviet and American sectors of control. The parallel, which ran across the middle of the Korean peninsula, dividing it into approximately equal halves (although the North contains some 8,500 more square miles of space than the South), seemed the most logical point of demarcation.

At first there was concern that the Soviets wouldn't agree. A young Army colonel named Dean Rusk, a future secretary of state and one of two committee members who initially recommended the 38th Parallel, worried that the line was too far north for the American military to enforce. But at the same time, Rusk said he "felt it important" to include Seoul, as the capital of Korea, in the area of American responsibility.

There was also concern among American diplomats that the Soviets might balk because most of Korea's light industry and best farmland lay within the proposed U.S. zone, and the population of the South was more than double that of the North (21 million to 9 million).

Even before the end of World War II, Rusk and others in the War Department had expressed concern about Soviet territorial ambitions in Asia, warning that Korea might offer "a tempting opportunity" for the Soviets to acquire ice-free ports and strengthen their economic resources in the Far East. In this case, however, the Soviets readily acquiesced.

As British historian Max Wells would observe some three decades later, "To neither side, at this period, did the peninsula seem to possess any inherent value, except as a testing ground for mutual intentions. The struggle for political control of China herself was beginning in earnest. Beside the fates and boundaries of great nations that were now being decided, Korea counted for little. Stalin was content to settle for half."

The Soviets weren't nearly so charitable in Eastern Europe, where they focused their attention for the next few years on welding together the Iron Curtain. In North Korea, they simply installed a native Marxist named Kim Il Sung as their surrogate head of state and made liberal use of their armaments and expertise to build a formidable army to support Kim.

Below the parallel, meanwhile, Major General John R. Hodge, who had commanded the Army's XXIV Corps in the Battle of Okinawa, was welcomed to Seoul by wildly cheering crowds. Hodge's orders from Washington were to treat the Koreans as a "liberated people" and help create a government "in harmony with U.S. policies."

Hodge had proved to be a tough, courageous battle commander, but he was, in the words of one historian, "a tactless man unsuited to any diplomacy beyond the barracks level." He committed a crucial blunder on the first day of the American occupation by allowing Japanese police in Korea to remain armed and in charge of maintaining order. Many Koreans who had cheered the Americans' arrival a short time earlier now joined mobs of rioters in the streets to protest Hodge's action.

Hodge himself seemed unconcerned. Far from viewing the Koreans as a "liberated people," he classified them as "the same breed of cat" as the Japanese and made it clear that he regarded them as conquered enemies. The Japanese police were disarmed and disbanded only after Army Chief of Staff General George C. Marshall ordered Hodge to do so and warned him to refrain from further insults to the Koreans, but the American occupation was off to a shaky start.

By December 1945, Hodge was so demoralized by the lack of stability and progress in Korea that he urged the U.S. Far East commander, General Douglas MacArthur (who forwarded Hodge's report to President Truman), to press for removal of all U.S. and Soviet troops. Hodge would remain in Korea as U.S. vice consul for four years, however, and his opinion of the Koreans never showed any signs of significant change during that period. Neither did the Koreans' opinion of him.

Admittedly, Hodge—who had no experience in governing civilians or trying to stabilize an economy, a society, and a political system in chaos—received little guidance from Washington, and few members of his staff even spoke Korean. Among his primary responsibilities was establishment of a police force that would form the nucleus of a South Korean military. It was a huge task at best, and one hampered at every turn by mutual distrust and inadequate communication between Americans and South Koreans.

Into this fractious atmosphere, in mid-October 1945, came Syngman Rhee, a fiery Korean anti-Communist who, as the war ended, had proclaimed himself head of an unrecognized "provisional Korean government" while living in exile in America. He was brought to Korea at the behest of

General MacArthur, who saw him as a leader who could rally widespread public support, and with the support of Chinese Nationalist leader Chiang Kai-shek and influential Korean exiles.

One of Rhee's major strengths in the beginning was that few Koreans knew very much about him. Most other prominent political figures in South Korea were stigmatized by a history of collaboration with the Japanese. Another strength was that the Americans, who were struggling to comprehend an alien culture and society, felt comfortable with Rhee. He spoke flawless English, was familiar with America and its institutions, and seemed an ideal father figure for South Korea despite his acerbic personality and uncompromising nationalism.

By 1948, Korea had become, in most surface respects, two separate nations, and the South seemed to be moving, albeit in fits and starts, toward something resembling independence. In May of that year, despite Communist terror tactics that left 100 people dead, nine-tenths of South Korea's registered voters went to the polls to elect Rhee the country's first president. By July, a constitution had been written and enacted.

From the beginning of his administration, Rhee's vehemence about uniting all of Korea under a democratic government and his castigation of his American sponsors for allowing the North to be controlled by the Soviets were major points of U.S. concern. The North Koreans also wanted the country united but under their own totalitarian regime, and toward that end, they had sent many saboteurs and collaborators into the South. For this reason, the idea of countrywide unification elections, proposed by some in the United Nations, had little appeal to Washington at this point.

What the Pentagon seemed to want more than anything else, once Rhee was installed in office, was disengagement. America's military leaders, increasingly pinched by ever-tightening budgets, began petitioning for withdrawal of the 40,000 U.S. occupation troops remaining in South Korea. Both the CIA and top State Department officials feared that without a significant ongoing American military presence to prop it up, the Rhee government couldn't survive, but the Pentagon was determined, and large-scale troop withdrawals began within weeks of Rhee's election.

By November 1948, amid a growing climate of violence and oppression by the government, Rhee tried to maintain control by imposing heavy restrictions on the Korean press and ordering the arrest of hundreds of citizens for political crimes. Kim Ku, widely regarded as Rhee's most creditable rival for the presidency, was assassinated the following June by suspected Rhee henchmen.

In stating the Pentagon's position, Undersecretary of the Army William H. Draper Jr. echoed the previously expressed sentiments of Secretary of State Acheson, describing Korea as of "little strategic interest" to the United States and emphasizing that the U.S. military withdrawal would be total. Leaving a reduced contingent of American troops in Korea—one small enough to be overwhelmed in a large-scale NKPA attack—would merely be inviting trouble, Draper contended. After months of study, the National Security Council agreed, expressing fear that if U.S. forces should be destroyed in Korea or forced to abandon the country in the face of an attack by the North, American prestige would be "seriously damaged."

Furthermore, Draper added—and this was the clincher—there was no money in the Army's budget for maintaining a substantial U.S. force in South Korea past early 1949.

Before the end of June 1948, the last U.S. occupation troops were gone from South Korea, leaving only the 500-member Korean Military Assistance Group to train the ROK Army. But since the Soviets had already removed all Red Army troops from the North, Washington turned a deaf ear to Rhee's demands for a larger continued U.S. military presence.

By any measure, the Soviets' unprecedented eagerness to rid Korea of all foreign troops should have been a clear indication of Moscow's belief that the North Korean People's Army was now potent enough not only to keep Premier Kim Il Sung in power but also to conquer South Korea all by itself. Still, U.S. disengagement from the South was now a fait accompli, and America's military leaders clearly had no intention of backtracking.

Five years after the end of World War II, Moscow's priorities had shifted dramatically. Eastern Europe was securely under the thumb of the Red Army and various Soviet puppet regimes, and Communist armies had completed the seizure of mainland China. Stalin was no longer content with half of anything.

North Korea had more than enough spies and saboteurs in the South to recognize the weaknesses and excesses that plagued the Rhee government. To the bitter disappointment of those who had backed Rhee to lead South Korea, the Korean people themselves developed a deep and growing distrust of their president and his rigid, totalitarian policies—and, by extension, for the Americans who had made it all possible.

Although Rhee clung ruthlessly to power, his steadily dwindling popularity was dramatically illustrated in May 1950 in elections for a new National Assembly. Right-wing candidates supported by Rhee won only 49 seats in the assembly—fewer than 30 percent—while independents and other parties captured 174.

"With the advantage of hindsight," wrote British historian Max Hastings, "it is evident that United States policy in postwar Korea was clumsy and ill-conceived. It reflected not only a lack of understanding, but a lack of interest in the country and its people beyond their potential as bricks in the wall against Communist aggression. This failure . . . lay close to the heart of the United States' difficulties not only with Korea, but also with China and subsequently with Vietnam."

In June 1950, when the target of Communist expansion became South Korea, it was merely the latest chapter in a long, repetitive story. The Soviets still weren't eager to challenge American arms directly, but based on past experience, Moscow and Peking had no reason to fear massive American intervention on the Korean peninsula. They assumed that the subjugation of the South would be completed in days. Meanwhile, they expected the United States to protest loudly to the United Nations, seek toothless UN resolutions condemning the attack, and perhaps threaten various empty economic sanctions. And that, they believed, would be the end of it.

This time they were wrong. This time Truman would make the strikingly bold decision to block further Communist expansion by committing U.S. ground forces to combat for the first time since VJ Day. But thanks to his own administration's relentless spree of cost-cutting, most of the troops at Truman's disposal were pathetically unprepared to fight in Korea or anyplace else.

"By June 1950, Harry Truman and Louis Johnson had all but wrecked the conventional military forces of the United States," charged historian Clay Blair. "The fault was Truman's alone."

By this point in his administration, however, there was no question that Truman possessed extraordinary inner resolve and a rare ability to make difficult decisions in times of crisis. To sidestep the need for congressional approval of U.S. military intervention in Korea, Truman refused to define the conflict as a "war." It was, he insisted, merely a "police action" taken under the auspices of the United Nations.

The bloody struggle to halt a Communist takeover of South Korea would eventually bring more than 1.3 million U.S. military personnel to Korea, claim more than 33,000 American lives, cost a total of 142,000 American combat casualties, and drag on for three years. It would cause the deaths of at least 1 million Koreans and untold thousands of Chinese. But it would never actually end the hostile stalemate between North and South. As this is written, no peace treaty has ever been signed between the belligerents, whose forces continue to face each other across a demilitarized no-man's-land where armed clashes still flare occasionally. In effect, the undeclared, not-so-sudden war that began in a divided Korea on June 25, 1950, continues today. Six full decades after Truman initiated his "police action," no permanent resolution is yet in sight.

These negatives notwithstanding, the Korean War could well have ended on a far more somber and damaging note for the United States. As the long, frenetic summer of 1950 unfolded, American forces' initial attempts to halt North Korea's aggression were both feeble and futile as the invaders swept south with impunity. But by the time that pivotal season faded into autumn, the war would see a stunning reversal of fortunes, one engineered by courageous U.S. Marines and Army GIs, who overcame seemingly hopeless odds to win the victories that saved South Korea from oblivion.

CHAPTER 2

★ ★ ★

AN ARMY IN DISARRAY

SHORTLY AFTER TEN o'clock on Saturday evening, June 24, 1950 (Sunday, June 25 in Korea), President Truman was relaxing in the library of his family home in Independence, Missouri, where he'd come for the weekend to attend to some pressing personal business. When the telephone rang and Truman lifted the receiver, he heard the distraught voice of Secretary of State Dean Acheson on the line.

"Mr. President, I have very serious news," Acheson said. "The North Koreans have invaded South Korea."

After Truman caught his breath, his first impulse was to return to Washington immediately, but Acheson persuaded him to wait until the next morning, when more detailed information would be available. In the meantime, Acheson would ask for an emergency meeting of the UN Security Council to condemn North Korea's aggression and demand a cease-fire. He would also alert the Joint Chiefs of Staff and the secretaries of the Army, Navy, and Air Force that Truman wanted to meet with them as soon as possible.

Back in the nation's capital the following day, Truman faced his top military advisers and digested their grim assessment that an all-out attack on South Korea was under way.

"I don't think the Russians are ready to start a war with us, Mr. President," said General Omar Bradley, chairman of the Joint Chiefs of Staff, who had returned a few hours earlier from a trip to the Far East with Defense Secretary Louis Johnson, "but they're obviously testing us. The line has to be drawn somewhere, and I think we ought to draw it now."

"I agree," Truman said. "The Russians are trying to get Korea by default. They're gambling that we're too afraid of starting a third world war to offer any resistance, but I think we're still holding the stronger hand—although it's hard to tell how much stronger."

Over the next two days, the situation deteriorated with sickening speed while UN demands for a cease-fire were ignored by the hard-charging North Koreans. On June 27, a message reached Truman's desk from General Douglas MacArthur, supreme commander of U.S. forces in the Far East, who had just returned from a flying visit to the battlefront near the city of Suwon. The message was rife with alarming information. Soviet-built tanks were entering the suburbs of Seoul. President Syngman Rhee and his government were fleeing south, to the city of Taegu. ROK units were in full retreat and "entirely incapable" of resisting an onrushing enemy supported by armor, artillery, and aircraft.

"The only assurance of holding the present line . . . is through the introduction of U.S. ground combat forces into the Korean battle area," MacArthur warned. "Unless provision is made for the full utilization of the Army-Navy-Air team in this shattered area, our mission will at best be needlessly costly in life, money, and prestige. At worst, it might even be doomed to failure."

MacArthur concluded by urging that a regimental combat team be rushed to Korea at the earliest possible moment, to be followed as soon as possible by two U.S. infantry divisions.

On that same day, Truman issued his first official public statement on the Korean crisis, which read in part, "The attack upon Korea makes it plain . . . that communism has passed beyond the use of subversion to conquer independent nations and will now use armed invasion and war."

In his memoirs, Truman would later add, "There was now no doubt! The Republic of Korea needed help at once if it was not to be overrun."

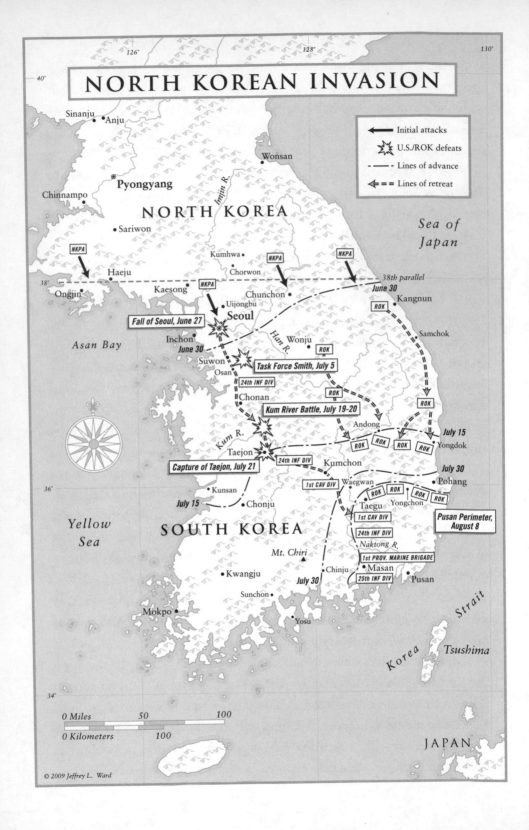

NORTH KOREAN INVASION

Initial attacks

U.S./ROK defeats

Lines of advance

Lines of retreat

Sinanju
Anju
Wonsan
Pyongyang
Chinnampo
Imjin R.
NORTH KOREA
Sea of Japan
Sariwon
Kumhwa
Chorwon
NKPA
NKPA
NKPA
Haeju
Kaesong
38th parallel
Ongjin
Chunchon
June 30
Kangnun
NKPA
Uijongbu
ROK
Seoul
Fall of Seoul, June 27
Samchok
Inchon
Wonju
June 30
Han R.
ROK
Asan Bay
Suwon
Task Force Smith, July 5
Osan
24th INF DIV
ROK
Chonan
Kum River Battle, July 19-20
ROK
Andong
ROK
Kum R.
Taejon
ROK ROK ROK ROK
July 15
Yongdok
Capture of Taejon, July 21
24th INF DIV
Kumchon
July 30
1st CAV DIV
Waegwan
Pohang
Kunsan
ROK ROK ROK ROK
July 15
Chonju
Taegu
Yongchon
Pusan Perimeter, August 8
SOUTH KOREA
1st CAV DIV
24th INF DIV
Mt. Chiri
Naktong R.
1st PROV. MARINE BRIGADE
Kwangju
Chinju
Masan
25th INF DIV
Pusan
Sunchon
July 30
Mokpo
Yellow Sea
Yosu
Korea Strait
Tsushima

0 Miles   50   100

0 Kilometers   100

JAPAN

© 2009 Jeffrey L. Ward

Finding that help, however, wouldn't be easy. Initially, Truman ordered all available U.S. air and naval forces in the area to provide whatever support they could to an ROK Army that seemed perilously close to disintegration. (MacArthur estimated that the ROKs had only about "25,000 effectives" remaining in the field, less than one-fifth of their preinvasion strength.) Getting the first American combat units on the ground in South Korea would take at least several days, and no amount of bold pronouncements could change that fact.

Even so, Truman politely declined Chinese Nationalist premier Chiang Kai-shek's offer to send 33,000 troops to Korea from Formosa if the United States could arrange transportation. After mulling it over, Truman decided that any potential benefit gained by accepting Chiang's proposal was heavily outweighed by the risk of drawing troops from mainland China into the Korean conflict.

Only as the full scope of America's deepening dilemma sank in on the president would he begin to realize how weak and ineffectual his "stronger hand" actually was.

Some of the gravest damage inflicted on U.S. military capabilities in the nation's history resulted from Truman's appointment in March 1950 of Louis Johnson to succeed James Forrestal as head of the recently created Department of Defense, which combined the old cabinet-level Departments of War and Navy.

A large, forceful, wealthy lawyer from West Virginia, Johnson already had a deserved reputation as a disruptive publicity hound. During World War II, he had been fired by President Roosevelt as an assistant secretary of war because of his self-serving meddling.

But Johnson had been a key supporter and fund-raiser for Truman during the 1948 presidential campaign, in which Truman was a heavy underdog. When Truman won, to the surprise of almost everyone, he returned Johnson's favor by naming him defense secretary, a job Johnson hoped to use as his own stepping-stone to the presidency. In the meantime, Johnson's main priorities were to slash military spending, make "heads roll" at the Pentagon, and help Truman realize an obsession to "unify" the Army, Navy,

Air Force, and Marines into a single, cut-rate military organization—a plan bitterly opposed by each service.

To Johnson, "unification" was synonymous with radical downsizing, and he set out to shrink the military by ruthlessly shutting off its funding. He pursued the task with tireless zeal and achieved what might best be termed a disastrous success. By June 1950, thanks to Truman, Johnson, and other budget cutters in Congress, total authorized manpower in the U.S. armed forces had plummeted from its 1945 high of more than 12 million personnel to just 1,070,000. During the same period, the annual defense budget had gone into free fall, plunging from $82 billion to $13 billion, with additional cuts anticipated at the time of the North Korean invasion.

While Johnson made political hay and received widespread public applause for these dramatic "savings" to American taxpayers, U.S. infantry divisions in the Far East were shorn of 62 percent of their firepower, and troops in Japan were left with barely a forty-five-day supply of ammunition. Virtually every Army regiment was reduced to only two battalions instead of the prescribed three, and every company lost one of its three authorized rifle platoons. Tanks and all other types of heavy equipment were in pathetically short supply, and often what *was* available was pathetically obsolete.

The dire lack of funds and equipment hovered like a vulture over the American military in the summer of 1950, and every member of every combat unit felt its impact. As young Second Lieutenant Addison Terry, an artillery forward observer with the Army's 27th "Wolfhound" Regiment of the 25th Infantry Division during the early fighting in Korea, would later muse:

"The jeep that my . . . party was assigned had come out of the ordnance depot in February 1942. This was the vehicle on which our lives depended day in and day out. The radio our party was carrying had come out of a depot in 1943. It was . . . declared obsolete and replaced in 1946 by . . . a more compact and efficient model. We had not seen any of these, however. Incidentally, in sixty-two days of combat, this particular radio worked for only one mission."

Whenever Terry thought of Secretary of Defense Johnson, he also thought of the ancient howitzers that his unit was forced to use; of the fact that the guns were truck-towed instead of self-propelled, like those of the NKPA; and of the myriad personnel problems facing the Army.

"Only six months ago," he observed, "many fine reserve officers had been relieved of active duty, not 'cutting an ounce of muscle, only the fat' (in Johnson's words). Yet at this very same time, of the four divisions in Japan, not a one was up to two-thirds strength. When we were ordered to Korea, it was necessary to rob [other divisions] to fill the 25th. . . .

"This was the 'powerful, well-equipped, well-trained, and well-manned Eighth Army,'" Terry added sarcastically, "of which our president, secretary of state, and secretary of defense were so proud and confident."

In light of such sad circumstances, Truman's decision to intervene in Korea with all available force and speed showed remarkable grit. Unfortunately, it also revealed the president's failure to grasp how incapable the financially starved U.S. Army was of expeditiously carrying out his commands. He was banking on the active involvement of armed forces from a dozen or more UN member nations to fill the gap, but this would take time that South Korea didn't have.

Truman had never risen above the rank of artillery captain during his Army service in World War I, yet he often claimed, in private conversations, to know more about military strategy than his "dumb, spendthrift" generals and admirals. In the years after World War II, historian Clay Blair observed, "Truman allowed his obsessive fiscal conservatism to dominate his military thinking and decisions."

To Truman's critics—and there were many—the attitudes and reactions of the nation's commander in chief remained those of a spiteful junior field officer whose view of the "big picture" was distorted by distrust and dislike of "brass hats." By some accounts, Truman delighted in putting his "spoiled, arrogant" admirals and generals in their place and keeping them there, a sentiment that figured strongly in his heavy-handed cuts in military funding. And in this effort, Defense Secretary Johnson was more than willing to serve as chief hatchet man.

T. R. Fehrenbach, an Army battalion commander in Korea and author of the 1963 book *This Kind of War: A Study in Unpreparedness*, described Johnson as "the most tragic figure" of the Korean War era. But Fehrenbach added pointedly, "When Louis Johnson began to cut the armed forces, it must be remembered [that] he was giving the bulk of the American public . . . precisely what it wanted."

Now, overnight and of urgent necessity, public priorities had to be set aside. On the afternoon of June 29, as chaos reigned across South Korea, the Joint Chiefs of Staff recommended unlimited retaliatory air and naval attacks against North Korean targets above the 38th Parallel. They also approved the immediate deployment of an Army regimental combat team (RCT), not to join the fighting north of the city of Suwon (a mere twenty-five miles due south of Seoul), as General MacArthur was urging, but to defend the vital port and airfield at Pusan, at the extreme southeastern tip of Korea, both of which were already in jeopardy.

In retrospect, MacArthur's idea that a single regimental combat team—with a strength of approximately 3,000 troops—could deploy and dig in in time to block the NKPA advance down the Suwon–Seoul corridor was pure fantasy. In the first place, even at this point, four and a half days into the war, it was already too late. By then, NKPA troops had crossed the Han River, occupied Seoul, and were driving south on Suwon. In the second place, no combat-ready RCT existed in or near Japan, and even if it had, no planes were immediately available to airlift it and its essential heavy equipment to Korea. The "chickens" hatched from the Truman-Johnson budget cuts were coming home to roost.

Nevertheless, Truman unhesitatingly approved the Joint Chiefs' recommendations. Fearing that the Korean invasion was merely one facet of a coordinated series of Soviet-directed acts of aggression in the Pacific and Asia, the president seemed almost as worried about Taiwan as he was about Korea. He ordered the U.S. Seventh Fleet into the Formosa Strait to serve as a buffer between Chiang's forces and those on the Communist mainland. In addition, Truman directed that U.S. forces in the Philippines be strengthened and that military help be sent to French forces fighting Marxist guerrillas in Indochina.

But how all these urgent strategic moves could be accomplished—short of sheer legerdemain—with the scant, scattered military resources at America's disposal remained a riddle. There were no easy solutions as Truman faced his greatest quandary since his decision to use the atomic bomb against Japan.

The closest available U.S. Army units to Korea were the 24th and 25th Infantry divisions and the First Cavalry Division (also an infantry outfit with a misleading name). All three were assigned to occupation duty in Japan, and most of their troops were about as far removed from combat readiness as soldiers on active duty could get. Their training for warfare had been minimal at best, and their assignment to leisurely duty with an occupation army in a generally docile defeated nation had left too many rank-and-file GIs soft, spoiled, and unfamiliar with either physical danger or hard work.

When an Associated Press correspondent interviewed some of the first Army troops of the 24th Infantry Division to reach Korea, he was stunned by their don't-give-a-damn attitude about the war. "I just want to get back to Japan to my little Sasebo Sadie," said one young PFC. "I got a place to live that beats the dump I lived in for fifteen years in Enid, Oklahoma. I get my meals cooked, my washing done, my socks mended, my orders obeyed like I was MacArthur myself, with no backtalk and all of everything a fellow wants, you know, and it all comes to $37 a month. I never had it so good."

All three divisions displayed a notable shortage of combat-tested junior officers and NCOs, and numerous squad and platoon leaders suffered from the same lack of energy, motivation, and toughness as the men they were supposed to command. Among the seasoned Army field commanders who recognized these problems and tried hard to correct them was Colonel John "Iron Mike" Michaelis. A twice-wounded veteran of D-day at Normandy and an alumnus of the 101st Airborne Division, Michaelis would later command the hard-fighting "Wolfhounds" of the 27th Infantry Regiment, and he pulled no punches about the Army's lack of combat readiness.

"In peacetime training, we've gone for too damn much folderol," Michaelis complained in an interview with the *Saturday Evening Post.* "We've put too much emphasis on information and education and not enough stress on rifle marksmanship, scouting, patrolling, and the organization of a defensive position. These kids of mine . . . spent a lot of time listening to lectures on the difference between communism and Americanism and not enough time crawling on their bellies . . . with live ammunition singing over them."

To compound the problem, the inexperienced young men from these occupation units labored under the smug misconception that troops of the NKPA would turn and flee north in terror at the first sight of uniformed American soldiers.

The attitude of Corporal Robert Fountain, a nineteen-year-old ex–Georgia farm boy now serving as a 24th Division rifleman, was typical. Before leaving Japan, Fountain had pegged the mission to Korea as a five-day job at most. He was so confident that he'd be back in time for a weekend liberty that he left nearly everything he owned—including his money—in his barracks.

"When the gooks hear who we are, they'll quit and go home," he told his squadmates with a grin.

Fountain and his buddies could not have been more mistaken. When the first U.S. Army troops were flown from Japan and thrown into the battle for South Korea—in pathetically small numbers—they learned the bitter truth. The NKPA attacked them with battle-toughened troops, superior firepower, and not the slightest hesitation. And the outgunned, outmanned Americans retreated before the enemy blitzkrieg in much the same haste and confusion as had the ROK Army before them.

At 9:00 PM on June 30, 1950, when the phone rang at Lieutenant Colonel Charles B. "Brad" Smith's home on the southernmost Japanese island of Kyushu, Smith was in such a deep slumber that his wife had to shake him awake. The officer had gone to bed early that evening to make up for lost sleep the night before when his unit, the First Battalion, 21st Infantry Regiment, 24th Infantry Division, had abruptly been placed on combat alert. It took his wife several seconds to make Smith understand that his regimental commander, Colonel Richard W. Stephens, was calling.

"It sounds urgent," she said.

Smith took the receiver from his wife's hand with a premonition of dread, and Stephens wasted no time in confirming it. "The lid's blown off, Brad," he said. "Get your clothes on, and get over to the CP as fast as you can."

Smith's wife frowned as he hung up the receiver, and he saw alarm in her eyes. "It's bad news, isn't it," she said. It was more a statement of fact than a question.

"I can't see how it could be anything else," Smith said.

A thirty-four-year-old career officer from Lambertville, New Jersey, Smith had seen his share of combat in World War II. As a second lieutenant less than two and a half years out of West Point, he'd commanded a company at Scofield Barracks in Hawaii when the Japanese attacked on December 7, 1941, and he'd spent the entire war as a front-line infantry officer in the Pacific. His commanding general at the time had praised him as a "bright officer" who showed "great promise."

At the regimental command post at Camp Wood on Kyushu, a short distance from Smith's home, Stephens didn't mince words. When he gave Smith the stunning news that he'd been chosen to lead the first U.S. ground troops into battle in Korea, the young battalion commander may have cringed inwardly, but he maintained an outward calm. Smith's B and C companies were ordered to grab their gear immediately and move out by truck before dawn for the seventy-five-mile trip to Itazuke Air Force Base on Kyushu, where planes were waiting to fly them to Korea.

Almost apologetically, Smith reminded his CO that several of his rifle platoons were shorthanded. "Borrow the men you need from the Third Battalion, and get ready to get on the road," Stephens replied.

"We'd celebrated payday night that Friday [June 30]," recalled Sergeant Phil Burke, a veteran NCO from Mississippi who'd carried a Browning automatic rifle into combat in the Philippines in 1944 but was now assigned as a corpsman in a medical platoon. "We'd hardly gotten to sleep when the call came to fall out. By about 2:00 AM on July 1, all thirty-one of us in the platoon were on our way."

By 3:00 AM, the departing troops were aboard trucks en route to the airfield, where Major General William F. Dean, commander of the 24th Division, would meet Colonel Smith to brief him on his mission. The orders given to Smith by Dean were terse, far from explicit, and not the least bit encouraging:

"We want to stop the North Koreans as far from Pusan as possible,"

Dean said, "so block the main road as far north as possible. Contact [Briga-dier] General [John H.] Church [head of the Army's advance party in Korea] if you can find him. If you can't find him, go on to Taejon and be-yond if you can get that far. Sorry I can't give you any more information. That's all I've got. Good luck, and God bless you and your men."

Dean's words conveyed the feeling to Smith that he and the 440 troops in his command were embarking on a suicide mission. Yet, as far-fetched as it seems, General MacArthur, who originated the order to send Smith's unit to Korea, had the loftiest of goals for the assignment. Presumably so did the planners who bestowed the overblown, almost ludicrous designation of "Task Force Smith" on the little group. Military brass hoped that the enemy would mistakenly identify the arrival of Smith's 440 GIs as—in MacArthur's terminology—an "arrogant display of strength" by the United States. Their ambition was to "fool" the NKPA into at least pausing in its headlong charge down the Korean peninsula until the rest of Dean's 24th Division, plus two other full U.S. infantry divisions, could be thrown into the fray.

At best, it was a long-shot gamble that defied all military logic. At worst, Smith and his men were heading into a death trap.

At Taejon, on July 2, Brad Smith had his first meeting with General Church, who had fumed a day or two earlier that he would willingly "trade the whole damned ROK Army for 100 New York policemen." The atmosphere was tense, but Church tried to be upbeat.

"We've got a little action going on up here," the general said, pointing out the village of Osan, some sixty-two miles north-northwest, on a wall map of Korea. "All we need is some men up there who won't run when they see tanks. We're going to move you up there to support the ROKs and give them some moral support."

Church must have known—or at least guessed—that this assessment wasn't quite as simple as he made it sound. As the members of Task Force Smith would soon learn, it was impossible to lend support to an ally you couldn't find.

While Smith's men traveled slowly north aboard a decrepit South Korean train, the young colonel and his staff piled into jeeps and drove up the main highway toward Osan in search of defensible high ground where their troops could make a stand. They found a promising spot about three miles north of the village, where a line of hills ran across the road, providing excellent visibility, protective cover for infantry, and good defensive positions for artillery.

For the troops, the trip north seemed to last forever—not that they were in any hurry to reach their destination. It took until Tuesday, July 4, for the train to arrive at Osan, where Smith's men were joined by a battery of 108 artillerymen and six 105-millimeter howitzers from the 52nd Field Artillery Battalion. The unit was commanded by Pennsylvania-born Lieutenant Colonel Miller O. Perry, a 1931 West Point graduate, who had trained Filipino artillery before the Pacific war broke out and later helped plan artillery support for the 1944 Normandy invasion.

By nightfall, the infantry had clambered aboard a collection of creaky, commandeered Korean buses and was ready to press on. But when the Korean drivers learned that they were expected to go north, they refused to budge.

"You Americans are stupid," one driver admonished Smith with the aid of an interpreter. "The war is that way," the driver said, gesturing north. "We must go the *other* way." Smith argued with the drivers. He alternately coaxed them and cursed them, but they were adamant. Finally, they all jumped out of their vehicles and disappeared into the darkness.

As soon as enough volunteer drivers could be found among the waiting GIs, the journey continued, but given a choice, many of Smith's men would have much preferred heading south with the departed Koreans. It wasn't that the young soldiers lacked confidence or that they were particularly afraid at this point. But they were what battalion-commander-turned-author T. R. Fehrenbach termed "the new breed of American regular." "[N]ot liking the service," Fehrenbach wrote, "[they] insisted, with public support, that the Army be made as much like civilian life and home as possible. Discipline had galled them, and their congressmen had seen to it that it did not become too onerous. They had grown fat. . . .

"It was not their fault that no one had told them that the real function of an army is to fight and that a soldier's destiny—which few escape—is to suffer, and if need be, to die."

Around midnight on July 4, Independence Day, Colonel Smith's infantrymen exited the buses and were loaded into trucks, still not knowing exactly where they were going or why. "All we were told," recalled Corporal Norman V. Fosness, a BAR man from Fargo, North Dakota, "was that we were going north to set up a roadblock, and we were to hold there until reinforcements showed up."

Nobody was even slightly optimistic about the assignment—and for good reason. Uneasiness spread through the ranks like a fast-moving infection as Fosness's First Platoon, B Company, awaited its first encounter with enemy invaders fresh from their conquest of Seoul.

Men who were normally lighthearted, upbeat, and good-humored were close to despair. Even Fosness's buddy PFC Vincent Vastano, known throughout the platoon as always good for a laugh, turned bitterly serious.

"Shit," he snapped as the trucks bounced along in the darkness, "by morning, the only thing left of this outfit will probably be a few handfuls of dog tags for the graves registration guys to pick up."

Across from Vastano, PFC Charles Hendrix sounded close to tears. "God, I wish I'd written my mother before we started out," he whispered to Fosness. "Now it's going to be too late."

Thus, in the predawn darkness of July 5, 1950, a few platoons of U.S. infantry and a handful of artillery troops crouched in newly dug foxholes and gun emplacements on hills overlooking a main north-south road about thirty miles south of the fallen capital city of Seoul. A few miles to their north lay the Suwon airfield, and in the opposite direction, the hamlet of Osan.

The Korean War was barely ten days old, and these soldiers were about to become the first American GIs to meet the onrushing and hitherto undefeated North Koreans in face-to-face combat.

Only five days removed from the leisurely "good life" of duty in Japan, where a six-bit carton of cigarettes from the PX would buy a weekend's worth of food, sake, and sexual favors, the men had been rushed to Korea aboard C-54 transports. Now they were cold, wet, disheveled, mosquito-bitten, confused, and exhausted from ninety-plus hours of stop-and-start travel by plane, train, truck, bus, and foot. Some were sick from drinking tainted local water, and all were repulsed by the pervasive stench of human excrement used to fertilize the ubiquitous Korean rice paddies.

There were exactly 548 Americans in this small, isolated band, including Brad Smith. For antitank firepower, they had Colonel Perry's lone battery of 105-millimeter howitzers, a couple of 75-millimeter recoilless rifle squads, a pair of 4.2-inch mortars, and a few handheld, small-caliber bazookas. One of the 105 crews had exactly six rounds of high-explosive antitank (HEAT) ammunition, constituting one-third of all that could be found in Japan before the artillery unit shipped out. The rest of the gunners had none at all.

"They looked like a bunch of Boy Scouts," said one American officer who watched the little group move out from Taejon toward what passed for a front. "I told Brad Smith, 'You're facing tried combat soldiers out there.' There was nothing he could answer."

This, then, was Task Force Smith, a few hundred men and a handful of officers under orders to halt—or at least slow down—the hordes of North Korean troops sweeping south toward them behind a phalanx of T-34 tanks.

The problem was, nobody had told them how.

The South Koreans hadn't been much help. Colonel Smith had been told that an ROK unit would meet his men on a designated hill to help them anchor a defensive line, but the hill was deserted when the GIs got there. Like the recalcitrant drivers at Osan, the ROKs had simply vanished.

Now, in the stark light of a new day, the men of Task Force Smith felt their optimism evaporating with the darkness. They fidgeted nervously along their thin, one-mile front, rubbing sleep from their eyes in a driving rain, pulling sodden uniforms away from their skin, and opening cans of cold C rations.

On a slight rise some 1,500 yards behind the dug-in infantry platoons, Colonel Perry's artillery battery had positioned five of its six 105-millimeter howitzers. The sixth gun, the one with the few available HEAT rounds, was pulled up only 400 yards behind the infantry units.

"We figured that the forward gun would have the best chance against enemy tanks," Perry recalled nearly fifty-eight years later. "We had only a half-dozen rounds capable of stopping them, and we wanted to make every shot count. The doughboys in the line had nothing that could slow a tank unless they managed to hit a tread."

Sergeant Burke, the medic from Mississippi, had laid out his field kit in a shallow depression to the rear of the infantry's foxholes, then caught a brief nap. When he awoke, dawn was beginning to filter through the leaden skies, but he felt little relief at being able to see his surroundings.

Colonel Smith himself was the first person to spot the enemy armored column—an indistinct gray mass still several miles up the road—at about 7:00 AM. He sent runners to spread the word that the enemy was approaching, and because of the shortage of ammo, he cautioned his gunners on the 75-millimeter recoilless rifles to hold their fire until their targets were within 700 yards.

At about 7:30 AM, a shout from Sergeant Loren Chambers to Lieutenant Phillip Day, his platoon commander, shattered the tense silence on one of the hillsides.

"Hey, look over there, Lieutenant," Chambers called, pointing toward the open plain in the direction of Suwon. "Can you believe that?"

Day turned to stare in that direction, and his eyes widened. Rumbling across the plain from the north on the main road was a long column of dark green armored vehicles.

"What the hell are they?" Day asked.

"They're T-34 tanks, sir," Chambers replied, "and I don't think they're going to be friendly."

They weren't.

The only U.S. media representative accompanying Task Force Smith that morning was Peter Kalischer, a veteran combat correspondent for United Press, who arrived on the scene just as the fighting erupted. His dispatch from the front, published in numerous Stateside newspapers on July 7, after Kalischer had erroneously been reported captured by the NKPA, included the following eyewitness observations:

American artillery a half-mile back opened up on the tanks just as I reported in to the battalion commander, Lieutenant Colonel Charles B. Smith.

Ten minutes later, from a foxhole, I saw the first Russian-made tanks rumble over the road I had taken to the command post. First one, then 10, then 20 Communist tanks rumbled past. They completely cut us off from our lines. I lost count after that.

The tanks began firing at the American artillery batteries, which had range of the road. But so far as I could tell, they scored no hits. The tanks were in single file, like ducks in a shooting gallery, but they knew what they were about. They would pause before the target spot, wait until American batteries fired, then spurt on ahead.

The soldiers fired mortars, bazookas, and new recoilless 75-millimeter rifles. But for the most part, missiles bounced off [the tanks] like ping-pong balls.

Clutching obsolete World War II–vintage 2.36-inch bazookas, three of Brad Smith's platoon leaders—Second Lieutenants Carl Bernard, Jansen Cox, and Ollie Connor—waited with their gunners until the tanks were practically in their laps before opening fire. Crouched in a ditch on the eastern side of the main road, Cox and Bernard allowed the first two tanks to pass their position, then struck at the rear of the T-34s, where their armor was alleged to be thinner and more vulnerable.

Bernard's bazooka scored eight straight hits on one tank without causing discernible damage. Meanwhile, Connor's fired twenty-two rounds at a point-blank range of fifteen yards from the top of a rocky knob with a similar lack of results. Some of the rounds were old and exploded prematurely, showering the American gunners with fragments that inflicted small but painful wounds.

"The seats in hell closest to the fire should be reserved for the Army officers who knew those 2.36-inch bazookas didn't work and didn't alert our soldiers to their inability to kill tanks," said Bernard, still incensed nearly six decades later. "They sent us that junk and kept the larger, much more effective 3.5-inch rocket launchers back in the States."

When the task force's only two 75-millimeter recoilless rifles opened fire from 700 yards, they were equally ineffective. Their high-explosive rounds burst as harmlessly as firecrackers against the tanks' turrets. Unperturbed, some of the tanks paused and returned fire, pounding U.S. positions on the ridge above them with their 85-millimeter cannons and heavy machine guns.

Meanwhile, the other T-34s continued their advance—at least thirty of them in all—seemingly oblivious to the explosions spewing up mud and flames around them.

"When we saw those tanks bearing down on us, I don't think any of us figured we'd ever get out of there alive," recalled PFC William Thornton, a twenty-year-old squad leader from Covington, Tennessee, who'd been nicknamed "Pop" by his teenage squadmates. "Our weapons and ammo were soaked from the rain, and M-1s are pretty useless against tanks, anyhow."

As Colonel Perry had expected, only the lone 105 howitzer armed with HEAT shells claimed an appreciable toll. It took the two lead tanks under fire, damaging both and forcing them to the roadside, where one burst into flames. Two crewmen scrambled away from the burning tank with hands raised, but a third jumped from the hatch, firing wildly with a burp gun toward an American machine-gun emplacement near the road. Before he and his two comrades died in a hail of bullets, the NKPA tanker fatally wounded an assistant gunner on the machine gun.

Because of the chaos in which he died, the dead GI's identity was never established. But as far as can be determined, he was the first American soldier to be killed in action in the Korean War.

During a two-hour period, waves of North Korean tanks rolled impudently past Task Force Smith's defensive positions, pounding them with machine-gun and cannon fire that killed or wounded at least twenty GIs. One of the artillery battery's six howitzers and most of its vehicles were destroyed. None of the enemy armored units stuck around for long, however, and all of them finally disappeared through a gap in the ridges to the south.

"If we'd had even a few antitank mines buried in the road, we probably could've temporarily stopped the whole North Korean tank column," Perry said. "But as it was, we didn't have a single one."

At about 11:00 AM, a massive column of trucks and walking North Korean infantry units came into sight, led by more tanks and stretching up the road to the north for an estimated six miles. Platoons of soldiers from the 16th and 18th regiments of the NKPA's Fourth Division quickly fanned out into the rice paddies on either side of the road, while others worked their way toward the flanks of Task Force Smith's fragile front. Soon the Americans were coming under intensive mortar, machine-gun, and small-arms fire from three sides and taking heavy casualties.

Dug in on a hillside, "Pop" Thornton and his First Platoon of L Company opened up on the North Korean infantry as soon as they came into range, and Thornton took grim satisfaction in seeing some of his targets fall as they tried to negotiate a shallow creekbed. But the survivors clambered up the hill toward him without slowing down.

"I shot at one of them and missed," Thornton said. "Then three of them closed in and sprayed our foxhole with burp guns. They shot my rifle to pieces, and one piece hit me in the arm. They'd have finished me off for sure if our platoon sergeant hadn't killed all three of them with a machine gun. By then we were almost out of ammo, anyway."

Fresh out of high school in Jersey City, New Jersey, John Doody had joined the Navy in 1943, but soon after completing basic training and getting his first shipboard assignment, he learned that he'd won an appointment to West Point. In June 1949, with a brand-new commission as an Army second lieutenant—and a brand-new wife as well—he'd shipped out for Japan to join Brad Smith's battalion of the 21st Infantry.

On July 5, 1950, Lieutenant Doody had been temporarily detached from the rifle platoon he usually led to take charge of the only two heavy 4.2-inch mortars possessed by Task Force Smith, and he was squatting on the back side of a ridge with ten tense mortarmen.

"For a while, we fired at those NK infantry columns as fast as we could drop rounds down our tubes," recalled Doody. "I know we did some damage, but we couldn't keep it up for long because we were critically short of ammo. Rounds for our guns weighed about forty pounds apiece, and our two gun crews hadn't been able to carry nearly as many as we needed."

With the closest other U.S. units many miles away, and the promised ROK troops nowhere to be found, Colonel Smith and his little band could expect neither reinforcement nor relief. Withdrawing south meant again facing the enemy tanks, yet staying where they were was nothing short of suicidal. By about 2:30 PM, the situation was desperate.

"We've got to get the hell out of here," somebody said.

At first Smith shook his head, but then he reluctantly agreed. "Okay," he said heavily, "this is a decision I'll probably regret for the rest of my days, but I guess we've got no choice but to withdraw."

By this point, Smith had no means of communicating with anyone beyond the range of his voice. He waved his arm and shouted, "Fall back!" Within seconds, every man on either side of him was scrambling for the rear.

"I was about thirty yards away from Brad when he gave the order, and I could see how upset he was," recalled Lieutenant Doody. "But I can tell you that if he'd waited even a few minutes longer, none of us would've gotten out. It was starting to look a lot like Custer's last stand."

Corporal Norman Fosness, the B Company BAR man from North Dakota, and his buddy PFC George Pleasant saw a runner from the company command post darting behind their positions, and they heard him yelling at the top of his lungs,

"Retreat! Retreat! Every man for himself! Retreat!"

Fosness emptied his weapon and hurled his two grenades down the hill toward the enemy. Then he and Pleasant jumped out of their foxhole and ran like rabbits through a swarm of machine-gun bullets.

Many other GIs never heard an order to retreat, but when they spotted other Americans bolting southward, they joined the exodus, abandoning weapons, equipment, helmets, and anything else that impeded their flight. When infantry began falling back on his artillery positions, Colonel Perry, who'd been hit in the right leg by small-arms fire and was barely able to walk, felt he had no option but to order his 105s abandoned. One gun had already been disabled by enemy fire, but the other five were still functional.

"If we'd tried to haul those 105s out, all of us would've been killed or captured," Perry said, "so I told the battery commander to strip the guns of their sights and breeches and get out of there."

Likewise, Lieutenant Doody wrecked his two mortars with rifle bullets and told their crews to leave. Some of the artillerymen were able to flee in the unit's jeeps and trucks, but because the enemy tanks dominated the road, the infantry platoons had no chance of using it as an escape route. Their troops would have to navigate the fields and the stinking rice paddies, taking advantage of whatever cover they could find.

Decades later, Lieutenant Day described the agony of the retreat: "It was every man for himself. When we moved out, we began taking more and more casualties. . . . Guys fell around me. Mortar rounds hit here and there. One of my young guys got it in the middle. Another got it in the throat and began spitting blood."

Cradling his wounded arm against his chest, PFC Thornton struggled out of his foxhole and ran as hard as he could go for the rear, strongly motivated by what he saw happening on the hill behind him. "When the gooks took the hill, they shot all the wounded that couldn't walk," he said. "We lost most of the company right there. Nearly the whole Second Platoon was captured."

The withdrawal disintegrated into a nightmare of panic, confusion, and death. Officially, Task Force Smith suffered 155 casualties in its brief battle. More GIs fell during the long retreat, and dozens were captured by the North Koreans. Many of those who escaped spent up to five harrowing days playing hide-and-seek with pursuing enemy troops before they managed to reach friendly territory and safety.

"I lost a lot of good friends there," recalled Corporal Fosness many years later. "Sixty-five out of 150 men in my company were either killed or captured—and a part of me died that day at Osan."

Over the next sixty years, the officers and enlisted men of Task Force Smith have been among the favorite "whipping boys" for Korean War historians and armchair critics. They've been targeted for the bitterest kind of condemnation and even outright ridicule for "bugging out" in the face of the enemy. But in truth, the majority of them—green, poorly trained, and shoddily equipped though they were—fought bravely in an untenable situation.

If the real culprits had been singled out, they could have been found in Washington, Tokyo, and Taejon, among the ill-advised commanders who sent 548 American soldiers into a battle they had no hope of winning against a tank-led army of thousands.

"Our orders were to fight a delaying action," said Colonel Perry. "We did that and then withdrew. That's all you can do when you're out of ammunition and outnumbered twenty to one."

Even as their comrades took flight, Sergeant Burke and four members of his medical team remained at their posts to tend to the seriously wounded. At the time, medics weren't issued weapons, so they had no means of defending themselves. As the medics worked, a young lieutenant ran past, heading for the rear. For a moment, the lieutenant's eyes met Burke's, and the officer paused long enough to hand Burke a grenade.

"Here, take this," he panted. "You may need it." Burke accepted the gift silently, and the lieutenant ran on, yelling "Good luck" over his shoulder.

When Peter Kalischer, the United Press reporter, heard GIs around him yelling "Here they come!" and firing down the north slope of their hill, he stayed in his foxhole long enough to see 100 or more North Koreans inching steadily forward. At that point, Kalischer abandoned his foxhole and fell back to the aid station, where the medics were frantically treating wounded men, wondering whether it was "unpatriotic of me to want to get out as much as I did."

A wounded sergeant stumbled toward him, gripping a bullet hole in his arm to stanch the bleeding. "I got one of those tanks with a bazooka," the sergeant muttered, "and one of the gooks inside crawled out like he wanted to surrender and shot me. He had his hands up, too, the son of a bitch."

The medics finally abandoned their own position a few moments later, carrying two men on stretchers and helping others who were still able to hobble along. As Burke lifted another wounded sergeant into his arms, he couldn't help thinking how naive and overconfident he and some of his comrades had been only a few days earlier, when Task Force Smith was flying to Korea.

"We figured to be there maybe a week, settle the gook thing, then go on back to Japan," Burke recalled with lingering chagrin many years later. "We never expected to face anything like what we faced. We had wounded men all over the place—including fifteen litter cases—and no way to transport them."

On their way down the hill, the medics and their patients came under intense fire from enemy artillery, mortars, and machine guns. Halfway to the bottom, a North Korean shell burst about fifty feet in front of Burke, killing the two corpsmen nearest him and sending the severed head of one of them rolling back toward Burke.

"I took cover with the wounded sergeant until the firing eased off," he recalled, "and when I got off the hill, everybody else had already pulled out. The wounded guy and I were all alone, and I was so pooped from carrying him I had to lay him down. I sat there for a couple of minutes, wondering what the hell I was going to do. Then I picked him up again and started wading across a rice paddy."

Lieutenant Bernard, suffering from painful wounds to his face and hands caused by one of his own malfunctioning bazooka shells, was still holding his hilltop position with the Second Platoon of L Company when he noticed that no fire seemed to be coming from other nearby American posts.

"All communication between units had been lost when the enemy tanks tore up our phone lines, and the rain knocked out our obsolete radios," Bernard recalled. "Effective artillery fire would've made a big difference when the North Korean infantry began moving in long lines around our positions, but most of our ammunition was exhausted by then. As it was, the enemy troops were out of the range of my platoon's .30-caliber machine guns and BARs until just before they dispersed to begin their assault."

Bernard sent a runner over to the company command post to see what was going on. In a few minutes, the breathless runner came back with a look of panic on his face.

"They're all gone!" he said with a gasp. "Nobody's there!"

Bernard, who had joined the Marines as a private in 1944, then switched to the Army after the war and won a commission in 1949, had been a last-minute addition to Task Force Smith. A trained parachutist, he'd been helping load equipment aboard the C-54 transports in the small hours of July 1 when Brad Smith paused in his rounds long enough to tell him, "Just stay on the plane when you're done, boy. You're going with us. I've got work for you."

Now Bernard held out no hope of ever getting back to Japan, but he knew he had no alternative but to order his men to retreat. The battle, such as it had been, was clearly over, and the good guys had lost. For more than six hours they'd thrown everything they had at the enemy, and none of it had done much good. But staying put any longer was only asking to be surrounded and annihilated. It was time to go.

When what was left of Bernard's platoon reached the bottom of the hill, they found several wounded soldiers being tended by medics—undoubtedly the same ones Sergeant Burke had been with before getting separated. Bernard and his men helped carry the wounded to a protected area, then moved on.

As they made their way south, aided by a map of Korea torn by Bernard from a geography book found in an abandoned schoolhouse, they had to take frequent detours to avoid NKPA infantry units. En route, the group was joined by other stragglers, including Burke and the wounded sergeant he was carrying. Gradually their number swelled to twenty-two men, all but one of whom were capable of walking under their own power.

After escaping several brushes with enemy tanks over the next couple of hours, the group happened upon a Korean farmer with a wheelbarrow, and Bernard offered to give the man an expensive gold watch he'd won in a poker game in return for hauling the injured man to the nearest U.S. unit.

"I also gave the farmer a note," Bernard recalled, "asking the first Americans he met to give him $100 for delivering the sergeant. I doubt if the farmer ever got his money, but he did his job well. He took the sergeant all the way to the coast, put him on a fishing boat, and by July 8, he was safe in Pusan."

Other retreating GIs also made valiant efforts to get wounded comrades to safety, but in many cases they were forced to leave behind men whose conditions appeared hopeless.

"It was July 9 before I finally made it back to friendly territory," said Burke, one of only 190 to reach safety out of the 548 officers and enlisted men in Task Force Smith. "Two of our medics were killed, and 11 others from our platoon were captured."

• • •

Under anything resembling normal circumstances, the remnants of Task Force Smith would have been given a few days' rest after their ordeal and narrow escape. But the situation in South Korea was far too desperate—and the number of defenders far too few—to allow this.

By the time Lieutenant Bernard had his shrapnel wounds patched up and had returned to duty, he and Burke, also hurting from shrapnel wounds and badly swollen feet, were folded into the 21st Infantry's Third Battalion along with the still-usable elements of Brad Smith's force. Soon they were back in combat around the villages of Chonui and Chochiwon, some twenty miles south of Osan and eighty-two miles below the 38th Parallel.

Early on July 10, units of the Third Battalion came under heavy attack by the NKPA and were unable to hold their positions. At about noon that day, the company to which Bernard had been reassigned—L Company of the 21st Infantry—found itself in a situation distressingly similar to the predicament at Osan five days earlier. Under orders to "hold at all costs," the company lost 101 men killed or captured out of a total of 130 on July 10–11 while defending against what historians termed "one of the most perfectly coordinated assaults ever launched by North Koreans against American troops." Thirty-three members of the company who surrendered were murdered by their captors—shot through the head with their hands tied behind their backs.

Bernard was awarded a Distinguished Service Cross for valor, but the platoon he led was wiped out almost to a man after destroying two enemy tanks with only rifles and gasoline.

"We got one tank when Sergeant Hugh Brown, the best fighting man I ever knew, put fifteen rounds from his M-2 through the tank's open port when the burp gunner paused to reload. We got the next tank by pouring a five-gallon can of gas on its hot engine compartment. Then we went back and burned the other tank.

"Did we hold? Hell, no, we didn't hold. We stayed too long in a losing fight, and a lot of good men died."

Bernard described that "hold at all costs" order with one word:

"Idiotic."

• • •

On July 12, Lieutenant General Walton Walker arrived in South Korea to set up headquarters for the U.S. Eighth Army and assume command of all American and UN forces in the country, most of which were still nonexistent.

In announcing Walker's appointment, President Truman took the opportunity to aim more tough talk at the folks at home. Appropriately, he praised "a small band of heroic youngsters" who were "holding off a landslide" in Korea. But he also castigated the American press for news stories that "spoke of entire units being wiped out and exaggerated the rout and confusion" there.

"The fact is," Truman would later write, "there was more panic among the civilians at home than among the soldiers in Korea."

Perhaps a commander in chief shouldn't be faulted for sugarcoating the facts while trying to reassure the jittery citizens of his abruptly embattled nation. In truth, however, there was plenty of panic to go around—in Korea as well as in the United States.

By July 9, Japan-based American B-29s were raining bombs on the North Korean capital of Pyongyang and other targets above the 38th Parallel. Offshore, the light cruiser *Juneau* and four U.S. destroyers pounded away at enemy troop concentrations. Meanwhile, the bulk of the 24th Infantry Division, some 16,000 men as opposed to Brad Smith's pitiful handful from the 24th, was either preparing to leave Japan for Pusan by ship or already on the way. Tanks, trucks, jeeps, artillery, heavy mortars, and even small-arms ammunition were still in painfully short supply, however.

With considerable justification, South Korean President Rhee was bitterly complaining that U.S. aid was "too little and too late." On the ground 150 miles south of the Parallel, near the embattled key city of Taejon, the defenders' situation continued to deteriorate, and an unpalatable dose of stark realism had erased the early cockiness of U.S. soldiers already there.

"How's morale among the troops?" *Time* correspondent Frank Gibney asked a stubble-faced infantryman with a cluster of hand grenades on his belt.

"Morale's fine," the GI answered. "We have the best morale in the world, but what can morale do against planes and tanks?"

CHAPTER 3

★ ★ ★

A Proud Corps
in Peril

WHILE BUDGET CUTS by the Truman administration and Congress had left the U.S. Army perilously unprepared for a shooting war, the Marine Corps was floundering in even more dire straits. By June 1950, in fact, it seemed to be teetering on the brink of extinction.

As unthinkable as it would have been five years earlier, when the Marines were bearing the brunt in the fight against Japan, America's most elite military organization was now down to two "shadow strength" divisions, with their major elements scattered thousands of miles apart. But top-echelon Marine commanders feared that the worst was still to come. They were unanimously alarmed at growing sentiment among the power brokers in Washington to reduce their Corps to a small, ceremonial unit with no combat capabilities.

President Truman himself had shown little sympathy for the Marines' plight and even less concern about their eroding ability to uphold their 175-year tradition of being "first to fight." He had pointedly denied Marine generals representation on the Joint Chiefs of Staff and made it clear that he saw no sense in the Navy maintaining "its own little army." Under the unification plan for major U.S. military branches that Truman had begun promoting in the late 1940s, the president foresaw the Marines being fully absorbed into the Navy and shorn of their separate identity and command structure.

Men such as General Clifton Cates, commandant of the Marine Corps, and General O. P. Smith, commander of the First Marine Division, would much rather have died than see this happen. But they were forced to concede privately that given the climate on Capitol Hill in 1950, it was no longer out of the question.

Lieutenant Colonel Bryghte D. Godbold, a staff officer at Marine Corps headquarters in Washington, was driving home from a friend's house on the afternoon of June 24, 1950 (June 25 in the Far East), when he heard a news flash on his car radio. Eight crack North Korean infantry divisions, spearheaded by one armored division, had invaded the Republic of South Korea and were driving the ill-trained, poorly equipped ROK Army back toward Seoul.

As it did to listeners across the nation, the report came as a shock to Godbold because it clearly represented the most serious threat by the Communist bloc since the start of the Cold War. "At the same time, though, I could almost feel a sense of relief," he recalled decades later. "In one of the darkest moments in the Corps' history, I thought it might mean the Marines would be going back into combat with a chance to prove once again how much the country needed them."

An officer in the Corps since his graduation from Auburn University in 1936, Godbold was no stranger to fierce fighting and physical suffering. As an artillery captain commanding an antiaircraft battery during the siege of Wake Island in December 1941, he'd overseen the destruction of some of the first Japanese planes in World War II and later endured forty-three months in a Japanese prison camp.

After the war, the rail-thin Alabama native watched in chagrin as the Corps dwindled from its wartime strength of 800,000 officers and enlisted men to a skeleton crew of just 74,000.

"We were down to two active Marine divisions—the First and Second," he recalled, "and there was a highly organized effort by the Army and some of the country's most powerful political figures to abolish the Marines entirely as a combat organization."

In response to a congressman's suggestion that the Marines should have a permanent representative on the Joint Chiefs of Staff, Truman himself delivered a stinging slap to the Corps. "For your information," the president responded tartly, "the Marine Corps is the Navy's police force, and as long as I'm president, that's what it will remain. They have a propaganda machine that's almost the equal of [Soviet Premier Joseph] Stalin's."

General of the Army Dwight D. Eisenhower, who would succeed Truman in the White House, and who, as supreme Allied commander in Europe, had had no dealings with the Marines in World War II, was prepared to go even farther after the war. In official documents prepared by the Joint Chiefs of Staff for presentation to the Defense Department during the late 1940s upheaval over unification of the services, Eisenhower, then chief of staff of the Army, expressed the belief that the Marines had duplicated the Army's role in World War II by serving as regular ground forces. Alone among the services, Eisenhower wrote, the Marine Corps should not be "appreciably expanded," and he added that he saw no justification in maintaining an all-purpose Marine aviation wing.

Other major figures in the Army's power structure voiced similar opinions and pressed Congress and the Truman administration to "drastically curtail" the Marine Corps to prevent it from duplicating the Army's ground and air forces.

General Carl A. Spaatz, former commander in chief of the Army Air Forces and first chief of staff of the newly created U.S. Air Force, called the Marines' World War II operations a "patent incursion" into Army and Air Force operations and urged limiting the Corps in the future to "lightly armed units no larger than a regiment."

"Eisenhower favored reducing the Corps to small, noncombat units with only ceremonial responsibilities," Godbold said. "Fortunately, we had a lot of retired Marines and other friends in Congress, but I think it's safe to say that the modern Corps was never on thinner ice where its future as a fighting force was concerned than it was in the late spring of 1950."

As he drove home that June afternoon, Godbold had a strong inkling that he'd soon be headed to Korea himself. He was right. Within hours after news of the invasion broke—and without waiting for orders from the Joint Chiefs of Staff—General Cates and General Lemuel Shepherd, commanding the Fleet Marine Force, Pacific (consisting of small units serving aboard Navy warships), quickly began drafting a Korean combat plan.

On June 27, the UN Security Council passed a resolution calling for its member nations to take all necessary means, including armed force, to repel the Communist invaders. The resolution would never have escaped a Soviet veto if Moscow hadn't been boycotting the Security Council at that time for its refusal to approve the admission of Red China to the United Nations. At any rate, General Cates quickly seized the initiative. He arranged to meet the next day with Navy Secretary Francis P. Matthews and Admiral Forrest Sherman, chief of naval operations, to offer the services of the Fleet Marine Force.

Because it was still uncertain at this early date—barely forty-eight hours into the war—whether U.S. ground forces would actually be sent to Korea, the response from Sherman and Matthews was noncommittal. But Cates acted out of instinct cultivated from long years of experience in combat readiness and crisis management. On that same afternoon of June 27, he dispatched a warning order to General O. P. Smith, telling him to get his First Marine Division ready to go to war.

One of General MacArthur's earliest moves after the fall of Seoul on June 28 was to deliver an urgent request to Washington for immediate deployment of a Marine regimental combat team to South Korea. On July 10, hours after MacArthur officially took command of UN forces in Korea and five days after the debacle of Task Force Smith, he met in Japan with General Shepherd, whom he'd gotten to know in 1943–44, when Shepherd was assistant commander of the First Marine Division.

As they conferred, ROK troops were falling back in disorder and U.S. Army units were being rushed to Korea in hopes of buying enough time through delaying actions to form a defensive line capable of withstanding the NKPA blitzkrieg. At that moment, no one was sure where that line would be—only that it should be as far as possible from the vital port of Pusan, at the extreme southeastern tip of the Korean peninsula. South Korea's defenders were giving ground rapidly, and the "front," such as it was, was in a constant state of southward flux.

To Shepherd, MacArthur laid out a bold strategic scheme for reversing the Red tide that threatened to obliterate the ROK Army and absorb South Korea into the Communist empire. At the heart of the plan was an amphibious landing behind enemy lines at the port of Inchon, west of Seoul. If it succeeded, the landing could isolate the invaders, sever their supply lines, and set them up for quick destruction. This was where the Marines, the world's most experienced specialists in amphibious warfare, came in.

For the plan to work, however, the U.S. military would have to hold and stabilize a defensive perimeter to protect Pusan until the amphibious operation could be organized and carried out. A secure Pusan could provide a crucial staging area for the Inchon landing. Strengthened sufficiently for a counterattack, Pusan's defenders also could serve as the other half of a pincer movement to squeeze to death enemy forces in South Korea. But if Pusan fell or came under intense NKPA pressure, any landing attempt at Inchon would almost certainly be doomed to failure. Securing Pusan and establishing a stable defensive perimeter around it had to come first, and much of that job, too, would fall to the Marines.

Turning to a map of Korea, MacArthur pointed to Inchon with the stem of his pipe. "If I only had the First Marine Division under my command again [as he had in World War II]," he told Shepherd, "I would land them here at Inchon and reverse the war. I would cut the North Korean armies attacking the Pusan Perimeter from their logistical support and cause their withdrawal and annihilation."

Shepherd needed no convincing. He and other high-ranking Marine officers were aching to prove once again that their Corps was combat-ready, and Pusan offered the earliest opportunity. When MacArthur asked if a Marine brigade could be at Pusan by early August and the entire First Marine Division assembled and transported across the Pacific in time for a September 15 landing at Inchon, Shepherd's replies were "Yes" and "Yes."

First, though, they'd have to sell the Joint Chiefs of Staff on the idea—and that wouldn't be easy.

Back in the States, Marine Corps brass moved with speed and determination—and without any formal approval by the Joint Chiefs—to pull together the widely scattered elements of the First Marine Division and shape them into a cohesive combat force. They had a daunting job ahead of them. At the time, the division's strength, including its accompanying aircraft wing, totaled fewer than 12,000 men, which was less than half the two units' full complement.

To fill the gap, reservists across the country were called back to active duty. Leaves were canceled, and Marine garrisons everywhere were placed on alert. Within hours after the Communist invasion, regular Marines of every rank had begun streaming into Camp Pendleton, the vast training complex on the California coast north of San Diego where the First Marine Division was based.

"As a PFC clerk, I was temporarily assigned to assist in processing men arriving from all over the world," recalled retired Marine Sergeant Charles Sands many years later. "I still remember incidents where men were returning to San Francisco from completed tours of duty overseas, some for two years or more, and who were expecting to go home on leave. Instead, they were put on trains and sent to Camp Pendleton for reassignment to the First Marine Division. Some of them were pretty upset, but it had to be done."

Sergeant Bill Finnegan, a veteran of three major Pacific battles in World War II, was among the ranks of the "pretty upset"—and with good reason. "I'd just gotten married a couple of months before the sky fell," he recalled decades later, "and my wife and I had just settled into a small apartment near the Great Lakes Naval Training Center, where I was doing MP duty and looking forward to a discharge in about a year. When I heard about the invasion on the radio and that all enlistments were being extended at least a year, I went home, broke the news to my bride, and dragged out my old seabag. I knew darn well I was headed for Korea."

Even so, Finnegan, assigned to I Company, Third Battalion, First Marines, didn't have to travel nearly as far as some others in his regiment to join the division. Commanded by Colonel Chesty Puller, a World War II legend, many members of the First Marines (in Corps parlance, Marine regiments are identified simply as First Marines, Fifth Marines, etc., while divisions are always identified by their full names, as in First Marine Division) would have to travel all the way from Camp Lejeune in North Carolina and through the Panama Canal to reach Pendleton and prepare for their long ocean voyage to Korea.

But the first order of business—and by far the most imperative—was to fold the Fifth Marines, the Corps' most battle-ready regiment, into a newly activated First Provisional Marine Brigade and speed it across the Pacific. Traveling with the Fifth Marines would be a battalion of artillery from the 11th Marines, a tank battalion, an air wing, an engineer battalion, and various support units. Named to command the 6,500-man brigade was tall, white-maned Brigadier General Edward A. "Eddie" Craig, a Marine officer since 1917 and a combat commander in some of the hottest Pacific battles of World War II. His responsibility: to have his brigade in action in the beleaguered Pusan Perimeter by the first days of August. Bolstering the brigade's command structure was Lieutenant Colonel Raymond Murray, CO of the Fifth Marines, plus a cadre of battle-tested battalion and company commanders, many of whom had been decorated for bravery under fire.

With a critical shortage of every type of military equipment, the Marines had a "secret weapon" stashed away at a huge desert depot near Barstow, California. In the months immediately after World War II, while other services had jettisoned countless vehicles and pieces of heavy equipment in the mad dash to get home, Marine supply officers had snatched up as many of these discards as possible for reconditioning and mothballing. There would be no room aboard the small convoy of ships carrying Craig's brigade to Korea, but ready and waiting at the obscure depot were all the trucks, jeeps, trailers, and amphibious tractors the First Marine Division would need a few weeks later to carry it into a new war.

The earliest Army troops to reach Korea frequently suffered casualties from "friendly fire" during attacks by Air Force and Navy planes that weren't in close contact with the ground forces, but the Marine brigade—and later the division—would have their own unified, coordinated air arm. While

General Craig's ground troops hurriedly familiarized themselves with such newer weapons as the M-26 Pershing tank, the 75-millimeter recoilless rifle, and the 3.5-inch rocket launcher, pilots of the First Marine Air Wing honed their skills at close air support at the El Toro Marine Air Station, a few miles north of Camp Pendleton.

The Navy, meanwhile, with most of its World War II transports in mothballs and a crucial shortage of able-bodied seamen to man its warships, also had plenty of scurrying and scrounging to do.

Youngsters such as seventeen-year-old Joe Maddox, who was just three weeks past his graduation from Pleasant Grove High School in Dallas when the war broke out—and facing an imminent date with his draft board—helped fill the Navy's manpower void.

"Along with a lot of other guys my age, I joined the Navy in August 1950 because I didn't want to be in the infantry, and I was placed in a special rush-rush program," Maddox recalled many years later. "We got only half the normal time in basic training before we shipped out for Japan." By December, Seaman Third Class Maddox would be aboard the aircraft carrier *Princeton* in the Yellow Sea, setting fuses in bombs bound for North Korea.

Somehow, the Navy had to find a way to assemble its largest task force since World War II. Transporting the First Marine Division and other troops for the Inchon operation would require a huge armada of ships. Meanwhile, a more immediate problem was cobbling together a ten-ship task force to carry the Marine brigade from San Diego to the Far East. The brigade's three infantry battalions would make the long voyage aboard three venerable veterans of the Pacific war—the attack transports (APAs) *Henrico*, referred to affectionately as "Happy Hank"; *George Clymer* (or "Greasy George," as it was known to its passengers); and *Pickaway*, which had yet to pick up a nickname. The convoy also would include two LSDs (landing ships, dock); two AKAs (cargo ships, attack); two other transports; and the light carrier *Badoeng Strait*, which would carry the men and planes of Marine Aircraft Group (MAG) 33.

General Craig, whose battlefield experience stretched from Haiti to Guadalcanal to Iwo Jima, had been awarded a Navy Cross for valor in the Battle of Guam and the Legion of Merit for his service at Iwo. He had a well-earned reputation as a tough, no-nonsense commander, but one who always made his men's welfare a top priority. In one of his first meetings with the assembled officers of his newly formed brigade, Craig reinforced both of these images.

"You've read the papers and seen the pictures from Korea," he told them. "You know the kind of enemy we'll meet and what they've done to wounded men left behind. As long as there's a Marine alive who can fire a rifle or throw a grenade, we will not leave a wounded or dead Marine on the field.

"It's been necessary," he continued, "for troops now fighting in Korea to pull back at times, but I'm stating to you now that no unit of this brigade will retreat except on orders from an authority higher than the First Marine Brigade. You will never receive an order to retreat from me. All I ask is that you fight as Marines have always fought. If you do that, I can ask no more."

Unlike many of the men who were required to travel long distances to reach Camp Pendleton during the frantic days of early July 1950, Navy Corpsman Herbert Pearce had already been stationed there for more than a year. A small-town boy from Wesson, Mississippi, who aspired to become a physician, Pearce had joined the Navy in May 1947 but had yet to serve a single day out of sight of land. When the Korean War broke out, he was a twenty-one-year-old MH-3 (equivalent to a three-stripe sergeant) attached to the First Weapons Battalion of the Fifth Marines.

"Everybody in the medical service was excited, and we all started packing our gear in anticipation of loading out," Pearce recalled decades later. "I'd already been warned that only two of the three corpsmen from our battalion would be going to Korea with the brigade, but I was hoping I'd be one of them. Sure enough, when the brigade started forming, the battalion was split into two units—a 75-millimeter recoilless rifle company and a 4.2-inch mortar company—and each was given one corpsman. I was assigned to the 75s, and my friend Conraid Pope went with the 4.2s."

Pope, a California native who had gotten married on June 12, 1950, and was in the process of being discharged from the Navy when the Korean War broke out, holds especially vivid memories of that hectic time. "My wife and I were on our way back from our honeymoon trip when we phoned my wife's mother, and she told us, 'Something's happened in a place called Korea.' Obviously, my plans to become a civilian immediately went on hold."

Pope and Pearce were in a pool of only about ten corpsmen at Pendleton at that time, but soon they were joined by dozens of others. "We were assigned to qualify on M-1s and carbines just like the infantry," Pope said. "By the time the brigade left for Korea, it included ninety-three corpsmen in all. By December of 1950, only thirteen of them were left."

Like Pearce and Pope, Sergeant Charlie Snow, a career Marine who had grown up in the Texas Panhandle, also arrived at Pendleton in 1949 to become a squad leader in the same recoilless rifle company where Pearce was assigned. Snow was quickly impressed with the Marine-like toughness and dedication to duty displayed by the tall, lanky Pearce.

"Whenever we went on a tough march during training, a corpsman always went with us," Snow recalled, "and that was how we met. Pearce picked up the nickname "Doc Rocket" even before we left for Korea because whenever a guy hollered "Corpsman!" he was on his way like a rocket. We never thought of him as a Navy guy. He was as much a Marine as any of us."

The corpsmen at Pendleton worked closely with their assigned Marine units, attending the same lectures and training sessions, and learning as much as they could of what the Marines already knew.

"General Craig really got things moving," Pearce remembered, "and it only took a total of six days from the time the brigade was activated until we embarked. On July 12, we were bused from Camp Pendleton to San Diego to board our ships. Mine was the *Pickaway.*"

That evening, Pearce went with other members of the company into San Diego for his last Stateside liberty. In high spirits after a few beers, he called home—never realizing how much was destined to happen to him and his comrades before he would talk with his parents again.

"After three years in the Navy, I was finally getting to go someplace and do something different, and I could hardly wait to get started," he remembered. "It was an adventure, and if it included a war, that was all right with me. I never once stopped to think that I might not survive."

Early on the morning of July 14, the *Pickaway* slipped her moorings and eased away from the dock while a band played the "Marine Hymn." The ship was initially headed for Sasebo, Japan, where the brigade and its air group were supposed to disembark for a quick round of air-ground maneuvers before going into battle. But soon the steadily worsening situation in South Korea would dictate a change in plans. When the ships were still in midocean, it was decided that even a brief delay for training was courting disaster, and the task force would be rerouted directly to Pusan. It wouldn't arrive a minute too soon.

As the sun rose above the mountains behind San Diego and the *Pickaway* cleared Point Loma, Herb Pearce and his fellow corpsmen ceremoniously tossed their Red Cross armbands overboard. "We believed that the armbands represented a target to the enemy, rather than protection for us," Pearce explained.

By noon that day, the young medic recalled, "I was so seasick that I didn't care if I lived or died."

No one in the brigade was more excited to be embarking for Korea that morning than three young platoon leaders in A Company, First Battalion, Fifth Marines. As the brigade was forming, the trio—Lieutenants Tom Johnston, Baldemero Lopez, and Francis Muetzel—had received identical orders transferring them out of the First Marine Division to attend a special school at Quantico, Virginia.

Their first move after the orders came through was to approach their company commander, Captain John R. "Blackjack" Stevens, and plead their case as a group.

"Please, sir," they chorused, "don't let them send us off to Quantico. What good can we do there? We want to go to Korea with you and the rest of Able Company. We're Marines. We can go to school later."

Stevens studied the three eager young faces in front of him. As a seasoned combat veteran, he knew they reflected the spirit and character that could inspire men—and win battles.

"Lots of guys'd jump at the chance to miss this one," Stevens said quietly. "It's gonna be nasty. Are you sure about this?"

"Absolutely, sir!"

"Okay, I'll see what I can do."

Within hours, the Quantico orders were rescinded.

Sergeant Frederick "Rusty" Russell, a career Marine from Cranston, Rhode Island, who had joined the Corps in August 1941 at seventeen and fought his way across the Pacific in World War II, had spent enough time aboard ships in midocean to develop a permanent immunity to seasickness. But he had at least two valid reasons for feeling tense and queasy as the convoy bearing the Marines—now designated as Task Group 53.7—headed out to sea.

For one thing, Russell and his antitank company were aboard the trouble-prone *Henrico*, which began having engine problems even before it was out of sight of land. But this was a minor concern compared to another, far more distressing one: Russell had been forced to leave his pregnant wife, Ruthie, behind just as she was going into labor. Now he was sweating bullets wondering (a) whether his child had been born, (b) whether it was a boy or a girl, and (c) whether mother and baby were both okay.

As luck would have it, however, one problem would end up negating the other, at least partially. "The *Henrico* broke down completely, and we had to put into Hunter's Point for repairs while the rest of the convoy sailed on," Russell recalled nearly six decades later. "While we were stuck there, I begged the chaplain to let me call my mother-in-law to check on my wife, and he finally said okay, but that he'd have to listen in to be sure I really had a legitimate reason for calling. Naturally, I agreed."

Russell learned that his son, Paul, had been born about two hours after the *Henrico* sailed and that mother and son were doing fine. Russell was tremendously relieved, and his ship was soon able to set out in pursuit of the rest of the convoy, but there *was*, indisputably, a down side to the story.

"Paul was born on July 14, 1950," said Russell, "but I didn't get to see him until April 1951."

As General Craig's brigade was preparing to sail, Colonel Godbold was among several staff officers at Marine headquarters in Washington who were ordered to Camp Pendleton. From there, after a short stay, Goldbold and ten others would be flown to Japan as an advance command unit for the Inchon operation.

"The Army units being sent to Korea at that time were thrown into combat piecemeal, and they were being cut to shreds," said Godbold. "By contrast, when all its major components were assembled, the First Marine Division was a reinforced unit of 20,000 troops, plus a battalion of 60 tanks and the 5,000-man First Marine Air Wing. It was a formidable outfit, and we never had any doubt that we could do whatever we were asked to do."

After the Joint Chiefs denied approval of MacArthur's plan to get the Marines involved immediately, arguing that the rapid mobilization required would weaken other Marine units, MacArthur turned up the heat.

"Most urgently request reconsideration of decision with reference to the First Marine Division," he wired the Pentagon. "There can be no demand for its potential use elsewhere that can equal the urgency of the immediate battle mission contemplated for it."

Fortunately, by the second week in July, the Joint Chiefs had relented. Meanwhile, the boundaries of the Pusan Perimeter continued to tighten like a noose around the necks of its defenders as NKPA forces drove steadily south, and U.S. Army units, now totaling about 6,000 men, tried in vain to stem the Red tide.

After the disastrous experience of Task Force Smith, the Army should have had no further illusions about the ability of small, poorly equipped American forces to impede the North Korean advance by their mere presence.

"The Americans who lived through the rigors of this battle [Task Force Smith at Osan] lost their contempt for the fighting ability of the North Koreans," wrote historian Orlando Ward in the book *Korea 1950*, commissioned by the Department of the Army and published before the end of the war. "It was evident that the enemy soldiers were excellently trained, led with skill, and equipped with an unexpected amount of firepower."

But before other American units in harm's way had a chance to take to heart the cruel lessons of Task Force Smith, similar debacles were destined to be repeated again and again. Next in line for a demoralizing learning experience were men of the 34th Infantry Regiment, who had set up a defensive line just north of the squalid village of Pyongtaek and some fifteen miles south of where Task Force Smith had been overwhelmed.

Four full U.S. Army divisions—close to 50,000 men—had by now been ordered to Korea, although only a fraction of that number had arrived in the combat zone. Among the first to join the fight were the remaining units of the 24th Infantry Division, plus the 25th Infantry Division, the First Cavalry Division, and elements of the Seventh Infantry Division. Every member of their ranks would be needed if the UN toehold on the Korean peninsula was to be maintained. But for the time being, sparse, scattered units of the 24th Division remained the only American troops in the path of the enemy advance.

The 24th's commander, General William F. Dean, a tall, handsome, fifty-year-old Illinois native, had flown to Korea on July 3 to take personal charge of U.S. defensive efforts in the area north of Taejon. After studying maps, Dean sent two battalions of the 34th Infantry Regiment to Pyongtaek.

Dean decided that this area, where an arm of the Yellow Sea protected the U.S. left flank and the Korean peninsula was narrower than it was farther south, offered the best chance of mounting a successful defense against the NKPA. He ordered the First Battalion of the 34th to set up its defenses in the hills north of Pyongtaek overlooking the main road and the railroad.

"Everything's going to be okay," the riflemen in the line were assured by officers and noncoms. "This is nothing but a police action. President Truman says so."

At daylight on July 6, in a scene hauntingly similar to that faced by Brad Smith and his men twenty-four hours earlier, the GIs of A Company of the First Battalion sat in a pouring rainstorm outside their flooded foxholes on the western side of the main road, awaiting their first look at the enemy. There were only 140 men in A Company, barely two-thirds of the company's authorized strength, and each man had exactly 100 rounds of ammunition for his M-1 or carbine. Each of the company's three shorthanded rifle platoons had a solitary BAR with 200 rounds of ammo. The weapons platoon had three puny 60-millimeter mortars, two 75-millimeter recoilless rifles—but no ammo for them—and three .30-caliber machine guns. There wasn't a single hand grenade among them.

Through the fog and mist along the road, they saw tanks approaching—a dozen or more—followed by endless lines of enemy infantry.

"Commence firing! Commence firing!" a few World War II veterans in the group yelled. But most of the GIs froze in their tracks, staring transfixed at the advancing North Koreans. Except for a handful with combat experience, almost none of them fired. Some dropped their weapons and ran.

They never had a chance.

By July 9, North Korean tanks and infantry had roared through both Pyongtaek and Chonan, the next town to the south and a key rail junction. There, what was left of the 34th Infantry Regiment lost its gallant commanding officer, Colonel Robert R. Martin, as he tried to rally his faltering troops by his own personal bravery.

With half a dozen enemy tanks blasting everything in sight in the center of Chonan, Colonel Martin raced through the streets, gathering a small group of men and firing an obsolete 2.36-inch bazooka. He was in the act of firing his last round at a tank less than fifteen yards away when he was blown in half by an 85-millimeter shell. (He was posthumously awarded the Korean War's first Distinguished Service Cross, the nation's second highest valor-based military decoration.)

When Martin was killed, the doomed effort to hold Chonan collapsed. The few Americans who escaped the carnage there tried to retreat by road from the ruined town, but they were caught in a murderous crossfire from enemy troops positioned on the high ground on both their flanks. "Bitter, haggard, tattered, and exhausted," Army historian Orlando Ward wrote of them, "they withdrew toward the Kum River and the town of Taejon."

Taejon, a city of about 40,000 people during normal times, now lay directly in the path of the principal North Korean thrust along the railroad that had, until recently, connected it with Seoul. Simultaneously, however, NKPA forces also were advancing in three parallel thrusts: one through central South Korea; another into the Ongjin peninsula, on the far west coast; and yet another down the east coast, toward the town of Samchok.

Ward painted a desolate portrait of the war-ravaged landscape and stricken civilians through which the Americans retreated. "Along the railroad between the Han and the Kum Rivers, the countryside was littered with wrecked and abandoned equipment—the huts, which had once been the homes of the now dispossessed population, were in ruins. Stately patriarchs in tall black hats, worried bands of women in high-waisted skirts and loose white blouses, bewildered children naked in the oppressive heat, and wiry Korean fathers stooped beneath the staggering weight of overloaded A-frames, clogged the highways to the south. Strafed at times by Russian-made Yak fighters, buffeted by friendly soldiers hurrying to the front, splattered with mud, soaked by cloudbursts, the homeless host of refugees contributed to the tragic confusion. . . . Mingling with innocent civilians, enemy personnel in native dress moved inconspicuously, waiting for opportunities to stampede the crowds, block bridges, and throw hand grenades into passing groups of U.S. soldiers."

The heart of South Korea's army had been ripped out during the early fighting, and many of its best soldiers had been lost during their futile attempt to defend Seoul. But two weeks after the NKPA's initial breakthrough, elements of the original eight ROK divisions attempted, with some success, to regroup. After July 10, in areas where North Korean infantry units were without tank support, ROK troops began giving a decent account of themselves for the first time. Also at this point, U.S. Air Force and Navy planes, bolstered by fighters of the Royal Australian Air Force, began dominating South Korean airspace. Soon, most of the Soviet-built aircraft that had terrorized both the ROKs and the civilian population were destroyed, leaving the skies firmly in control of UN air forces. In a concerted effort to delay the North Koreans' progress, U.S. B-29s flew repeated bombing missions from bases in Japan against enemy troop concentrations, a role that the world's heaviest bombers had seldom, if ever, been called upon to fill in their storied past.

The overall picture remained bleak, but there were occasional bright spots. On July 10, American fliers had a field day north of the town of Chonui, where they spotted an NKPA mechanized column stalled at a blown-out bridge. The Fifth Air Force ordered every available plane to the area, ranging from F-80 and F-82 jet fighters to creaking old World War II–era B-26 medium bombers. Observers counted 38 enemy tanks and 117 trucks destroyed. Coupled with damage inflicted in U.S. air attacks in the same area a day earlier, North Korean armor probably suffered its worst losses of the war during this single thirty-six-hour period.

But by far the most important factor slowing the pace of the NKPA advance at this critical juncture was a new, and largely unwarranted, cautiousness among its commanders. On the ground, the enemy had gained a huge tactical advantage during the first two weeks of the war, and it still possessed a crushing superiority in weaponry: 122-millimeter Soviet howitzers vs. the old 105-millimeter U.S. version; scores of medium and heavy tanks vs. a handful of outdated Shermans and M-24 light reconnaissance tanks on the U.S. side; and 120-millimeter mortars vs. many American mortars only half that size.

Fortunately, though, the North Koreans failed to take full advantage of this superiority in men and armaments. Facing only a few depleted, thinly spread U.S. units and an ROK Army still struggling for cohesion, they turned hesitant at the precise moment when they should have pressed their offensive to the utmost.

"At that time," historian Ward observed, "an all-out enemy assault against [the engaged portion of] the 24th Division might well have resulted in its destruction, leaving the route to Taejon, Taegu, and Pusan bare of defenders."

Brief as it was, the resulting respite of two or three days was a godsend for American and South Korean forces. It gave them a chance to catch their breath. It also allowed more fresh troops and advanced weapons to reach the war zone. But when it was over, the defeats, retreats—and a deepening sense of desperation—started all over again.

On July 12, 1950, as the First Provisional Marine Brigade was being bused to San Diego to board its Korea-bound ships, Lieutenant General Walton H. Walker, commanding general of the U.S. Eighth Army, assumed command of all UN ground forces in South Korea. Several days earlier, Walker had visited General Dean's 24th Division headquarters at Taejon to assure Dean that significant help was on the way. The first elements of the 25th

Infantry Division were expected to arrive from Japan in a few days, and the First Cavalry Division would be close behind.

In addition, General MacArthur was pressing the Joint Chiefs of Staff to commit the Second Infantry Division, stationed at Fort Lewis, Washington, and a regimental combat team from the 82nd Airborne Division to combat in Korea. Furthermore, Dean was informed, the first major reinforcements from the States—the Marine Brigade that MacArthur had so urgently sought—were now en route to Pusan. Accompanying the brigade were its own artillery batteries, sixty-vehicle tank battalion, and Corsair air group.

That was the good news. In the interim, however, the burden of holding the line along the Kum River, one of the last defendable natural obstacles to the NKPA's drive toward Pusan, would rest almost entirely on Dean's own 24th Division.

The river, which formed a ragged semicircle curving from east to west about ten miles north of Taejon, was 200 to 300 yards wide, but both its banks and its water level were shallow in many places. The enemy's next major goal was to cross the Kum in strength at several points and seize positions on its south bank. If that could be accomplished, it would become almost impossible for the Americans to keep Taejon itself from falling into enemy hands. To prevent such a catastrophe, Dean would have to rely on his three infantry regiments already close at hand—the untested 19th, the severely bloodied 21st, and the badly battered 34th.

"The Kum River line must be held at all costs," read Dean's orders to his three regimental commanders. He might as well have been asking them to walk on water.

That was the bad news, but there was worse to come.

On July 12, the 19th Infantry Regiment—famed as the "Rock of Chickamauga" in the Civil War and still known proudly as the Chicks—relieved the decimated 21st Infantry (now reduced to fewer than 1,100 effectives and with more than 1,400 dead or missing) on the south bank of the Kum. The 19th had 2,276 men in its ranks, the vast majority of whom had never fired a shot in anger. They spread themselves out over thirty miles of riverfront, necessarily leaving wide gaps between units. Then they dug in and waited.

At about one o'clock on the afternoon of July 14, enemy tanks opened fire on the 19th from fortified positions north of the river. Before daylight the next morning, NKPA infantrymen began wading and swimming across the Kum in small groups. Several hundred of them slipped behind the 19th to set up a roadblock, shutting off the Americans' only escape route to the south as well as any efforts to resupply them.

At precisely 3:00 AM on July 16, a single enemy scout plane dropped a flare above the river, and the North Koreans attacked in force. As enemy artillery, tank cannons, mortars, machine guns, and small-arms fire pounded American positions, enemy infantry poured into the Kum "like a swarm of rats," in the words of one historian. Where sandbars were handy, some waded across on foot; others came in rafts and small boats. Within an hour, they held a secure foothold on the south side of the river.

By dawn, North Korean infiltrators were everywhere—on both the Americans' flanks, peppering them with fire; behind them in rear areas, chopping up support and service troops; in their midst, dressed as white-clad Korean farmers.

Corporal Wilbert "Shorty" Estabrook had never seen anything to match the first sights that greeted him on the morning of July 16 as he awoke in a trench on the south bank of the Kum River.

"The first enemy artillery round came in almost vertically, and I looked up in time to see it hit dead center on a trailer filled with Old Nick candy bars only about twenty yards from me," Estabrook recalled a long time later. "It blew pieces of candy over about an acre of ground and got me wide awake in a hurry."

When the dust cleared a little, Estabrook peered out at an even more alarming spectacle on the opposite side of the river. "Here came thousands of North Koreans," he said, "looking like a bunch of fire ants boiling out of a mound—and every one of them coming straight at me."

Until a couple of days earlier, the twenty-year-old soldier from Maine (whose nickname stemmed from the fact that he stood an even five feet tall in his combat boots) had been just another dogface in B Company, First Battalion, of the 19th Infantry Regiment. But then he'd been picked for se-

curity duty at battalion headquarters and separated from the buddies he'd
served with for the past two years.

"Those of us on the security detail were bits and pieces picked up from
every part of the regiment," said Estabrook. "None of us knew anybody
else in the detail, and that made it tough—especially when the fit hit the
shan that morning. Next thing I knew, most of the guys around me were
hit. Quite a few were killed on the spot, and as far as I could tell, there was
just me and an old medic left. I only had one bandoleer of ammo for my
M-1, and it didn't last long. Then I didn't have anything—no grenades, no
nuthin'."

Men were scrambling for the rear in all directions, but many were trying
to follow a road leading away from the river and in the direction of Taejon.
"We hadn't gone far when we ran head-on into heavy fire from an enemy
roadblock. It looked to have been there for a while because the North Koreans were well dug in."

A sergeant ran past, calling for volunteers to try to take out the roadblock. Having picked up additional ammunition for his M-1, Estabrook
joined the group, but its attempt almost immediately failed, and many of its
members were cut down.

"I heard bullets whizzing past my ears," he recalled, "and all of a sudden,
I was the only man still standing. I saw several guys taking cover in a low
spot to the right of the road, and I jumped in there with them, right beside
a lieutenant, who was lying still and not moving."

"We'd better get going, Lieutenant," Estabrook said. He shook the officer
vigorously for several seconds before realizing that the man was dead.

"It was the most god-awful nightmare you could ever imagine," Estabrook recalled. "There was no way to tell which way to turn, and I've never
been so scared in my whole life. I spotted about fifteen Americans running
toward a bend in the river, and I ran after them. Thank God I never caught
up with them because one of our jets came in low and just made chowder
out of them. Our troops and the enemy were so mixed together on both
sides of the river that the Air Force couldn't tell them apart."

Estabrook kept running blindly until he came to a steep hill that appeared unoccupied. It took him most of the rest of the day to inch his way

to the top of it on hands and knees. Once, along the way, he heard voices talking in Korean, and he froze in his tracks for an hour or more before daring to slither on. As night fell, he dragged himself under a clump of brush and lay there, trembling with exhaustion and almost mad with thirst.

Finally, he passed out.

The Battle of the Kum River, if such it can be called, was lost almost before it started. As the NKPA struck across the Kum, the remnants of the 24th Division reeled backward toward Taejon to avoid being surrounded. Meanwhile, the convoy carrying the First Provisional Marine Brigade was following the Great Northern Circle route toward the Asian mainland, with one of its three principal troopships—the venerable *Henrico*—lagging well behind with mechanical troubles. Somewhere south of Alaska, the convoy was still a full two weeks' sail from Pusan.

Those two weeks would try the heart and soul of America's military like nothing since Pearl Harbor.

CHAPTER 4

★ ★ ★

MISSIONS IMPOSSIBLE

EARLY ON JULY 18, as the broken, bleeding remains of Major General William F. Dean's 24th Infantry Division attempted to make another defensive stand in the cramped ten miles between the shattered Kum River line and Taejon, Eighth Army commander General Walton Walker again flew to the front. This time, he had two crucial objectives in mind.

In this darkest hour ever faced by the 24th Division, Walker's first concern was reviving the crushed spirits of Dean, his field commanders, and their troops sufficiently to draw from them one final all-out effort. Walker must have known by now that, in its pathetic condition, the 24th couldn't hope to hold Taejon for long by itself. But he was bringing encouraging news that might inspire Dean's scarecrows to hang on for a few more days.

Another, no less urgent objective of Walker's trip was determining the next feasible line of defense where American troops could make a last-ditch stand before Pusan if Taejon should fall to the Communists. Barring some miracle, it was much more a question of *when* than *if* in Walker's mind.

After studying all available maps, Walker concluded that the only remaining geographic feature favorable to such a stand was the Naktong River, most of which flows in a north–south line that passes some sixty miles east of Taejon. The Naktong outlines a section of extreme southeastern Korea measuring about sixty by ninety miles. The river rises near the east coast, flows almost due west for fifty miles or so, then turns abruptly south before curving sharply back to the east and emptying into the Korea Strait only a couple of miles west of Pusan. In the weeks ahead, the meandering course of the Naktong would become virtually synonymous with the boundary lines of the besieged Pusan Perimeter.

Simply put, the Naktong was to Pusan what the Kum River was to Taejon. If the Naktong were breached by the North Koreans, Pusan—and the war—would be as good as lost.

For obvious reasons, Walker didn't say much about this latter objective to General Dean. Instead, he informed Dean that the entire Eighth Army was coming to Korea to join the fight. In fact, the First Cavalry Division was landing that very morning at Pohang-dong, on the east coast, and would be in combat position between the 24th and ROK units to the east in a day or two.

Meanwhile, elements of the 25th Infantry Division, including Colonel Mike Michaelis's 27th "Wolfhound" Infantry Regiment, had been in Korea since July 10. Teamed with the Eighth Field Artillery Battalion to form the 27th Regimental Combat Team, the Wolfhounds also would be on their way to the Taejon front as soon as they secured a vital airfield on the east coast. Some of their officers had already been to the front on a reconnoitering mission.

Walker brought additional encouragement by revealing that a few Sherman tanks and a shipment of 3.5-inch bazookas would be in Taejon within hours. The powerful new rocket launchers, which fired a nine-pound round with a shaped charge designed to burn through the heaviest armor, would be the first fully reliable antitank weapons to reach American infantry in Korea. (A total of 316 launchers had reached Korea on July 12, accompanied by slightly more than 1,300 rockets—only about four per weapon—and one three-man team of trainers to show American troops how to fire them. Sixty of these 3.5s were designated for the 24th Division, and they arrived in Taejon on July 18, but for reasons that remain unclear, none was put into action until early on July 20.)

Nevertheless, the cold, hard truth remained distressingly clear: Dean's crippled division had nowhere near enough weapons or troops to hold the NKPA at bay for long. Walker asked the 24th for at least forty-eight hours, and Dean promised to do his best, but both of them realized the odds were heavily stacked against them. As noted Army historian Colonel Roy A. Appleman explained:

"In any deployment of his forces against the North Koreans in front of Taejon, Dean . . . had only the remnants of three defeated regiments. Each of them could muster little more than a battalion of troops. In addition to numerical weakness, all the troops were tired, and their morale was not the best. General Dean . . . himself was as worn as his troops; for the past two weeks, he had faced daily crises and had pushed himself to the limit."

The casualties already suffered by the three regiments prior to the battle for Taejon had been disastrous. The 21st Infantry had lost 1,433 men (some 57 percent of its total strength), with only 1,100 troops remaining fit for combat, yet it was in better shape than the other two units. The 34th Infantry reported 2,002 killed or wounded, while three-fourths of the 19th Infantry—some 2,400 men—had fallen in battle.

Among those listed as killed, wounded, or missing in the 19th were Corporal Shorty Estabrook and the two young buck privates he'd happened upon after fleeing the Kum River and wandering alone for a time. All three were tired, hungry, thirsty—and utterly lost. They knew they couldn't be far from Taejon, but they had no idea how to get there, or even in which direction they were traveling.

Estabrook had awakened to a bright sun and total solitude on the morning after his escape from the collapsing American lines. From the far distance, he could hear the sound of artillery fire, but in the immediate area, it was amazingly quiet.

He was so starved for food and water that he wasn't sure at first if he could even stand up, but after a few minutes he managed to struggle to his feet, easing his way slowly down the hill where he'd spent the night. He'd gone only about 100 yards when he caught sight of a Korean hut and heard indistinct voices inside.

Estabrook still clutched his M-1, although its barrel was clogged with mud and probably would've exploded in his face if he'd tried to fire it, and he kept the weapon at the ready as he approached the door of the hut. He knew that almost all Koreans spoke Japanese, and during two years in Japan, he'd picked up enough of the language to communicate.

"I'm an American," he told the man who appeared in the doorway. "I'm lost, and I need food and water."

The man nodded, and to Estabrook's immense relief, he soon brought out a jug of water and a bowl of rice. When Estabrook had eaten and drunk as much as he could hold, he asked directions to Taejon, and the man gestured toward a crease in the hills.

"That way," he said in Japanese.

A couple of hours later, Estabrook met up with the two GIs. Both were about eighteen, and they'd jettisoned all their equipment except for a .45 automatic with one remaining round in the barrel.

"We kept walking toward the crease in the hills until we spotted some men in ROK Army uniforms," Estabrook recalled. "But when we yelled at them, they started shooting at us, and we knew something was wrong. They were North Koreans dressed as ROKs."

"What're we gonna do?" one of the privates asked Estabrook after they ducked for cover. "You outrank us, so you decide."

"My rifle's no good; the barrel's clogged," Estabrook told him, "and your one bullet ain't gonna go far. They'll probably shoot us on the spot, but I don't see any choice but to surrender."

Estabrook waved a white handkerchief and held his breath. He'd seen numerous dead Americans with their hands tied behind them and bullet holes in the backs of their heads.

The North Koreans didn't shoot the three captive Americans, but they beat them unmercifully until they lay groaning on the ground. It was Estabrook's first small taste of life as an NKPA prisoner of war.

Harsh weather—a devilish mixture of monsoon rains and furnacelike daytime temperatures—plus long marches over brutal terrain and long days with little rest had taken a fearsome physical toll on the 24th Division GIs still listed as on duty and able-bodied. "Only foot soldiers who have labored up the steep Korean slopes in mid-summer," historian Appleman observed, "can know how quickly exhaustion overcomes the body unless it is inured to such conditions by training and experience."

Unfortunately, the survivors of General Dean's command had the benefit of neither.

Nevertheless, Dean himself was heartened by the news from Walker, and although he ordered his divisional headquarters moved east to a more secure location at the town of Yongdong, he chose to stay behind with his troops in Taejon.

After conferring with Dean, Walker departed for the small city of Taegu, seventy miles to the southeast, where his own headquarters was being set up. When his chief of staff asked Walker how much liberty he'd given Dean in deciding the fate of Taejon, the Eighth Army commander replied, "I told him that I had every confidence in him, and that, if it became necessary to abandon Taejon earlier, to make his own decision, and I'd sustain him. Dean's a fighter. He won't give an inch if he can help it."

White-haired, square-jawed Bill Dean had dreamed as a teenager of attending West Point, but mediocre grades prevented him from getting an appointment. He won his Army commission by virtue of completing an ROTC program at the University of California, although he left without earning a sought-after law degree.

Dean proved to be competent and courageous in battle, and he won recognition during World War II as a "can do" assistant commander of the 44th Infantry Division. He served in Europe on a severely burned left leg, suffered in a training accident, after ignoring a surgeon's recommendation that the leg be amputated, and he was awarded the Distinguished Service Cross for personally leading a platoon through savage German artillery fire. Dean also knew Korea well, having previously spent a year in the country as a senior adviser to the South Korean police and constabulary. Now, true to Walker's assessment of him, he was ready to do everything in his power to stop or slow the NKPA onslaught.

As he would later recall, in justifying his decision to stay with his troops at Taejon rather than retreat to his divisional headquarters at Yongdong, "My reasons for staying were simple, although, of course, there can be much argument about them. (I spent a great deal of time later trying to second-guess myself about them.) But these reasons were compounded of poor communications . . . and the old feeling that I could do the job better—that is, make the hour-to-hour decisions necessary—if I stayed in close contact with what was happening. . . . Very few of the things I did in the next twenty-four hours could not have been done by any competent sergeant— and such a sergeant would have done some of them better. I have no intention of alibiing my presence in Taejon. At the time, I thought it was the place to be."

Dean felt, with some justification, that the sight of the division commander fighting shoulder to shoulder with his enlisted men might stiffen their resolve. He also hoped that he might set a positive example for the few ROK commanders and staff officers who hadn't already hopped aboard the "Pusan Express" and headed south. And finally, Dean had a professional soldier's angry yearning to inflict as much pain and suffering as he could on the ruthless invaders who had slaughtered and maimed so many of the young men in his charge.

Yet remaining in Taejon was a decision Dean would have cause to regret for the rest of his life. He was, beyond question, a brave man—one who would be awarded the Medal of Honor for valor in the Korean War—and his task was among the most daunting ever faced by an American military leader of his rank. But driven by desperation amid the bloody chaos of Taejon on July 19–20, 1950, he took foolhardy risks and extreme chances that even the most valiant division commander should never take—and he paid dearly for them.

Dean's isolated actions during this period have drawn both praise for his courage and harsh criticism for failure to accept his larger responsibilities as a division commander. "Fundamentally, he was a silly man," said one of Dean's fellow officers. "He still didn't know what war was."

Corporal Lacy Barnett, company clerk of the 34th Infantry Regiment's medical unit during the deluge of casualties suffered in the fighting along the Kum River and north of Taejon, went from being one of the luckiest men in the U.S. Army to being one of the unluckiest in two or three days.

Barnett, an Alabama native who had been stationed in Pusan in 1948–49, then returned a week after the war started, was scheduled for discharge on July 19, 1950. As a farewell assignment on his way out, he'd had the good fortune to be sent south to division headquarters at Yongdong on July 15 to take care of some casualty reports before heading home, thereby missing the bloodbath at Taejon on July 18–20.

"My enlistment was supposed to be up on July 19," Barnett recalled decades later, "but my orders weren't cut until the next morning. Then I caught a train to Pusan, where I boarded an LST for Yokohama and the trip back to the States."

Halfway to Japan, the LST stopped, and a first sergeant broke the bad news to the would-be civilians. "You guys ain't going Stateside after all," he announced. "Congress just passed a bill extending all enlistments for one year, so the only place you're going is back to Korea."

Barnett was back with his medical company a few days later. When the decimated 34th Infantry was dissolved in September 1950, he would be one of just 184 surviving original members of the 2,000-man unit that had landed at Pusan on July 2.

Nearly sixty years later, Barnett, a retired Army major, remained bitter about the slaughter of the 34th at Taejon—a tragedy he narrowly missed and one he blamed largely on General Dean. Barnett based his condemnation of his division commander on years of extensive research for a yet-unpublished book.

"The whole setup was stupid," he said. "I learned conclusively that General Walker had ordered Dean to be out of Taejon before daylight on July 20. Instead, Dean fiddled around until almost nightfall. If he'd followed orders, the division could've gotten away with a lot fewer casualties. Hundreds of lives could've been saved. In my opinion, Dean was one of the worst division commanders in the history of the U.S. Army."

Although General Lawton Collins, the Army's chief of staff, was considerably more diplomatic, his comments hardly constituted approval of Dean's actions. "The personal involvement of a senior commander in the combat of small units or in one small segment of an action," Collins observed, "tends to divert his mind from larger issues."

Dean's job would surely have been less onerous if the GIs who served under him had been better trained and more fully prepared to fight, and as their commander, he doubtlessly bears a portion of the blame for the fact that they were not. On the other hand, Dean could do nothing to alter the fact that his troops had neither the tools nor the numbers to succeed against their much larger, more powerful foe, or that the supplies and equipment issued to them were nothing short of a national disgrace.

And it certainly wasn't Dean's fault that his division was being asked, yet again, to do the impossible. As Dean himself phrased it at the time, "Stopping the gooks is like trying to keep water from coming through a fishnet."

By the early morning of July 20, battered survivors of the 34th Infantry huddled among whatever cover they could find in the countryside north of Taejon, unnerved and uncertain of what to do next.

Fragments of two battalions of the 34th—fewer than 1,000 riflemen— had begun a slow retreat before noon the previous day from positions between Taejon and the Kum River, pulling back to avoid being surrounded and annihilated by a force of 17,000 North Koreans. The enemy troops, supported as always by tanks and artillery, had poured through a mile-wide gap between the 34th's First Battalion and the 19th Infantry, then launched a broad flanking movement aimed at cutting off all escape routes for the Americans defending Taejon.

The gravity of the situation had become apparent on the night of July 19 after Colonel Harold Ayres, commanding the 34th's First Battalion, sent out a patrol to investigate what sounded like tanks moving on his flank. The patrol never returned, and later, another patrol was turned back by enemy troops blocking the main road six miles south of Taejon. In the meantime, Colonel Charles E. Beauchamp, who had assumed command of the regiment after Colonel Robert Martin was killed, ordered his Third Battalion to attack in the gap between the 19th and the 34th. To the GIs' dismay, however, they arrived to find the gap already occupied by North Korean infantry supported by six tanks.

The entire Third Battalion might have been wiped out if not for the self-sacrificial action of First Sergeant Robert E. Dare, who took up a defensive position with a BAR and laid down a curtain of fire to cover the advance platoon's withdrawal. Dare paid for his heroism with his life, but most of his comrades managed to escape.

At this point, Colonel Ayres was more than ready to quit the battle altogether and make a run for the mountains to the south or east. Ayres suggested this to Beauchamp, who rejected the idea, knowing how determined General Dean was to hold Taejon for at least one more day.

But now hundreds of enemy infiltrators, many clad in white to mingle undetected with civilian refugees who moved freely among the American troops, were all around the men of the 34th. There was no safe haven from snipers firing rifles and tossing grenades from scores of buildings, and soon after daylight, NKPA tanks rumbled into the city.

Aided by detailed reports on the locations of various American units, either by disguised NKPA soldiers or civilian collaborators, the tanks proceeded directly to the position occupied by the 34th's service company. There, they methodically killed most of the 150 mechanics, drivers, cooks, and clerks manning the compound, destroyed all vehicles in the motor pool, and blew up an ammunition truck before moving on. Their obvious intention, beyond the slaughter of Americans, was to trap as many of Taejon's defenders as possible with no motorized means of getting away.

Meanwhile, the fast-moving enemy assault north of the city passed virtually unmolested through Colonel Ayres's bazooka teams and rifle platoons. By dawn, Ayres's command post was in enemy hands, and the First Battalion Headquarters and Heavy Weapons Company were frantically fleeing into the mountains in search of refuge.

The confusion mounted steadily as the morning wore on, with communication cut off among all engaged 24th Division units. Soon the Second Battalion of the 19th Infantry also abandoned its defensive positions and went into hiding in the mountains. By midday, not one unit of the division was still in its assigned position on General Dean's maps.

On the night of July 19, Dean and a small group of aides had crept into an abandoned house in Taejon, where the general had fallen into a fitful sleep to the sound of gunfire. When he awoke before dawn the next morning, the explosions were louder, and they were punctuated by the crackle of small-arms fire at close range. Dazed and weary American soldiers stumbled past Dean's makeshift command post in full retreat. The scent of defeat hung heavy in the air, but Dean refused to give up hope.

At 6:30 AM one of the general's staff officers, Lieutenant Arthur Clarke, appeared with grim news. "We've got reports of North Korean tanks within the city," he said. "We thought our lines were still holding to the north and west, but headquarters has lost contact with two battalions, and that may be where the tanks broke through."

This revelation left Dean feeling sick, but it also stoked his fierce urge to strike back at the enemy. It no longer made sense to sit and wait, he reasoned, or try to do the things that generals did under normal conditions. Besides, he was spoiling for a fight.

Dean stared at Clarke for a long moment, then at Jimmy Kim, his young Korean interpreter.

"Let's go tank-hunting," the general said.

At this point, the situation in Taejon itself wasn't as grave as that to the north and west of the city. From Dean's severely limited perspective, the battle seemed to be going reasonably well within the town, and that feeling was reinforced by the troops' enthusiasm over the newly arrived 3.5-inch bazookas. For the first time in the war, the powerful rocket launchers enabled small enclaves of American troops to disable or destroy the NKPA's dreaded T-34 tanks on a predictable basis.

Dean wanted the new weapons employed to the utmost. The only thing he wanted more was to get his own hands on one of the 3.5s. There were plenty of targets around that morning, including one enemy tank that headed straight for Dean's position. But at the time, the only weapon at the general's disposal was a truck-mounted 75-millimeter recoilless rifle.

"I succeeded in getting the driver's attention and redirected him back toward the tank," Dean recalled. "But even though we reached a firing position, we accomplished nothing. The gunner either was too nervous or was unfamiliar with his weapon, and none of our four or five rounds of remaining ammunition scored a hit."

Later in the day, Dean's group finally hooked up with a soldier carrying a 3.5 bazooka, but he had only one round of ammunition left for it, and apparently he was nervous, too. When a pair of enemy tanks lumbered into sight, the bazooka man fired at one of them from 100 yards, but the round fell dismally short.

In an outburst of anger, Dean drew his .45 automatic and emptied it at the unscathed T-34, cursing it roundly as it ground past him less than twenty yards away.

"This was our day for bad shooting," he said later. "Some people who escaped from Taejon that day reported that they had last seen me firing a pistol at a tank. Well, they did, but I'm not proud of it. . . . I wasn't silly enough to think I could *do* anything with a pistol. It was plain rage and frustration."

In his group's third encounter with enemy armor that day—its second with a 3.5 bazooka—Dean's luck changed for the better, however. After pursuing a T-34 on foot for blocks through a series of abandoned stores and shops, the general's team of tank-hunters ran through a courtyard, climbed to the second floor of a corner building, and entered a small, plastered room.

"Quietly, I slipped up beside the street window and looked around the side of it with one eye—directly into the muzzle of the tank's cannon," Dean recalled. "I could have spat down the barrel."

Dean signaled to the man with the bazooka, who eased forward into firing position. Then Dean pointed to a spot at the base of the cannon, where the turret and the body of the tank came together.

"Aim there," he said softly.

A second later, the deafening blast from the bazooka shook the room like a miniearthquake, sending fragments of plaster raining down on Dean and the gunner and filling the room with smoke and fumes. Ear-piercing screams came from the tank.

"Hit him again!" Dean snapped.

The gunner fired a second round, and more plaster poured from the ceiling. When the bazooka roared a third time, smoke billowed from the tank, and the screaming stopped.

Other American bazooka teams were equally successful. At least ten T-34s were destroyed in the streets of Taejon that afternoon by 3.5-inch rockets, and U.S. air strikes knocked out five or six more. When word of these unprecedented successes got around, GI morale in Taejon took a brief but dramatic leap.

While Dean was patrolling the edges of Taejon and jousting with tanks during most of the day on July 20, he clung to the mistaken belief that his troops were holding their own. In reality, the battle for the town was being lost a short distance to the north and west, and the unknowing Americans in Taejon proper were effectively being surrounded by the NKPA.

At about noon that day, Dean had driven north to Colonel Beauchamp's command post and shared a quick lunch of C rations with the 34th Infantry's commander. Although Beauchamp also seemed to feel that the situation in Taejon wasn't yet at the desperate stage, he and Dean agreed that General Walker's plea to hold the enemy for two more days had now been fulfilled. The time had come, they decided, to begin an orderly withdrawal while continuing to fight a rearguard delaying action.

With no effective phone or radio communication, Beauchamp sent out runners to spread the word to the First Battalion of the 34th and the Second Battalion of the 19th, unaware that both were already fleeing into the mountains. The runners were never heard from again, and the withdrawal order failed to reach the 34th's still-entrenched Third Battalion.

With these developments, the unraveling American front lost any semblance of cohesion. Panic gripped the troops holding the line north of the city as the situation grew more chaotic by the minute. In an effort to calm down his men, Beauchamp left his command post and set out by jeep to contact his scattered units. But for reasons that remain hazy six decades later, the colonel ended up miles to the southeast at the town of Okchon, where he found Brigadier General Pearson Menoher, assistant commander of the 24th Division, and reported the deteriorating situation to the north.

Back in Taejon, Dean was stunned to discover that Beauchamp was missing from his command post and that no one seemed to know where he'd gone—only that he hadn't been seen or heard from for more than two hours. The general had no way of knowing that Beauchamp had tried to return to Taejon from Okchon but was unable to penetrate enemy road-blocks, even with the help of several tanks.

With the surrounded city now coming under heavy artillery fire, and a number of buildings blazing furiously, Dean had little time to worry about Beauchamp's whereabouts. At about 5:00 PM on July 20, he summoned Lieutenant Colonel Robert L. "Pappy" Wadlington, an old comrade from World War II who was now executive officer of the 34th Infantry.

"We've got to evacuate the city immediately," Dean told him. "Get the show on the road as soon as you can."

It was easier said than done. For one thing, there was the American artillery to consider. Leaving valuable heavy weaponry behind in a retreat had become a distressingly common practice in the division over the past two weeks, and Dean was determined not to repeat it. Yet the North Koreans were already perilously close to the big guns, and the artillery positions were under heavy sniper fire.

Dean managed to get a message through to his headquarters at Yong-dong, pleading for American armor to be sent up, but time was running out. In desperation, he organized a counterattack force from kitchen police, messengers, clerks, and other rear-echelon personnel, and Major S. C. McDaniel, commanding the artillery battalion, also threw his headquarters staff into the fray. Together, this contingent of unlikely warriors managed to drive the enemy back temporarily, allowing some of the guns to be towed away by tractors. The rest were wrecked and abandoned.

Genuine safety was still a long, arduous journey away, however, and many who tried to escape Taejon that evening never made it that far.

By 6:00 PM virtually every road leading south and east from Taejon was blocked by NKPA forces, and long stretches of the roadways were subject to intense enemy mortar, machine-gun, and small-arms fire from ridges on both sides. As darkness fell and General Dean's convoy prepared to run this gauntlet, a detachment of light tanks from the First Cavalry Division miraculously managed to fight its way into the city to help cover Dean's withdrawal.

But taking personal advantage of the tanks ran against Dean's nature. He insisted instead that the tankers accompany the headquarters company of the 34th Infantry, adding that he and his convoy would follow shortly. He also declined an offer from Colonel Wadlington to call for more armor to shield their own withdrawal. Dean did, however, send another message, asking for tanks to clear an enemy roadblock he had heard about east of the city. Then he and the rest of his party climbed into their vehicles and drove through the gathering darkness in the direction the tanks had gone.

Wadlington led the way, but near the center of town, with the convoy under heavy machine-gun fire, the colonel's jeep and dozens of others following it became lost and ended up on a dead-end street that dissolved into a schoolyard. Panic-stricken and unable to turn around, the Americans set fire to their vehicles and fled on foot toward the mountains outside Taejon.

Meanwhile, Dean's party, continuing on the main road toward Okchon, came upon the flaming remains of an earlier convoy that had been ambushed by NKPA infiltrators hiding along the route. Wrecked and burning trucks littered the street, and buildings on both sides were ablaze. At the edge of the roadway, a ferocious firefight raged between American infantrymen and enemy troops.

"Keep driving!" Dean yelled to his driver. "Everybody down!"

Somehow Dean's jeep made it through the searing heat and the tangle of stalled vehicles. Swerving wildly with tires squealing, it veered back onto the straightaway, and the driver jammed the accelerator to the floor. A block farther on, as the jeep zoomed through an intersection with snipers' bullets slapping the pavement on all sides, Dean heard his aide Lieutenant Clarke shout a warning:

"Stop! We missed our turn!"

"No!" Dean told the driver. "We can't stop here! Keep going straight ahead! We'll have to go the long way around!"

Disoriented in the darkness after leaving Taejon, Dean's small party continued on in several jeeps through unfamiliar, enemy-infested countryside on a road that, according to Dean's maps, headed in the general direction of the town of Kumsan. At an S-curve along the route, they ran into an enemy roadblock and were forced to jump from their jeeps and take cover in a ditch. As they dashed for safety, Clarke took a bullet in his shoulder.

"Here I realized that I no longer had any weapon," Dean would recall much later. "I'd left my M-1 behind when I jumped for the ditch, and my pistol had been lost somewhere. The holster dangled empty at my hip."

They crawled away from the road in pitch blackness, trying not to make a sound that would give them away to the North Koreans. They dragged along a severely wounded man, who became delirious as the night wore on. The man drank every drop of the party's water before anyone realized what was happening, then loudly demanded more.

About midnight, while his thirsty, exhausted comrades dozed, Dean thought he heard water running somewhere nearby, perhaps a spring or a small stream. Without a weapon of any kind—or even a canteen—he set out alone in search of the water's source. He hadn't gone more than a few dozen yards when he blundered unexpectedly onto a steep hill, and before he could stop himself, he was half-running, half-stumbling down its slope.

Then he lost his footing and fell.

After searching vainly for their commander and dodging enemy patrols for approximately sixty hours, Lieutenant Clarke and other members of the party finally made their way back to U.S. lines on July 23. General Dean wouldn't be seen again by friendly forces for almost three years.

The First Cavalry Division, commanded by Major General Hobart R. Gay, had sailed from Japan on July 15 aboard a hodgepodge collection of U.S. and British ships. Its hurriedly planned assignment was to make the first amphibious landing of the Korean War at the small east coast fishing port of Pohangdong, and its objectives were twofold.

The first was to put more American troops on the ground in Korea as quickly—and as close to the combat zone—as possible. By landing up the coast at Pohangdong, this could be accomplished without adding to the frenzied congestion at Pusan, sixty-three miles to the south. The second objective was to shore up the threatened right flank of the UN line, previously manned only by ROK troops.

The First Cav's landing on July 18 has frequently been described as unopposed, and it's true that the Americans encountered no resistance as they disembarked from their ships. But as they marched inland a short time later, NKPA artillery wasn't far away, and it made its presence felt by firing sporadic rounds in the direction of the U.S. advance.

Corporal Jack Brooks had been ashore for only an hour or two when he saw his best friend, PFC Bill Meckley, fatally wounded by an exploding enemy shell.

"All of a sudden, we were under attack," Brooks remembered. "I was within fifteen or twenty yards of Meckley when he was hit. I saw him go down, and I ran over and picked him up in my arms and started looking for a medic. By the time I found one, I realized Bill was dead."

Brooks recalled several other men being wounded that day, but Meckley, a Pennsylvania youngster whom Brooks had met several months earlier at Fort Benning, Georgia, may have been the first member of the First Cavalry to die in action in Korea. He would be far from the last. In the course of the war, the division would see 3,811 men killed in action and 12,086 wounded.

By July 22, two days after the fall of Taejon, troops of the First Cav and the 25th Infantry Division were deployed in relief of the battered and virtually leaderless 24th Division, and the 24th was finally sent into reserve. (General John Church assumed command of the division three days after General Dean went missing, but many other officers also had been lost, and few replacements were available.) In its failed effort to hold Taejon, the division had lost an additional 1,150 dead, missing, or wounded out of a total remaining strength of about 4,000. Most of the missing would later be confirmed as KIAs, many of them murdered in cold blood after being captured.

The First Cav dug in near the town of Kumchon, in the center of the UN front, with the 25th Infantry Division, commanded by Major General William B. Kean, on its right. ROK units, meanwhile, continued to retreat—although more gradually than before—along the east coast. The American soldiers now facing the North Koreans were at least fresh and better equipped than their predecessors, yet for the most part, they were no better trained, no better led, and totally lacking in combat experience.

Ready or not, though, their turn in the cauldron was coming, and it wouldn't be pretty.

• • •

On July 20, the same day that U.S. forces were routed at Taejon, units of the 25th Division had begun reaching Yongdong to relieve the gaunt survivors of the 24th Division. Two days later, the 25th moved into the line near Sangju while the First Cav went into action at Yongdong. The results of these newly arrived divisions' first encounters with the NKPA were disheartening similar to all that had gone before. The fighting was bloody and hellish. Yongdong was lost. So was Sangju. Once again, the American front moved south and east.

General Walker now realized that even reinforced by two full divisions, his Eighth Army was plunging deeper and deeper into crisis. Some of the new troops turned in creditable performances on the battlefield, but they were unable to stem the tide. In particular, the 25th Division's failure to hold Sangju galled Walker, and he gave General Kean a stern dressing-down about it.

Among the principal targets of blame for the loss of Sangju was the 24th Infantry Regiment (not to be confused with the 24th Infantry Division), an all-black unit led by white officers and commanded by Colonel Horton White. Its reputation for "bugging out" under fire began on July 20, when the regiment became the first unit of the 25th Division to face the North Koreans at the town of Yechon, northeast of Sangju.

After only a brief exchange of fire, panicky troops of the 24th broke and ran before even catching sight of the enemy. Field officers on the scene claimed that the regiment was attacked by a "vastly superior" NKPA force, but when a scouting party entered the town the next day, no evidence could be found that any enemy troops had even been there. Fires that broke out in the town and contributed to the defenders' fright were apparently caused by the Americans' own artillery.

A day or two later, the regiment's Second Battalion—close to 1,000 men—retreated in disorder after encountering a minor roadblock and being fired on by one light mortar and a few automatic weapons. The next morning, when the roadblock was stormed and overrun by ROK troops, they found only two small-caliber machine guns, the single mortar, and about thirty guerrillas.

When the ROKs were ordered east to counter North Korean forces driving south along the coast, the 24th Regiment was left alone to protect the western approach to Sangju—only to disgrace itself again. An official U.S. Army history of the Korean conflict summed up the charges against the regiment in these words:

"The tendency to panic continued in nearly all the 24th Infantry operations west of Sangju. Men left their position and straggled to the rear. They abandoned weapons on position. On one occasion, the Third Battalion withdrew from a hill and left behind twelve .30-caliber and three .50-caliber machine guns, eight 60-millimeter mortars, three 81-millimeter mortars, four 3.5-inch rocket launchers, and 102 rifles."

The combat modus operandi of the 24th was to hold its positions during daylight hours, when the NKPA tended to lie low because of American air superiority, but when darkness fell, many men would slip out of their foxholes and disappear.

Angry, disgusted officers ordered roadblocks set up behind the 24th to deal with fleeing deserters. Walker soon realized that the regiment could be employed only as an outpost force, whose flight would alert other units to enemy assaults. But this required placing other units in reserve to the rear of the 24th to plug the inevitable hole left in the line when members of the regiment went AWOL.

The lyrics of a derisive little tune called the "Bug-Out Boogie" reflected the disdain felt by other GIs for the 24th Regiment:

> *When those old gook mortars begin to chug,*
> *That old deuce-four begins to bug!*

If there was one positive factor in the shameful debacle suffered by the 24th, it was the long-overdue revelation to the nation's leaders that segregation of the U.S. military was a tragically bad idea. The plight of the 24th provided vital impetus in the full integration of America's armed forces. Army Chief of Staff General Lawton Collins was among the most outspoken proponents of this change.

As he put it, "Negro soldiers, when properly trained and fully integrated with their white comrades, would fight as well and would readily be accepted as equals."

Maligned as it was, there were some truly courageous individuals in the ranks of the 24th. One notable example was PFC William Thompson of New York City, a machine gunner in M Company of the regiment's Third Battalion.

When two rifle companies of his battalion stampeded like cattle during an enemy ambush, trampling their officers underfoot in their haste to get away, Thompson stayed at his .30-caliber weapon, mowing down the attackers right and left.

"Come on, Willie," Thompson's platoon leader urged. "We gotta get outta here while we still can!"

Thompson continued firing. "You go on," he said. "I'll cover you."

A passing corporal tried to pull Thompson away from the machine gun, but the husky gunner shook him off and waved him away.

"Maybe I won't get out," he said, "but I'm gonna take a whole lotta them with me."

After the others reached safer positions, they could still hear Thompson's gun chattering. Then several enemy grenades exploded, followed briefly by total silence. Months later, Thompson was posthumously awarded the Medal of Honor.

On July 29, the First Cavalry, defeated at Yongdong by the same enemy flanking attacks that had spelled disaster for so many other U.S. units during the month, was forced to retreat toward Kumchon. The following day, the 25th Division also began falling back, yielding Sangju to the North Koreans.

Now the major concern for Eighth Army commander General Walker was the city of Taegu, where his own headquarters was and which lay squarely in the path of the NKPA advance, just sixty-two miles northwest of Pusan. A key highway and rail center, Taegu also was the site of the only operational airport in the region. Responsibility for holding it rested squarely with General Kean's 25th Division.

The situation south and east of Taejon was sliding from bad to worse, with no remedy in sight. But while the attention of U.S. commanders was focused on that area, a threat of even greater urgency was taking shape west of Taegu, in territory where no organized UN defensive lines existed.

Faced with stiffening resistance and sharply rising casualties along the established front—more than 50,000 NKPA troops had by now been lost since the war began—the Communists staged a surprise "end run" that caught the Americans badly off guard. Two full NKPA divisions suddenly swept past U.S. troop concentrations stretching from the center of South Korea to the east coast, then raced southward unimpeded down the west side of the peninsula. Their target was the area south of where the short Han River branched off from the larger Naktong on a more westerly course and the Naktong itself curved sharply east, passing too close to Pusan to serve as a feasible line of defense. This territory between the two rivers constituted a vulnerable soft spot, where Walker's troops would be forced to defend positions west of the Naktong.

Before the resulting threat was fully recognized by the Americans, the attacking enemy force was at the extreme southern tip of Korea and driving east through unprotected countryside toward the towns of Chinju and Masan, the nearer of which was just thirty-one miles from Pusan.

It took a nearly superhuman effort by elements of the Eighth Army, particularly General Kean's 25th Division, to avert total disaster—at least for the moment. As of nightfall on August 1, units of the 25th still faced NKPA forces in the lines southeast of Sangju. But by sunrise the following morning, in one of the most deftly executed strategic redeployments in military history, the bulk of the 25th had slipped away from the Sangju front, boarded trucks, and made the 150-mile journey south to the vicinity of Masan to block the enemy advance.

At the same time, General Walker dispatched two battalions of the 29th Infantry Regiment, recently rushed to Korea from Okinawa, to perform a similar blocking operation at Chinju, twenty-three miles west of Masan. The men of the 29th had first been promised ten days of field training before being committed to battle; then the preparation time was cut to three days to draw equipment and test weapons. In reality, however, these troops were herded aboard trucks almost as soon as they set foot ashore and driven immediately to Chinju. They arrived there the next day with their machine guns still clogged with Cosmoline, their mortars yet unfired, and their M-1s still not zeroed in.

Even the exhausted survivors of the 24th Infantry Division were pulled out of reserve and sent south to further shore up the Chinju–Masan defenses. "I'm sorry to have to do this," Walker told General John Church soon after Church had assumed command of the 24th as General Dean's successor, "but our whole left flank is open, and the Koreans are moving in. I want you to cover the area from Chinju up to near Kumchon."

This portion of the fluid new front stretched about sixty-five air miles from north to south—quite a chunk of real estate for the remains of a thoroughly defeated division to defend.

On July 31, all units of Walker's beleaguered army except those struggling to hold back the NKPA around Chinju and Masan retreated across the Naktong River under orders to make a stand on the south and east sides of the stream—or else.

"No more retreating, withdrawal, or whatever you call it," Walker warned his soldiers. "There is no line behind us to which we can retreat. This isn't going to be another Dunkirk or Bataan. A retreat to Pusan would result in one of the greatest butcheries in history. We must fight to the end. Capture by these people is worse than death itself.

"We will fight as a team. If some of us must die, we will die fighting together. I want everybody to understand we are going to hold this line. We are going to win!"

The Eighth Army held strong defensive positions on steep hills along the Naktong's banks. It was far bigger and much better armed than it had been two or three weeks earlier. But a premature end to the monsoon season and searing summer heat had left the river shallow and easily forded in many places, and that was a major problem.

The biggest problem, though, was that the young Americans dug in on this last line of defense in the UN effort to save South Korea had, as yet, no experience at winning. They had been thrown into the teeth of too many missions impossible. Thus far they had learned only how to fight losing battles and then retreat. Regardless of the potential consequences that might await them this time, many of them were gripped by an alarming lack of faith that they could hold their ground.

Facing them were ten divisions of enemy troops—including the NKPA's crack Sixth Division, commanded by General Pang Ho San—none of which had yet learned to lose. "Comrades, the enemy is demoralized," Pang told his troops as they surged south. "The task given to us is the liberation of Masan and Chinju and the annihilation of the remnants of the enemy. The liberation of Chinju and Masan means the final battle to cut off the windpipe of the enemy."

Here, on the craggy ridges above the Korea Strait, and with only the sea at its back, the fate of General Walker's Eighth Army—and the future of South Korea—would be decided.

CHAPTER 5

★ ★ ★

ENTER THE
"FIRE BRIGADE"

B Y AUGUST 1, when the first elements of the First Provisional Marine Brigade finally reached Pusan, a suffocating blanket of gloom hung over
the city. The air was full of contradictory rumors that had only one thing in
common: all were prophesies of inevitable catastrophe.

Almost no one believed that the shrunken perimeter around Pusan
could be held. Boat owners were selling space aboard their craft for exorbi-
tant prices in preparation for the massive evacuation that was believed to be
only a few days—perhaps hours—away. Total hopelessness hovered just
below the surface.

Bloated to ten times its normal size—from a prewar population of about
200,000 to more than 2 million—South Korea's last remaining open port
swarmed with fretful activity. Thousands of homeless refugees (and more
than a few Communist spies and collaborators) mingled with wounded,
dying, and newly arrived UN troops. Stevedores unloaded ships while beg-
gars, prostitutes, thieves, smugglers, and black marketers plied their trades.
The town and its dock area were a crazy-quilt maze of teeming dirt streets,

corrugated metal buildings, military convoys, packed and raucous markets, naked children, festering shantytowns, disagreeable smells—and thinly veiled hysteria.

It was a day later, on the afternoon of August 2, as the sun was sinking behind the rugged hills above Pusan, when most of the ships of Task Group 53.7 steamed into the port. The *George Clymer*, one of the three transports carrying Marine ground forces, was first to arrive at dockside. Awaiting it was General Craig, the brigade commander, who had flown to Korea several days earlier and had already been to the front on a reconnoitering mission. During a brief welcoming ceremony for his troops, Craig received a bouquet of flowers from the mayor of Pusan, Kin Chu Han.

"Thank you for bringing the Marines," Kin said. "The panic will leave my people now."

"There are more of us on the way, many more," Craig replied.

Moments later, Craig waved a greeting to the men lining the rail of the "Greasy George" as a South Korean band blared out a tinny, off-key rendition of the "Marine Hymn."

Nearby, shaking their fists in salute, stood twenty Marine guards from the defunct U.S. Embassy in Seoul, who had been, until now, their Corps' only representatives in South Korea. Commanded by Master Sergeant John Runch, the embassy Marines had won high praise from Ambassador John Muccio for protecting him and his staff and helping them escape from the capital city in late June as enemy troops closed in.

"What the hell took you so long?" yelled Sergeant Augustus Siefkin, one of the guards, to the shipboard Marines. "We thought you'd never get here!"

Few others in Pusan apparently shared Mayor Kin's and Sergeant Siefkin's upbeat attitude that afternoon, however. Defeatism and despair were clearly the prevailing sentiments, and they were particularly noticeable among the workers on the overcrowded docks, who lost no time in bombarding the newcomers with wild rumors of impending calamity.

"Damn, these people are just like Chicken Little," said a frowning young Marine rifleman as he disembarked. "You know, 'The sky is falling! The sky is falling!'"

A Marine officer noticed the tension in the air immediately. "You could sense—almost feel—the fear," he said. "The people were scared to death. The North Koreans were very close."

"Everything seemed in turmoil," added Lieutenant Colonel Robert Taplett, commanding the Third Battalion, Fifth Marines. "There were too many people with a wild stare in their eyes. We encountered badly frightened military and civilian personnel who demonstrated an attitude of 'doomsday is coming.'"

Although many of the Army troops along the waterfront were gratified to see the Marines, some offered their traditional barbed greetings to the Leathernecks, occasionally with a touch of grim humor.

"Welcome to Korea, jarheads," yelled one GI. "I guess this means the rest of us can go home now, right?"

General Craig was unquestionably happy to see his men, but his pleasure was quickly dimmed by the frustrations and foul-ups associated with bringing a Marine force into an Army-dominated theater of operations. One of Craig's first discoveries was that his carefully crafted operations plan, spelling out assignments for various brigade units and informing commanders that their troops should expect to move out as soon as they arrived, had never been delivered. As a result, the troops were clueless as to what was expected of them now. No ammunition or rations had been issued and, as desperate as the situation was, no decision had been made about where the brigade would be deployed initially.

Craig was shocked to see Marines casually leaning over the rails to watch their ships dock after he'd issued explicit orders through Army channels for every member of the brigade to be prepared to march ashore combat-ready and with weapons loaded.

"Which battalion is the advance guard?" Craig shouted from the dock to Colonel Edward Snedeker, his chief of staff, who was still aboard ship. Snedeker's only response was a puzzled frown. He had no idea what Craig was talking about.

"Did you get my orders?" Craig shouted to Lieutenant Colonel Raymond L. Murray, commander of the Fifth Marines, as the *Pickaway*, the second troop ship to reach port, tied up at the dock.

"No, sir!" Murray replied, shaking his head.

Although the shipboard Marines understood that the situation was grave, they had only the sketchiest knowledge of what was happening at the front. They'd seen situation maps showing the steady gains made by the North Koreans, but otherwise they knew virtually nothing about the foe they would shortly face or the life-or-death situation confronting them in a country most of them had never heard of five weeks earlier.

"While en route, intelligence on the NK Army was zero," Colonel Taplett complained, "and information on the progress of the war on the peninsula was practically nonexistent, except for occasional commercial radio broadcasts. The lack of enemy intelligence was a serious deficiency."

To clear up the confusion, Craig ordered an immediate conference of all brigade staff officers, battalion commanders, and leaders of supporting units with himself and Colonel Murray. When the briefing convened in the wardroom of the *George Clymer* at 9:00 PM on August 2, the first order of business was a summary of current battlefield conditions by Lieutenant Colonel Ellsworth Van Orman, brigade intelligence officer.

The news was disturbing enough to dispel any remaining mood of celebration among the officers at having reached their destination. On the central front, NKPA forces were poised at the Naktong River; on the east coast, they were battling ROK units for control of the secondary port of Pohangdong; and in the far south, they were driving on the town of Masan, only thirty-one miles from Pusan. In all, eleven divisions of well-armed, battle-tested North Korean troops—estimated total strength, 90,000 to 100,000 men—had been thrown into the fight. Their commanders fully expected them to be in Pusan by August 15 at the latest.

Opposing the invaders were eight depleted, exhausted divisions—four American and four ROK—whose lines stretched over 120 miles of ridges and riverfront, and whose battered troops had yet to defeat the enemy or drive him back. Token military contingents from five UN countries had by now reached Korea, but only the British had enough combat-ready ground troops in the country to make an appreciable difference on the front lines.

Although the Marine brigade, with a total of 6,534 men, including its aviation components, wasn't nearly large enough to even the numerical odds faced by UN forces, it would at least help level the playing field. Each

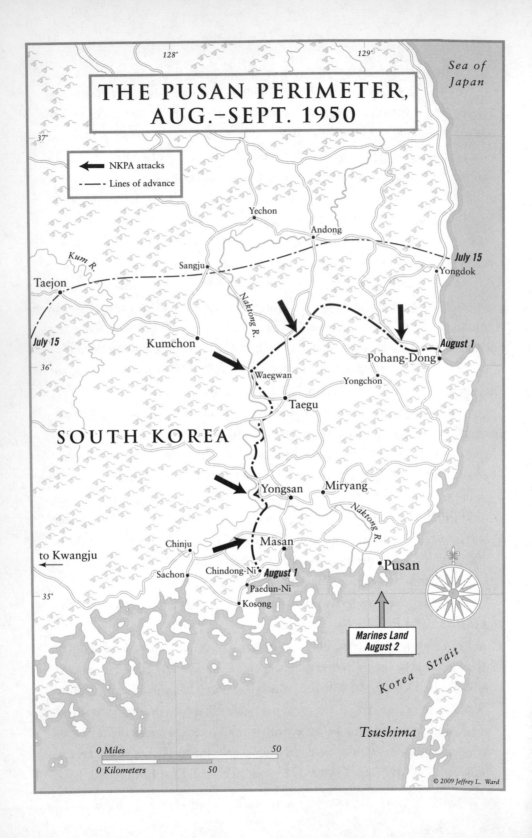

THE PUSAN PERIMETER, AUG.–SEPT. 1950

Sea of Japan

→ NKPA attacks

–·– Lines of advance

Yechon

Andong

Kum R.

Sangju

Taejon

July 15

Yongdok

July 15

Kumchon

Naktong R.

Pohang-Dong

August 1

Waegwan

Yongchon

Taegu

SOUTH KOREA

Yongsan

Miryang

Naktong R.

to Kwangju

Chinju

Masan

Pusan

Sachon

Chindong-Ni

August 1

Paedun-Ni

Kosong

Marines Land August 2

Korea Strait

Tsushima

0 Miles   50

0 Kilometers   50

© 2009 Jeffrey L. Ward

128°   129°

37°

36°

35°

of the three battalions of infantry was short one entire rifle company (about 235 men) out of its normal three, but the infantry was augmented by a wide range of specialized auxiliary units borrowed from the First Marine Division. These included engineer, ordnance, and tank battalions; signal, motor transport, medical, reconnaissance, and amphibian tractor companies; and various smaller detachments. Also attached was an artillery battalion with three firing batteries drawn from the 11th Marines to give the brigade its own coordinated heavy-weapons support.

In addition, the men of the Marine brigade brought with them one intangible yet indispensable asset—a unique esprit de corps that was almost mystical. This was the essence of their confidence, their swagger. It was what set them apart. They hadn't joined their Corps to see the world or vacation comfortably in a foreign land. Their only mission was to fight, and they had been prepared to fulfill that mission from their first day in boot camp.

"The Marine Corps was not made pleasant for men who served in it," wrote author T. R. Fehrenbach. "It remained the same hard, brutal way of life it had always been. They were only young men like those about them in Korea, but they were conscious of a standard to live up to. . . . [T]hey had had good training, and it had been impressed upon them that they were United States Marines."

Added historian Clay Blair, "The ranks were filled with physically tough young men who had joined the Corps to fight, not to sightsee, [and they] had superior firepower in squads, platoons, and companies."

"The situation is serious, gentlemen," General Craig told the officers as the conference aboard the *George Clymer* began. "With the forces available, it's obvious that the perimeter can't be held in strength. Eighth Army has adopted a plan of holding thinly and counterattacking enemy penetrations to keep them off-balance and prevent them from launching a coordinated effort."

At the moment, Craig continued, General Walker was undecided where the Marines would be used first. They could be sent north of Taegu to support the left flank of the First Cavalry Division, or they might go west to block an enemy advance along the Masan road. It all depended on where the greater threat developed.

The only thing of which Craig was absolutely certain was that General Walker was counting on the Marines to launch the first American offensive of the war—wherever it might be. This came as no surprise to any of the assembled officers. They'd known from the get-go that this would be their job. Attacking and destroying the enemy were what Marines were all about.

"We're going into battle against a vicious, well-trained enemy in what will be an extended land campaign," Craig said. "Much of our moving will be done on foot. We'll leave all nonessential supplies and equipment in storage on the docks here. We'll carry with us two days of rations and two units of fire [enough ammunition to last, theoretically, for two days]."

Craig compared the Pusan Perimeter to a weakened dike, one that could spring a leak almost anywhere at any time. "We'll be used to plug holes as they open," he said. "We're a brigade—a fire brigade—and we'll be in costly fighting against a numerically superior enemy. Marines have never yet lost a battle, and this brigade isn't going to be the first to set such a precedent. Unloading will begin at once. We move out at 0600 [six o'clock] tomorrow morning."

After dark, the atmosphere on the Pusan waterfront usually turned even more urgent and confusing than it was in daylight, and the humid evening of August 2 was no exception. Despite their early-morning travel orders, the Marines would get no sleep that night. They had tons of equipment and supplies to unload.

As the hours passed, the scene degenerated into near bedlam, with thousands of bone-weary Marines hauling weapons, ammunition, rations, and other essentials from ships' holds to Army warehouses; collecting their personal gear; regaining their "land legs" after nineteen days at sea; and frequently swearing at each other. On one level, the men were apprehensive about what the coming day would bring. On another, they were relieved to be ashore and able to move around freely beyond their cramped shipboard quarters.

First Lieutenant Francis I. "Ike" Fenton, executive officer of the brigade's B Company, First Battalion, felt tired but strangely energized as he surveyed the dockside activity. For the twenty-seven-year-old World War II veteran from Long Beach, California, the trip across the Pacific had seemed to last forever, especially after the Marines learned that an anticipated stopover in Japan for loading combat supplies and equipment had been canceled.

"We were looking forward to a few days in Japan, where we could let the new guys fire their weapons, something they hadn't had the opportunity to do at Pendleton," Fenton recalled. "We were also hoping to get in one or two days of platoon tactics in the hills of Japan."

All these hopes went down the drain, however, as the situation around Pusan deteriorated, and the brigade was ordered directly to Korea. Many of the men were combat veterans, but there had been no chance for any type of active training on the creaking old transports of the task group because space was too limited. Conditions on the breakdown-prone *Henrico*, where Fenton was assigned, were especially bad.

"It was impossible to get the whole company together at one location," said Fenton. "Consequently, we used passageways, boat decks, holds—any space we could find to lecture to the men and give them what little information we had on what was happening in Korea. A lot of time was spent on blackboard tactics for the fire teams, platoons, and company. We also emphasized first aid, hygiene, water discipline, and no eating of native foods. We were very conscious of the fact that dysentery could be just as big an enemy as the North Koreans themselves."

The brigade was equipped with the powerful new 3.5-inch rocket launchers, Fenton noted, but none of the men had ever fired one. Now, because there'd been no stop in Japan, they still hadn't.

"Our big worry," Fenton said, "was how we were going to combat those enemy tanks that seemed to be breaking through wherever they approached our lines."

Like most of his shipmates, Corpsman Herb "Doc Rocket" Pearce had sharply mixed emotions about his arrival at Pusan. For several days after leaving San Francisco, Pearce had remained too seasick to venture topside. Not even the open-ocean transfer of Colonel Murray, commander of the Fifth Marines, from the stricken *Henrico* to Pearce's ship, the *Pickaway*, could lure Pearce abovedecks. Eventually the nausea and dizziness had eased, but during the rest of the long voyage across the Pacific, an almost equally distasteful bout of boredom had set in.

The troops aboard the *Pickaway* had dreamed up various diversions—some creative and some merely silly—to combat the dreary routine. "We'd start some kind of rumor early in the morning, then time it to see how long it took to get back to us," Pearce recalled. "Or a long line of us would stand at the rail and read the same paperback book. After the first man read a page, he'd tear it out and pass it to the next guy while the first guy read the second page, and so on. This way, the whole book made its way down the line one page at a time."

As the voyage dragged on, however, Pearce and other "green" corpsmen found more constructive ways to spend their time. "I volunteered to work in sick bay to help take care of a Marine who'd lost an arm in an accident in the ship's laundry," he remembered. "We also got briefings from some of the World War II corpsmen about what to expect when we went into combat. It was time well spent, and their advice paid real dividends later, both for us and the men we treated on the battlefield."

Pearce spent the night of August 2–3 working alongside the Marines in the massive unloading job. Early the next morning, as many of the men scurried back aboard the *Pickaway* for what was expected to be their last hot breakfast for a long time, they still faced at least one major problem.

Since the brigade had been forced to leave many of its trucks behind in the States because of a lack of shipboard space, a severe shortage of motor transport now became obvious. But even one truck would be better than none, and the recoilless-rifle platoon to which Pearce was assigned was fortunate to have more than its share of enterprising and innovative scroungers. Thus the transport problem was soon alleviated.

"We 'liberated' an unattended Army truck, spruced it up with a new coat of Marine-green paint and some really neat new yellow numbers, and calmly loaded our gear aboard," said Pearce, pausing to laugh. "You know, the Army never did get that truck back!"

It was after 11:00 PM on August 2 when the orders that General Craig had been awaiting finally came through from Eighth Army headquarters. The

Marine brigade's initial destination was to be the town of Changwon, forty miles west of Pusan, where it was instructed to bivouac and await further orders.

At six o'clock the next morning, Lieutenant Colonel George R. Newton's First Battalion, including Lieutenant Ike Fenton's Baker Company, set out for Changwon by truck as advance guard for the rest of the brigade. Before departure, the men received a ringing send-off message from the Marine Corps commander, General Clifton Cates: "The pride and honor of many generations of Marines is entrusted to you today. You are the Old Breed. With you moves the heart and soul and spirit of all who ever bore the title United States Marine. Good luck and Godspeed."

The rough, narrow roads made for slow going in the oppressive heat, and the trucks kicked up stifling clouds of dust. "We had a water shortage right from the first, which didn't help matters," said Fenton. "A lot of the men left for Changwon without much water in their canteens, and we didn't get a chance to refill them until that afternoon."

It was 2:00 PM before the thirsty, dust-covered advance battalion reached a point about a mile west of the town and set up a defensive line on high ground astride the Changwon–Masan road to the rear of the 25th Infantry Division. The Army's Fifth Regimental Combat Team also was in the area.

The main body of the Marine brigade had left Pusan by road and rail between 6:30 and 7:00 AM, with its new M-26 Pershing tanks and other heavy equipment being transported on flatcars. The primitive Korean trains, with old wooden coaches dating back to the era of Japanese rule, were no faster or more comfortable than traveling by truck over the terrible roads, and they frequently jolted to sudden stops for no apparent reason.

"The Marines inside showed almost no interest in the slowly passing scenery," wrote *Life* magazine reporter-photographer David Douglas Duncan, who was embedded with the brigade. "They ate their rations, oiled their weapons, slept in the vestibules between cars with their rifles held close. They were professional men riding to work."

"Each time our train stalled in the tunnels," said Colonel Robert Taplett of the Third Battalion, "I thought we'd suffocate in the bitter black smoke belching from the overworked steam engine." By 4:00 PM, however, all combat and support elements of the brigade, except for one tank platoon, had reached the Changwon area.

Despite orders to bivouac in the town itself, Craig was wary. The NKPA lines west of Masan were too close for comfort, and there was heavy fighting a few miles away, at the important road junction of Chindong-ni. "We felt that going into bivouac would leave us wide open for surprise," the brigade commander said. "To ensure our security and be prepared for any eventuality, I deployed the brigade tactically. A major penetration of the Army lines at Chindong-ni could've been fatal to us if we'd been caught in bivouac."

Consequently, Craig positioned his troops in a defensive perimeter on high ground west of Changwon and placed them on full alert. Lieutenant Colonel Harold Roise's Second Battalion dug in atop a dominating hill, which was surrounded on all sides by rice paddies and provided an excellent overview of the surrounding countryside. Craig established his own command post immediately behind Roise's position, in a small basin shielded by hills on the edge of Changwon, with close-in protection provided for the CP by the engineering company and various headquarters units. The brigade's tank platoons and the batteries of Lieutenant Colonel Ransom H. Wood's artillery battalion were scattered throughout the interior of the bivouac area.

"The area assigned to B Company was on a ridge," said Lieutenant Fenton, "where we put two of our three platoons on line and the other in support. We were told the enemy was infiltrating through the 25th Division and coming back into rear areas and that we'd be responsible for our own security at night, so we had the men prepare two-man 'buddy-buddy' foxholes. We wanted to keep 50 percent of the men awake at all times that night. The guys were kind of nervous, and we wanted to be ready for anything."

While the ground elements of the First Provisional Marine Brigade were unloading at Pusan on the night of August 2, Marine Air Group 33, commanded by Brigadier General Thomas J. Cushman, was at Kobe, Japan, where two fighter squadrons were preparing for their first action in Korea.

Between them, the "Death Rattlers" of Marine fighter squadron VMF-323, assigned to the escort carrier *Badoeng Strait*, and the "Black Sheep" of VMF-214, based on the escort carrier *Sicily*, had a combined total of sixty gull-winged F4U Corsairs, all of which would be busy in the skies above the Pusan Perimeter in early August. They would be augmented by the planes and pilots of VMF(N)-513, a night-fighter squadron based at Itazuke Airfield on the Japanese island of Kyushu.

Eight planes from VMF-214 drew first blood on August 3, when they struck troops of the NKPA's Sixth Division at the villages of Chinju and Sinban-ni, northwest of Pusan, with incendiary bombs and rockets. A series of strafing runs capped off the attack, giving the enemy a small taste of the havoc to be wreaked by Marine air in the weeks ahead. The close support provided by the Corsairs would be a major factor in sustaining the Marines' ground offensive.

"Not only was 50 percent of our pilot training devoted to close-air support, but before we went to Korea, we were also sent to Camp Pendleton to train as infantrymen, so we'd know something about how the ground troops lived," recalled Captain Lyle Bradley of VMF-214, who had flown Corsairs at Okinawa in 1945.

"The Corsair itself gave us a decided advantage over the pilots of other services," added Bradley, an Iowa native who had left college to enlist in the Marines in 1942. "It was a fabulous airplane, faster than other Navy fighters, highly maneuverable, and capable of carrying over 4,000 pounds of external ordnance—that meant up to eight 500-pound bombs. Whatever the job was, the Corsairs just did it better."

A fourth major aerial asset for the brigade was VMO-6, a squadron of four "Grasshopper" light observation planes and four new Sikorsky HO3S-1 helicopters. The latter aircraft were making their first appearance in actual combat with any branch of the U.S. military.

On the morning of August 3, as the brigade was moving out for Changwon, General Craig climbed aboard one of the helicopters and proceeded to demonstrate their amazing versatility by covering at least ten times the distance he could have traveled that day by any other means. He first stopped to brief the advance battalion on its route, then paused long enough to pick a site for his forward command post. Next, he hopped on to Masan to confer with General Walker and General Kean, commander of the 25th Division, to which the Marine brigade would be attached. Finally, on his return trip, Craig touched down three more times to meet with various field commanders.

"Time was always pressing," he remarked later, "but fortunately, Marine helicopters were always available for observation, communications, and control. These aircraft made my day! Without them, I don't think we would've had nearly the success we did."

During the meeting at Masan, Craig requested that some of the thousands of new, relatively untrained ROK recruits be attached to the brigade to serve with the Marines as scouts, interpreters, and rear-area guards. Walker agreed to the request and also arranged to provide arms for the recruits.

The three generals then reviewed the tactical situation on the Eighth Army's southern flank, which Walker characterized as tenuous at best. This brought them to the primary purpose of the meeting.

"Your brigade should be prepared to go on the offensive anytime after the evening of August 5," said Walker. "The time has come when we've got to quit giving up ground and equipment. The enemy has driven us back so rapidly that his supply lines are stretched to the limit. The time has come to hit him hard, and I'm counting on your men to do it. Are they ready?"

"Yes, General," Craig said. "We may be a little trigger-happy, but we're spoiling for a fight."

As the sun sank low in the western sky on the hot afternoon of August 3, Corpsman Herb Pearce dug in on a small hill along with other men of the Second Platoon of the recoilless gun company to which he was assigned. From his vantage point, Pearce could look down on an American motor pool and the Third Battalion aid station, in an abandoned schoolhouse at the foot of the hill.

Except for the subdued sound of tired men talking, everything was quiet and seemingly secure. To all outward appearances, the enemy could have been hundreds of miles away. But the Marines' first night in the trenches was rapidly approaching, and as darkness descended, everything began to change. The "trigger-happiness" to which Craig had referred was about to become an epidemic, and even a stable twenty-one-year-old such as Herb Pearce wasn't immune to its effects.

"I thought about not having a weapon of any kind to call my own, and I worried about it," Pearce recalled much later. "In the morning, I told myself, I'll go down to the battalion CP and see if I can find a spare carbine. Meanwhile, it was going to be a long night."

In the words of the official Marine Corps history of the Pusan campaign, "an army of phantoms invaded the brigade's perimeter" on the night of August 3. To this day, many Marines who were there remain uncertain whether these phantoms were real, imagined, or a combination of both.

"The reaction of green troops was typical of men new to combat," wrote Corps historian Lynn Montross. "As nerve-taut men stared fixedly into the blackness, forms that had been harmless bushes and rocks took on the guise of Communist infiltrators."

The uproar started shortly after 10:00 PM when a single rifle shot rang out. After a few seconds of silence, it was quickly followed by others, and from there, the volume of firing continued to swell.

Although most of the brigade's NCOs were combat veterans of World War II, a majority of the rank-and-file troops had never before heard a shot fired in anger, and their reaction was predictable. By midnight, the firing had swelled into a continuous crackle and seemed heaviest in the vicinity of Craig's CP. "Palpitating hearts pounded even more strenuously," noted Montross, "when two Marine machine guns began chattering in positions occupied by brigade headquarters troops."

No one present could estimate how many shots were fired altogether that night, and few Marines wanted to talk much about it later. But at least one, PFC Fred F. Davidson, gave this admission of his own participation:

"I raised my carbine and squeezed the trigger. The muzzle flash blinded me. For the next few seconds, I saw lights and stars. Then Andy [Davidson's foxhole buddy] shouted, 'Hey, you almost hit me!' I thought, *Oh, God, I didn't know I was aiming in that direction. It was so dark I couldn't see my front sight. You better take it easy, ol' buddy, before you kill some Marine.*"

Neighboring Marines soon began following Davidson's example. "Over to my rear, someone else pulled off a round," he recalled. "Next it was someone to my front. Then the firing pinballed from place to place all over the hill and back down toward the railroad track. Finally, all firing ceased. The rest of the night, I lay awake, scared, with my finger on the trigger."

The principal reason for the cease-fire, which took effect at about 3:00 AM on August 4, was that numerous NCOs took their lives in their hands by moving among their units and ordering the troops in the strongest possible terms to "Knock it off, dammitt!"

At dawn, a furious General Craig called in the leaders of the worst-offending units and administered a dressing-down that none of them would ever forget. By then at least three Marine casualties had been reported, one resulting from a random shot, one from a case of mistaken identity, and one when a weapon discharged accidentally. Fortunately, none of the wounds was fatal.

If any flesh-and-blood enemy infiltrators actually ventured into the brigade's area that night, no evidence of their presence could be found the next morning. Despite Craig's stern warning, at least three more firing outbreaks were recorded on the night of August 4, but this time they appeared to have been more justified. What looked to be an NKPA observation post, manned by seven soldiers with radios, was spotted atop a nearby ridge overlooking the brigade area that afternoon, and an infantry platoon was sent to confront them. But by the time the Marines scaled the height—several of them suffering heat prostration along the way—the intruders had vanished.

"On our second night at Changwon, one of our listening posts reported a group of armed North Koreans heading toward our positions," recalled B Company's Lieutenant Fenton. "About an hour later, the listening post said the Koreans had fired on them, and they were returning fire. This skirmish lasted only about fifteen minutes, but the whole line remained awake that night. The following day, we couldn't find any bodies or used cartridges, so I'm not certain if we had enemy infiltrators or just shadows."

Unlike the haunted nights, the daylight hours during the brigade's three-day stay at Changwon served several useful purposes. "This period was our first chance to get the men oriented, and we took advantage of it," said Lieutenant Hugh "Nick" Schryver, leader of B Company's First Platoon. "It gave us a chance to shake off our sea legs and get somewhat acclimated to Korea's hostile summer climate. We conducted patrols in the high ground on our right and updated the men on battlefield developments since we'd left San Diego. We were in for a tough time, and we knew it."

While General Walker and his field commanders laid plans for an offensive that they hoped would change the entire climate of the war, the task of keeping the NKPA sufficiently off-balance to prevent a major enemy attack in the interim fell largely to U.S., British, and Australian naval and air units.

On August 5, the British cruisers *Belfast* and *Kenya*, joined by Marine aircraft from the carrier *Sicily*, bombarded North Korean facilities around the port of Inchon, some 200 miles northwest of the Marines' position at Changwon. The *Sicily*'s planes battered airfields, factories, warehouses, railroads, bridges, and harbor installations in raids designed to interdict the flow of enemy supplies to the south.

On the east coast, the U.S. cruisers *Toledo* and *Helena* turned their eight-inch guns on troop concentrations near the town of Yongdok, preventing any North Korean advances. The ROK Navy also got into the act when one of its ships destroyed several boatloads of North Korean troops attempting a seaborne flanking maneuver south of Yongdok.

Meanwhile, to the immediate front of Eighth Army positions, Marine Corsairs from the *Sicily* and the *Badoeng Strait* flew dozens of sorties between August 4 and 6 against NKPA troop concentrations, vehicles, and supply dumps.

"The planes paved the way for that first offensive of ours," recalled Sergeant Mackie Wheeler of A Company, First Battalion, Fifth Marines (A/1/5), a ten-year veteran of the Corps who had fought the Japanese at Wake Island in 1941. "We couldn't have gotten to first base without them."

Late on August 5, after two days and nights in defensive positions near Changwon, the Marine brigade got orders to begin moving out the next morning. Its destination was Chindong-ni, where the NKPA's Sixth Division and 83rd Motorcycle Regiment were exerting heavy pressure on thinly spread elements of the Army's Fifth Regimental Combat Team and the 27th "Wolfhound" Infantry Regiment. The brigade's assignment was to spearhead the first large-scale American offensive action since the invasion. For the Marines, now temporarily attached to the 25th Infantry Division, the "shadow war" was over. The real thing was about to begin in earnest.

In addition to the brigade, General Walker also had assigned the Fifth Regimental Combat Team and two regiments of the 25th Division to the attacking force, which would be known as Task Force Kean, a name borrowed from the commanding general of the 25th. The launch date for the offensive was set for August 7, the eighth anniversary of the first U.S. ground offensive of World War II—the Marines' amphibious assault on the Japanese island fortress of Guadalcanal on August 7, 1942.

Choosing this date may or may not have been a coincidence, but senior noncoms made sure that younger members of their units realized its significance.

"We were already aching to kick the hell out of somebody," recalled Sergeant Wheeler of A/1/5, "but the tie-in to Guadalcanal made us want it even more."

Several hours before daylight on the morning of August 7, Corpsman Herb Pearce was awakened by enemy mortar fire. None of the rounds hit anywhere near Pearce's foxhole, and the firing soon tapered off, then stopped altogether. But it was obvious to Pearce that the shells came from an all-too-human enemy, rather than the "phantoms" of the past few nights. Unquestionably, the brigade's positions were under actual attack for the first time.

Pearce's first concern was that he was still weaponless. Several times over the past few days, he'd inquired around the brigade CP about unattached rifles or carbines, but none had been available.

After a few minutes of silence, the sporadic firing resumed, still with the same degree of inaccuracy, and Pearce listened to the explosions—all of them seemingly several hundred yards away—with a curious sense of detachment.

"For someone who'd never been under fire before, I wasn't really scared at all," he recalled. "In fact, I was totally unimpressed. I thought, 'Hey, these guys are really lousy shots.' It didn't take long for me to get over that idea."

Shortly after daybreak, another mortar barrage erupted, and this time the enemy gunners showed alarmingly better aim. A mortar round hit within about fifty feet of Pearce, and he saw Marines in a neighboring foxhole blown up into the air in a cloud of dust and smoke.

"Corpsman!" somebody yelled almost before the sound of the blast had died, and true to his nickname, "Doc Rocket" Pearce was immediately on his way.

Moments later, with mortar rounds still falling in the vicinity, he was squatting beside a bleeding, unconscious victim of the mortar round in the battalion aid station and treating his first gravely wounded Marine as other casualties were carried in by stretcher bearers. Pearce's patient was young, no more than eighteen at the most, and his arm had almost been blown off above the elbow. Pearce wasn't sure if the shattered mass of flesh could be saved, but he did what he could. Nearby lay the mangled bodies of two other Marines killed by the same shell.

"Now I *was* impressed with those enemy gunners," Pearce said, "and I was stunned at how much damage one piece of shrapnel could do."

Before leaving the aid station, he made sure to pick up a carbine that had belonged to one of the dead or wounded.

I've spent my last day without having something to fight back with! he told himself grimly.

"You okay, Doc?" asked Pearce's friend Sergeant Charlie Snow as the bloodstained corpsman returned to the area where their recoilless gun company was preparing for the trip to Chindong-ni.

"I guess so," Pearce said, holding up his new carbine. "I know this thing's no protection against mortars, but I feel better having it, anyway."

"You're probably gonna need it," Snow said. "We just got word that we'll be right on the point with the infantry when we move out. I hear the gooks would a lot rather zap a corpsman than an ordinary grunt like me." He grinned at Pearce. "You think you could really shoot one of the bastards, Doc?"

Pearce thought of the maimed youngster he'd just attended, and he nodded. "I know I could," he said.

CHAPTER 6

★ ★ ★

A MELEE OF CONFUSION AND CHAOS

T HE EIGHTH ARMY'S first attempt at taking the offensive began quietly enough on the morning of August 6, as the trucks bearing Colonel Robert Taplett's Third Battalion, Fifth Marines, drove through a drifting mist along the road to Chindong-ni.

"South Korea actually looked like the legendary 'Land of the Morning Calm' as we moved out that morning," Taplett remembered many years later. But the tranquil atmosphere obscured an ominous truth. Neither Taplett nor any of his troops yet knew that the town toward which they were traveling was under savage attack by the North Koreans at that very moment. As a result, the optimistic plan for the U.S. offensive was running into serious trouble even before it officially started.

The plan hammered out by Generals Walker, Kean, and Craig looked fundamentally sound on paper, at least at the time it was conceived. The problem was that the plan took too long to execute, and the North Koreans refused to wait. Just as the Eighth Army was set to launch its three-pronged assault, the NKPA's Sixth Division unleashed a new offensive of its own—

one that the Army units holding the line at Chindong-ni were too beaten up and worn out to withstand.

As during the earlier journey from Pusan to Changwon, Taplett's Third Battalion had been designated as the Marine brigade's lead unit for the advance toward Chindong-ni. The infantry companies were augmented by a battalion of artillery, a platoon of 75-millimeter recoilless guns, and an engineer platoon.

By 1:00 PM on August 6, Taplett's men were within one and a half miles of the town, where they relieved a battered Army battalion and took up defensive positions on imposing high ground along both sides of the main road from Masan.

The attack plan called for them to be joined by a second Marine battalion early the following day, but General Craig wasn't to assume command until both battalions were assembled and ready to launch a coordinated assault. Until then, Taplett's unit would be under the operational control of Colonel John Michaelis, commander of the Army's 27th Infantry Regiment.

Michaelis's "Wolfhounds" had spent the first week of August fighting off repeated attempts by the NKPA to break through American lines and drive on to Pusan, only about forty miles away. The 27th had sustained heavy casualties, and many of the survivors were at the point of exhaustion.

If there was a crucial flaw in the plan for Task Force Kean, it was the same lack of combat-capable troops that had plagued the Eighth Army from the outset. Except for the Marine brigade, there were no fresh American units standing in the path of the North Koreans. Each of the Army's four infantry divisions—comprising the bulk of the task force—had been skeletonized by losses, and the troops still on line were little more than zombies. "It was a disaster in the making," said Taplett.

The planned offensive suffered a further setback at about 1:30 AM on August 7 when Taplett received an urgent—and totally unexpected—radio message from Michaelis, who was relaying a directive from General Kean's 25th Division headquarters.

"Dog Company of the Fifth Regimental Combat Team is on Hill 342 west of Sangyong-ni," Michaelis said. "They've been under heavy attack for some time, and they may not be able to hold. This high ground commands the road junction, and we've got to hold it, or the attack tomorrow can't move. I can't spare anything to help them, so you'll have to send a platoon. There's a guide in my CP who'll lead your men to the area."

Taplett wasn't happy with the order, and he let Michaelis know it. "My battalion's supposed to hit the enemy with everything we've got in a few hours," he said. "Under the circumstances, how can I afford to tie up one of my six rifle platoons to bail out these troops?"

"I'm sorry," Michaelis replied, "but there's no other way. We're under orders from General Kean to hold Hill 342 at all costs."

When Taplett contacted First Lieutenant Robert "Dewey" Bohn, CO of G Company, and explained the situation, Bohn assigned Second Lieutenant John J. "Blackie" Cahill's First Platoon to become the first Marine infantry unit committed to combat in the Korean War.

Cahill was grim-faced as he called his NCOs together a short time later to brief them on the mission. "Pass the word to go easy on the water," he warned. "No telling how long we'll be up there, or when we'll get more."

Reinforced by a machine-gun squad and a radio operator, Cahill's platoon jumped off at 2:15 AM on August 7 in search of the command post of the Fifth RCT's Second Battalion. When the Marines arrived there, Cahill was astonished to learn that his small force was expected to relieve an entire Army company and hold Hill 342 by itself. The young lieutenant had no recourse but to bite his lip and march on.

More problems arose when the Army guide assigned to the platoon led the Marines off the road and through a series of rice paddies, where they had to pick their way from dike to dike and progress was slowed to a snail's pace. Sporadic enemy mortar fire forced further delays, and Cahill's men also came under "friendly fire" from troops of the Fifth RCT.

"We're Marines!" Cahill shouted. "For Christ's sake, knock it off!"

The firing abruptly stopped, but two Marines were down with painful wounds, one hit in the foot, the other in the shoulder.

An apologetic Army medic appeared from somewhere. "Sorry, we didn't know you were in the area," he told Cahill. "We've got an aid station about 300 yards from here. We'll take your men there."

As the Marine platoon tackled a series of climbs toward the crest of Hill 342, the sun rose, and the soaring heat took a vicious toll. The temperature would reach 112 degrees by afternoon, and despite Cahill's warning, canteens were soon dry. In addition to casualties inflicted by enemy fire, men began collapsing with nausea and heat prostration.

In the growing morning light, the dark mass of Hill 342 towered above the sweating Marines like a giant, jagged tooth. "This thing's too steep for tactical climbing," Cahill told Sergeant Lee Buettner, one of his squad leaders. "It's gonna be grab and hold all the way up. Keep the ranks closed up tight, and tell every man to help his buddy."

Buettner and Sergeant Tom Blackmon, the platoon guide, moved quickly among the men, gasping words of encouragement. Later, they'd have reason to wish they'd saved their breath. After they'd clawed their way to the crest of the hill, the Army guide cursed and made a devastating confession. "Damn it, I took a wrong turn, and we're in the wrong place. We'll have to backtrack."

The mistake forced the platoon to return almost to the base of the hill, then make the climb all over again following a different route. Only thirty-seven of the fifty-two Marines who originally started up the hill reached the top on the second try. En route, Sergeant Blackmon was severely wounded by a burst of enemy fire. He was taken to the Army aid station where the other casualties had gone.

Using every ounce of strength they could muster, Cahill, Buettner, and the Army guide forged ahead of the rest of the platoon. It was shortly after 8:00 AM when they dragged themselves over the edge of the summit and onto a narrow, brush-covered plateau swept by periodic volleys of enemy small-arms fire frequently punctuated by mortar rounds. Cahill crawled over and introduced himself to a haggard Army officer slumped in a foxhole.

"Are you relieving us?" the officer asked. His voice was hollow with weariness.

"Reinforcing you," Cahill corrected. "We've got to hold here, and a platoon's all I've got. You'd probably lose a lot of men if you tried to get off the hill right now, anyway."

The hope that had flashed briefly in the officer's eyes quickly died there.

• • •

The main body of the platoon, led by Sergeant Jack Macy, now the group's senior NCO, reached the summit at about 8:30 AM. Additional casualties on the way up and the assignment of men to transport the wounded to the Army aid station had reduced the number of Marines with Macy to thirty-four.

"These Army guys are totally bushed," Cahill told Macy. "They're dead on their feet, short of ammo, and worse off for water than we are. You and Buettner start feeding Marines into the Army foxholes one at a time. Stay low and be careful."

On the way up the slope, Cahill had been unable to reach George Company's headquarters by radio, but when he had the radio operator try again, he was able to get through to Lieutenant Bohn.

"We made the high ground," Cahill said. "We're in contact with the Army and in position on the plateau. We're getting small-arms and mortar fire, and we took some casualties coming up, but we're okay. We desperately need artillery support and air drops of water and ammo."

Bohn notified Colonel Taplett's headquarters, and an Air Force transport was dispatched to a drop zone atop Hill 342, but snafus continued to plague the men on the ground. Most of the precious cargo fell into enemy territory, and the only retrievable packet contained nothing but carbine ammunition. Nobody in the platoon was carrying a carbine.

Next, the Brigade Air Section turned the drop assignment over to VMO-6, the Marine observation squadron, whose small, maneuverable planes were more capable of hitting the confined area within the American perimeter. Every available five-gallon water can was donated for the job, but the containers burst on striking the rocky ground, and the defenders on the hill were able to salvage only a few mouthfuls of water apiece.

Meanwhile, as Sergeants Macy and Buettner took on the tedious, high-risk task of placing Marine riflemen in Army foxholes, enemy snipers continued to take a toll. Inching along on his belly, Macy was leading PFCs William Tome and Melvin Brooks toward a well-located BAR position that could serve as a defensive strongpoint against attack. Then an enemy machine gunner spotted them.

Flattened against the ground, all three men were digging frantically to deepen an existing hole in the rocky soil when a burst of fire tore through Tome's body. Macy returned fire with the BAR and yelled over his shoulder at Brooks.

"Tome's hit! See if you can help him."

Brooks scrambled over to the stricken Marine. "It's no use!" he yelled back. "He's dead!"

Macy reached out and grabbed Brooks by the shoulder. "They're zeroed in on this spot," he said. "We gotta—"

Another burst from the machine gun cut off Macy's words and slammed through Brooks's chest, killing him instantly. As Brooks fell across Tome's body, Macy saw PFC Lonzo Barnett, a Marine to his immediate right, hurl a grenade toward the machine gun. When the grenade exploded, the firing stopped.

On his way back to the area of the Army CP, Macy learned of a third Marine KIA. As PFC John Johnson had tried to repair a machine gun damaged in the climb, a sniper's bullet had crashed into his skull.

Crouching uneasily in their new positions, the remaining Marines were shocked by their losses and the intensity of the enemy fire. Cahill did his best to reassure them, although his heart wasn't in it.

"Stand fast, and we'll be okay," he said. "Colonel Taplett says the Second Battalion's coming up here to help us out."

Dear God, let 'em hurry, he thought.

Before the morning was over, the marooned GIs and Marines on Hill 342 sustained eight additional casualties, among them the commander of the Army company, who was evacuated with a wound. But somehow they managed to hold the North Koreans at bay.

One of the day's most courageous feats was carried out by Sergeant Macy and a small group of Marines who formed an all-volunteer patrol to search for water. Braving intense enemy fire, they descended the southeastern slope of Hill 342 and reached a stream that Macy had spotted from the crest.

After gulping all the water they could hold—without pausing to use the purification tablets that each man carried—they filled their own canteens and three five-gallon canvas water bags, then hauled their liquid treasure back to the top. When the water was divided, each of their swollen-tongued comrades on the summit received only about four ounces, but even this small amount was a godsend.

All across the front, Task Force Kean's would-be offensive sputtered and struggled throughout the day on August 7. Unforeseen problems and severe logistical foul-ups seemed to crop up everywhere at once.

While the Second Battalion, Fifth Marines, under Lieutenant Colonel Harold Roise, tried to reach and reinforce the GIs and Marines clinging to the crest of Hill 342, Lieutenant Colonel George Newton's First Battalion was immobilized at Chindong-ni because an Army battalion had taken the wrong road, then stalled.

"When we got to the crossroads where we were supposed to take the left fork toward Sachon," recalled B Company's Lieutenant Ike Fenton, "we found Army troops bogged down by an enemy roadblock that was supposed to have been cleared. We had to fall back about a mile, go into defensive positions, and try again later."

Meanwhile, Colonel Taplett's Third Battalion, less Cahill's platoon, came under attack as it tried to move into reserve in the rear. The Second Battalion of the Fifth RCT, minus the men of D Company trapped on Hill 342, jumped off on schedule but ran squarely into the teeth of the NKPA Sixth Division's offensive and was halted in its tracks.

Arriving at Chindong-ni at seven o'clock that morning, General Craig faced what he called "the most confused situation that I've encountered in the Marine Corps." An official Army history described the scene in and around Chindong-ni as "a general melee," which didn't end until Craig was placed in charge of all involved Army units.

"Finally, due to the inability of the Army to clear the road junction and the holdup of our offensive," Craig later explained, "General Kean put all troops in that area under the Marine brigade commander, and I was given the brigade plus the [Army's] 24th Regiment and the Fifth RCT."

Once in charge, Craig went immediately to the front lines, convinced that this was the best place to sort matters out and get his forces moving. He was disappointed to find the Fifth RCT, commanded by Colonel Godwin L. Ordway Jr., still stymied, although enemy resistance was minimal. But the plight of the Army unit brought Craig to the crucial realization that for the American offensive to materialize at all, a series of aggressive attacks by every Marine unit in the brigade, closely supported by heavy artillery and airpower, had to begin right away.

It was getting late in the game—but not quite *too* late.

Early on August 8, in a series of aggressive thrusts by D Company, Second Battalion, under the command of Captain John Finn Jr., the Marines fought their way to the top of Hill 342. Resistance was light at first, as all three of the company's rifle platoons jumped off abreast along the hill's southern face and swiftly reached the top, where they were greeted with great relief by Lieutenant Cahill and other thirsty, bone-tired survivors.

Once there, however, the new arrivals came under a storm of fire from enemy positions ringing the north side of the hill. Marine artillery and air support silenced the firing long enough to allow the shattered company of the Fifth RCT and the remnants of Cahill's platoon to withdraw. Eighteen Marines—more than a third of the group that had left Chindong-ni not quite thirty hours earlier—had by now been killed or wounded. (For his valiant leadership in reaching the trapped Army unit, then holding the hill until help arrived, Cahill would be awarded the Silver Star.)

Even after the relief mission was accomplished, the situation on the hilltop remained touch and go for most of the morning of August 8. Buffeted repeatedly by determined NKPA counterattacks, Captain Finn's company fared no better at first than its predecessors in securing the tenuous American perimeter on 342's summit or in clearing upper slopes crawling with enemy troops.

The enemy's intent was to sever the main UN supply route between Chindong-ni and Pusan. To accomplish this, the Communists had to gain and maintain control of 342. Only then could they apply the insidious flanking and encirclement tactics that had worked so well and so often during the past six weeks.

This time, the stakes could not have been higher. If this last major American force could be cut off from its base and destroyed, the victorious NKPA would be able to march into Pusan virtually unopposed.

There were no blatant frontal assaults by the North Koreans—Hill 342 was too steep for that—but snipers firing burp guns and machine guns from concealed vantage points were constant threats to the defenders. They kept the Marines pinned down while NKPA riflemen painstakingly wormed their way up the hill's approaches and inched perilously close to American positions. Fierce, hand-to-hand fighting broke out several times after small enemy forces penetrated to within a few yards of the Marines' lines, but again and again, the attackers were thrown back down the hill.

Before noon on August 8, all three of D Company's platoon leaders had been lost in the struggle. Both Second Lieutenant Wallace J. Reid, commanding the First Platoon, and Second Lieutenant Arthur A. Oakley, commanding the Second Platoon, were killed outright. Second Lieutenant Edward T. Emmelman, Third Platoon commander, suffered a severe head wound as he pointed out targets for one of his machine gunners.

Captain Finn himself narrowly escaped death when he crawled forward in an effort to recover Reid's body. "He may still be alive," Finn told Sergeant Sydney Dickerson, who was hugging the ground next to him.

But before he could reach Reid, Finn was struck by enemy bullets in the head and shoulder. Almost blinded by blood from a gaping head wound, Finn dragged himself back toward his lines with Dickerson's help. Under continuing heavy fire, a corpsman applied first aid, and the sergeant guided Finn downhill toward an aid station.

En route, Finn and the sergeant met First Lieutenant Robert T. Hanifin, the company executive officer, who was leading a 60-millimeter mortar section uphill toward its firing positions.

"You're in command now, Bob," Finn whispered. "The bastards got me."

Hanifin was clearly feeling the heat on his steep climb. "Sorry, John," he muttered shakily. "I'll do my best."

At about 11:30 AM, after the Marines had repelled yet another enemy attack with rifles, machine guns, and grenades, Hanifin received a phone call from Colonel Roise, his battalion commander. As D Company's new

CO picked up the receiver, he collapsed to the ground, unconscious. Moments later, he was evacuated with heat exhaustion.

With the company's command structure in shambles and thirty-one of its men either killed or wounded, a veteran NCO and a green young officer stepped up to fill what could have been a disastrous void.

Master Sergeant Harold Reeves, a thirty-year Marine Corps veteran, took charge of the company's three rifle platoons and led them with a confidence born of numerous past firefights. Second Lieutenant Leroy Wirth, a forward artillery observer, assumed responsibility for all supporting arms, including the Marine fighter squadrons operating overhead. Both men moved out far ahead of the front lines to pinpoint NKPA positions for artillery and air strikes and to provide up-to-date situation reports at regular intervals.

Heat and the ongoing shortage of water also were eating away at other Marine units. By the time Lieutenant Fenton's B Company had crossed a huge rice paddy and taken up new positions along a ridgeline, it was 9:00 AM on August 9. At that point, the unit's orders were abruptly changed. The men were told to move off the high ground, go back down to the road, and continue advancing toward the village of Paedun-ni.

"By now, the heat was terrific, and most of the men were out of water," Fenton said. "The heat prostration cases in the company grew to an alarming number. Our men were dropping like flies, and two of them were completely out of their heads and frothing at the mouth. They got so bad that we had to call in a helicopter to take them off."

Captain Tobin, the company commander, was in bad shape himself and too weak to stand. Despite orders from First Battalion headquarters to move out and follow A Company to the road, only thirty men—less than 15 percent of Baker Company—had the strength to get off the ridge without collapsing.

"Captain Tobin stayed on the hill, while one other officer and I led the thirty men who were able down to the road," said Fenton. "The rest just couldn't make it. They were lying on the ground where they'd fallen, out cold or trying to crawl under bushes to find a little shade. Those that weren't unconscious tried to place themselves where they could cover their buddies in case of enemy attack, but I personally doubt if all the Marines on that hill put together could've held off ten enemy soldiers. They were that bad off."

The descent down the ridgeline was steep and tortuous, and the temperature was approaching an afternoon high of 114 degrees. Fenton made it to the road with his little group; then he, too, passed out.

After being revived, watered down, and given an hour's rest in the shade, Fenton and the others were sufficiently recovered to fall in on the tail end of the battalion column as it moved toward Paedun-ni. Slowed by heavy sniper fire, they'd covered only about a mile and a half by 5:00 PM, when the column was ordered to halt for the night and take up defensive positions on hills overlooking the road.

"The irony of this," Fenton recalled much later, "was that B Company was assigned to protect the battalion's left flank, which put us on the same high ground we'd just left a few hours earlier. Fortunately, 85 percent of the company was still there, and, this time, we had civilian laborers with us to haul up loads of water and carry the fifteen worst heat cases down to the battalion aid station."

In effect, Company B was right back where it had started that morning. But by this point Fenton and the other survivors were too drained to care.

The entire American offensive might have wilted and died in the murderous heat if not for the constant presence of the two fighter squadrons of Marine Air Group 33, whose planes and pilots wrote a whole new definition for the term "close air support" during this critical period.

The Communist invaders had never before encountered such powerful precision aerial attacks, and their devastating effects on the enemy are difficult to exaggerate. Directed to their targets by panels laid out to mark friendly ground positions, Vought F4U-4 Corsair fighters struck so near Marine lines that their spent machine-gun cartridges rained down on their comrades below.

During the daylight hours, the Corsairs were on call continuously—and capable of responding within seconds. Their deftly orchestrated strikes and pinpoint accuracy were indispensable facets of General Craig's strategy to force a general retreat by the North Koreans.

The lightweight Marine observation planes, or OYs, also played a key role. Their pilots were experts at spotting targets for both bombing runs and heavy artillery, a job in which the planes' slow speed proved an asset, albeit a dangerous one. As Lieutenant Pat Sivert, one of the pilots, explained,

"In this type of terrain, the enemy was so adept at camouflage that . . . high-performance aircraft were just too fast to get down and search out a target. We in the slower-moving aircraft were able to get much lower and take our time in spotting a target. Too, we were using the same maps as the ground commanders. They could give us targets and pinpoint them with exact coordinates."

In the first three days of combat, the two fighter squadrons attached to the Marine brigade flew more than 100 sorties. The constant overhead presence of four to ten Corsairs was perhaps the most decisive factor in the fight for Hill 342, first in enabling the hard-pressed Americans to hang on, then in forcing the North Koreans to withdraw, leaving hundreds of their dead littering the hillsides.

"This was more than the previously all-victorious NKPA had bargained for," wrote Captain John C. Chapin of the Marine Corps Historical Division. "Their firing slacked off, and the crucial hilltop held. Some 600 enemy attackers had failed in their attempt to cut the task force's main supply route."

At about noon on August 8, the combined efforts of the Corsairs and D Company broke the back of the NKPA's last sustained attack on Hill 342, and never again was the hilltop seriously threatened. By the morning of August 9, there was only desultory small-arms fire in the vicinity of 342, and soon even it died away. That afternoon, brigade intelligence reported the enemy gradually withdrawing to the north.

Meanwhile, Colonel Robert Taplett's 3/5 had taken on the job of dislodging the North Koreans from another strategic piece of high ground, designated as Hill 255. Like Hill 342, it also overlooked the main supply route toward the rear and Pusan, and it was protected by well-dug-in enemy troops on a stair-step lower hill that blocked access to 255.

Early on August 8, the Marines' first small-scale probing attack on the lower hill by the First Platoon of H Company was sharply repulsed by NKPA small arms and grenades. A short time later, Captain Joseph C. Fegan, H Company's CO, relayed Taplett's order for the Third Platoon to pass through the First to resume the assault—a much-practiced Marine strategy to keep fresh troops always at the point of attack—but the lieutenant leading the Third Platoon failed to respond.

Rushing forward from his CP, Fegan confronted the young officer. "I told you to attack," he said. "What the hell's the matter with you?"

"We've already taken casualties, and I've seen my wounded rolling helplessly down the hill, sir," the lieutenant replied. "I've got no stomach for sending more men to their deaths."

Fegan shook his head in disbelief. The recalcitrant officer had compiled an outstanding record at Camp Pendleton, but in the cauldron of actual combat, his nerves had snapped. "Then you've got no business leading a platoon," Fegan said. "I'm giving you an order, Lieutenant."

"I can't do it, sir," the lieutenant said, staring at the ground.

"Then I'm relieving you," Fegan snapped. "Get out of here, and go back to the battalion CP."

Moments later, with Fegan personally in command, the platoon moved forward with restored confidence, inspired both by their captain's example and the encouragement of a small cadre of veteran NCOs. The riflemen charged across the exposed tableland toward Hill 255 in a wedge formation, with one squad at the apex and two others slightly to the rear, taking more casualties as they went but never faltering.

In this case, air strikes and artillery had little effect against enemy troops dug into the rocky crags of 255 itself, and the final assault was bloody and hand to hand. While leading his squad, Sergeant John I. Wheatley fell severely wounded, along with several of his men. Sergeant Edward F. Barrett, with bullet wounds in his elbow and hip, lay helpless and exposed to enemy fire until Fegan carried him to safety.

In the struggle for the summit, Fegan's men had to clear the ridge one enemy foxhole at a time, with many NKPA troops fighting to the death. A squad led by Corporal Melvin James rolled up the enemy's left flank, earning James a Distinguished Service Cross, while an assault spearheaded by Sergeant Ray Morgan and PFC Donald Terrio, each of whom wiped out an enemy machine gun and its crew, shattered the right flank. Both Morgan and Terrio were awarded Silver Stars.

By late afternoon, Captain Fegan reported to Taplett that Hill 255 was secure. H Company had suffered six men killed and thirty-two wounded, but the Third Platoon had obliterated the main enemy position, and three squads had driven all the way to the towering 800-foot crest of 255. Other elements of the company were pursuing the fleeing NKPA survivors with assistance from Marine air and artillery.

By 6:30 PM, when they were ordered to dig in for the night, Fegan's men had advanced more than 1,400 yards in nine-plus hours against a stubborn foe and over some of South Korea's roughest terrain.

"Fegan's action ensured the security of the main supply route to Pusan," said Taplett, "but the insurance policy cost the Third Battalion a total of twenty-six KIAs and thirty-six WIAs—as well as the career of one lieutenant. Neither Fegan nor I would subject our Marines to such an officer."

Fegan was later awarded a Gold Star in lieu of a second Silver Star in recognition of his courageous leadership. General Craig's reward, on reporting to General Kean that the enemy had been driven from the high ground and that the Army's Fifth RCT had occupied the crossroads at Chindong-ni without opposition, was to be relieved of his responsibilities as sector commander. Craig was ordered to move his Marines by night toward Paedun-ni, fifteen miles to the southwest.

The brigade's first forty-eight hours of sustained combat had claimed the lives of 33 Marines and left 141 others with wounds requiring evacuation. Hundreds of men also had been felled by heat prostration, but almost all were able to return to action after being rested and revived.

Colonel Harold Roise's Second Battalion, which had been relieved on the high ground by troops of the Army's 24th Infantry Regiment just before nightfall on August 9, drew the assignment as lead unit for the advance on Paedun-ni, with Colonel Taplett's Third Battalion following. Attached to Roise's battalion for the night march was a battery of artillery, an engineering platoon, three Pershing M-26 tanks, and a platoon of 75-millimeter recoilless guns.

In the absence of so many fallen officers, a largely new cast of company commanders and platoon leaders had been assembled. Captain Andy Zimmer had been transferred from the Fifth Marines' regimental staff to take command of D Company, replacing wounded Captain John Finn, and Lieutenant William Sweeney had replaced wounded Captain George Kittredge as CO of E Company. Sergeant T. Albert Crowson retained command of D Company's First Platoon after the death of Lieutenant Arthur Oakley, and Second Lieutenant Mike Shinka had taken over as leader of the Third Platoon for wounded Lieutenant Edward Emmelman. Second Lieutenant Ralph Sullivan was the new leader of the Second Platoon, replacing Lieutenant Wallace Reid, another KIA.

"Although the men were very tired, and I hesitated to carry out the night movement," said Craig later, "I considered that if we could surprise the North Koreans and keep moving when the other American troops had already stopped for the night, we might gain some added advantage—and this proved to be the case. We marched throughout the night and gained quite a bit of distance, with only occasional shots being fired."

With strict blackout conditions imposed on the march, the tanks had to be preceded by men on foot with hooded flashlights leading the way, and progress was necessarily slow. It was reasonably steady, however, until shortly before daybreak, when the lead tank, carrying a dozen or so infantrymen, came to a small bridge. The tank paused while its crewmen climbed out to inspect the fourteen-inch-thick slab of concrete over which the forty-ton Pershing would have to pass and confer with First Lieutenant William Pomeroy, the armored platoon commander.

"I think it'll be okay," Pomeroy decided. "We've got to give it a try."

After the hitchhiking riflemen were ordered to walk, the tank rolled forward—immediately collapsing the bridge and crashing through to the dry streambed below. Pomeroy suffered a broken hand when the tank's hatch slammed shut on it, and a crewman was hit in the foot when the jolt of the fall caused the coaxial machine gun on the M-26 to fire accidentally.

In desperation, a second tank tried to make its way through the streambed but threw a track halfway across, creating a total bottleneck. The engineers, stuck at the rear of the column, had great difficulty getting their heavy equipment past other vehicles on the narrow, winding road to reach the scene. When they got there, early estimates placed the projected delay at a full day.

Once General Craig and Fifth Marines commander Colonel Murray arrived to take charge, however, the estimates were rapidly scaled down. Utilizing civilian labor to help construct a bypass, the engineers had the column on its way again within about four hours. By 8:00 AM on August 10, the entire battalion had reached Paedun-ni to find the village empty of enemy troops.

The Marines collectively sighed with relief and looked forward to a few hours' rest after three full days of almost constant marching, climbing, and fighting.

It was not to be. By 9:30 AM, they were on the move again. A four-jeep reconnaissance detachment from D Company, Second Battalion, led the column, followed by two D Company rifle platoons plus mortar and machine-gun sections aboard six more jeeps and five trucks. Then the rest of the battalion re-formed and set out on foot again along the dusty road toward Kosong, the next town to the southwest, about ten miles distant.

Some two and a half miles ahead of the column, where the road narrowed, made a sharp turn, and passed beneath a large hill, an ugly surprise lurked. At a 1,000-yard-long defile called Taedabok Pass, some 300 North Koreans with mortars, antitank guns, and artillery were waiting in camouflaged positions to spring an ambush.

For the Marines, it was going to be another in a series of long, bloody days.

General Craig was acutely aware of the NKPA's skill in the arts of ambush and envelopment. This was why he usually sent up helicopters and observation planes to check out suspicious areas in advance, and why he also assigned motorized reconnaissance teams to the high-risk job of scouting the route ahead of the main body of troops and protecting the advance guard.

On the morning of August 10, however, based on intelligence reports that the area between Paedun-ni and Kosong was free of enemy troops, the Marine column received neither air cover nor artillery support, and observation planes were unable to spot the danger because of the enemy's adept use of camouflage.

The D Company men in the recon detachment were the first to suffer the consequences. A young PFC, riding in one of the lead jeeps, later described the scene.

"We were rolling down the road, thinking how quiet it was, when the North Koreans suddenly opened up on us. They cut up the first couple of jeeps pretty bad, and my group tumbled out and ran for the ditch, where I landed calf-deep in warm water. I heard machine guns chattering around me and kicking up dirt along the road, now lined with abandoned jeeps."

Sergeant Sidney Dickerson, also a passenger in one of the jeeps, quickly sized up the situation and yelled at his comrades above the whine of bullets and the roar of mortar shells.

"Get over to those little hills on the right!" he ordered. "We gotta get over there to return fire. Now do it!"

At almost that same instant, an OY observation plane, skimming the ridges at an altitude of fifty feet, spotted the ambush and radioed a warning that reached the main body of Marines, still traveling by foot a considerable distance away.

With their cover blown and all hope of trapping the entire Marine column now lost, the Communist troops poured a savage avalanche of fire down on every visible target. An NKPA antitank gun blew one of the abandoned jeeps to pieces, but most of the Marines from the recon team were able to withdraw from their exposed positions and fall back gradually on D Company's First Platoon, commanded by Captain Zimmer.

"Let's get those tubes in firing position up there," Zimmer told his 60-millimeter mortar section, pointing to the low ridges at the right side of the road. "I think I know where that gook antitank gun is."

Although the mortarmen used every available round of ammo to do the job, the antitank gun was finally silenced. Zimmer then ordered his men to lie low and hold their ground until reinforcements arrived. Two Pershing tanks showed up about an hour later and used their 90-millimeter cannons to drive the remaining NKPA troops deep into their holes. After that, the enemy firing tailed off to nothing.

The attempted ambush was thwarted, and Colonel Murray, the regimental commander, ordered the advance to continue. More snafus, however, lay just down the road.

After winding up its final security mission in the area of Chindong-ni and boarding trucks bound for Kosong, Colonel Taplett's 3/5 reached the entrance to Taedabok Pass after the firefight at the roadblock had subsided. Murray's orders to Taplett were to pass through Colonel Roise's 2/5 and lead the advance south to seize Kosong, where major NKPA units were concentrated, then drive west, toward the town of Sachon.

Colonel Newton's 1/5 had been relieved as advance guard by Roise's 2/5 because of excessive heat casualties and a lack of accurate maps that caused some of Newton's units to take the wrong roads. But then 2/5 faltered as well, also plagued by heat exhaustion and hit by a rash of casualties from enemy small-arms fire. Late on the afternoon of August 10, the Marine advance ground to a halt about five miles short of Kosong, pending the arrival of Taplett's platoon.

When Taplett reached the scene, a sweating, fuming Colonel Murray hurried to Taplett's CP. "Damn it, I can't locate Hal Roise," Murray said. "We need to push on to Kosong, but I've lost radio contact with the 2/5 command post, and I'm really not sure where the battalion's front-line units are."

To Taplett, "confusion galore" seemed to be the order of the day. To clarify the situation, he and Murray climbed to the top of a nearby hill, from which they had a clear view of Kosong in the distance. Smoke was rising from the village as a result of earlier strikes by Marine air and artillery. Although there were no visible signs of enemy activity in the intervening area, Taplett had no doubt that a strong NKPA force was concealed in the rugged terrain ahead.

"We can't afford to stay stalled here," Murray said. "We're supposed to be attacking simultaneously with the Army's Fifth RCT to our north, so go ahead and move your battalion. Maybe we can still get into Kosong before dark."

This sounded like wishful—and potentially dangerous—thinking to Taplett. Moving his battalion through 2/5 without knowing the other battalion's location seemed virtually impossible, and with night approaching, trying to do so could be courting disaster.

Nevertheless, he ordered Lieutenant Dewey Bohn's G Company to continue the advance, with Captain Joe Fegan's H Company following in support. Within minutes, Bohn got his men off their trucks and moving forward on foot, but there was scarcely an hour of daylight left by the time they launched their attack on both sides of the narrow main road.

By dusk, G Company had gained almost two miles against stiff enemy resistance. But as the blistering sun settled beyond the ridges to the west, Bohn's men were halted by fire from two NKPA machine guns on a dominating height where the road made a wide right turn about a mile from the village. Several Marines on the point of the attack were hit, and a 2/5 jeep that entered the area unaware was riddled with bullets, fatally wounding Major Morgan J. McNeeley, the 2/5 operations officer, along with his driver and two other Marines. From his command post, Taplett had spotted the jeep heading for trouble, but his radioed warning to Bohn to stop the jeep was too late to save the victims.

Taplett would later muse bitterly about the calamity, "Why McNeeley was unaware of the confusing situation and that my battalion had already taken over the attack from 2/5, we will probably never know—or why Lieutenant Colonel Roise apparently lost control. Strange things do happen in war when a unit commander loses control in combat."

Knocking out the two machine guns used up what remained of the daylight, but it at least allowed G Company's Lieutenant Jack Westerman and PFC Fred Davidson to recover the bodies of the McNeeley party. The major was still clinging to life when he was pulled from the wreckage of the jeep, but he died a short time later at the 3/5 aid station. Westerman was later awarded the Navy Cross for his part in the daring rescue attempt.

On that note, the attack was suspended for the night. Taplett's battalion was ordered to dig in on the hills overlooking the road and continue the assault on Kosong at 8:00 AM the following morning, August 11. But before sunrise, Lieutenant Bohn's G/3/5 was struck by a furious NKPA counterattack, and it took half an hour of hand-to-hand fighting to beat off the enemy onslaught. Bohn was wounded twice by grenade fragments during the action but continued to lead his company until the North Koreans gave up the assault and withdrew.

"In spite of this enemy delaying action, [Bohn] was able to commence his attack a scant eight minutes after the 0800 [8:00 AM] deadline, Taplett noted. "My staff and I, of course, received a heated blast from Murray for not jumping off as ordered."

The actual drive into Kosong was anticlimactic. G and H companies moved swiftly through the town, with only minor resistance. Then, aided by close air support, they stormed and seized Red Hill, a strip of high ground overlooking Kosong.

Once again, the Corsairs of the 33rd Marine Air Group played a decisive role, rapidly turning what began as a crucial test for the Marines into the most disastrous rout of NKPA forces up to that point in the war. As it hastily pulled out of Kosong to the west in an effort to escape U.S. artillery fire, the enemy's crack 83rd Motorcycle Regiment was caught in open ground by planes from VMF-323. The resulting slaughter is famed in Corps annals as the "Kosong Turkey Shoot."

"The pilots could hardly believe the tempting targets arrayed before their eyes," wrote a Marine historian. "The Corsairs swung low up and down the frantic NKPA column, raining death and destruction in a hail of fire from rockets and 20-millimeter cannon. . . . It was a scene of wild chaos: vehicles crashing into each other, overturned in ditches, afire, and exploding; troops fleeing for safety in every direction."

Sandwiched between forty or more wrecked and burning vehicles front and rear, the rest of the motorized column was trapped with no place to turn, as another flight of Corsairs arrived, joined by a squadron of Air Force F-51s. When the air attacks ended, 118 jeeps, motorcycles, and trucks had been destroyed and scores of enemy troops killed. It was the NKPA's greatest one-day loss to date and the first clear-cut victory for American arms.

By noontime on August 11, U.S. ground forces had gained full control of Kosong, and advance units were passing through the scenes of devastation west of the town as they continued the advance toward Sachon. Among the twisted, charred wreckage, the Marines found some enemy vehicles that had been abandoned in flawless condition. Many of the trucks and jeeps were powered by familiar Ford engines, apparent leftovers from America's World War II Lend-Lease shipments to the Soviet Union. Also in the wreckage were several American jeeps, captured earlier by the NKPA.

Except for occasional sniper fire, Kosong proper was relatively secure, and a makeshift aid station was set up in an abandoned schoolhouse to treat victims of wounds and heat prostration. Between patients, Corpsman Herb Pearce and a friend, feeling fairly relaxed after the high-tension events of the morning, took a break to grab a quick C ration lunch.

Within the next few minutes, as Pearce recalled nearly sixty years later, both the grim humor—and the abject horror—of the war would be driven home to him in an awesome, unforgettable way.

"The two of us were standing there several feet apart, spooning down our C rations, when a sniper fired a single round in our direction," Pearce said. "I don't think he was actually aiming at us, but we could hear the bullet coming with a high-pitched whine that reached a real crescendo as it passed directly between us, missing each of us by two or three feet at best."

Pearce and his friend stared at one another for a moment as the sound tailed off. Then, without saying a word, his friend carefully set down his can of C rations, dropped his pants, squatted on the ground, and answered nature's call then and there.

"I fell on the ground laughing," said Pearce, "but I understood exactly how the poor guy felt. I also realized for the first time that it was really physically possible to have the you-know-what scared out of you."

A short time later, as Pearce moved out toward Sachon with the recoilless gun platoon to which he was attached, one of a pair of enemy antitank guns opened fire from a hidden position above the road. The shell struck a jeep-ambulance driven by Pearce's friend and fellow corpsman William H. Anderson, killing him instantly.

Pearce was approximately fifty feet away when the shell hit, and as he ran toward the ruined jeep, he saw his friend's mangled body sprawled in the road. "He never knew what hit him," Pearce said, "and that was my only comfort—that he never suffered. The shell hit him in the upper abdomen and almost cut him in half."

Anderson had already been wounded twice that day, but he'd refused to be evacuated, and he was on his way to pick up another casualty when he was killed. His death had a lasting impact on Pearce.

"It sobered me like nothing I'd ever experienced," he said. "I didn't laugh again for quite a while."

For the first time in the war, the North Koreans had been forced into a general withdrawal. For once, their faith in their own invincibility had been shaken, at least slightly. A Marine historian described the enemy as seeming "disorganized if not actually demoralized," and an NKPA major captured near Kosong confirmed as much when he told his American interrogators, "Panic sweeps my men when they see the Marines in the yellow leggings coming at them."

But the enemy was still strong and full of fight, still certain that Pusan was within his grasp, and still determined to sweep the UN forces into the sea. If the Marines and GIs were to turn the tide, innumerable hills remained to be climbed and conquered. Along the way, countless other comrades were still to be mourned.

CHAPTER 7

★ ★ ★

TRIUMPH, TRAGEDY, TRAPS, AND TEARS

LIEUTENANT IKE FENTON had never felt more pride in the men of his company.

As the First Battalion of the Marine brigade moved out toward Sachon on the early morning of August 12, the executive officer of Baker Company could sense a newfound optimism and eagerness resonating among the troops. He could even detect a slight swagger in their step, despite the blisters on their feet, and Fenton knew exactly what had put it there.

"We moved at a very rapid pace, knowing that we were close to Sachon," he recalled. "We were all anxious to get there because we knew the Army was moving right along parallel to us on another route, and we wanted to keep after the enemy while we had them rolling. We felt that we had them on the run, and we wanted to finish them off."

The First Battalion, commanded by Colonel George Newton, was responsible for the southern half of a two-pronged attack. The Army's Fifth Regimental Combat Team was to follow a more northerly course toward the town of Chinju, another major objective of Task Force Kean, some seven miles north of Sachon. Many Marines regarded the attack as a race with the Army, and they hoped to seize Sachon before the Fifth RCT reached Chinju.

In terms of air miles, each of the objectives was about the same distance from the road junction near Chindong-ni, where the Army and Marine units had separated on August 9. But by road, the Marines would have to cover a total of thirty-four miles, while the Army troops would travel only twenty-eight. The Marines looked forward to the challenge.

Baker Company, commanded by Captain John Tobin, was designated as lead unit for the Marines' portion of the attack. It was preceded only by a jeepborne fifteen-man detachment of Captain Kenneth J. Houghton's Recon Company, which ranged about a mile ahead of the column to serve as advance guard on the point.

Following the reconnaissance team was Baker Company's First Platoon, commanded by Lieutenant Hugh Schryver and separated by two M-26 Pershing tanks from Lieutenant David "Scotty" Taylor's Second Platoon. Close behind marched the Third Platoon, under Lieutenant Dave Cowling, followed by three more M-26s. Strung out to B Company's rear was the rest of the First Battalion. Helicopters and observation planes guarded the flanks on both sides of the road, scouring the countryside for any trace of the NKPA.

At 6:30 AM on August 12, when A and B companies of the First Battalion had passed through Colonel Robert Taplett's 3/5 to assume the forward position in the advance, no signs of enemy activity had been detected in the area. The rest of the morning was equally quiet—unnaturally so, in the minds of some veteran NCOs—as the column advanced about eleven miles before noon, encountering virtually no opposition.

"Our guys took a lot of pride in the fact that we'd done all this moving on foot," Fenton noted, "while Army units moved mostly by motor. Our morale was very high."

Along the roadsides as the Marines passed lay telltale signs of the recent flight of NKPA troops over this route and of the havoc wreaked on them by Marine air. An estimated 1,900 North Koreans had been killed or wounded in the combined air-ground assaults of the past two days.

"We saw evidence of considerable enemy disorganization," said Fenton. "Abandoned equipment, vehicles still smoldering from direct hits, and quite a few dead bodies."

Among the scores of demolished vehicles were some sidecar-equipped motorcycles that were still in running condition, and Fenton and other officers looked the other way while a few footsore Marines appropriated the machines for their own use.

As one PFC observed to his buddy in the sidecar as they zipped along on a sleek, black, Russian-built motorcycle, "The only good thing about being in the lead is that you get first grabs on stuff like this."

By 2:00 PM on August 12, the column had advanced sixteen miles from Kosong and a total of thirty-one miles from Chindong-ni since the day before. Thus far during the day, they had taken only three rest breaks along the way despite the brutal heat, and Sachon was only about three miles farther on. "The men were tired, but we kept encouraging them and telling them we were almost there," Fenton said. "A big creek that ran beside the road helped with the heat and eased the drain on our water supply. Men would wade in and completely soak themselves, and this gave them an added lift."

After ten days in Korea—days of constant climbing across endless ridges and wading through miles of rice paddies—the Marines were also tougher now and better acclimated to the peninsula's extreme weather conditions. Because of more rigorous training, they'd already been in better physical shape than their Army counterparts, and the hardships they'd faced had merely increased their strength. As one author put it, "[T]he constant fighting and marching was boiling off the fat. The brigade was fast becoming a lean, hard outfit with fewer and fewer men succumbing to the heat."

This was extremely fortunate because unmitigated havoc was about to descend on the Marine column. Over the next twenty-four hours, the men of Baker Company would need every ounce of stamina, resolve, and courage they could muster.

Near the hamlet of Changchon, the main road entered a broad valley of the same name, framed on both sides by 600-foot hills. Between the hills and the road were large rice paddies, encompassing an area about 500 yards wide and offering no appreciable cover. Directly behind Changchon village and running perpendicular to the Marines' line of march rose another stretch of high ground, in the shape of a large "U," with its open end providing the Marine column its sole entry point into the valley. Its code name on the maps was Hill 202.

It was a made-to-order spot for an ambush, and Captain Houghton, commanding the Recon Company advance guard, was immediately suspicious. But when the Grasshopper OY planes overhead were unable to spot any enemy activity, Houghton cautiously ordered his jeeps forward. Lieutenant Schryver's First Platoon of B Company followed a few hundred yards behind.

Just as the Recon Company crossed a bridge at the edge of Changchon, two enemy soldiers jumped from their hiding places and ran toward the village center. The Marines, thinking they'd simply flushed out a couple of stragglers, fired a few rounds at the North Koreans—the first they'd seen all day—as they disappeared.

The echoes of the rifle shots died away, followed by an instant of eerie silence. Then, as one Marine historian wrote, "The reply was thunderous. From the hills ahead and on either side of the road, all hell broke loose, as 500 of the NKPA poured in fire from carefully camouflaged positions above the Marines."

"We didn't know it at the time," said Lieutenant Fenton, "but we'd engaged the rear guard of the North Korean 83rd Motorized Regiment. There was machine-gun fire from the front, left, right, and right rear, and no cover or concealment could be found in those fields along the road."

Houghton's advance guard quickly deployed in shallow ditches and returned fire, but there was no way for his handful of men to cope with the situation, especially when they could see nothing to shoot at. "We're taking more than we can handle up here!" Houghton yelled to Captain Tobin over the radio. "We're in a crossfire, and we're getting murdered!"

"Try to hold on," Tobin urged. "I'm sending up Schryver's platoon and two tanks."

Tobin himself accompanied the reinforcements, leaving Fenton to set up a company command post, organize an aid station, recruit stretcher bearers to retrieve wounded under heavy fire, and put in a call for close air support.

"We were taking a lot of fire, but we couldn't pinpoint the enemy's guns because their camouflage was outstanding," Fenton said. "We asked battalion to have the planes strafe the whole general area where the enemy was dug in, and we kept trying to locate their machine guns, so we could get our tanks on them."

Riflemen floundered through muddy roadside ditches and rice paddies covered by two feet of water, vainly searching for effective firing positions. Radios fell into the muck and were knocked out. Tanks sat helplessly in the road, unable to deploy or find targets for their cannons and machine guns.

Meanwhile, so many wounded began flooding in that the two corpsmen assigned to B Company were unable to keep pace. "Give us a hand here," one medic implored. "Anybody who knows first aid, come on!"

Awaiting treatment on a stretcher, a bloodstained young Marine gestured toward the hills and swore brokenly, "They got a fuckin' division up there, and we can't even see the bastards."

Tobin, accompanied by two runners, had made it less than 100 yards up the road when an enemy machine gunner opened up on the trio, forcing them to seek cover behind the meager protection of a rice paddy dike. As they hunkered down in the fetid water, Tobin noticed one of his runners shaking violently.

"What's the matter with you, son?" Tobin demanded.

"I'm . . . I'm scared, sir."

Tobin scowled at the kid. "Shape up, lad," he said. "You know Marines are never scared."

The words had scarcely left Tobin's lips when the enemy machine gunner zeroed in on them, and a hail of bullets began eating away at the top of the dike and kicking up mud and water around the three Marines. "On second thought, son, I see what you mean," Tobin said. "Let's get the hell out of here!"

They ran like rabbits for the ditch on the far side of the road. Miraculously, all three made it safely. After catching their breath, they began inching their way forward.

• • •

What the Marines didn't know when the shooting started was that, after the NKPA's disaster at Kosong, several hundred survivors of the 83rd Motorized Regiment had been ordered to make a stand in the high ground above Changchon Valley. Reinforcements also had been sent forward from Sachon, and the enemy troops had worked all night to dig in and camouflage their fortifications, laying an intricate trap that was invisible from the air when daylight returned.

The North Koreans had planned to wait to spring the trap until the bulk of the Marine column had passed through the U-shaped entrance to the valley and into their interlocking fields of fire. But when Houghton's men had opened fire on the two enemy soldiers in the village, the gunners hiding in the hills had reacted prematurely.

If the enemy troops had held their fire for a few more minutes, hundreds of Marines might have been massacred at Changchon. The results were grim enough as it was, but the alert reaction by the recon team unquestionably averted a potential catastrophe.

Miles to the northeast, meanwhile, the Army's Fifth RCT, commanded by Colonel Godwin Ordway Jr., had run headlong into an even more devastating situation than the one facing the Marines at Changchon. As it turned out, the Marines needn't have worried about the Fifth RCT reaching its assigned objective before they reached theirs. The Army unit had bogged down almost before it got started, making its rear echelon a sitting duck for an enveloping surprise attack from behind. Meanwhile, the Marines had covered more than three times as much distance.

Plagued with problems since the onset of Task Force Kean's offensive, the Fifth RCT had left Chindong-ni on August 11, the day before the Marine column departed Kosong, But by the afternoon of August 12, the Army unit had advanced only about five miles before being stymied by what Ordway described to General Kean as a large enemy force. Kean doubted the accuracy of Ordway's report, but he promised to send up a battalion from the 24th Infantry Regiment to protect Ordway's right flank.

The promised battalion failed to show up, and a series of communications breakdowns added further confusion. Then Ordway's headquarters lost contact with one entire company of his Second Battalion. An outbreak of firing was heard from the company's position, followed by flashing light signals from that same locale. Numerous attempts were made to contact the company by radio and telephone. None succeeded.

What had happened, it was later learned, was that the Army troops had failed to spot an undetermined number of North Koreans hiding in the hills along the Fifth RCT's route and bypassed the enemy force. This allowed the North Koreans to reorganize and strike at the rear of the American position, where attached units of the 90th and 555th (Triple Nickel) Field Artillery battalions were concentrated.

By the time Ordway's men realized what was happening, the Fifth RCT was caught up in what one historian termed "an epic disaster." Swarms of NKPA infiltrators had cut the main road behind them and overrun the unsuspecting artillery units, killing or wounding 300 American troops.

Fearing a frontal attack, Ordway had at first ignored pleas from other officers to move his supply train and artillery through a critical mountain pass. Then, after the company's disappearance, he'd changed his mind, only to have the narrow road through the pass blocked by a wrecked ambulance, whose overanxious driver had tried to cut into the column from the side. For more than an hour after that, no vehicle in the column had been able to move more than twenty feet.

When the sun came up on the morning of August 12 (at about the same time that the Marines of the First Battalion were setting out for Sachon), the enemy force had fallen on the stalled and exposed main body of the Fifth RCT with a vengeance.

General Kean's only hope of saving the besieged unit was to call on General Craig's Marine brigade, several miles away, for immediate help. With the Americans' main supply route again threatened and the entire right flank of the offensive vulnerable to attack, Craig again ordered Colonel Taplett's 3/5 to the rescue.

Taplett and Craig's operations officer, Lieutenant Colonel Joseph Stewart, took off in Craig's helicopter later that morning with instructions to reconnoiter the area and rendezvous with an Army liaison officer. According to their instructions, the officer would be waiting for them in a red-paneled jeep at a bridge a couple of miles west of Chindong-ni, where more explicit orders would be forthcoming.

"Looks like another doomsday affair to save some more Army butts, Tap," Stewart remarked as the chopper clattered northeast.

"Yeah, Joe, and probably ours, too," Taplett replied.

After an extensive search, they found the designated bridge, and the helicopter pilot landed in a dry streambed. The Army liaison officer and his red-paneled jeep were nowhere to be found, but a short distance down the streambed, Taplett and Stewart came upon an armored personnel carrier. Inside the vehicle was an Army first lieutenant, who climbed out to greet them.

"I haven't seen any liaison officer or anybody else in this area," the lieutenant said, "but I'll be glad to drive you down the main road toward Chindong-ni and see if we can find the 25th Division command post."

"Aren't you in radio contact with division headquarters?" Taplett asked.

"No sir," said the lieutenant. "I'm not in contact with anybody. But as far as I know, nobody's passed this way since I posted a sentry over on the main road early this morning."

As they rode east in the armored vehicle, Taplett noticed tangles of Army field telephone lines along the roadside, and the lieutenant agreed to stop and try to tap into one of them. Eventually the lieutenant located a line to 25th Division headquarters, and after a long delay, Colonel Stewart was connected with the division's G-3 operations officer.

"I don't know where the liaison man is, but he's supposed to have all the orders for your battalion," the G-3 said.

"Well, we've looked everywhere, and we can't find him," Stewart said. "So what the hell are we supposed to do now?"

"Attack to the north, I guess," the G-3 said vaguely, "or just look the situation over and decide for yourself."

Realizing that further conversation was pointless, Stewart broke the connection. Moments later, as he and Taplett were climbing back into the lieutenant's vehicle, they saw several trucks approaching, each of them heavily loaded with troops.

Taplett stepped out into the road and stopped the first truck. He later described it as "bulging with black troops, some of them hanging off the sides."

"I'm Colonel Taplett, Third Battalion, Fifth Marines," he told the driver. "Where are you people going?"

"To the rear, sir," the driver said. "Our outfit's been hit hard, and we're getting out of here."

Taplett tried to argue. "You're needed up here where you are," he said. "Now I want you to turn that truck around and head back to your posts. Are there any officers with you?"

There was no reply from the driver, but a towering black trooper climbed onto the cab of the truck and pointed a BAR squarely at Taplett's chest.

"Get outta the way, white boy," he said. "We's headed for Pusan."

Taplett was both shaken and disgusted, but he stood his ground for a moment until he heard Stewart yelling at him, "Come on, Tap, let 'em go before you get shot. They wouldn't do us any good here, anyway."

The truck roared past as Taplett stepped out of the way. Then he and Stewart got back into the lieutenant's vehicle and returned to the dry streambed, where a very nervous helicopter pilot was waiting. As they took off and flew along the streambed, they saw a scene that was unlike anything Taplett had ever witnessed before.

"The riverbed was littered with [American] dead, mutilated bodies, and burned-out, destroyed guns, motor transport, and equipment were strewn all over the area," he recalled. "Not a sign of life anywhere."

The carnage below marked the spot where much of the 555th Field Artillery Battalion had been annihilated in the NKPA attack. As Taplett later learned, the truckloads of fleeing black troops who had defied his order to turn around were apparently the only GIs to survive the massacre.

In addition to 300 KIAs, the Army artillery had lost six 105-millimeter howitzers, six 155-millimeter howitzers, and close to 100 vehicles in the attack at "Bloody Gulch," as the dry streambed became known.

On learning of the slaughter, General Craig was appalled. Marine artillerymen—like all other members of the Corps, regardless of their specific jobs—considered themselves riflemen first and foremost, and they were well schooled in security measures. "They were armed with bazookas,

.50-calibers, and everything that infantrymen would need to defend a position," Craig noted. "As a result, we never had a gun taken or overrun, whereas the Army on a number of occasions in the perimeter lost whole batteries. It was simply because the [Army] artillerymen weren't trained along the same lines as the Marines."

The Army estimated that 2,000 to 2,500 enemy troops had attacked elements of the 555th and 90th Field Artillery battalions from the rear at Bloody Gulch, then melted away into the ridges. But after reconnoitering the area and attracting fire from only a handful of North Koreans hiding in some huts in a small village, Taplett discounted the estimate and pegged the enemy's strength at no more than a few hundred.

When his battalion arrived on the scene, Taplett ordered H Company, under Captain Joe Fegan, to lead the assault on the suspected enemy-held ridges, followed by Lieutenant Bob Bohn's G Company and supported by a convenient flight of Corsairs.

As the attack was jumping off, Taplett received word from General Craig that Brigadier General George B. Barth, assistant commander of the 25th Infantry Division, would arrive shortly to take charge of the operation. But with the sun rapidly descending behind the western ridges, Taplett felt he couldn't afford to wait.

"I told Craig that we'd attacked immediately after arriving and that Joe Fegan's H Company was in the process of clearing the first of the enemy ridgelines with the help of our Corsairs," Taplett recalled. A few minutes later, G Company cleared the second portion of the ridge against light resistance.

It was after sunset when Barth arrived to take command. "How soon will your men be ready to attack?" he asked when Taplett reported to him.

Taplett almost had to bite his lip to keep from grinning. "Sir, we've already done that," he said, "and my men are now digging in on top of the ridge to protect our main supply route. We'll continue the attack in the morning to eliminate any other enemy threats in the area."

The Army general was surprised and clearly a bit embarrassed, but his response was gracious.

"Good job, Colonel," he said. "My congratulations on your speed and efficiency."

Barth departed a short time later, and Taplett never saw him again. But Taplett later admitted being deeply disturbed by what he had witnessed that day.

"That night was exceptionally quiet," he recalled, "and I had time to dwell on the Army disaster upstream, the deterioration of the proud U.S. Army, and the leadership competence of its generals and field officers. I felt sorry for their poor soldiers."

Back in Changchon Valley, meanwhile, the Marines remained locked in a bloody stalemate with a North Korean force whose strength they initially underestimated. After a firefight that raged much of the afternoon on August 12, the American column was no closer to Sachon than it had been when the first shots were fired more than three hours earlier. All three platoons of B Company, First Battalion, had suffered casualties.

Captain Tobin was still pinned down near the head of the column with the recon unit and Lieutenant Schryver's First Platoon. But by radio, Tobin approved a request by Ike Fenton to send Lieutenant Dave Cowling's Third Platoon across the rice paddies on his right to flush out the troublesome enemy machine guns on the ridge beyond, identified on maps as Hill 202.

"We had no indication that the enemy was up there in great strength, and I thought one platoon, with the tanks covering them as they moved up, could take that high ground," Fenton recalled. "But when they got to the top of the ridge, about 100 North Koreans attacked from the reverse side of the hill."

The enemy troops had been lying in wait for the Marines, and, aided by their machine guns, they struck with such force that Cowling's men were driven off the ridge. One Marine was killed, and Cowling himself was among four others wounded. As soon as Fenton found out what had happened, he ordered the Third Platoon back to safer ground to wait for Marine air, artillery, and mortars to "work the area over with everything available."

After three or four strafing runs by the Corsairs, a half-hour artillery barrage, and blanketing fire from every available 60-millimeter mortar, the enemy firing subsided.

By this time it was almost 6:00 PM, and as darkness approached, Colonel Newton, the regimental commander, ordered B Company to establish a defensive perimeter for the night on the high ground to the left of the road to Sachon. The order came as a relief to Fenton, since almost all of the company's radios had been knocked out by the high water in the rice paddies, and many of its weapons also were waterlogged or mudclogged and useless until they could be broken down and thoroughly cleaned.

Using a radio borrowed from the tank platoon commander, Fenton asked battalion headquarters to send up replacement radios and weapons. Battalion promised to resupply the unit as soon as possible, but because of the lateness of the hour, Fenton was told to move his men forward.

"We immediately sent Lieutenant Scotty Taylor's Second Platoon to seize the right portion of the high ground, while the Third Platoon moved up to take the other part of the ridge," Fenton said. "Evidently, after our air attacks, the enemy had pulled out. The machine gun that had bothered us was silent now, and we encountered only a little sniper fire as we went up."

While Taylor's men climbed one side of the ridgeline, however, an NKPA patrol was coming up the other side. "Fortunately," Fenton recalled, "Taylor was able to get his platoon to the top about five minutes ahead of the North Koreans, and he spotted the enemy in time to set up an ambush."

Moments later, when the Marines stopped firing, thirty-eight members of the enemy patrol lay dead. The sole survivor, a young lieutenant with serious wounds, died en route to the battalion CP.

Full darkness descended over the First Battalion's thinly manned lines well before the Marines were ready for it. As the last light faded, B Company counted three men killed, thirteen wounded, and two missing in the action of August 12. To bolster the Marine front, Captain Stevens's A Company had been ordered to join B Company's three shorthanded platoons on the high ground, with Stevens's men assigned to the right side of the Sachon road.

"We were really short of people," recalled Sergeant Mackie Wheeler, a squad leader in A Company. "We were the only two rifle companies in the battalion at that point. We didn't get Charlie Company until later on, but God knows we sure needed 'em that night."

Even with A Company's additional manpower, it was impossible to defend the ridgeline adequately. "Quite a bit of the terrain had to be covered by mortar and artillery fire directed from battalion headquarters," Lieutenant Fenton said, "and this situation left a gap of 800 to 900 yards—a half mile or more—between A and B companies. Each company was, in all respects, out there by itself."

It was a far from comfortable situation for Tobin, Fenton, and the two remaining B Company platoon leaders, Taylor and Schryver. One bit of good luck was that there was little need to dig fresh foxholes, since the ones recently vacated by NKPA troops were well positioned on the ridgeline. Nevertheless, it was close to midnight when the setup for the night was completed, and everybody was jumpy.

"If there were any enemy in the area, we knew we'd be hit that night," said Fenton. "We cautioned all our squad leaders to keep at least 25 percent of their men awake. Later, we changed that to 50 percent, but that was a mistake. The men had been moving continuously for three days, and they were dead tired."

The prevailing feeling during this period was that no place was safe— not even a regimental command post—and Corporal Bob Speights of A Company, First Engineer Battalion, learned that the feeling was well justified.

"I was waiting outside Colonel Ray Murray's CP when a sniper's bullet hit me across the left cheek," recalled Speights, who had departed his Texas home for Marine boot camp in San Diego on his sixteenth birthday in 1946. "I jerked my head around when I felt the sting, and damned if I didn't immediately get grazed again across the right cheek. No more 'turning the other cheek' for me after that!"

A minute or two before 5:00 AM on August 13, an enemy flare lit the sky above Hill 202, and the North Koreans came screaming up the slope out of the muggy darkness, throwing themselves in human waves on the thinly stretched lines of Baker Company.

Lieutenant Hugh Schryver's First Platoon was dug in near the main thrust of the attack. The instant the flare went off, the densely wooded hillside to the platoon's front became a maelstrom of sound and movement, but it was almost impossible to pick out individual enemy soldiers.

"Christ, they're right in our faces!" said Schryver with a gasp. He grabbed for his carbine in the shallow foxhole he shared with his runner/radioman and yelled down the line, "Fire! Fire!"

"I hear 'em, but I can't see nothin' for all the damned brush!" a Marine shouted from an adjacent foxhole as M-1s and BARs spat fire into the tangled undergrowth.

"Just keep firing!" Schryver shouted back. "Open up with everything you've got. There's so many of 'em, you're bound to hit something!"

Schryver tried to sound confident, but he knew the platoon would need a miracle to hold its ground. An Iowa-born World War II veteran who'd joined the Corps in April 1941 and served for seven years as an enlisted man before qualifying for officer candidate school, Schryver knew there were several Marine tanks on the road barely a hundred yards away, but there was no way they could get through the heavy foliage to help his riflemen.

Early the previous afternoon, Schryver had seen bedlam descend on his platoon, and now things were going from bad to worse. In less than eighteen hours, B Company was destined to suffer more combat deaths than any Marine unit since the Battle of Okinawa.

"Get Captain Tobin on the horn if you can," Schryver told the radio operator above the near-continuous roar of rifle fire. "We may not be able to hold this position for long."

Private First Class Ben Wray, a designated BAR man in B Company's Second Rifle Platoon, who had turned eighteen aboard his troopship bound for Korea, grabbed his weapon and listened intently to harsh grunts and threshing noises in the gloom a few yards away.

A tough kid from Austin, Texas, who had dropped out of the tenth grade to join the Marine Corps, Wray had met his first North Korean face to face at about two o'clock the afternoon before. "He was hiding, and I walked right up on him," he recalled decades later. "I was only about five yards away when I unloaded about twenty rounds in him from the BAR. Thank God, he was alone."

In the melee that followed, Wray had fired at numerous other enemy soldiers, but none had been nearly as close as that first one. Now, though, the sounds erupting from the undergrowth in front of him signaled that another close encounter was only seconds away.

"Sounds like a bunch of damned hogs out there," whispered the Marine at Wray's elbow.

An instant later, they heard the raspy rattle of automatic weapons fire and the whistle of bullets ripping through the brush.

"Hogs, my ass," Wray said. "Hogs don't carry burp guns. The gooks are coming straight up the hill at us. They're right between us and our machine gun section." He braced the BAR against his shoulder, peering into the curtain of darkness in search of a target. A second later, he saw a dim suggestion of movement and opened fire.

From the company command post, where Lieutenant Ike Fenton squinted into the darkness, the enemy attack on the knob of high ground called Hill 202 seemed eerily reminiscent of the fanatic Japanese banzai charges he'd seen in World War II—with one major difference. Instead of bayonets, every North Korean seemed to have an automatic weapon—and all of them were firing at once.

As Fenton squatted in the erstwhile enemy foxhole that served as Baker Company's makeshift headquarters, his eyes met those of his commanding officer, Captain John Tobin, who clutched a phone in one hand and a .45 automatic in the other.

"The First and Second platoons are both catching hell to their front," Tobin said. "The gooks slipped in right under their noses when a lot of guys who were supposed to be on watch went to sleep. Looks like we've lost some machine guns out there."

In most combat situations, falling asleep on watch was an unpardonable sin, but in this case, Fenton could almost sympathize with the culprits. He and Tobin themselves were bone-tired and red-eyed from five almost-sleepless days and nights of marching at double time, assaulting one enemy-held hill after another, dodging machine-gun and mortar fire, and fighting off counterattacks. Along the way, they'd advanced twenty-nine miles with little rest in scorching midday temperatures. It seemed miraculous that anyone in the company was still able to stand.

"The gooks have knocked out the artillery's radio, and they're chopping us to pieces on the left flank," Tobin told Fenton. "Get mortars on the line, and tell them to blanket that area with fire on the double."

Seconds after Fenton grabbed a phone and shouted the order, he heard Lieutenant Dick Christolas's 81-millimeter mortar section open up with a roar. But almost before the echoes died, the First Platoon's Lieutenant Schryver reported fierce enemy pressure continuing against his position.

Tobin turned to Fenton. "Schryver's guys look to be catching the worst of this thing," he said. "The enemy's trying to drive a wedge along the ravine between the First and Second platoons, and Schryver doubts he can hold. Two of the Third Platoon's machine guns have been overrun, and the gooks are using them against our guys. We've got a bunch of men down—at least ten dead in the machine-gun section—and others are cut off. The gooks have cut our wire to the Third Platoon, so we'll have to use runners. We're in a helluva shape."

Since Fenton had been assigned to Tobin's unit at Camp Pendleton four weeks earlier, they'd had a few differences, but now the two were in total agreement about the urgency of their situation.

"Schryver has to pull back, and so do we," Fenton said. "Hell, the gooks'll be right here in our laps if we don't. What does battalion say?"

"The phones are screwed up, and I can't get through to battalion," Tobin said, "but you're right—we can't wait around."

Within the next few moments, Tobin managed to get word to Schryver to pull his men back into the area held by Lieutenant Taylor's Second Platoon. But when he tried to reach Staff Sergeant Alfred Cirinelli, who had assumed command of the Third Platoon after Lieutenant Cowling was evacuated with a bullet in his left foot, that phone line was dead, too.

"Send out runners, and tell all three platoons to pull back and reorganize their lines while we work the gooks over with mortars and artillery," Tobin said. "Have Schryver's First Platoon serve as a rear guard to cover us while we move our CP to a safer position."

• • •

The really infuriating part of all this, Tobin thought, was that the whole company was going to have to withdraw as soon as the sun came up, anyway. The pull-out order from the Eighth Army, relayed through General Craig's headquarters, had reached Tobin late the evening before, soon after B Company had managed—at least for the time being—to stabilize its defensive perimeter. It had been bitterly frustrating news—so frustrating that Tobin had temporarily resisted sharing it, even with Fenton.

The company's cost in casualties was already ruinously high. In addition to the dead and wounded, more than a few were still missing. The rest of the company was physically and emotionally drained, but, to a man, they would've chosen to stay and fight rather than yield this hard-won ground. Pulling out now meant that all their sacrifices had been for nothing, but an order was an order, no matter how distasteful it might be.

Word of the withdrawal had been late reaching Tobin because of phone lines severed by the enemy, but Colonel Newton, commanding the First Battalion, left no doubt that the order took precedence over everything else. By then, however, Tobin's exhausted troops were bedded down for the night, and he saw no harm in letting them grab an hour or two of rest before relaying the bad news to the units holding Hill 202. Then the enemy's predawn attack had screwed up everything. (The following exchange between Fenton and Tobin is based on three principal sources: Fenton's official debriefing interview in early 1951; a reconstruction of the two officers' conversation quoted in Andrew Geer's *The New Breed*, published in 1952; and author interviews with Lieutenant Hugh Schryver in 2007 and 2008.)

As Tobin turned to face him, Fenton could tell from his captain's pained expression that something was terribly wrong. "I may as well tell you right now, Ike," Tobin said. "We've been ordered to pull out at first light and head for the Naktong River. The gooks have broken through over there, and General Craig says the situation's desperate. They're sending trucks to pick us up, and we've got to be ready to roll by 0700 [7:00 AM]."

The words hit Fenton like a punch in the gut. He'd lost his only brother on Okinawa in 1945, but except for that tragedy, this was the worst news he'd ever heard. It made him feel like vomiting.

"We've got a bunch of guys cut off out there, John," Fenton said. "We'll have to wait till daylight to find them, and it's almost dawn now. Damn, we can't just walk off and leave them."

"We've got no choice," Tobin said. "Colonel Newton says we've got to withdraw with all possible speed and head for a place called Miryang, south of the Naktong." He quickly explained that the enemy had crossed the river and opened a major gap in American lines. If the gap wasn't closed in a hurry, Tobin said, the whole Pusan Perimeter could collapse like a house of cards.

"Maybe they can justify flushing the twenty-nine bloody, sweaty miles we've gained down the drain," Fenton argued. "But Christ, John, we can't abandon all those guys out there to the mercy of the North Koreans. Marines don't do things like that. Sure, most of them are probably dead, but some may still be alive. We can drive the gooks back and get to those kids in an hour or less."

Tobin shook his head wearily, and he had trouble holding his voice steady when he replied. "I've already asked the colonel, Ike, but he said no. I hate it as bad as you do, but there's no time. If the NKs collapse this perimeter we're hanging on to, there's no way we can hold Pusan—and if we lose Pusan, we lose South Korea. Now take what's left of the Third Platoon, collect our wounded, and get down to the road."

Fenton turned away, wiping clumsily at the tears on his face. "Telling Cirinelli and his men to leave those Marines behind is gonna be the worst job I ever had," he said as he stumbled away.

With the surprise assault by the North Koreans threatening all three rifle platoons with annihilation, and communications again disrupted, the pull-out order didn't reach the men in the ranks until a few minutes before departure time. When they got the word, riflemen of A and B companies were stunned. They'd been expecting an order to counterattack to reclaim lost ground and collect the dead, wounded, and missing men they'd been forced to leave on the field.

As platoon sergeants and squad leaders spread the word about the pull-out, telling the men to grab their gear and move downhill away from the enemy-held area of the ridge, many Marines fell into sullen silence. Others started cursing and kicking things. The cursing gradually intensified until even some senior NCOs joined in.

"We gotta get them boys off that hill before we go," a buck sergeant squad leader from Schryver's First Platoon pleaded to Fenton. "Please, sir, Marines don't abandon their own like this. Alive or dead, it don't matter."

"Nobody's sorrier about it than I am," Fenton replied through tight lips. "But we've got our orders, Sergeant. It's out of our hands. We'll try to come back for them later." Fenton knew as he spoke how empty and futile his words sounded.

"But my buddy, Arkie Parrish, is out there someplace, sir, and there's others from our platoon that are missing, too. I think some of 'em could still be alive, but they won't be for long if we don't go after 'em. Just give me a few minutes. I'll take my squad and get through to 'em—or, by God, we'll die tryin'."

Fenton bit his lip and clapped the sergeant on the shoulder. "We've lost enough good men as it is, Sergeant," he said. "We can't afford to lose you, too. Now try to get hold of yourself and move out. The trucks are waiting, and we've got to go."

"Shit!" the sergeant whispered, but he did as he was told.

At least twenty members of Baker Company never left Hill 202 that day. How many of these men were already dead when the trucks bearing their comrades rolled away has never been determined. Fenton's informal count of casualties during that morning's NKPA counterattack showed twelve dead, sixteen wounded, and nine missing. All of the MIA designations were eventually changed to "killed in action."

In all, twenty-four B Company Marines were confirmed dead in the August 12–13 action. There would be many more casualties to come, but this period would rank as the company's costliest twenty-four hours of the entire Korean War.

While they waited to board trucks, Marines who hadn't had a hot meal, or even a cup of hot coffee, since their first morning in Pusan, and who were still wearing the same filthy uniforms they'd worn for eleven days, watched disconsolately as small mountains of food and fresh clothing were set afire. Because there was no room for them on the trucks, all nonessential materials were ordered burned to keep them from falling into enemy hands.

Crates of B rations, heat-and-eat meals that were much preferred over cold C rations, were among the goods consigned to the flames as bulldozers broke up and buried many types of kitchen supplies and equipment that couldn't be moved. On top of everything else that had happened that morning, it was a heartbreaking sight.

"The men were whipped," Fenton recalled many years later, his voice still hoarse with emotion, "and a lot of them were crying. The word was out now that we were pulling out of the area altogether, that we couldn't continue our advance toward Sachon, which was only about three miles to our immediate front.

"It was hard to see men sitting around—veterans of the last war, older men—with tears running down their cheeks. They just didn't give a good 'hoot' anymore. They were tired and disgusted. People just couldn't understand this part of the war. But the thing that hurt the worst was that we couldn't go in there after those men. We couldn't even bring out their dog tags or anything. They were all listed as MIAs, but we knew we'd never see any of them alive again."

The survivors of Hill 202 would have plenty of time to ponder these unhappy facts as they traveled toward Miryang by truck, rail, and landing craft. By the morning of August 17, they and the rest of the Marine brigade would be under fire again, with the fate of the Pusan Perimeter—and the entire South Korean nation—resting squarely on their shoulders.

CHAPTER 8

★ ★ ★

NIGHTMARE ON THE NAKTONG

I T WAS SEVENTY-FIVE miles from Hill 202 near Sachon to the town of Miryang, now threatened by an estimated 7,000 enemy troops, who had waded across the shallow Naktong River, towing crude rafts loaded with heavy weapons, vehicles, and supplies. By August 8, an entire reinforced North Korean regiment had established a bridgehead on the east bank of the river, which was the last natural barrier between the Communist army and Pusan.

Over the next few days, the NKPA had steadily broadened its foothold until most of its crack Fourth Division—the same unit that had shared in the capture of Seoul, then routed Task Force Smith—was on the American side of the stream, opening a yawning gap in U.S. lines. The gap was in a cluster of rugged hills, where a sharp bend in the river surrounded a thumb-shaped strip of land on three sides to form a topographical oddity that the Americans called the Naktong Bulge. Unless the gap could be closed, the main supply route between Pusan and the inland city of Taegu, headquarters of General Walker's Eighth Army, was in danger, and Taegu itself might be overrun.

In his first attempt to dislodge the enemy troops, Walker ordered the recently arrived Second Infantry Division's Ninth Regiment, commanded by Colonel John G. Hill, to join elements of General John Church's 24th Division to create Task Force Hill. In addition to his own regiment, Hill was placed in control of all 24th Division units in Church's southern sector— giving him a force equal to three full infantry regiments—and ordered to assault the enemy bridgehead.

To Walker's distress, however, the attack by Task Force Hill on August 11 met a reception hauntingly similar to those encountered by previous Walker task forces. The attack lost its momentum and dissolved in confusion when the North Koreans attacked at the same time. Hill tried twice more, on August 14 and 15, but his troops ran into a stone wall of resistance, and bad weather deprived them of air support.

During this interval, the enemy had spirited more than 100 machine guns, considerable artillery (including a number of American 105s seized at Taejon), and even several tanks across the river. Entrenched in the high ground and with superior weaponry, the NKPA force was simply too strong, and Hill was forced to break off the attack and take up defensive positions east of the enemy stronghold.

By now, Walker's patience was frayed to the breaking point. He minced no words when he told Church, "I'm giving you the Marine brigade, and I want this situation cleaned up—and quick!"

On their arrival at Miryang on the afternoon of August 15, General Craig and his men confronted stakes that could not have been higher. The consensus among high-echelon UN commanders was that if Miryang fell, neither Taegu nor Pusan could be held. Walker himself pledged to fight in the streets if the enemy got into Taegu.

"And you'd better be prepared to do likewise," he told one field commander, whose reticence and excuses brought Walker to the boiling point. "Now get back to your division and fight it! I don't want to see you back from the front again unless it's in your coffin."

Meanwhile, by August 15, more than 400,000 Korean refugees had crowded into Taegu, and the ROK government, fearing its security could no longer be guaranteed in the city, packed up and moved to Pusan.

In addition to the precarious situation at the Naktong Bulge, Walker faced serious problems all across the front. The First Cavalry Division, charged with anchoring a tremendously wide section of the front west of Taegu, had repulsed repeated NKPA incursions across the Naktong farther to the north but remained under heavy pressure from the enemy. In the far southwest, although the Marine attacks had left NKPA forces weakened and disorganized, Army lines continued to develop leaks after the Marines' hurried withdrawal from Sachon. On the east side of the peninsula, the ROK Third Division was forced out of the secondary port of Pohang-dong and evacuated under cover of American air and naval forces, then relanded farther south. With NKPA troops only a few hundred yards from its runways, the U.S. Fifth Air Force abandoned Yonil Airfield, its only base on the east coast, and moved its desperately needed F-51 squadrons back to Japan. The entire eastern front looked to be hovering on the verge of collapse.

If there was any small shred of hope remaining, it lay with the Marines. As a British military observer attached to the 24th Division observed in a wire dispatched on the morning of August 16, as Craig's brigade prepared for its new mission,

"The situation is critical, and Miryang may be lost. The enemy has driven a division-sized salient across the Naktong. More will cross the river tonight. If Miryang is lost . . . we will be faced with a withdrawal from Korea. I am heartened that the Marine brigade will move against the Naktong salient tomorrow. They are faced with impossible odds, and I have no valid reason to substantiate it, but I have the feeling they will halt the enemy. . . .

"These Marines have the swagger, confidence, and hardness that must have been in Stonewall Jackson's Army of the Shenandoah. They remind me of the Coldstreams at Dunkirk. Upon this thin line of reasoning, I cling to the hope of victory."

When the Marines reached Miryang, however, they were dragging their heels rather than swaggering. To a man, they were drained, hungry, caked with dirt, and red-eyed from lack of sleep. Many of the troops had had to march most of the previous night after a promised convoy of trucks failed to show up, and the forced journey, after days of heavy fighting, had been

1

Task Force Smith, the first U.S. military unit to see action in the Korean War, arrived at Taejon on July 3, 1950 (above), led by young Lieutenant Colonel Charles B. "Brad" Smith (below left). Major Miller Perry (below right), commanding the small artillery unit attached to Task Force Smith, suffered a severe leg wound in the outmanned Americans' resounding defeat near the village of Osan on July 5.

2

3

4

In the early days of the war, small groups of U.S. troops like the GIs manning a machine gun in the top photo were routed again and again by the tank-led invaders and forced to retreat steadily south. Lightly trained and poorly equipped soldiers of the 24th and 25th Infantry Divisions, rushed from occupation duty in Japan and commanded respectively by General William F. Dean (far left) and General William B. Kean (left), proved no match for the enemy in the early fighting.

5

6

7

Weak delaying actions constituted the only strategy available to General Walton Walker (center) and his Eighth Army staff as the Americans were pushed into a shallow defensive perimeter around the beleaguered port city of Pusan at Korea's southeastern tip.

One of the Eighth Army's most critical deficiencies was a shortage of artillery. Heavy weapons like this 105-millimeter howitzer (above) were transported from Japan with great difficulty, but many were lost to the advancing North Koreans. Meanwhile, treating American wounded in makeshift aid stations (below) became an around-the-clock task.

10

Back in the States, a Marine Corps shrunken by federal budget cuts scrambled to assemble a fighting force capable of ending the string of U.S. defeats in Korea. Sergeant Bill Finnegan (center, left) and his buddies gathered at Camp Pendleton, California, where Corpsman Herb "Doc Rocket" Pearce (below left) and Sergeant Charlie Snow (below right) were already stationed. There, General O. P. Smith (bottom left), commanding the First Marine Division, and General Eddie Craig (bottom right), assigned to lead the newly activated First Provisional Marine Brigade, moved swiftly, enabling the Brigade to sail for Korea in mid-July.

11

12

13

14

15

The attack transports *Pickaway* (left) and *Henrico* (center left) were among the convoy carrying the First Provisional Marine Brigade from San Diego to Pusan, where the North Koreans were about to drive U.S. forces into the sea. Once there, Marines armed with 75-millimeter recoilless guns (bottom) scored some of the earliest victories against formerly unstoppable NKPA tanks. Meanwhile, Marine Lieutenant Colonel Bryghte Godbold (below) joined an interservice team in Japan to plan a daring assault behind enemy lines at the port of Inchon.

16

17

18

Docking at Pusan, the ships bearing the Marine Brigade received a warm welcome from a South Korean color guard and band (above). Earlier, during the long voyage from San Diego, the Marines underwent as much training as possible in the limited space available, including an introduction to the light machine guns they would soon be using against the North Koreans (below).

As the Marines prepared to move inland for their first combat, Sergeant Mackie Wheeler (center above) and two buddies unloaded cases of hand grenades for distribution to the infantrymen in A Company, First Battalion, Fifth Marines. Accompanying the ground troops into combat—and giving them a decided advantage over U.S. Army troops in close air support— were several squadrons of Corsair fighters from Marine Air Group 33, like these (right) aboard the aircraft carrier *Badoeng Strait.*

One of the last defensible natural barriers to the conquest of Pusan—and a disastrous end to the war—was the Naktong River, where A and B Companies of the Fifth Marines dug in for a climactic stand. The face of Captain Ike Fenton, commander of B Company, mirrors the frustration and exhaustion of his men in this classic photo (left) by photographer David Douglas Duncan. To Captain John "Blackjack" Stevens, commander of A Company (inset, below), the Naktong action was the "toughest" ever faced in Korea, and the Marines charging a contested ridge along the river (bottom) would attest to that description.

24

Fifth Marines field commanders convened briefly to plan the next phase of the Naktong campaign with regimental CO Colonel Ray Murray (above lower left). Others pictured include (clockwise from upper left) battalion commanders Colonels Hal Roise, George Newton, and Robert Taplett, and Murray's executive officer, Colonel Larry Hayes. After a confrontation with the Marines' 3.5-inch rockets and 75-millimeter recoilless rifles, three enemy tanks sprawled disabled (below).

Marines board a landing craft in Inchon harbor (above) as their three-pronged amphibious operation hits full stride. Right, General Douglas MacArthur watches approvingly from the bridge of his command ship as the Marines wrest Wolmi-do Island from the North Koreans with minimal resistance. Standing at right behind MacArthur is General Ned Almond, commander of the X Corps invasion force.

On Inchon's Red and Blue Beaches, the Marines needed scaling ladders to get over a massive seawall onto solid ground. After several of his troops ran into difficulty using the ladders, platoon leader Lieutenant Baldomero Lopez (right) grabbed a ladder and led the charge over the wall (below). But moments later, Lopez was fatally wounded when he smothered an errant hand grenade with his own body to protect his men. He was posthumously awarded the Medal of Honor.

32

Marine tanks like this M-26 Pershing (above), manned by driver Corporal Murdoch Ford (sitting on deck of tank) and his crew, helped to secure the Inchon beachhead (below), then led the way into the South Korean capital of Seoul, overpowering the enemy armor they encountered en route. During the street fighting in Seoul, U.S. tanks played a vital role in breaching the huge barricades erected by NKPA troops at major intersections.

33

Under heavy fire on a main street in Seoul, Marine riflemen evacuated a wounded buddy (left) during a block-by-block battle that lasted several days in late September.

Some North Koreans fought hard to slow the American advance, but many others chose to surrender (right). With gunfire still echoing through the city, troops of Colonel Robert Taplett's Third Battalion, Fifth Marines, hauled down the North Korean flag at Government House (below) and raised the Stars and Stripes.

37

In early October, with victorious U.S. and ROK troops poised to cross into North Korea and veiled threats coming from Red China, President Harry Truman and General MacArthur met at Wake Island (left) to discuss limiting the scope of the war. Yet no firm decision was made as to how far the Americans should advance toward the Chinese province of Manchuria.

38

As winter descended, Marines of an antitank platoon (above) huddled around their frozen weapon and struggled to stay warm. By December, temperatures plunged to 40 below, and Lieutenant Hugh Schryver (right), a rifle platoon leader in B/1/5, tried in vain to fight the cold with hot coffee, cigarettes, and bulky winter gear.

Marines cut off and trapped by hordes of Chinese troops near North Korea's Chosin Reservoir (above) began a brutal march southward toward the port of Hamhung and their only hope of escape. Along with wounds inflicted by relentless enemy attacks, thousands of Marines suffered crippling frostbite on the way. Many others froze to death (below) and were buried in mass graves blasted into the ground with TNT.

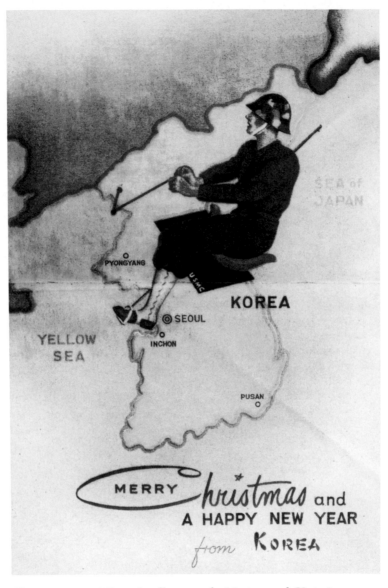

Christmastime 1950 was hardly merry for Marines and GIs trying desperately to free themselves from the Chinese trap, but this holiday greeting card—prepared weeks in advance for men of the First Marine Division to mail home to their families—conveyed the grossly misleading message that U.S. forces were "sitting pretty" in North Korea. The war would go on for more than two and a half years, until July 1953.

an ordeal for everyone. "By that time," recalled PFC Ben Wray, a native Texan and a BAR man in the First Battalion's Second Platoon, "we looked and felt like an old horse that had been rode hard and put away wet."

During the withdrawal from near Sachon, the situation had been so hectic that Colonel Harold Roise, commanding the Second Battalion, received his only orders for the move scribbled on a scrap of paper. The terse message, written by Colonel Joe Stewart, Craig's operations officer, and left with a fleet of parked vehicles, read simply, "These are your trucks. Move to Naktong at once."

After all this, Miryang proved to be an unexpectedly pleasant surprise.

Compared to the sun-baked, unforgiving hills they'd just left, the picturesque village was the closest thing to paradise the Marines had seen since leaving the States. To Colonel Robert Taplett of 3/5, it looked like "a heavenly oasis" and "an ideal spot for a picnic," and *Saturday Evening Post* writer Harold H. Martin, embedded with the brigade, called it "the most beautiful bivouac in all Korea."

"Our bivouac area was in a cool grove of trees on the grassy banks of the Miryang River, which would soon be our bedroom, bathroom, and laundry," Taplett recalled. "Everyone looked forward to our first night of uninterrupted sleep, a dip in the river, a change of clothes, and our first hot meal since leaving the USS *Pickaway*."

After a dozen days of living and fighting in the same field dungarees, Taplett and his troops were, in his words, as dirty and smelly as "a herd of goats." They took to the river in droves while dozens of native women, recruited by unit supply officers and paid with wages of cigarettes, washed grimy Marine uniforms and laid them out on the riverbank to dry.

Medical officers tried to warn the Marines that the pristine-looking stream might harbor potentially dangerous contaminants, but the warnings were ignored. Even normally cautious Navy corpsman Herb Pearce joined in the splashfest. But, as he observed later, "My enjoyment of the swim was lessened somewhat when I got out of the stream and discovered that some Koreans were busily skinning a dog in the water just around the bend from us."

• • •

The Marines realized that their interlude of rest and rehabilitation would be brief and that another brutal ordeal loomed ahead. On August 16, barely twenty hours after their arrival at Miryang, they received orders to move west about twenty-four miles to the area of Yongsan, a village less than ten miles from the Naktong. This would be the jumping-off place for their attack.

Intelligence reports indicated that the enemy was almost ready to break out of his Naktong salient, seize Miryang, and split UN forces into northern and southern halves. Miryang lay astride the double-track railroad over which vital supplies flowed between Pusan and Taegu. If Communist forces gained control of the rail line or cut it, Taegu would be cut off from supply and reinforcement.

That night, Fifth Marines commander Colonel Ray Murray met with Colonel Harold Roise, whose Second Battalion had been chosen to lead a frontal assault the next morning on Obong-ni Ridge, part of a jumbled mass of high ground held in strength by the NKPA. Roise's battalion would be followed by Taplett's 3/5, with Colonel Newton's 1/5, which had been badly battered in the fight for Sachon, in brigade reserve.

"Obong-ni Ridge sprawled across the Marine front like some huge pre-historic reptile," wrote Marine historian Lynn Montross. "Its blunt head overlooked the main supply route . . . and the elongated body stretched to the southeast more than 2,000 yards before losing its identity in a complex of swamps and irregular hill formations."

The ridgeline included half a dozen dominating peaks (identified by number, from north to south, as Hills 102, 109, 117, 143, 147, and 153), several smaller hills, and a succession of steep spurs, separated by deep gullies that ran all the way down to a series of rice paddies on the plain below. It presented a vast, demonic puzzle for the men of the Second Battalion's D and E companies assigned as the first Marines to climb it.

"You *must* take that ground tomorrow," Murray told Roise. "You *have* to get on that ridge and hold it. Understood?"

"Understood," Roise assured him. "This battalion goes only one way—straight ahead!"

Dug in and waiting for the American "yellow legs," as the North Koreans now called the Marines, were confident, seasoned troops of the NKPA's

Fourth Division. "Intelligence says we are to expect an attack by American Marines," said Colonel Chang Ky Dok, veteran commander of the division's 16th Regiment, in a speech to his officers. "To us comes the honor of being the first to defeat these Marines soldiers. We will win where others have failed. I consider our positions impregnable. We occupy the high ground, and they must attack up a steep slope. Go to your men, and tell them there will be no retreat. I will take instant action against anyone who shows weakness."

H-hour for the brigade's attack was set for 8:00 AM on August 17 as part of a general offensive by the entire 24th Infantry Division, reinforced by the Marines and the Ninth Infantry Regiment. The Marines had a long, historic relationship with the Ninth Infantry, having served with the Army unit during the Boxer Rebellion in China at the turn of the twentieth century and again in France during World War I. But in the futile attacks by Task Force Hill, the Ninth had sustained heavy losses in recent days, and when Craig visited Colonel Hill's command post, he was less than reassured by the condition of Hill's troops and the thinness of their lines.

Fifth Marines commander Colonel Murray also met with Hill, and he was even more concerned than Craig about the battle-weariness and generally poor condition of the Ninth. The two agreed, however, that the Marine battalion would attack on the left side of the main road against the multiple peaks of Obong-ni Ridge, while the Ninth attacked to the right of the road against two other formidable pieces of high ground, designated as Hill 125 and Observation Hill.

For the Marines, a ragged, red-clay gully near the center of Obong-ni would form the dividing line between two attacking companies. (Because of the ridge's confusing topography and the number of separate hills involved, American news correspondents covering the action were soon referring to Obong-ni in their dispatches as "No Name Ridge," while the Marines called it "Red Slash Hill," in reference to the gully that divided it.) Marine air and artillery were scheduled to pound the ridge for forty-five minutes before the infantry attacked, but problems largely negated their efforts. The shelling was so inaccurate that many observing 2/5 officers thought there had been no artillery preparation at all. Then two supporting squadrons of Corsairs from the carriers *Badoeng Strait* and *Sicily* arrived late at the target area and had time for only one bombing run before the two rifle companies jumped off abreast. The end result was that enemy fortifications were scarcely touched.

On the right of the Marine attack was D Company, commanded by Captain Andy Zimmer, and on the left was First Lieutenant Bill Sweeney's E Company. After placing his Second Platoon in reserve to provide covering fire, Zimmer sent his Third Platoon, led by Second Lieutenant Mike Shinka, off the main road and across three rice paddies toward the foot of Hill 109. Advancing close behind Shinka's unit was the First Platoon, led by Staff Sergeant T. Albert Crowson. A rocket section trailing Crowson's unit stopped near the road and set up its weapons to protect the main supply route.

After struggling up a gully, Shinka and his men were almost halfway to the top of the ridge when dozens of NKPA machine guns opened fire at once from all directions, much of the outburst coming from the crests of Hills 117 and 143 on the left. Simultaneously, from directly above, at the top of Hill 109, enemy troops in holes on the reverse slope hurled down scores of hand grenades on the Marine riflemen. But the costliest fire—and by far the most difficult to defend against—came from Hill 125, almost directly behind the Marines on the opposite (right) side of the road.

Hill 125 was one of the Ninth Infantry's major objectives, but in the planned order of battle, the Army unit had been told to delay its attack on 125 until the Marines had secured 109. Now, however, it was obvious that the Ninth's part of the attack needed to commence at once. Otherwise, all of Shinka's Third Platoon stood to be slaughtered.

Despite the intense hail of bullets, and even after enemy mortars joined in, the Third Platoon continued to inch forward up the steep slope. But Shinka lost fully one-third of his thirty-man force on the hellish climb up the barren face of 109, and he lost several more within minutes after reaching the crest. Shinka's men were the only Americans to claw their way to the top that morning, but they were so cruelly exposed that any man's slightest movement invited sudden death. With only fifteen unwounded Marines remaining, they were unable to hold the ground and too isolated for reinforcements to reach them.

"It's too hot to stay up here!" Shinka yelled to his platoon sergeant. "Collect the wounded and weapons, and let's get back down the hill."

Dragging their wounded on ponchos, the Marines slid and stumbled down the same gully they'd ascended to a point about three-fourths of the way to the base of 109. There, with a reasonable amount of protective cover, surviving members of the platoon huddled together. Shinka counted only six men who were still able to fight.

"I decided to go forward to find out if we'd left any of our wounded behind," Shinka later recalled. "As I crawled along our former position [on the crest of 109], I came across a wounded Marine between two dead. As I grabbed him under the arms and pulled him out of the foxhole, a bullet shattered my chin. Blood ran into my throat, and I couldn't breathe."

Choking on his own blood, Shinka was hit again, this time in the arm. The impact sent him rolling helplessly down the hill for a considerable distance, but he survived to receive a Bronze Star for valor. Sergeant Crowson, leading the First Platoon, single-handedly wiped out two of the enemy machine guns that had taken such a horrendous toll on the Marines. He was awarded the Distinguished Service Cross by order of General MacArthur.

Meanwhile, one platoon of E Company, commanded by Second Lieutenant Nickolas Arkadis, moved into Obong-ni Village at the foot of Hills 143 and 147, where it also came under heavy fire. Arkadis and his men fought their way to the lower slopes of the ridge, then bogged down with mounting casualties.

After the GIs of the Ninth Infantry were beaten back in their first attack on Hill 125, they regrouped and stormed the hill again. This time they succeeded in ending the deadly flanking fire that had decimated D Company's two platoons, but by now the Marines' chance to seize Obong-ni Ridge had, for the time being, been bled away.

At 3:00 PM on August 17, with D and E companies suffering a combined total for the day of 142 casualties—almost 60 percent of the 240 infantrymen who had begun the attack that morning—and no replacements available, Colonel Murray ordered the Second Battalion to pull back.

By noon it had been one of the bloodiest days yet for the Marines in Korea. "The worst day I've ever seen," said a doctor at the First Battalion aid station. "But 146 men have come in here so far, and all but one of them have gone out of here alive."

Unfortunately, both the day—and the bloodshed—were far from over.

At midafternoon on August 17, Colonel Roise's Second Battalion was ordered to break off its efforts to advance and hold where it was, while Colonel Newton's First Battalion passed through to take the lead position in the attack. Captain John "Blackjack" Stevens's A Company was assigned to the left flank, in relief of the Second Battalion's E Company, and Captain John Tobin's B Company was to relieve D Company on the right.

The troop exchange quickly drew enemy fire. Tobin had just gone forward to a ridgeline running parallel to Obong-ni to be briefed by D Company commander Captain Zimmer when both Zimmer and his radio operator were wounded and had to be evacuated.

Tobin immediately called Lieutenant Ike Fenton, his executive officer, and told Fenton and his three platoon leaders to meet him at a point where the main road passed through a saddle in the ridgeline, so that Tobin could point out the route of attack.

"We'd barely arrived at the meeting place when a North Korean machine gun opened up and severely wounded Captain Tobin in the chest and arm," Fenton recalled. "After he was evacuated, I contacted battalion and told Colonel Newton I was assuming command of the company. A minute or two later, we jumped off in the attack with the First and Second platoons on line and the Third Platoon in support."

Almost instantly, both lead platoons came under savage enemy fire, and neither was able to advance until Lieutenant Nick Schryver, commanding the Second Platoon, adjusted his mortar section's aim and had it pound the enemy positions for twenty minutes without letup. Then Schryver's men surged forward with renewed determination.

From an observation post in the distant high ground, where he could view the full sweep of Obong-ni Ridge through his field glasses, General Craig watched the men of Able and Baker companies fighting their way up Hill 109, and he winced at what he saw.

"They're getting hurt," Craig said, as Colonel Joe Stewart, his operations officer, and other members of the brigade staff stood by. "I can see them bringing the wounded down." Suddenly Craig stiffened and began to count aloud. "One . . . two . . . three . . . four . . . five! Hey, they're making it to the top! There's twenty of them in that little saddle to the right. Now thirty of them . . . now forty! By God, Baker Company's up there! Now, if they can only hold!"

Once the men of B Company had seized their sector of the ridge (the part to the right of the red slash), they were able to relieve some of the pressure on the Second Platoon's front, and by 5:00 PM the company's sector of Obong-ni was secure.

Meanwhile, out on the left flank, the men of Able Company were being hammered hard by relentless enemy fire. Their stubborn, repeated attempts to reach the tops of Hills 117 and 143 yielded some ground, but despite the aggressive leadership of Captain Stevens and his veteran gunnery sergeant, they were pinned down and stopped short of both objectives.

"Our seizure of the right portion of the ridge did relieve a little pressure on A Company," said Fenton, "but their casualties were heavy, and they were having great difficulty securing the high points on the left."

Second Lieutenant Francis W. Muetzel, commanding A Company's machine gun section, took cover in an abandoned gun pit, along with one of his riflemen and another officer. It was a grave mistake because the enemy mortars and artillery were already registered in on the emplacement, and the three Marines instantly came under fire.

"Four rounds from 82-millimeter mortars landed around it," Muetzel said. "The blast lifted me off the ground, and my helmet flew off. A human body to my left disintegrated. Being rather shook up and unable to hear, I crawled back to the CP."

As soon as Muetzel's hearing returned and he regained his equilibrium, he made his way back to the gun pit to look for the rifleman from his platoon. When he found him, he wished he hadn't. "One of the mortar rounds must have landed in the small of his back," Muetzel recalled. "Only a pelvis and legs were left. The stretcher bearers gathered up the remains with a shovel."

By dusk, however, the battered survivors of A Company had established a foothold on Obong-ni and extended their front from the southern portion of Hill 109 to the center of the saddle separating 109 from 117. Hoping that the First Battalion was now capable of holding this bloody ground, General Craig directed his unit commanders to consolidate their positions for the night.

"I want you to account for the location of every individual and be prepared for a counterattack," Craig warned. "Prepare plans of fire both within and to the rear of your positions."

At about 7:00 PM on August 17, a lull fell over the embattled ridgeline, and A and B companies were able to tie their lines together for increased security. Lieutenant Fenton, now commanding B Company in relief of Captain Tobin, decided to take extra precautions. "I'd learned my lesson at Changchon," Fenton said, "so to make sure we maintained contact with all our units, I made up my mind to lay two lines of telephone wire to all three platoons as well as battalion headquarters."

Less than an hour later, with the last vestiges of daylight still lingering amid hurried defensive preparations, one of Fenton's Marines ran up to him in alarm.

"Sir," he said, "some gook tanks are coming this way, and they're headed straight for our position!"

Fenton grabbed his field glasses and took a quick look. About 5,000 yards up the road to the battalion's immediate front, he spotted two Russian-built T-34s coming on in no particular hurry. A moment later, he made out a third enemy tank trailing a few hundred yards behind the first two. A fourth was still farther back, beyond Fenton's field of vision.

Fenton felt an adrenaline rush as he hit the "flash" signal on his telephone, alerting all units on the battalion network. "Enemy tanks in the area," he said. "They're coming right up the road like they own the world."

During the past few weeks, the Marines had heard a lot about the supposed invincibility of the North Korean tanks, but because of the rugged terrain in which they'd been continuously fighting, they'd yet to come face to face with enemy armor. Now, with their first confrontation obviously only minutes away, even a hardened combat veteran such as Fenton was swept up in the excitement.

"It was like sitting on the 50-yard line of the Rose Bowl about 150 feet up," he recalled much later. "We had a great seat for the show that was about to take place."

Then Fenton heard Colonel Newton's voice on the phone. "Just hold your fire and let the tanks pass through, Lieutenant," he said. "Our antitank platoon and 3.5 rocket section are primed and ready to deal with them as soon as they get into range, and our own tanks are refueling and almost ready to roll."

"Aye, sir." Fenton's voice was calm, but he'd already watched a flight of F-51s try—and fail—to stop the tanks, and his thoughts were troubled:

Whatever you say, Colonel. But by then, those T-34s are going to be practically sitting in your lap!

It had been a tense, agonizing day at General Craig's headquarters, and runnerborne casualty reports filtering in from the First and Second battalions at sunset on August 17 did nothing to brighten the prevailing mood.

According to a detailed account of the battle published in the *Saturday Evening Post*, each of the four companies committed on Obong-ni Ridge had counted about 200 enlisted men and seven officers when the day began. Now A Company had 4 officers and 68 riflemen still combat-capable, and some of these had minor wounds but had refused evacuation. B Company had 103 riflemen and only 2 officers left; D Company had 85 riflemen and 2 officers; and E Company reported 3 officers and 78 riflemen in fighting shape. Based on these figures, the four companies' rifle platoons had lost close to 55 percent of their total strength since morning.

Craig and his staff were mulling over this bleak news when the phone rang. Colonel Joe Stewart yanked up the receiver, listened for a moment, then grunted and hung up.

"Regiment says three gook tanks are coming up the road toward the First Battalion CP," Stewart told Craig. "The observation plane spotted them, and they're already behind our positions on the hill."

When Navy Captain Eugene Hering, the brigade surgeon, heard what Stewart was saying, he jumped to his feet. "God almighty," he said. "The aid station's just a quarter mile from there! If those tanks break through—"

"Don't worry; they won't," Craig reassured Hering. "Colonel Newton will know what to do."

The general's faith in his First Battalion commander was well placed. A Pacific veteran of World War II, Newton was no stranger to crisis command situations, and fortunately the early tip-off from the pilot of the Grasshopper plane had given him ample time to ready a network of defenses as the North Korean tanks approached.

"We set up two of our guns in record time in a rice paddy near the road," said Sergeant Rusty Russell, a squad leader in the 75-millimeter recoilless rifle platoon attached to the First Battalion, "and our 3.5 rocket launchers were positioned off to our left in the ditches along the roadside. We also had two M-26 tanks on the road with 90-millimeter cannon. We were sick of hearing about how 'unstoppable' these Commie tanks were, and we intended to find out for ourselves."

Corporal Edward T. "Red" Martin, a Minnesota native and an assistant gunner in another section of 75s, was helping pull a machine-gun cart carrying his weapon up a small hill to get it into firing position on the opposite side of the road from Russell when a Marine in a passing jeep slowed down and shouted,

"Better run, you SOBs! Those tanks are just around the bend!"

"To hell with that!" Martin yelled back. "They're the ones who'd better run!"

Not far away, at the battalion aid station, when PFC Don Kennedy, a rifleman being treated for a shrapnel wound in his shoulder, heard about the tanks, he grabbed his M-1 and made his way a short distance up the road to a small hill, where he lay down to observe the action.

"It was after sundown, but there was still plenty of light," Kennedy recalled. "I watched the bend in the road, where it came around the nose of the hill. You could see the dust rising, and then this long, bulb-nosed gun sort of poked around the corner."

Texas-born Second Lieutenant Charles M. C. Jones, commander of the recoilless rifle platoon, was understandably nervous. But he told his men to hold their fire until the tanks came within point-blank range.

"They were less than fifty yards away when we opened fire," Jones recalled many years later, "and we tore them up."

"We were looking right down the barrels of their guns," added Sergeant Russell of the recoilless gun unit, "when Corporal Victor Malacara, the gunner in our seven-man squad, blew the hell out of them."

As the first tank rounded the bend in the road and rumbled toward the First Battalion CP, it was met almost simultaneously by 3.5 rocket fire from the ditches and 75-millimeter recoilless rifle rounds from either side of the road.

"It came on slow," said PFC Kennedy, still watching from his vantage point on a nearby hill, "and then all of a sudden, the bazooka men started throwing those big rockets into its flanks. . . . It stopped and began to swing right and left, like an elephant swinging its head, but not moving forward, and it was firing all its guns, but it was firing wild."

When the first rounds from the 75s struck the tank, they tore through its armored hide as if it were tissue paper. One of its machine-gun mounts was ripped out by the roots, and all firing from the tank immediately stopped. The turret swung open, sending flames leaping skyward as the crew tried to scramble out, but Marine rifle fire sent them tumbling back into the blazing tank.

"I put my first round into him broadside between the body and turret of the tank, using a HEAT shell," said Corporal Robert Whited of Laramie, Wyoming, a gunner on one of the 75s. "It made a hole no bigger than a .50-caliber slug, but it sprayed molten metal all through the inside of the tank and set the whole thing on fire."

Trying to escape a similar fate, the second tank attempted to pull around the first one on the narrow road, but it had gone only a few feet when it was hit in the track and skidded off the road, where the cannon fire from one of the M-26s finished it off.

"It only took us about a minute and a half to take out all three tanks," said Red Martin. "Our only casualty was PFC Bob Strand, a friend of mine from Minnesota, who was hit in the leg by a stray machine-gun bullet. Doc Rocket Pearce took good care of him, and he was able to rejoin us a few weeks later."

"This was one time that the tanks could easily have maneuvered because there was plenty of firm ground on both sides of the road," said Ike Fenton. "But the third tank made the same mistake as the second by trying to stay on the road and squeeze past the other two tanks. One of our M-26s took it out with a direct hit. No one escaped from any of the tanks."

The fourth T-34, well to the rear of the others, fell victim to Marine air. The 75-millimeter antitank unit was credited with two of the four kills, the other going to the M-26 tankers.

"What happened that evening gave us confidence and helped solidify us as a unit," said Corporal Whited, who would advance to the rank of captain during his Marine career. "We were never in awe of those Russian T-34s again."

Long after full darkness descended, Marines of Able and Baker companies continued to dig foxholes and organize their defenses. Wires were strung and attached to trip flares in front of their lines. Artillery of the 11th Marines was zeroed in on likely enemy approaches, while Korean laborers hauled supplies to the ridgeline and carried casualties back to the rear. During much of this preparation, the battalion was forced to dodge sporadic sniper fire from the crest of Hill 117.

Not a single man among the Marines on Obong-ni Ridge had the slightest doubt that the North Koreans would strike before morning with all the firepower they could muster. "We were quite worried about another night counterattack," said Ike Fenton, "and we cautioned all the men to maintain a 25 percent listening watch."

What the Marines didn't know was that heavy losses, coupled with a shortage of food, weapons, ammunition, and medical supplies, had prompted Colonel Chang Ky Dok, veteran commander of the NKPA's 16th Regiment, to ask permission to withdraw that night back to the west bank of the Naktong. Late in the afternoon, elements of the U.S. Ninth, 19th, and 34th Infantry regiments had launched a series of punishing attacks against the right flank of the NKPA salient, and Chang sensed that his dwindling force couldn't withstand another day of intense pressure on the ground and fierce pounding from the air.

Chang's request was denied, but in the meantime—also unknown to the Americans—he'd obtained a captured U.S. SCR-300 field radio tuned to Marine frequencies. Consequently, he knew from monitoring on-air messages that the First Battalion had relieved 2/5 as well as the exact locations where Companies A and B were dug in on the ridge.

His only hope, Chang decided, was to hurl his remaining troops, under cover of darkness, in an all-out assault against the Marines' thin lines on Obong-ni before the Americans could deliver a knock-out punch of their own.

"This had been the longest day I could remember," recalled Sergeant Mackie Wheeler of A Company. "I had no way of knowing it at the time, but the night coming up was going to be even longer."

The night remained eerily quiet until about 2:30 AM on August 18, when lookouts of the First Battalion's Second Platoon reported suspicious activity to its immediate front. Moments later, a green signal flare lit the sky above Obong-ni Ridge, and the North Koreans struck with frenzied fury at the precise point where A and B companies were tied together.

The enemy's clear intent was to separate the two companies by driving a wedge between them, then to envelop and annihilate them one at a time. The ferocity of the attack produced a quick breakthrough on B Company's left flank, held by Lieutenant Scotty Taylor's Second Platoon. As soon as Lieutenant Fenton realized what had happened, he grabbed the phone and managed to reach Taylor.

"They're all over us, Ike," Taylor yelled. "It's hand to hand, and we can't hold."

"You've got to pull back fast, Scotty," Fenton told him. "Fall back toward the company CP, and form a perimeter defense with the other platoons."

Meanwhile, Fenton got word that the men of A Company were catching hell all along their front. Their left flank was being pushed back, and their right flank had already been turned. Enemy troops were almost certainly moving through the gap between the two companies, and the sound of small-arms fire at close range told Fenton that the enemy was only a few yards from his command post.

The telephone rang, and Fenton heard Colonel Newton's tense voice on the line.

"I know you're under heavy pressure up there," Newton said, "but you've got to hold your position at all costs. I'm pouring in all the supporting mortar and artillery support I can. A Company's got three major breakthroughs on their front, and if your company gets pushed off the ridge, we'll have it all to do over in the morning."

"We'll do our best, sir," said Fenton, "but we've got gooks all around us, and they've turned my left flank. The situation's very confused, and we can't see a damn thing."

"I understand, Lieutenant, but I'm asking you—can you hang on till daylight?"

Fenton ground his teeth as he replied: "Don't worry, Colonel. The only Marines that leave this ridge tonight will be dead ones."

The first Marines to feel the enemy's wrath that pitch-black morning were those of A Company's mortar section, set up in a gully near the company CP. Because of the intercepted radio messages, the North Koreans knew precisely where the mortarmen were, and they took full advantage of that knowledge.

At about 2:00 AM, the Marines in the gully heard the telltale whine and rattle of incoming fire and ducked low in their foxholes. Then the explosions started, enveloping the position with sheets of flame from deadly white phosphorus rounds. Virtually every man in the gully suffered painful wounds, leaving Captain Blackjack Stevens's company with no remaining mortar defense.

The edge of the NKPA barrage also struck the area occupied by the Third Platoon, wounding First Lieutenant George Fox, the platoon commander, and half a dozen of his men. Two riflemen were evacuated, but Fox and the others remained on the line after receiving first aid.

Half an hour later, the full-scale enemy assault began with a hail of machine-gun fire from the crest of Hill 117 and an avalanche of grenades from directly above the Marines. Then a platoon of NKPA infantry charged down the slopes and pounced directly on Stevens's reeling troops, cutting the company in half and forcing its survivors to withdraw part of the way toward Hill 109.

"Me and my buddy, Sergeant R. D. Lopez, were together in our foxhole when four North Koreans ran right up on us," recalled Sergeant Mackie Wheeler, who served as a runner and radio operator for Stevens. "They were within ten feet of us when we opened fire. They didn't get any closer."

At about the same time, Lieutenant Tom Johnston led his Second Platoon up a shallow defile toward the saddle between Hills 117 and 143 until they were pinned down by machine-gun fire about seventy-five yards from their goal. After maneuvering Corporal Cleylon Camper into firing position with a BAR, Johnston borrowed a grenade from PFC Billy Lindley to augment the two he already carried.

"Now gimme some heat!" Johnston yelled and charged up the slope. He hurled one grenade, hitting the deck an instant before it exploded, then jumping back to his feet and running on. As he threw a second grenade, an enemy grenade exploded within a few feet of him, killing him instantly.

All told, the Second Platoon slugged it out for a full half hour with an enemy force three times its size, thanks in large measure to the courage and leadership of Tech Sergeant Frank J. Lawson, who took command after Johnston's death, staying at his guns and refusing evacuation despite three painful wounds.

Eventually, though, the platoon's survivors were forced to give ground, along with all the rest of A Company. As the attackers penetrated the Marines' lines, Captain Stevens was cut off from many of his men, and several enemy soldiers with burp guns invaded his command post. Stevens and his headquarters staff were forced to make a fighting retreat down a nearby draw, but the attackers were wiped out.

Because of confusion among the attackers, deadly accuracy by Marine mortars and artillery, heavy NKPA casualties suffered in the attack, or a combination of all these factors, only a single squad of enemy troops slipped through the hole punched in the brigade's front. When no reinforcements arrived to join them, this small group was soon overwhelmed. As a result, although both companies of the First Battalion suffered horrific losses, they retained their foothold on Obong-ni.

On learning that A Company's lines had been breached, Colonel Newton ordered continuous artillery and mortar barrages on all enemy approaches to the ridge. Supporting fire from the brigade's 4.2-inch mortar section proved especially valuable because the high trajectory of its rounds allowed them to strike shielded enemy positions that artillery couldn't reach. The First Battalion's own 81-millimeter mortar section also joined in, although it had to borrow most of 2/5's available ammo to keep firing.

When daylight returned, Marine air quickly entered the picture as well. At this point, a single enemy machine gun was keeping A Company's right flank pinned down. To take the gun out, Captain Stevens called for a high-risk air strike within 100 yards of his own lines.

"The plane came in and actually pinpointed the target with a direct hit," recalled Lieutenant Fenton, who observed the action from where B Company still held fast to Hills 102 and 109. "After this bomb hit, a few strafing runs and a napalm strike were called. Then A Company was able to move up and retake their sector of the ridge."

Fenton had high praise for his company's veteran NCOs, who had taken the lead in regrouping their ravaged, officer-short units and inspiring their riflemen to fight like fiends to hold their ground. He called them "the finest batch of noncommissioned officers ever assembled in any Marine regiment."

His rank-and-file infantrymen also drew plaudits from their new company commander. "In some cases, it wasn't just noncoms," Fenton said. "It was the PFCs and privates holding the job of a fire team leader or squad leader. It was their fine leadership, outstanding initiative, and control of the men that turned a possible defeat into a sweet victory."

Also singled out for special recognition were Lieutenant Nick Schryver, commanding B Company's First Platoon, and Lieutenant Francis W. Muetzel, who was transferred from command of A Company's machine-gun section to take over the company's Second Platoon, replacing Muetzel's fallen friend Tom Johnston.

Although suffering head and facial wounds from a grenade that exploded a few feet in front him, Schryver refused evacuation, had himself patched up by a corpsman, and continued to lead his men with what his subsequent citation for valor called "fierce determination."

"I didn't even have to come to Korea in the first place, because my wife was pregnant at the time, and my daughter had been born the day after we sailed," Schryver recalled many years later. "But I figured as long as I was there, I might as well earn my keep. Ike Fenton and I were the only two officers left in the company because Scotty Taylor had been fatally wounded that morning [he died later at the Army field surgical hospital at Miryang], and I didn't want to let Ike down. He was a fine officer and an outstanding human being."

Muetzel, who had been wounded and left for dead in his foxhole after the enemy breakthrough, had regained consciousness to find himself completely alone except for the enemy. Dragging his wounded leg behind him, he fought his way past several NKPA soldiers until he reached the Marines' new lines.

Both Muetzel and Schryver were awarded the Silver Star.

By sunup on August 18, the enemy attacks on Obong-ni had spent themselves, and the attackers were in disorganized retreat. On an adjacent ridge, the Army's Ninth Infantry also had been rolled back by a nighttime assault but had counterattacked and reclaimed the lost ground.

At seven o'clock that morning, General Craig ordered a resumption of the Marines' attack, and the ragtag remnants of the First Battalion swept forward again to secure more of the high ground. "The Second Platoon, which had borne the brunt of the night attack, had only eleven riflemen left [out of its normal complement of forty]," said Ike Fenton. "We were shot up, but morale was good. The boys felt like they'd done a pretty fine job of holding our line that night."

A couple of hours later, Colonel Robert Taplett's 3/5 moved through 1/5 and took the lead in the attack on the Marines' next objective, driving beyond Obong-ni Ridge against feeble resistance toward a piece of high ground designated as Hill 207. The First Battalion remained behind to rest its battle-scarred bones and count the dead bodies and abandoned weapons left by the North Koreans. Their finds included forty machine guns, numerous small arms, a 3.5-inch rocket launcher, four antitank rifles, and large amounts of ammunition and hand grenades—many of which had been forfeited earlier by retreating American troops. They also found the captured SCR-300 field radio that had allowed the enemy to listen in on 1/5's tactical net and enabled him to pinpoint Marine positions.

By late morning on August 19, all three of the Marines' objectives in the Naktong Bulge were secure, and Army and Marine troops met on the east bank of the river while hundreds of fleeing enemy soldiers swam frantically toward the other side. Repeated strafing runs by Marine Corsairs and massive shelling by U.S. artillery left the river "definitely discolored with blood," in the words of one American pilot.

Fewer than 3,000 North Koreans made it back across the Naktong. Behind them, they left more than 1,200 dead, plus vast quantities of arms and equipment, including thirty-four artillery pieces, hundreds of automatic weapons, and thousands of rifles. The NKPA Fourth Division had been shattered beyond repair in what an official Army history termed "the greatest setback suffered thus far by the North Korean Army."

Marine losses totaled 66 dead, 278 wounded, and 1 missing in action. The First Battle of the Naktong was over. There would be a second.

CHAPTER 9

★ ★ ★

COMMANDERS
IN CONFLICT

WHILE AMERICAN TROOPS were hanging on by their fingernails against an increasingly impatient foe in the Pusan Perimeter, a small team of high-level U.S. officers was piecing together an operation aimed at dramatically reversing the course of the war.

By late August 1950, handpicked groups of planners from the Army, Navy, Air Force, and Marines were quartered aboard the command ship *Mt. McKinley* in Tokyo Bay and spending long days confronting an awesome array of problems. The largest of these was not knowing whether the plans they were making would ever reach fruition.

Considering the atmosphere in which it was conceived, General Douglas MacArthur's grand scheme for turning the tables on the North Koreans was strikingly bold. He proposed to land the First Marine Division far behind enemy lines at the port of Inchon on Korea's west coast, catch the NKPA invaders unaware, trap them between the Inchon assault force and a breakout offensive by Pusan's defenders, then destroy them.

As bold as it was, however, MacArthur's Inchon plan was far from a new

or original idea. "Military history shows quite a few examples of the successful application of MacArthur's Inchon strategy," wrote Department of
the Army combat historian Bevin Alexander, citing similar tactics by Napoleon, Hannibal, and other early military leaders. Alexander also compared the Inchon strategy to the island-hopping approach developed by
MacArthur in the Pacific during World War II, in which several Japanese
strongholds were bypassed and left to wither, effectively removing their
garrisons from the war.

Still, as a tentative mid-September assault date approached, MacArthur's
plan was by no means set in concrete. Numerous logistical concerns remained to be addressed, and a chorus of dissenting voices—including those
of the Joint Chiefs of Staff—could be heard all the way from Washington.

MacArthur had a well-demonstrated talent for infuriating Army Chief
of Staff General J. Lawton "Joe" Collins, and MacArthur's arrogant postur-
ing and repeated refusal to consult the JCS as planning proceeded for the
Inchon operation became almost more than Collins could bear.

From the beginning, Collins had cited a host of disadvantages that, in
his mind, made Inchon a debatable—if not potentially disastrous—choice
as a landing spot. Among them:

1. The port was accessible from the sea only by a single, narrow deep-
   water channel that was easily mined or blocked, meaning that even
   one sunken or disabled ship could stymie the entire operation.
2. Strong, peculiar tides made the harbor an impassable mass of mud
   during much of the day, and landing ships that entered on the morning tide couldn't unload quickly enough to avoid being stranded
   there for twelve hours until the tide returned in the evening.
3. A 350-foot hill on the small, inner-harbor island of Wolmi-do dominated the main landing area and would have to be secured by forces
   arriving on the morning tide, but the rest of the landing force would
   have to wait for the evening tide, eliminating the element of surprise.
4. Most of the waterfront was protected by massive twelve-to-fourteen-
   foot-high seawalls that would have to be scaled with ladders.
5. One segment of the assault force would go ashore near the center of

a city of 250,000 people, facing the risk of house-to-house urban warfare and the possibility of North Korean troops using civilians as human shields.

6. The time frame proposed for the landing fell within Korea's September typhoon season, raising the possibility of a coinciding storm.

7. The wide expanse of the Han River separated Inchon from the Korean mainland, requiring what amounted to a second amphibious operation to secure the beachhead.

For all these reasons, Collins argued for landing the proposed 70,000-man invasion force at the smaller port of Kunsan, 109 miles south of Inchon, putting the amphibious assault force closer to the breakout force at Pusan and making the two more mutually supporting. Both Admiral Forrest Sherman, chief of naval operations, and General O. P. Smith, commander of the First Marine Division, basically agreed as to the liabilities of Inchon, but Sherman and Smith weren't totally sold on Kunsan as an alternative.

It seems appropriate to emphasize at this point that the men who directed U.S. military efforts in Korea in 1950 frequently disagreed on strategy and often had difficulty concealing their personal dislike for each other.

Collins was definitely not the same caliber of risk-taker as MacArthur, and the latter's impulsiveness made the cautious Collins nervous. Early in the war, in fact, Collins had drawn the ire of retired General of the Army Dwight Eisenhower, former supreme commander of Allied forces in Europe, who was then president of Columbia University but who would assume command of the North Atlantic Treaty Organization in December 1950. During a visit to Washington, Eisenhower administered a tough dressing-down to Collins; General Matthew Ridgway, Collins's deputy chief of staff for administration (often referred to as the Army's "general manager"); and their assistants for what Ike considered complacency and indecisiveness. Afterward, Eisenhower made the following caustic notes in his diary: "My whole contention [in chewing out the other generals] was that an appeal to force cannot, by its nature, be a partial one. This appeal having been made, for God's sake, get ready! Do everything possible under the law to get us going."

But Eisenhower, who had served directly under MacArthur twice during his career, was no great fan of his World War II Pacific counterpart either. "In commenting on General MacArthur," Ridgway wrote in his journal following their meeting, "Ike expressed the wish that he would like to see a younger general out there, rather than, as he expressed it, 'an untouchable' whose actions you cannot predict."

When MacArthur's Inchon strategy was spelled out to Truman, he took note of Collins's "misgivings" but termed the proposed amphibious operation "a bold plan worthy of a master strategist." From this point on, Truman seemed willing to let MacArthur and the JCS hash out their differences on their own.

For his part, MacArthur remained, as usual, theatrically inflexible as he plunged ahead with the Inchon plan. Collins was particularly upset when, without bothering to consult the Army chief in advance, MacArthur picked his own chief of staff, General Edward M. "Ned" Almond, to command the Inchon landing force.

According to observers, Collins leaped from his chair and yelled, "*What?*" on hearing the news of Almond's appointment. Almond was a military lightweight with no experience leading amphibious assault forces, but he was adept at flattering MacArthur's super-sized ego, so they got along splendidly. Many of Almond's fellow senior officers considered him the most feckless, incompetent—and irritating—general in the entire U.S. Army. They saw it as the height of folly to place him in charge of such a delicate, demanding operation, although few would have said as much to MacArthur.

"The best that could be said of Almond was that he was overly optimistic to the point of being delusional," recalled retired Marine Brigadier General Bryghte Godbold, one of the planners working aboard the *Mt. McKinley* that summer. "He was frequently out of touch with reality, and his manner was so condescending that other officers hated being around him."

Among those other officers was Eighth Army commander General Walton Walker, whose dislike for MacArthur was widely known and whose relationship with Almond was described by Colonel Mike Michaelis, one of Walker's senior field commanders, as "horrible."

"I'd be in Walker's office and the phone would ring," Michaelis recalled. 'Walker, this is Almond.' Mind you, this is a two-star talking to a three-star. Almond would say, 'I want you to do so-and-so.' And Walker would ask, 'Is this Almond speaking or Almond speaking for MacArthur?' They just couldn't get along."

Thomas J. Marnane, secretary of the Eighth Army general staff, stated the case against Almond even more succinctly: "Almond was impossible. Very snotty. I soon developed a very low opinion of him. He gave Walker a hard time."

There were other valid reasons, however, for Collins's consternation. For one thing, almost all the assault troops involved in the Inchon landing would be Marines, so logic suggested that a Marine Corps general should be in charge. (It had been widely assumed that General Lemuel Shepherd, commander of the Fleet Marine Force, Pacific, and a veteran leader of amphibious operations at Guadalcanal, Cape Gloucester, Guam, and Okinawa, would get the job.) For another, Collins didn't like the idea that Almond would also continue to serve as MacArthur's chief of staff or that the Inchon assault force, designated as X Corps, would be, in effect, a "separate army" under MacArthur's total control.

Collins was far from the only powerful Washington figure who was fuming at MacArthur at this juncture. John Foster Dulles, a future secretary of state who was then helping negotiate a peace treaty with Japan; current Secretary of State Dean Acheson; and President Truman himself were equally furious but for a different reason. During the same week as Almond's X Corps appointment, MacArthur had sent a message to the annual national encampment of the Veterans of Foreign Wars that was not only insulting to the Truman administration but also a blatant challenge to Communist China.

"Nothing could be more fallacious," the message read, "than the threadbare argument by those who advocate appeasement and defeatism in the Pacific that if we defend Formosa [Taiwan], we alienate continental Asia. Those who speak thus do not understand the Orient. They do not grasp that it is in the pattern of Oriental psychology to respect and follow aggressive, resolute, and dynamic leadership—to quickly turn from leadership characterized by timidity or vacillation."

Coming, as it did, on the heels of an unauthorized visit by MacArthur to Formosa to meet with Nationalist leader Chiang Kai-shek, the VFW message was like salt in an open wound to official Washington. Just a few weeks earlier, Truman had delivered a message to Congress expressing America's desire "that Formosa not become embroiled in hostilities disturbing to the peace of the Pacific, and that all questions affecting Formosa be settled by peaceful means."

Clearly, MacArthur's statement to the VFW collided head-on with Truman's sentiments about a "neutralized" Formosa. Secretary Acheson later described the statement as an "affront" with "damaging effect at home and abroad."

As damage control, Truman ordered Defense Secretary Louis Johnson to send a letter to MacArthur demanding that he "withdraw" his message to the VFW because it was "in conflict with the policy of the United States." After Johnson spent most of a day trying to dissuade Truman, the exasperated president dictated the letter personally and forced Johnson to send it.

Although MacArthur's message hadn't yet been read to the VFW gathering at the time Truman obtained a copy, the general's public relations staff had already released the full text to the U.S. media. It was being quoted prominently in many newspapers and had been published in full in *U.S. News & World Report*. "It was my opinion," said Truman, "that this statement could only serve to confuse the world as to just what our Formosa policy was."

Under heavy pressure from the Pentagon, Truman had already decided to replace Louis Johnson, who was universally despised by U.S. military leaders, and had persuaded General George C. Marshall, venerable former secretary of state and wartime chairman of the JCS, to take over as defense secretary. For several days, the president also gave serious consideration to stripping MacArthur of his command and power base and "hauling him back to the States," as Dulles had angrily recommended. Finally, Truman changed his mind about MacArthur, but in early September, he forced

Johnson to sign a letter of resignation in a pathetic scene that ended with Johnson weeping and begging for his job.

Johnson's ouster was universally cheered by America's military, but it was genuinely painful for Truman. "I've never felt quite so uncomfortable," he would later recall. "He [Johnson] looked like he had been beaten."

Where MacArthur was concerned, however, Truman's "white-lipped" anger—in the words of one presidential aide—was deep-running and lingering. In months to come, MacArthur's arrogance and repeated refusal to accept direction from Washington would create an irreparable rift between the president and his supreme commander in the Far East.

Truman's irritation at the VFW message was amply justified. It not only aroused Communist China's suspicions about U.S. intentions but also gave the U.S.S.R. a propaganda victory at the United Nations, where Soviet Ambassador Andrei Vishinsky railed at MacArthur's "cynical candor" about turning Formosa into a U.S. base "at all costs."

MacArthur added fuel to the fire when he ignored a cable from the Joint Chiefs, received in Tokyo on August 28, diplomatically suggesting Kunsan as an alternate location for the Korea landing. Two days later, MacArthur issued firm orders for the Inchon operation to proceed according to plan. Copies of the order, however, weren't delivered to the Pentagon until September 8—just a week before D-day at Inchon—when the massive machinery for the operation was fully in motion, and MacArthur knew it was too late for the JCS to halt it.

Lieutenant Colonel Lynn D. Smith, the courier assigned to hand-carry full details about the operation, didn't leave Tokyo until September 10, however, at which time MacArthur told him lightly, "Don't get there too soon." Smith didn't reach Washington until late evening on September 13, and it was almost noon the next day when Smith actually presented his paperwork to the JCS.

By then, it didn't really matter anyway. The military chiefs had held a final conference on Inchon on September 8, with Truman sitting in, then capitulated and endorsed the Inchon landing. "We approve your plan, and the president has been so informed," they cabled MacArthur.

• • •

At only a few other moments in the 230-plus years of America's history have U.S. military commanders, as a class, endured levels of stress, confusion, dissention, and loss of confidence equal to what they faced in Korea in the summer of 1950.

The plight of George Washington's ragtag army in the winter of 1776–77 stands out among the darkest moments of the American Revolution. The panicked flight of Union soldiers after their rout at the First Battle of Bull Run in 1861 ranks as the U.S. Army's lowest point in the Civil War. And the interval of shock and dismay following the Japanese attack on Pearl Harbor in 1941 surely represents the rock bottom of our military leadership's confidence and public image during World War II.

Arguably, though, no trial of flesh and spirit has tested the U.S. officer corps more severely or cast it in a more negative light than the ordeal of July and August 1950, when the defenders of the Pusan Perimeter barely avoided being swept from the Asian mainland into the sea. Never have our armed forces seemed more impotent. Never have senior military decision-makers been more prone to costly ineptitude and miscalculation or broader disagreement on how to prosecute the war. Never have unit-level commanders who led U.S. troops into battle been less combat-experienced or exposed to greater personal risk of injury and death.

As discussed earlier, the problem originated at the very apex of the military pecking order. It began with President Truman, a commander in chief who had allowed, even promoted, disastrous deterioration of America's armed forces. But it extended downward through every echelon of command, from five-star generals to "shavetail" second lieutenants.

Among front-line U.S. commanders in Korea in 1950, Brigadier General Edward A. Craig stands out for his energy, initiative, common sense, personal bravery, and compassion for the men who served under him. The high respect in which "Eddie" Craig was held throughout Marine command circles was why he'd been chosen to lead the First Provisional Marine Brigade in the long-odds effort to hold the Pusan Perimeter in the first place.

Yet in terms of battlefield strategy during a thirty-two-year tour of duty that had taken him from Haiti to the Philippines and from Guadalcanal to Iwo Jima, Craig had always tended toward the tried and true—not the experimental or unorthodox.

When he arrived at Pusan at the end of July, Craig was fifty-four years old and nearing the end of an illustrious, but fairly predictable, career that would earn him a Bronze Star, a Silver Star, a Navy Cross, and assorted other decorations before he retired.

After World War II, dozens of Marines whom Craig had led in the Pacific demonstrated their devotion by naming their firstborn sons after him, and the men who served under him in Korea held him in near-unanimous reverence. "I'd follow General Craig anywhere he wanted to go," wrote Navy Corpsman Herb Pearce in a letter to his parents from the Naktong Bulge. "It makes you feel good to know that he'd never send you anywhere that he wouldn't go himself." Yet never since he became a Marine officer in 1917 had Craig been considered a cutting-edge innovator or tactical visionary.

All that changed in early August 1950, when the silver-haired Connecticut Yankee from Danbury transformed himself into "Chopper Eddie" as the first American general to make daily use of helicopters in battlefield situations. Four new, three-seat Sikorsky HO3S-1 choppers were attached to the Marine brigade, and Craig lost no time introducing them to combat—and making them a vital factor in rescuing the Pusan Perimeter from a Communist takeover.

"Having helicopters attached to my command in Korea was a most rewarding experience," Craig wrote in a daily journal titled "Incidents of Service," which he kept throughout his career. "Without them, the brigade would have been seriously hampered, and my opportunities for personal command and reconnaissance limited."

With his personal pilot, Captain Gus Lueddeke, at the controls, and his aide, First Lieutenant John A. "Jack" Buck, usually occupying the only other passenger seat, Craig racked up a long list of "firsts" with his helicopters during August. He conducted the first combat reconnaissance missions by helicopter, first helicopter casualty evacuations, and first helicopter supply missions to forward troops, all within the first few days after his brigade went into action. "Chopper Eddie" also was aboard the first U.S. helicopter to come under enemy artillery and mortar fire and the first to rescue downed American pilots in enemy-held areas.

"I accompanied General Craig on most of his flights," recalled Lieutenant Buck, "and we often came under enemy machine-gun and rocket fire, but we were lucky, and nobody in the chopper ever got hit. I was the only one aboard with an M-1, so if anybody was going to return fire, it had to be me."

Brooklyn-born Buck had met Craig at Camp Pendleton in 1949 when the general was interviewing men to be his aide-de-camp. "We seemed to hit it off right from the beginning, and Craig told me soon after the interview that I was the one," Buck recalled. "I think one thing that affected his decision was the fact that I'd gone to air observer school at Quantico, and I was comfortable in the air. Craig knew even then that if he was ever back in a combat situation, he'd want to use helicopters as much as possible."

The choppers allowed Craig to perform feats that were almost miraculous in the eyes of the Marines he commanded. A prime example was his ability, on one occasion, to direct attacks by two of his battalions as they occurred simultaneously twenty-six miles apart.

When Craig needed to consult with Army generals at their command posts, he invariably traveled by chopper, amazing his hosts with the amount of ground he was able to cover. Buck recalled an incident during the fighting in the Naktong Bulge when Craig visited an "old and tired-looking" General John Church, commander of the 24th Infantry Division, at Church's CP thirteen miles behind the front lines.

"Church invited us to stay for dinner that evening, and one of his aides told me they were serving freshly killed pheasant, which sounded a lot better than the C rations we were used to," Buck remembered. "But Craig graciously declined. 'I've got to stop off and check on several of my units on my return trip,' he said, 'and still get back to my CP in time to plan tomorrow morning's attack.' Without the chopper, there was no way on earth he could've done all that."

The contrasts between Craig and Church ranged well beyond their respective dinner menus or their schedules on a particular day. In a sense, their divergent styles and priorities defined the sharp differences between the performances of U.S. Army and Marine officers in Korea during the summer of 1950.

At fifty-eight, Church was only four years senior to Craig, but in demeanor, physical condition, and battlefield acumen, he seemed much older, as Buck observed. In a military career spanning thirty-plus years, Church had performed gallantly in two world wars. He'd been wounded twice in France in 1918 and awarded a Distinguished Service Cross. In 1943 he'd served as chief of staff of the 45th Infantry Division as it clawed its way up the "boot" of Italy from Sicily through Salerno and Anzio. Later, while serving in Germany and Holland, Church had been wounded again and earned two Silver Stars for valor.

But by the time he was thrust into the chaos of South Korea on June 27, 1950—just two days after the Communist invasion—Church was frail beyond his years and suffering from severe arthritis that kept him in constant pain. "To many . . . it seemed that Church's time had come and gone," wrote historian Clay Blair, "that to send him off to yet another war at his age and in his poor state of health was unfair and unwise." According to Blair, Church kept a bottle of whiskey "close at hand" as a pain reliever, a practice that, along with his feverish joints, may have clouded his judgment or undermined his resolve at times.

Church and other Army commanders at the divisional and regimental levels in Korea also may have been handicapped by the fact that most of their combat experience had been in Europe, against German troops. Hence they were strangers to many defensive and offensive traits peculiar to Asian armies, whereas Craig and most other Marine officers had spent all of World War II fighting the Japanese, whose tactics the North Koreans tried to imitate.

"We didn't find the North Koreans as tenacious or fanatical as the Japanese," recalled Lieutenant Ike Fenton, who saw plenty of both, "and we didn't find the NKs pressing home their advantage once they were separated from their leaders. Their attacks would start suddenly and end just as suddenly. Most of the time, they'd probe the center of our defense, then hit us on our flanks. They liked to attack at night, but we generally broke the attack when daylight came around."

Church and other Army commanders repeatedly failed to recognize these tendencies or to counter these flanking movements effectively, and NKPA troops were consistently able to circle behind Army units to cut off supply and escape routes and infiltrate rear-echelon areas.

Church's original assignment in Korea was basically a fact-finding mission, not one involving brutal, close-up combat. But within hours, he'd found himself serving as the de facto commander of a battered, disorganized ROK Army. A few days later, it had been Church's misfortune to send Task Force Smith into the bloody debacle at Osan.

When Church assumed command of the 24th Division in late July, replacing the captured General William Dean, a change of leadership personalities certainly seemed to be in order. Dean's impulsiveness and lack of solid communication and control had contributed directly to his division's collapse at Taejon and to landing Dean himself in a North Korean POW camp for the duration of the war. Church's more cautious style might have been expected to reassure his troops, but during the First Battle of the Naktong, a full month after Church took over, the deficiencies plaguing the division under Dean remained much the same.

As a detailed study prepared decades later for the Army's Command and General Staff College at Fort Leavenworth, Kansas, concluded, "The [First Naktong] battle exposed several flaws in the operations of the 24th Division's staff. Intelligence estimates of North Korean capabilities and intentions were extremely conservative. . . . Even an attack by infiltrators on an artillery battery some distance behind the front was disregarded. . . . In fact, the North Korean Fourth Division was simply following the same pattern of operations it had been using since the war's outbreak."

A commander's staff usually reflects the level of discipline, intensity, and foresight offered by the officer in charge, particularly under unyielding pressure. Because Church was in no physical condition to run a tight ship, a tendency toward missteps and malfunctions grew to be systemwide in the 24th Division.

Craig, however, had assembled a brigade staff that he could rely on in any situation—men who knew as well as he did what to do and how to get it done. They also knew that Craig might show up suddenly at any moment, day or night, to see for himself if his troops were doing their jobs.

A few days before the brigade shipped out for Korea, First Sergeant John Farritor was surprised in an artillery storeroom by an unexpected 2:00 AM visit by Craig. "He said he just wanted to know how things were going," Farritor recalled. "He was a real hands-on general."

"I learned early in my career to rely on my noncommissioned officers," Craig explained, "and they never let me down."

If the stresses of mortal combat were difficult for ill-prepared or worn-out high-level commanders, they were many times greater for junior officers leading troops under fire—and the risks faced by these young, inexperienced officers in Korea were in a class by themselves.

"What happened to the West Point class of 1949 in Korea was an utter tragedy," recalled retired Army Lieutenant Colonel Fred Wilmot many years later. "They should have been assigned as company commanders, but most of them went into battle in Korea as infantry platoon leaders—the most dangerous job in the Army—and 60 percent of them were killed."

Wilmot himself would have been a member of that same West Point class, and might well have suffered a similar fate, if his life hadn't taken some unusual twists and turns along the way. A native of Nevada, Missouri, he'd entered the Army as a private in 1943 and earned a Bronze Star in the Battle of the Bulge. Shortly after surviving that last great German offensive, Wilmot had been accepted at West Point. At the Military Academy, however, he'd chafed under the immaturity of some cadet officers and resigned after a year. Later, he enrolled at the University of Arkansas, became cadet commander of its ROTC unit, and earned a regular Army commission.

Assigned to the Seventh Infantry Division in Japan, Second Lieutenant Wilmot was named executive officer of B Company, First Battalion, 17th Infantry Regiment, largely on the strength of his previous combat experience. Nobody else in the company, including Captain Earl "Lucky" Meridith, the CO, had ever been in battle.

"The company consisted of 77 Americans and 100 South Koreans, who got three weeks of training before we shipped out," Wilmot recalled. "The Koreans were pretty poor soldiers, and my GIs were badly trained and used to the easy life. They had to learn on the job and under fire—and it cost us."

It also cost Wilmot his best friend, Second Lieutenant Hap Ware, one of those young infantry platoon leaders to whom Wilmot referred. "He was leading his platoon forward when the North Koreans ambushed him," Wilmot recalled. "On the way to Korea, Hap told me he had a premonition that he'd be killed, and he gave me a fountain pen as a keepsake. I tried to talk him out of the idea, but I knew from experience that when a guy has feelings like that, they have a way of coming true. I still have his pen."

Barely two months after his graduation from the U.S. Naval Academy, Second Lieutenant Charles M. C. Jones, a former Navy football star, found himself fighting side by side with Marine infantrymen at the Naktong Bulge. While many of his classmates at Annapolis were reporting for duty aboard Navy ships, Jones had been assigned to the Marine base at Quantico, Virginia. Then, hours after war broke out in Korea, he was placed in command of a 75-millimeter recoilless rifle platoon in the Antitank Company of General Craig's Pusan-bound brigade.

"I may have been the 'most junior' Marine officer in the whole deal," Jones recalled. "Three of us from the class of 1950 were sent over with the brigade, partly because we were football players, and [Marine Corps commander] General [Clifton] Cates wanted to break up what he called 'that beef trust' at Quantico.

"We were incredibly hard up for Marines of all ranks in those days. Each battalion was without one of its usual three rifle companies, and my platoon of 75s was expected to move right out there with the infantry in the toughest, nastiest fighting of the war. We used bigger weapons, and we used them against enemy gun emplacements as well as against tanks. That was the only difference between us and the infantry."

Young Marine platoon leaders such as Jones were fortunate to have a network of battle-tested junior officers and noncoms for support, while their Army counterparts often did not. In cultivating the ability to make rational decisions in the heat of battle, nothing replaces training and experience. All battles differ in some respects, but they also share many similarities, and only leaders who have learned to survive in harm's way can fully recognize this fact and communicate it to those they command.

"When I arrived in Korea and had the opportunity to take over a company," said Lieutenant Ike Fenton, a World War II veteran, "I found that the tactics hadn't changed. Regardless of how different the situation might have looked, I could always find the basic tactic that should be employed. Admittedly, I had to do things a little out of the ordinary sometimes, but I'm not a person who believes you can ever throw away the book. All the tactics and principles that I learned previously were of great value to me in Korea."

Fenton's training and background were mirrored by a vast majority of Marine junior officers and noncoms, and with several weeks of bitter, near-constant Korean combat now under their belts, surviving front-line Army officers also were doing a much better job. As one example, Army battalion commander-turned-author T. R. Fehrenbach cited the improved conditions in First Lieutenant Frank Muñoz's G Company, Ninth Infantry, Second Infantry Division, as of late August 1950.

"When . . . G Company went back on line [after the First Battle of the Naktong] . . . the company had only seventy effectives," Fehrenbach wrote. "But within a few days, while the front remained fairly quiet, George [Company] gradually built up to 300 men. Most of the replacements were men who had been wounded slightly and returned to duty or who had collapsed from illness or heat in the first days; all had had at least a brush with combat. . . . George was beginning to pull together. Good leadership could do a great deal, given time."

All along the front, Army units were showing the same sort of progress, and by this time UN forces had also tipped the scales in their favor numerically. Casualties had reduced the NKPA invasion force to about 100,000 men, and close to a third of these were hastily recruited South Koreans with little training and scant motivation to fight for a homeland unified under communism.

Many of the tough NKPA veterans of the China wars had by now been lost to death or severe wounds. Barely a third of the 300 Soviet-built tanks available at the time of the June invasion remained in operating condition, and although 100 new T-34s were added in late August, enemy armor was still outnumbered by about three to one by American tanks. U.S. ground forces also now claimed a heavy advantage in supporting artillery. Air

Force, Navy, and Marine aircraft ruled the skies above Korea, and Navy ships fully controlled the seas around it.

The entire UN force had swelled by this point to more than 170,000 personnel, although only a fraction of these were combat troops. Nearly 70,000 more were assigned to the Inchon landing, but the success or failure of the operation would rest on the 20,000-man assault force of the First Marine Division.

As the end of August arrived, time was clearly running short for the North Koreans, but it also was running out for Craig's Marines. In less than a week, the "Fire Brigade" would have to withdraw from action in the perimeter and return to Pusan to prepare to rejoin the rest of the First Marine Division in the assault at Inchon.

Marshal Choe Yong Gun, in command of all NKPA operations, had no knowledge of the Marines' imminent commitment elsewhere, but he picked this critical moment to order a massive offensive. On September 1, he would throw almost every man at his disposal—some 98,000 troops—against the thinly held UN lines at five key points along a front stretching more than 250 miles. The strongest attack would come at the same Naktong Bulge where Choe's soldiers had been beaten ten days earlier. But intense pressure also would be exerted simultaneously in the far south, in the vicinity of Taegu, and on the eastern front between Taegu and the coast. Choe was confident that his forces would break through somewhere.

As the North Korean blitz took shape, MacArthur's surprise strike at the invaders' rear was, at best, still half a month away. If Choe's offensive succeeded, the Inchon landing would come too late to save Pusan.

"If Pusan should fall to the North Koreans before our landing force was committed—or even if our perimeter forces were unable to break out as part of a coordinated attack—it would change the whole complexion of the Inchon operation," recalled retired Marine General Bryghte Godbold, one of its planners.

At this point, the tug-of-war between Washington and Tokyo remained unresolved. General Collins, the rest of the JCS, and other opponents of Inchon still insisted on employing traditional military tactics, while Mac-

Arthur was determined to toss tradition aside. Yet, because of the NKPA's refusal to cooperate, MacArthur's impending victory in his confrontation with Washington would produce no guarantee of his Inchon plan's success.

What happened at Inchon on September 15—if, indeed, it happened at all—would depend almost entirely on what took place during the next five or six days in the Pusan Perimeter.

CHAPTER 10

★ ★ ★

THE ENEMY
GOES FOR BROKE

AFTER SECURING OBONG-NI Ridge and chasing the North Koreans back across the Naktong River on August 19–20, the Marines received congratulations from Eighth Army commander General Walker for their "excellent leadership, grit, and determination." General Church, commanding the 24th Infantry Division, added his praise for the Marine brigade's "decisive and valiant" actions.

During this time, General Craig hopped aboard his helicopter and flew over to Eighth Army headquarters to confer with Army Chief of Staff General J. Lawton Collins, who was making his first wartime visit to Korea and wanted to find out more about the Marines' successful tactics against NKPA tanks. Collins, too, extended his congratulations and thanks to the brigade.

But more important than all these plaudits to General Craig's exhausted troops was the opportunity for their first extended rest since reaching Korea nearly three weeks earlier. On August 21, after being detached from the 24th Division and placed in Eighth Army reserve, the brigade went into bivouac near Masan in a now-famous area still known in Marine lore as the Bean Patch. It was exactly that—a soybean field large enough to accommodate the whole brigade—where the troops ate their first hot meals in weeks, received letters from home, and even got their first beer ration in Korea. They watched truckloads of supplies roll in from Pusan, enjoyed an improvised stage show by students from Seoul University, and greeted 800 fresh replacements who arrived to fill some of the yawning gaps in their ranks. No tents were available, but few men complained about sleeping in the open as long as no enemy shells exploded nearby and there were no rocky heights to scale.

"Korean barbers were brought in, and we all sat on logs to get our hair cut with their hand-operated clippers," recalled Corpsman Herb Pearce. "Afterward, we had unit pictures taken by Marine photographers. An outbreak of dysentery was quickly quelled by distributing small jars of flown-in cheese spread to each of the affected men."

Almost before the Marines could fully relax, however, General Craig was summoned to 25th Infantry Division headquarters, where General William Kean, the division commander, delivered unpleasant news: the situation in the 25th's sector had deteriorated sharply since the Marines' departure, and the enemy had penetrated American lines in several places.

"I need help from your artillery, and I've cleared it with General Walker," Kean told Craig. "I may need your infantry, too."

Thus, the next day, after less than twenty-four hours in the Bean Patch, the First Battalion, 11th Marines, moved out with its 105-millimeter batteries to the familiar area around Chindong-ni to support a counterattack by Kean's rifle companies. At the same time, Eighth Army headquarters alerted Craig's infantry to be ready to join the counterattack if necessary.

Overnight, though, it was decided that the Marines wouldn't be needed except to conduct patrols to the rear of the 25th Division lines to check for infiltrators. Otherwise, the infantry's stay at the Bean Patch turned into a ten-day respite from combat, highlighted by a congratulatory visit from South Korean President Syngman Rhee and a mass awarding of eighty-seven Purple Hearts to brigade members who'd returned to duty after being wounded.

For Tech Sergeant Ernest DeFazio, the award was his third Purple Heart, and Second Lieutenant Francis W. Muetzel and Corporal Marvin Wells received two medals apiece. (The Silver Star awarded to Muetzel for his valor at Obong-ni Ridge would come later.) Because of an ongoing shortage of replacement uniforms, however, Muetzel, a platoon leader, found it hard to look his best for the ceremony.

"My leggings had been thrown away, my trousers were out at both knees, my right boot had two bullet holes in it, and my dungaree jacket had corporal's stripes on the sleeves," Muetzel later recalled. Nevertheless, he "grabbed a fast shave with cold water, hard soap, and a dull blade," borrowed a set of second lieutenant's bars from another officer, and made an appearance.

Meanwhile, amid the leisurely atmosphere that prevailed in the Bean Patch, rumors of an impending U.S. amphibious operation in Korea, fueled by the daily departure for Pusan of trucks loaded with heavy equipment, filtered down to every enlisted man in the brigade. The Marines knew they'd be part of the operation, and speculation was soon running rampant as to when and where the landing would come.

"We knew something was in the wind," said Ike Fenton, who'd just received word of his promotion to captain. "Company commanders were called in and given the information—classified as top secret—that we were going to load out and make an amphibious landing with the First Marine Division and that we should start preparing accordingly. The men always seemed to have a way of getting the information, whether it was classified or not, and when they heard that the First Division had arrived in Japan, it did wonderful things for their morale."

It was in this atmosphere that Able and Baker companies received their first group of replacements. Among them was PFC Ray Walker, a native Californian who'd joined the Marines in October 1948 at age seventeen, assigned to fill one of the gaps in Able's hard-hit 60-millimeter mortar section. But when Walker arrived on August 22, he was too nervous to share in the veterans' excitement, and within a few hours he was "sick as a dog" from the intense heat that the other Marines were already able to take in stride.

"It was about 120 degrees in the shade the day I got there, and by the second day, I was totally wiped out by the heat," Walker recalled many years later. "I fell out on the ground with heat stroke and laid there unconscious for over an hour. After that, I learned to take salt tablets and drink lots of water."

Herb Pearce, who recalled feeling "down in the dumps" while treating the heavy casualties from the First Battle of the Naktong, was now especially buoyed by the upbeat scuttlebutt. "I was as gung ho as any Marine by this time," said the Navy corpsman, "and I figured we could whip anybody anywhere anytime."

Pearce's optimism was reflected in a random prediction (that somehow escaped the censor's attention) in a letter to his parents dated August 30. Despite a lack of hard supporting evidence, Pearce expressed his firm belief that Inchon would be the Marines' target, then added, "Once we land at Inchon, we should be in Seoul within ten days." Both of his off-the-wall prophesies would turn out to be accurate.

Despite all the encouraging news and positive vibes circulating around the Bean Patch, the Marines would have little time over the next few days to dwell on the looming amphibious operation. The Marine brigade was about to be officially deactivated and its troops reattached to the First Marine Division for the Inchon landing, now just over two weeks away.

But in the meantime, there would be one final conflagration for the "Fire Brigade" to deal with in the Pusan Perimeter—and it would be the hottest one yet.

On the afternoon of August 31, Lieutenant Frank Muñoz, commanding G Company, Ninth Infantry Regiment, Second Infantry Division, noticed a worrisome state of restiveness among the native Korean laborers attached to his unit. They were demanding to be paid that same day, and when Muñoz reminded them that the following day, September 1, was the established payday for employees of the U.S. Army, the Koreans grumbled that they couldn't wait. As dusk fell, every last one of the workers melted into the gathering darkness and disappeared in a mass bug-out.

Something's not right here, Muñoz thought. *What do these guys know that we don't?*

Muñoz hunted down Lieutenant Pete Sudduth, the battalion intelligence officer, and asked what he thought the Koreans' sudden, unexplained departure might mean.

"I'd say it means you should expect something hot tonight, Frank," Sudduth said.

"So should I continue the patrols you wanted in front of my own lines?" Muñoz inquired.

"Yeah," said Sudduth, "and tell your guys to be careful."

A few minutes later, Muñoz called aside the young sergeant assigned to take a four-man patrol out to the east bank of the Naktong River and delivered a vague warning. "Just keep your eyes and ears open," Muñoz said. "If you see or hear anything funny, call me on the radio—*pronto*!"

The sergeant and his men had scarcely moved into position on the riverbank when they heard the soft but unmistakable sounds of human movement. As they took cover, they saw small boats and rafts filled with enemy soldiers paddling across the river. Other North Koreans were slithering through the scrub brush on the bank the Marines were facing. In the clear, moonless night, still others had already moved in behind the patrol, the sergeant realized.

With one hand he motioned his men to stay down and clutched the walkie-talkie in the other, trying to call Muñoz.

"Oh, Jesus!" he whispered. "This damned thing won't work!"

"What do we do now?" one of the men asked.

"Shut up and lie still," said the sergeant, "and hope to God the bastards don't trip over us."

Late on the night of August 31, the NKPA troops spotted by Muñoz's patrol—parts of four full divisions—hurled themselves en masse against American lines. Long rows of enemy skirmishers smashed head-on into Muñoz's G Company, the bursts of flame from their rifles and burp guns punctuated by their shrill shouts:

Manzai! Manzai! Manzai!

Muñoz quickly lost contact with his Third Platoon, exposed on the spur of a ridge below the rest of the company, and when firing abruptly stopped in that area, he knew the platoon had either scattered or been wiped out.

But he managed to call in artillery fire that turned the main thrust of the enemy attack to G Company's right, where the 23rd Regiment took the brunt of the charge. Then Muñoz and the rest of the company clung helplessly to their positions, listening to periodic outbursts of firing to their rear and thankful that the attackers had bypassed them, at least for the moment.

By shortly after midnight on September 1, the ferocious enemy assault, centered on the area held by three regiments of the Second Infantry Division, had literally sliced the division in half, with the 23rd and 38th regiments isolated on the north and the Ninth Regiment and division headquarters forced to the south. Whole companies were either cut off or totally overrun, and their survivors were sent reeling backward almost to the village of Yongsan. The five members of the isolated patrol that Lieutenant Muñoz had sent out were luckier. At daylight, they found their way back to the company area, along with a few stragglers from G Company's Third Platoon, most of which had been killed or wounded.

By the following noon, the North Koreans had gouged a hole six miles wide and eight miles deep through the heart of the Second Division and were again threatening the vital road and rail junction at Miryang. For the second time in a week and a half, the main supply route between Taegu and Pusan was in grave danger of being cut.

Obong-ni Ridge, bought and paid for with Marine blood eleven days earlier, was once more in enemy hands. Everything gained in the First Battle of the Naktong had been lost.

Fifty-five-year-old Major General Laurence B. "Dutch" Keiser, commanding the Second Division, had won a Silver Star as a battalion commander in World War I, but he hadn't been on an active battlefield in more than three decades. He stuck close to the safety of his command post, and some of his fellow officers, including Eighth Army commander General Walker, had come to doubt his courage in the situation he now faced. As journalist-historian David Halberstam observed in his book *The Coldest Winter: America and the Korean War*, "Sometimes men who are exceptionally brave in one war, when they are young, do not age well as soldiers. So it was with Keiser."

Furthermore, none of Keiser's three regimental commanders had ever led troops in combat before—much less troops threatened with envelopment and annihilation—and their reaction verged on panic.

"Our situation's desperate," Keiser told Walker by phone. "We can't hold without heavy reinforcements."

Later that day, September 1, Walker flew low over the Naktong battlefield in a light plane, and he was enraged and sickened by what he saw. In the area that was supposed to be occupied by the Second Division's Ninth Regiment, he spotted an entire infantry company retreating in hurried disarray along a creekbed, although no enemy troops were anywhere near. In the process, the GIs were bypassing excellent defensive positions that could have been used effectively to slow the NK advance.

Walker had his pilot cut the plane's engine and descend to within about fifty feet of the ground. Then the Eighth Army commander leaned out as far as his five-foot, five-inch frame would allow and held a bullhorn to his lips, shouting,

"Stop, you yellow sons of bitches! Go back! You aren't under attack! Go back!"

The fleeing troops paid no heed to Walker's ranting, and he soon gave up the effort. But he ordered the pilot to fly on to the headquarters of the Second Division commander. Then he stalked into Keiser's CP with fire in his eye.

"Dutch, where's your division?" he demanded. "Where are your reserves? What are you doing about positioning your reserves? You've got to hold at Yongsan. If you don't, we could lose Miryang, and if we lose Miryang, we could lose Pusan. You're in the heart of this thing, and you don't even know what's going on!"

When Keiser stammered that he was waiting for his liaison people to bring back reports on the locations of various units, then tried to describe the condition of his division, Walker cut him off short.

"That's not it at all," he raged. "I've just flown over your front line. Now you get this division under control, or I'll take control of it, and I'll run you out of the Army! I'm not going to lose this battle!"

Walker's pilot, Mike Lynch, later recalled Walker weeping on the flight back to his own headquarters. "I can't let this Army be destroyed," Lynch quoted Walker as saying, "but I'm losing the whole Army, and I don't know what to do to stop it."

Although Keiser was left in command of the Second Division, Colonel John G. Hill, commander of the Ninth Regiment, wasn't so fortunate. Hill had already incurred the wrath of his superiors by ordering an ill-fated probing attack on the west bank of the Naktong just as an overwhelmingly superior enemy force was crossing the river. The American attack had ended in disaster, and the resulting losses and confusion had contributed to the subsequent rout of Hill's regiment.

On the morning of September 2, an angry Brigadier General Sladen Bradley, Second Division assistant commander, stormed into Hill's CP and demanded to know what was going on.

"Colonel, where's your First Battalion?" Bradley inquired.

"I don't know, General," Hill replied. "I haven't heard from them since midnight."

"Where's your Second Battalion?" Bradley pressed.

Hill shrugged helplessly. "I haven't heard from them either," he said.

"Well, this situation is out of control, Colonel," Bradley said, "and I'm assuming command of this regiment."

Moments later, Bradley ordered Lieutenant Lee Beahler, commander of D Company of the division's Second Engineer Battalion, to take his men to Yongsan immediately, where they would fight as infantry to hold the town until the Marines could get there.

In his rage, Bradley also relieved Beahler's battalion commander, Lieutenant Colonel Joe McEachern, who tried to argue about the order when told that his men would have to "stand and die" if necessary to stop the enemy at Yongsan.

"But sir," McEachern protested, "these men are specialists. They aren't infantrymen. You have to understand that they're technicians."

"Do you not understand *me*, Colonel?" Bradley flared. "I said stand and die, and I meant stand and die—and they *will* fight as infantrymen. You're relieved!"

Then Bradley turned to Major Charles Fry, the engineer battalion exec, giving every indication that he was ready to relieve Fry as well at the slightest hint of backtalk.

"Do you understand the order, Major?" Bradley asked.

"Yes, sir!" Fry said without hesitation.

For General Walker, the next step in this ongoing drama was pure agony, but he had no other options. As historian Clay Blair put it, "Once again, [Walker] would have to call on Eddie Craig's Marines for help. The decision was drastic, both because of the humiliation it would again cause the Army and because Craig's Marines were a vital element in the Inchon invasion plan."

At this crucial juncture, the Marines were scheduled to load out within forty-eight hours for the truck trip to Pusan, then board ships to join other elements of the First Marine Division for the landing at Inchon. But Walker's decision meant that the schedule would have to be rewritten.

Just beyond this dilemma lay an additional thorny problem for Walker. There was only one "Fire Brigade," but at this moment, there were several separate emergencies facing the Eighth Army at key points along the front. Near Taegu, the First Cavalry Division was hanging on by the skin of its teeth against constant fanatical enemy attempts to overrun the city. In the far south, west of Masan, two NKPA divisions had launched fierce attacks against elements of the U.S. 25th Division positioned along the Nam River near its confluence with the Naktong. Simultaneously, a third NK division had torn another huge hole through two battalions of the 25th's much-maligned 24th Regiment west of the village of Haman when most of the American troops broke and ran at first contact with the enemy. Both battalions had ceased to exist as fighting units, and the North Koreans were driving east against meager resistance.

But after assessing all the bad news, Walker decided that the gravest danger was in the Naktong Bulge, where the Second Division was now left with virtually no effective infantry units to defend Yongsan. Jolted into action by Walker's outburst, Keiser was trying to pull together a scratch force, including Lieutenant Beahler's engineers, a reconnaissance company, a tank battalion, and a few hundred survivors of the division's collapse to block the enemy advance toward Miryang.

Risking a furious reaction from General MacArthur, Walker issued a warning order to Craig's brigade, including the artillery of the 11th Marines, to move immediately to an assembly area at Miryang and prepare to take over the fight for Yongsan. Among Craig's troops, the reaction was predictable: initial bewilderment followed by anger and disgust.

"Okay, you guys, saddle up!" a platoon sergeant yelled to his men in the Bean Patch. "Vacation's over. We're movin' out."

"Hot damn!" an unknowing PFC yelled back. "We're headed for Pusan, right?"

"In your dreams," the platoon sergeant responded. "We're headed back to the Naktong to clean up another friggin' mess."

"We couldn't imagine how the Army could've let the NKs back across the river," said Corpsman Herb Pearce. "We were afraid this meant we'd miss out on the Inchon invasion, and nobody was happy about that. Every man I talked to was mad as hell about having to do the Army's work for them—*again*—and I felt the same way."

Because of overwhelming U.S. air superiority, the North Koreans had seldom fared well in daytime attacks, and after their defeat in the First Battle of the Naktong, their commanders had ordered all subsequent assaults to be staged under cover of darkness and carefully divided into phases. As Major General Pang Ho San, commander of the NKPA's Sixth Division, explained in a memo to his field officers,

"From now on, use daylight hours for full combat preparation, and commence attacks soon after sunset. Concentrate your battle actions mostly at night and capture enemy base positions. From midnight on, engage enemy in close combat by approaching to within 100 to 150 meters of him. Then, even with the break of dawn, the enemy planes will not be able to distinguish friend from foe, which will enable you to prevent great losses."

Effectively utilizing these tactics, a strong North Korean force captured Yongsan during the night of September 1–2, but Keiser's scratch force managed, for the time being, to prevent their further advance toward Miryang. At about 3:00 AM on September 2, enemy troops struck the Army engineers' positions overlooking the main roads south and east of Yongsan, triggering an intense firefight that lasted the rest of the morning.

Although the engineers lacked both artillery and mortars, they used bazookas, machine guns, rifles, grenades, and a quad-50 antiaircraft piece to inflict massive casualties on the charging enemy. M-26 Pershing tanks of the 72nd Tank Battalion also ravaged the attackers with heavy shellfire. Hundreds of North Korean bodies were left littering the hillsides, but the engineers also suffered heavy losses. In D Company of the engineer battalion, Lieutenant Beahler remained the only officer alive and unwounded when daylight returned.

To the men around him, it was a miracle that Beahler lived to see the sun rise. He stayed on the move constantly during three separate enemy assaults, racing along the line, reassuring his men, and trying to see that they all had enough ammunition.

"They came, and they came, and they kept coming," recalled Corporal Jesse Haskins. "We kept killing them, and I began to wonder if we could kill them fast enough. There seemed to be so many of them, and they just kept coming."

Twelve members of D Company were killed that night and early morning, and eighteen others were wounded, but Beahler somehow came through without a scratch. "I never saw a braver man in my life," said PFC Charles "Butch" Hammel. "I never saw a man so cool under fire."

Beahler's insistence, when the company was first hit, on leaving a vulnerable position in a rice paddy and moving to higher ground—defying an order from the already relieved Colonel Hill in the process—was probably all that saved the entire company from annihilation. Hill was so angry that he later tried to have Beahler court-martialed for insubordination until General Bradley told him to drop the matter or end up "looking like a fool." Beahler was awarded the Distinguished Service Cross instead.

On the afternoon of September 2, with 800 men who had fled the Ninth Regiment's collapse on the Naktong added to the scratch force at Yongsan, the Americans managed to regain control of the ravaged town. U.S. air strikes and bazooka teams knocked out several North Korean tanks, and by day's end, the enemy troops had been driven into the hills west of Yongsan.

On the same afternoon, after setting up his CP at Miryang and handing control of his brigade over to the Second Infantry Division, General Craig met with General Keiser and other Army brass to determine how to deploy the Marines. The first words out of Keiser's mouth were an abject apology.

"General Craig, I'm horribly embarrassed that you have to do this," Keiser said. "My men lost the ground that you took in a severe fight."

Craig graciously shrugged off the apology, saying, "It might just as easily have happened to me." But when he learned a few moments later that Keiser and the other Army officers wanted the Marine brigade thrown into the battle piecemeal and at once, rather than as a cohesive force in a carefully coordinated attack, his temper flared.

"This was the only heated discussion I had in Korea with the Army," Craig said afterward. "Only two of my battalions had arrived at Miryang; all my artillery wasn't available yet; and my air support was still on the road. The Army also wanted me to attack on a very broad front, and I also objected to this. I knew if we were committed to combat piecemeal that we'd be defeated in detail, and the Marine Corps would be finished in Korea and in the public eye. General Keiser and Eighth Army finally agreed, and we firmed up the plans for the attack on a narrow front."

H-hour for the brigade's jump-off was set for 8:00 AM on September 3—about the same time that Craig had originally planned to have his troops board trucks for the trip to Pusan. This time, even "Chopper Eddie" couldn't figure out how to have his "yellow legs" in two places at once.

At half an hour past midnight on September 3, the First and Second battalions of the Fifth Marines marched west from Miryang on the Yongsan road, with Colonel Newton's 1/5 leading the advance on the left and Colonel Roise's 2/5 close behind on the right. Colonel Taplett's 3/5 was in reserve for the moment, assigned to block the southern approaches to Yongsan.

"We followed in trace of the Second Battalion, which was to pass through the Army and occupy the Army's positions," said freshly promoted Captain Ike Fenton, commanding B/1/5. "When the Second Battalion was in position, we were to move up abreast and jump off in the attack at 0800 [8:00 AM]."

Unforeseen delays quickly developed, however. Enemy mortar and small-arms fire halted the Second Battalion on the eastern outskirts of Yongsan and held it up for an hour. Then the Marines found that during the night the Army had pulled back its defensive lines under enemy pressure and taken up new positions 1,000 yards to the east. This meant that the Marines' attack would be launched from farther back than expected and that the original planned point of departure would be their first objective.

Colonel Roise of 2/5 ordered Lieutenant Robert Winter's platoon of M-26 tanks forward to cover the Army withdrawal with their 90-millimeter guns, and this consumed more time.

Despite all this, both battalions were on line abreast and ready to jump off at 9:00 AM in what would be the Marines' first two-battalion assault in Korea. Until now, because of questionable flanking support from Army units, a single Marine battalion had been designated to lead, with a second backing it up. In this case, both had long rice paddies to cross before they could reach the now-familiar and much-hated bulk of Obong-ni "No Name" Ridge. The Second Battalion's route was somewhat longer than 1/5's, however, and its paddy was studded with several small hills that had to be secured during the advance.

Probably no Marine in either battalion was less enthusiastic about the task ahead than eighteen-year-old PFC Ben Wray, a designated BAR man in a B Company rifle squad and a Texan so proud of his home state that he flew a Lone Star flag in front of his foxhole. Wray had been evacuated with grenade wounds in his back and legs during the First Battle of the Naktong, but had recovered sufficiently during the respite in the Bean Patch to return to duty. Now he would've felt fortunate to be back in the hospital.

"Talk about bad timing!" Wray said. "I'd been in a recon squad in the first battle, and when I got back, because of the wounds, they said they'd put me in headquarters platoon. But then I'll be damned if they didn't give me my BAR back. Before the day was over, I was glad they had."

In the words of acclaimed combat photographer David Douglas Duncan, embedded with the Marine brigade, Captain Fenton's Baker Company "drew the short straw" that morning—the assignment to lead the First Battalion's portion of the assault. "Our mission was to seize the high ground to our immediate front," Fenton recalled, "at which time the Second Battalion would move out and take the high ground to our right front."

An eerie silence prevailed as the company crossed the coverless rice paddy under banks of dark clouds and started up the nearest small slopes. No one expected the calm to last long—and it didn't. The first rifle squads had just reached the rising ground at the foot of the slope when a wall of fire and lead erupted in front of them.

"Then everything happened at once," wrote photographer Duncan. "The stillness was broken forever as machine guns opened fire from all along the ridge ahead. Marine machine guns threw back answering fire. Other Marines were on their bellies, firing, waiting."

At almost the same moment, the leaden skies opened up, unleashing a driving rainstorm, cutting visibility sharply, and drenching the crouching Marines. Fortuitously, though, the deluge also offered a measure of protection as the last members of B Company slogged out of the knee-deep mud of the rice paddy and took cover in every available wrinkle of the earth. A squadron of Corsairs defied the nasty weather to scorch NKPA positions with napalm, taking just seven minutes from the time it was called to complete the mission.

This was the first time that many Army officers had gotten a firsthand look at the close air support delivered by Marine Air Group 33, whose fliers had worked out a shuttle system that kept one squadron constantly on station while another returned to its carrier to refuel and rearm. Colonel Paul Freeman, commanding the 23rd Infantry Regiment on the Marines' right flank, was particularly impressed with the coordination between air and ground units. As he observed in a letter to General Matthew Ridgway in Washington, "The Marines on our left were a sight to behold. . . . They had squadrons of air in direct support, and they used it like artillery. They had it *day and night*. . . . General, we just have to have air support like that, or we might as well disband the infantry and join the Marines!"

The Marines on the ground were equally appreciative. "Those planes saved our bacon again that day," said Sergeant Mackie Wheeler of A Company. "They roasted those gooks but good."

Meanwhile, Fenton peered through the downpour at signals conveying unsettling news from forward observers on the lip of the hill. The Second Battalion was pinned down and taking heavy casualties, and the NKPA's Ninth Division was mounting an attack of its own, under cover of heavy mortar and machine-gun fire, from the opposite side of the ridge, with the obvious aim of seizing the crest before the Americans could get there. But to the immediate front of B Company, there was no apparent enemy activity.

"I don't believe the enemy realized that we had a battalion to the left of the road," Fenton later recalled, "because they were preparing to go for that high ground themselves. As familiar as we were with the lay of the land, I thought if we hurried, we could beat them there by a good ten minutes."

Fenton stood poised for a moment, close behind his riflemen. Then he jumped to his feet and waved his men forward.

"Attack! Attack!" he shouted down the line.

A and B companies of 1/5 charged up the hill side by side, with covering fire from their 81-millimeter mortar sections. Shortly before 11:00 AM, Fenton reported to battalion headquarters that he was on the forward slope of Obong-ni and scrambling for the crest in his race with the enemy.

As Fenton had hoped, Baker Company made it with time to spare—about twenty minutes' worth, to be exact—giving the Marines a chance to catch their breath and take up defensive positions while the advancing North Koreans were still in a rice paddy far below.

"Fire at will," Fenton told his men, "and keep it up as long as you've got a target."

The company responded with massive volleys of small-arms, machine-gun, and mortar fire. With amazing accuracy, the Marine riflemen calmly picked off enemy soldiers with their M-1s from 400 or 500 yards away. Scores of North Koreans fell. Not one made it anywhere near the top.

"We really had ourselves a turkey shoot," said Fenton. When it was over, PFC Ben Wray's BAR was almost hot enough to blister his hands.

By shattering the NKPA attack and securing the crest of the ridge, A and B companies were able to provide vital fire support for the bogged-down

Second Battalion, allowing it to move forward a short distance to more secure positions. Then, as the enemy soldiers tried to flee the open ground, the 105s of the 11th Marines, the brigade's artillery outfit, blasted more gaping holes in their ranks.

Finally, as darkness neared on the evening of September 3, both battalions were ordered to hold what they had and set up their defenses for the night. Fenton's B Company was ordered to move down onto a smaller ridgeline that ran off the main mass of high ground to form what looked like an upside-down T. Captain John Stevens's A Company was assigned to defend high ground to the rear of B Company and another ridge on B Company's left flank.

This positioning left Fenton worried—and for good reason. As Marine historian Captain John Chapin described it, "The First Battalion's right flank was dangling in air; it was trying to cover a front of nearly a mile, and its two rifle companies were 200 yards apart."

"Once again we were faced with the situation of having nothing on our right flank," Fenton said. "The Second Battalion was about 900 yards to our rear, leaving us exposed on the right, like the point of an arrow ready to be shot from the bow." The position held by 2/5, stretching over a 2,000-yard front, was perhaps even more precarious, with its D Company totally isolated from the rest of the battalion.

The fact that the Marines had driven the North Koreans back two miles west of Yongsan during the afternoon was of small consolation. Marine losses had been heavy—34 killed and 157 wounded in the two engaged battalions—and many more casualties seemed inevitable before the next dawn. Nearly a month of grinding combat, plus the rigors of having to do the same bloody job all over again, had eaten away at morale.

The thoughts of Second Lieutenant Frank Muetzel, commanding A Company's First Platoon, were typical. "I knew this couldn't keep up," he said. "We, me, all of us were eventually going to get it; it was just a matter of when and how bad. . . . It was just a god-awful mess—inadequate replacements, insufficient ammo, worn-out clothes and boots. No one much gave a rap about anything. Outside discipline was no longer a threat. What could the brass do to us that was worse than what we were doing?"

Three key factors combined to spare the Marines of 1/5 and 2/5 the agony they were expecting on the night of September 3–4. One was the work of a Marine engineering unit that sowed a solid field of antipersonnel mines, wired hand grenades, and TNT charges along the two battalions' flanks. Another was timely intervention from the Corsairs and Tigercats of VMF(N)-513, the only squadron of single-engine night fighters then operating in Korea. In total darkness, these planes flew six close air support missions that strongly curbed nocturnal activity by the NKPA. And finally, the continuing heavy rain, miserable as it was for the Marines, may have washed out any plans for a major NKPA counterattack.

But the overriding truth of the situation was that the North Koreans were simply "running out of gas." Their supply lines were extended to the limit and constantly under threat of UN air attacks; they were critically short of food and ammo; and their troops were even more exhausted than the Americans. When the invaders met a force that yielded ground and allowed them to encircle and get behind it—as had so often happened with Army units—they usually had little trouble consolidating their victory. But when the NKPA faced a stubborn foe who held his ground, then counterattacked in force, it was often a different story.

To this day, historians and military observers generally agree that the invaders bled themselves to death in repeated small-scale attacks by platoons or companies, in which they left a combined total of thousands dead on the field. If they had, instead, concentrated the strength of entire available divisions at any one of several points along the fragile U.S. front, tactical experts believe, the struggle for the Pusan Perimeter might well have ended much differently.

As it was, despite periods of heavy shelling by the NKPA and the fears of every Marine and GI manning defensive positions west of Yongsan, there would be no major enemy attack during the night of September 3–4. In B/1/5's sector, except for a few easily repulsed probes by handfuls of enemy soldiers, the night passed with uncharacteristic calm. Before dawn, Fenton and his men got the distinct feeling that the North Koreans were withdrawing.

At 6:00 AM on September 4, the First Battalion was ordered to resume its attack, in tandem with Colonel Taplett's 3/5, which relieved and passed through 2/5 to take over its portion of the advance. Now the worries about the Marines' right flank were inherited by Taplett and his company commanders.

"Supposedly, the Ninth Infantry would attack abreast of us on the right, but the Army unit didn't appear," Taplett recounted. "As we moved west to begin the attack, we passed through the burning and completely destroyed village of Yongsan. The dense smoke and usual morning mist combined to reduce visibility to near zero."

After clearing the village, Taplett and his troops came upon a bloodcurdling sight. A group of thirty to forty fleeing civilians—women, children, and old men—had been caught in a crossfire and slaughtered. "Retreating Army tanks had run over the bodies," said Taplett, "grinding up the remains in their treads."

Pressing on past the carnage, 3/5 reached its first objective about twenty minutes after the jump-off, then stormed up a ridge identified as Hill 117 against a notable absence of enemy fire. Forty minutes into the attack, Taplett's men reached the top of the hill, finding it deserted except for fifteen NK dead. "The remainder of the enemy force had fled west . . . fighting a delaying action as they withdrew," Taplett recalled.

Meanwhile, A and B companies of 1/5 also were pressing rapidly ahead against a near-total lack of enemy resistance. Within twenty minutes, Fenton's suspicions that the North Koreans had quit the fight in the area were confirmed when his men overran the NKPA Ninth Division's vacant command post.

"Their tents were still up, and equipment was scattered all around," Fenton said. "They'd obviously pulled out in a hurry, leaving behind two T-34 tanks in excellent condition [the first undamaged enemy armor to be captured by U.S. forces]. In the vicinity was a big ammunition dump, which we accidentally blew up with a stray mortar round."

As the Marines pushed on westward toward the Naktong, they encountered other telltale signs of a disintegrating enemy. Hundreds of North Korean bodies lay sprawled along the main road among piles of abandoned equipment.

"We had them on the run," said Fenton, "and we started to take in our first big batch of prisoners. By noon, we'd collected a dozen of them."

By 3:15 PM on September 4, both companies of 1/5 were on high ground a short distance northeast of the site of the First Battle of the Naktong on Obong-ni Ridge. A couple of hours later, when they dug in for the night, the two Marine battalions had advanced a total of about three miles through the relentless rain since morning. Tied in on the First Battalion's right flank was the Ninth Infantry Regiment. It was depleted and disheveled, but at least it was where it was supposed to be. As darkness fell, everything was quiet.

The bitter fighting in the Naktong Bulge wasn't yet over, however. The North Koreans were marshaling their flagging strength for one great, last-gasp effort—a rare, all-out offensive in broad daylight.

In Tokyo, meanwhile, General MacArthur's Far East Command headquarters was operating in full crisis mode. On one hand, FECOM was deluged with vehement protests by General Walker over the Eighth Army's impending loss of the First Provisional Marine Brigade. On the other, architects of the Inchon invasion clamored for immediate release of the Fifth Marines, the infantry heart of the brigade, as an indispensable component of the approaching amphibious operation. General O. P. Smith, commander of the First Marine Division, was quietly but firmly opposed to the landing unless his most battle-tested infantry outfit was there to lead it.

Without the Fifth Marines, the main Inchon assault force would have only one Marine infantry regiment—Colonel Chesty Puller's First Marines—to secure the beaches and seawalls. This was because the Seventh Marines, the division's third infantry regiment, was having to travel all the way from the Mediterranean. It would be unavailable for the amphibious assault but would reach Korea in time to join the drive on Seoul. Troops of the Army's Seventh Infantry Division also would take part in the Inchon operation, but plans called for the initial, and most hotly contested, landings to be handled entirely by the Marines.

In the words of retired Marine General Bryghte Godbold, at the time a First Marine Division staff officer assigned to the Inchon planning team,

"Chesty Puller was a tough commander, and his men were tough Marines, but it was impossible for any single regiment to seize an objective as large and difficult as Inchon. To try it would've been utter lunacy."

In a meeting on September 3, General Ned Almond, appointed by MacArthur as overall commander of the Inchon operation, proposed leaving the Fifth Marines in the Pusan Perimeter and sending the 32nd Regiment of the Seventh Infantry Division to Inchon in its place. Facing an impasse after this idea was flatly rejected by General Smith, Almond and MacArthur retired to a private office where, for once, Almond spoke out candidly to his boss.

"It's no use, General," Almond said. "Smith and the Navy simply won't go into Inchon without the Fifth Marines."

MacArthur set his jaw for a moment, then relaxed it. "All right," he said, "then tell Walker he'll just have to give up the Marines."

The following day, MacArthur sent Major General Edwin K. Wright, his G-3 operations officer, to Taegu to hand-carry the order to Walker. It specified that the Marines had to be released by the Eighth Army no later than the night of September 5–6. To soften the impact, Wright told Walker that the 17th Regiment of the Seventh Infantry Division was being withdrawn from the Inchon operation and designated as a "floating reserve," to be rushed to Pusan if needed. Wright added that the 65th Regiment of the Third Division, due to reach the Far East on about September 18, would be sent directly to Pusan to bolster Walker's forces.

Walker, under what must have been the greatest stress of his career at this point, was far from overjoyed with the arrangement. It was better than nothing, but substituting a green, unbloodied Army regiment for the battle-hardened Fifth Marines was hardly an even trade. And September 18, when the other Army regiment would arrive, was still two full weeks away. As Walker knew from recent experience, a lot of bad things could happen in two weeks, and the question of whether the Naktong line could be held—even for another *two days*—was still very much up in the air.

Within the next forty-eight hours, Walker would have to make the most fateful decision of his life. If the Naktong front became untenable, his sole remaining option would be to order a withdrawal to what was loosely referred to among Eighth Army staff as the "Davidson Line." Named for Brigadier General Garrison H. Davidson, an engineering officer who had laid it out in August, the line defined a much reduced, and theoretically more defensible, Pusan Perimeter. To Walker, however, it bore an ominous resemblance to the besieged British pocket at Dunkirk on the French coast in June 1940. Dunkirk had worked miraculously well as a desperation escape hatch for a defeated army, but Walker had already promised his troops that Pusan would never become another Dunkirk.

On September 5, Walker discussed a possible retreat to the Davidson Line with his staff and his top field commanders, painfully aware that such a move would severely impact—if not totally derail—the counteroffensive out of the Pusan Perimeter, timed to coincide with the Inchon landing. He made no firm decision, but that afternoon he had orders prepared for the withdrawal "just in case."

At first light on September 5, Captain Ike Fenton had an excellent view from his command post of the day's primary objective: Obong-ni Ridge. Through his binoculars, Fenton was looking over practically the same ground that his company had crossed during its first drive on the Naktong Bulge.

Once again, the previous night had been disarmingly uneventful except for the pouring rain. There'd been quite a bit of enemy mortar and artillery fire in the area of the First Battalion command post, and at one point the men of B Company had heard tanks—presumably North Korean T-34s—moving to their immediate front. But Fenton had had the foresight to ask the engineers to mine the roads and booby-trap every approach to the area, and the enemy armor never made an appearance.

The order to continue the attack came at 6:00 AM, with jump-off set for two hours later. B/1/5 was designated as the right flank company, and the Ninth Infantry Regiment was supposed to come abreast of Fenton's unit so they could jump off together. But as inevitably seemed to be the case, the Army troops failed to show up, so A and B companies were instructed to attack by themselves.

"I keep hearing about these Army troops that are supposed to be right alongside us," Sergeant Mackie Wheeler muttered to his A Company buddy Sergeant R. D. Lopez, "but damned if I've ever seen any of 'em."

In the meantime, word reached the company that battalion was sending up the first hot coffee the men had seen since leaving the Bean Patch, but that also turned into a disappointment.

"Just as the coffee arrived," said Fenton, "we got the word to move out. We didn't get a drop of coffee distributed, which didn't do morale any good because the men were already soaking wet and grouchy. But they were anxious to get this thing over with, too. All of us were."

Amid the grousing, Fenton turned to Lieutenant Nick Schryver, commander of the First Platoon. "Tell your guys I think we've got a good chance of running the gooks right back across the river today," Fenton said.

Schryver nodded. "Yeah, if we can get any breaks at all, Ike," he said, "we're gonna break their damned backs today. The men can feel it."

The resistance was scattered at first—a few mortar rounds, some sniper fire, and an occasional burst from an enemy machine gun—and it slowed the Marines' advance only slightly. A and B companies worked in close harmony, with one storming a piece of high ground while the other provided a solid base of covering fire, then reversing the process. In this manner, they advanced about 3,000 yards to a ridgeline running parallel to Obong-ni and only about 400 yards away.

Here, Colonel Newton, the First Battalion commander, received urgent orders from General Craig to have both his companies stop where they were and dig in until the tardy Ninth Infantry could finally come up abreast of them. Fenton's battle-savvy instincts almost immediately told him why.

"It was my belief and the belief of all the men with me that the enemy had withdrawn to Obong-ni Ridge to prepare his main line of defense," Fenton later recalled. "They wanted us to come over our little ridgeline and get down in that rice paddy field where we'd been before. Then they were going to open up with everything they had."

Now, with the American advance halted, the NKPA decided not to wait. In the ceaseless rain, as the Marines were digging as hard as they could, they launched one of their most savage bombardments of the war.

"Everything broke loose," said Fenton. "We were pinned down and couldn't move, with the entire ridgeline swept with fire, and it was raining too hard to call in air support."

To make matters worse, every rain-soaked radio in the company went out at once. Fenton couldn't reach his supporting mortars or artillery. He lost all communication with battalion.

A runner raced up, dodging bullets, and jumped into the hole beside Fenton. "The Army's coming up on your right flank," the man said, panting, "but they're still about 1,800 yards away."

The North Koreans didn't wait. About 400 enemy infantrymen launched a powerful counterattack directly at B Company's positions, screened out front by three T-34s.

Fenton sent a runner of his own back to the Ninth Regiment to plead for artillery support. He dispatched another runner to Colonel Newton's CP to alert him to the situation and a third one to warn Marine tanks on the main road that NK armor was headed their way.

The enemy tanks rumbled eastward, following the same route as the ones the Marines had destroyed earlier in the First Battle of the Naktong, but this time it was the Pershings that were caught unaware, with their 90-millimeter guns pointed in the wrong direction as they rounded a curve. Two Marine tanks and one Army tank were knocked out almost immediately, and the others withdrew to blocking positions beyond the curve.

"We need maximum supporting fire from your artillery, and we need it *now*!" PFC William A. Wilson, the twenty-two-year-old runner sent by Fenton, said with a gasp as he ran up to a Ninth Regiment artillery officer.

"Come on and show me where," the officer said as both rushed toward a nearby observation post.

"Right in that area!" Wilson yelled, pointing. "See, just beyond that ridge!"

But before the officer could radio instructions to his battery, a burst of machine-gun fire knocked him to the ground. Wilson screamed for a medic, then grabbed the radio himself. He'd never tried to direct artillery fire before, but he was about to learn.

Moments later, clouds of smoke and fire from Army 105s blossomed in clusters along the routes of approach to B Company's ridgeline and on the crest of Obong-ni itself.

The Army's artillery barrage slowed the enemy infantrymen, but they still came on in charging groups of 40 to 100 with fixed bayonets and spewing burp guns.

"Every man grab a rifle and get on the line!" Fenton shouted. "That means mortarmen, rocketmen, corpsmen—everybody!"

During the frenetic minutes that followed, the bewhiskered young captain drew his .45 and joined the firing, but he doubted that anything could stop the onrushing North Koreans. The worst part of all was that the company was critically low on ammunition.

"I gotta have grenades!" a Marine yelled. "I'm down to my last one!"

"Make it count," Fenton yelled back. "Things don't look too rosy! We're practically out!"

At that moment, as if on cue, a platoon of crouching Marines from A Company scrambled up to Fenton's foxhole. Among them, they were manhandling five cases of hand grenades and other ammunition.

"Compliments of A Company," muttered Lieutenant Frank Muetzel, the platoon leader, as he hit the deck. "Colonel Newton said you might need these."

"Thank the colonel for me," Fenton said. *And thank God!* he thought.

He and Muetzel and the rest of the A Company men broke open the boxes and began tossing grenades forward to Marines on the line, who caught and threw them as fast as they could pull the pins. By this time, the latest wave of enemy soldiers was only a few dozen yards away. They didn't get much closer.

In the tension-charged lull that followed the breakdown of the enemy charge, Fenton discovered that Master Sergeant Leonard R. Young, the oldest of the old-timers among B Company's NCOs, had been hit in the chest by machine-gun fire as he moved along the line, rallying the troops.

"God, I'm sorry, Cap'n," Young whispered as Fenton leaned over him, his hand touching the dripping-wet canvas of the poncho-litter on which

Young lay. "I'm really sorry, but don't let the men fall back. Please don't let 'em fall back."

As the stretcher bearers started down the hill in the rain, Fenton shook his head, bit his lip, and turned away, unable to reply.

The men of A and B companies *didn't* fall back. With the help of Army artillery and an 81-millimeter Marine mortar barrage ordered by Colonel Newton—which hurled rounds within fifty feet of Fenton's lines—the North Koreans were stopped. Then, after about forty-five minutes of constant, unmitigated hell, their desperation attacks ceased altogether.

"We finally did get a few breaks," said Lieutenant Schryver many years later, "and we *did* break their backs."

Later that afternoon, bone-tired Marines of A and B companies could see the NKPA withdrawing from its positions on Obong-ni Ridge and retreating toward the riverbank—a clear signal that the invaders were thoroughly defeated. At about the same time, *Life* photographer David Duncan strolled up to Lieutenant Fenton with a choice piece of news.

"Hey, Ike, I just heard that the brigade's pulling out tonight and going back to Pusan," Duncan said.

"That sounds too good to be true, Dave," Fenton said. The skepticism was plain in his voice.

"I got the word at battalion," Duncan said. "All the battalion COs were told by General Craig and Colonel Murray. I hear you'll be moving out around midnight."

Fenton shrugged. He was too worn out to laugh. "I'll believe it when I see it happen," he said.

At about seven o'clock that evening, when the company got orders to dig in but not to set up "too elaborate" a defense for the night, Fenton *did* start to believe. About three and a half hours later, when an Army lieutenant showed up with a grand total of forty men to relieve B Company, Fenton was finally convinced.

"It was the same old story," he said. "The Army was going to relieve a company with a platoon, and the first time the enemy started to feel out their line, they'd probably pull out."

But it wasn't Fenton's problem anymore. Shortly before midnight, the men of B Company started hiking back toward Yongsan, where a convoy of trucks was waiting to take them to Pusan. From its first combat on August 11 through the day just past, September 5, the company had suffered 151 casualties, including 27 dead and the 9 presumed dead left behind at Sachon. The Marine brigade as a whole had lost 903 killed or wounded since coming ashore on August 2.

The Second Battle of the Naktong was over. Inchon awaited.

CHAPTER 11

★ ★ ★

A 5,000-TO-ONE "SURE THING"

THE PREVAILING ATTITUDE in Pusan had changed dramatically for the better when the First Provisional Marine Brigade returned there on the morning of September 7. The gloom and doom of early August had given way to a positive sense of purpose and preparation.

"Organized confusion was everywhere," said Navy Corpsman Herb "Doc Rocket" Pearce, "with people, supplies, and equipment moving in all directions at once. Now there were even some rules that had to be obeyed, but there were still plenty of others that could be bent or broken. Our outfit bought a trailerload of beer and soft drinks from the Army and iced it down. Then, for two days, any of us could stop by for a cold one anytime."

"It was a strange situation," added Corporal Red Martin. "You could stand in line for an hour to buy two legal cans of beer, or you could buy fifty cases on the black market. We opted for the fifty cases."

With a month's worth of accumulated pay in men's pockets, games of poker, dice, and blackjack weren't difficult to find, and Pearce won a considerable sum in one of them. Like the serious-minded young man he was, he sent most of his winnings home to Mississippi for his parents to save for him.

Two of the Marine battalions, 1/5 and 2/5, were quartered in dockside warehouses, where the men had their first chance to rest and clean up since leaving the Bean Patch. Colonel Robert Taplett's less fortunate 3/5 was assigned to what Taplett described as a "skeletonized" Pusan University building with neither windows nor a roof. With the approach of fall, he noted, the blistering heat of August had subsided, and the nights had turned noticeably cooler. "We bedded down on the concrete floor with just our ponchos and field jackets to keep us warm," Taplett said, "and the Good Lord kept the rain away." Hot meals—a luxury the brigade had all but forgotten—were served three times a day aboard Navy transports tied up to the docks.

The Marines were past due to be reequipped with weaponry, uniforms, boots, and other basic essentials. Most men's grimy dungarees were thoroughly rotted from the effect of constant mud, rain, and sweat, and their boots were falling to pieces, but it quickly became apparent that there was a shortage of almost everything in the teeming port city.

"There was such a shortage of Marine utility clothes that we had to outfit the men with Army stuff," said Captain Ike Fenton. "Shoes were also a great problem. We looked all over town at Army supply installations, and we were able to pick up a pair here and there, but a lot of men had to settle for the wrong sizes."

When thrice-wounded Marine Lieutenant Frank Muetzel, looking, in his own words, "like a damned refugee," strode into a supply depot and told a neatly dressed Army major that he needed a new pair of boots, the officer at first tried to tell Muetzel that none was available. Muetzel, however, refused to be put off.

"Listen, Major," he said, "I'm an infantry platoon leader just off the line, and I'm going right back on the line in a few days." At that point, Muetzel pulled up the legs of his tattered dungarees and showed the major several bullet holes in his boots. "I don't have a helluva lot to lose," he said with a growl, "and I want a pair of boots right now."

Without another word, the major went back to a stockroom, returned with a new pair of Army parachute jump boots, and handed them to Muetzel.

"I was ready to fight for those boots," Muetzel recalled later, "and the major knew it."

When it came to replacing lost or worn-out machine guns, the Marines were totally out of luck; there was simply none available. It also was impossible to find replacements for lost ammo magazines for Browning automatic rifles. Each BAR man was supposed to be equipped with nineteen magazines, but in B/1/5, only six per man could be located.

Since efforts to secure equipment through proper channels often failed, the Marines frequently resorted to illegal scrounging, especially of vehicles. "The worst offense I saw," recalled Lieutenant Muetzel, "was the theft of the MP company commander's jeep. After a fast coat of green paint and phony numbers were slapped on, it was presented to Lieutenant Colonel Newton, our battalion CO."

One commodity that *was* in good supply was "new blood" for the Fifth Marines' three infantry battalions. Up to now, each battalion had been fighting with only two of its three prescribed rifle companies, but on the Marines' arrival in Pusan, each battalion found its third company already there and waiting.

"Man, it was great to see that the guys from Charlie Company had finally arrived from the States," said Sergeant Mackie Wheeler of A/1/5. "It was like losing one of your arms and then getting it back."

Each battalion also received a third 17-member machine-gun section, and overall, the regiment welcomed 1,135 replacements to bring each company back up to its standard wartime strength of 5 officers and approximately 215 enlisted men. The Fifth Marines as a whole swelled to its full complement of 3,611.

In addition to gambling and scrounging, other popular pastimes included the age-old games of "Guess Where" and "Guess When." Everyone realized by now that an amphibious operation was in the offing, and although there was still no official word as to the time or place, scuttlebutt was everywhere. One set of rumors placed the landing somewhere on the west coast. Another favored the east coast. Yet another insisted that the

brigade would sail to Japan to be reunited with the rest of the division before making the landing.

Possibly in hopes of misleading omnipresent spies and Communist
sympathizers, Fifth Marines headquarters circulated a memo containing
detailed information on a landing beach at the small port of Kunsan (the
site favored by the JCS). "The papers were marked confidential," recalled
Ike Fenton, "but we had orders to read them to the troops in the warehouse,
and I do believe that a copy or two managed to get lost."

For all concerned, there was much to be done, and a very short time in
which to do it. The landing plan for Inchon was incredibly detailed and
complex, involving positioning for units as small as fire teams, and it would
be essential for every man in the operation to know precisely where he had
to be after going ashore. This task was complicated by the fact that except
for company and battalion commanders and their staffs, none of the participants would even be briefed on their mission until two or three days
before the landing, when they were already en route to Inchon.

The first component of the invasion force to embark from Pusan was
Colonel Taplett's 3/5, assigned to secure the small island of Wolmi-do at the
mouth of Inchon Harbor. By the time the battalion boarded ship on the
afternoon of September 8, Taplett and his staff were already at sea—in more
ways than one. "Never in the history of the Marine Corps had a major amphibious operation been planned in such a short, complex, and awkward
manner," Taplett grumbled. "The battalion staff and I faced a horrendous
task, and I wondered if 3/5 would be ready."

Taplett sometimes tended to overstate his own case, but General O. P.
Smith, commander of the First Marine Division, also was concerned. Smith
considered the early capture of Wolmi-do ("Moontip Island" in English)
"the key to the whole operation."

The island was connected to the city of Inchon by a 600-yard-long
causeway, and it was believed to be defended by about 500 North Korean
troops. Smith's plan called for 3/5 to land across Wolmi-do's Green Beach
on the morning tide of September 15 and eliminate whatever threat the
island's garrison might pose to the other two landing beaches on the
mainland—Red and Blue. Then 3/5 was to hold its ground for the next

twelve hours, until the rest of the Marine division could complete the landings on the evening tide. During that period, 3/5 would be left high and dry,
beyond the reach—or help—of other American ground forces. Only artillery and air support would be available.

(The tides at Inchon were among the world's most extreme and peculiar.
Except for one maximum high-tide period in the morning—ranging from
less than half an hour to more than an hour, depending on the phases of the
moon—and another of similar duration twelve hours later, in the evening,
the port was virtually inaccessible to any but the most shallow-draft vessels.
At other times of the day, when the tide receded, the harbor was clogged by
vast, impassable expanses of mudflats. The periods of high tide on September 15 were among the shortest of the month.)

Clearly, Taplett had ample reason to be nervous, but Smith's worries
were eased somewhat during his first face-to-face meeting of the war with
General MacArthur, who greeted Smith warmly aboard the command ship
Mt. McKinley and assured him, "The landing of the Marines at Inchon will
be decisive. It will win the war, and the status of the Marine Corps should
never again be in doubt."

Smith left the meeting convinced that MacArthur would never change
his mind about Inchon, and from that moment on, he told his staff to concentrate on plans for the quick seizure of Kimpo Airfield, the crossing of the
Han River, and the capture of Seoul.

If there was unease and confusion at Pusan, in Tokyo, and on board the
Mt. McKinley, the situation in Washington was even more fraught with tension and misgivings as September 15 drew nearer. General Matthew Ridgway, deputy chief of staff of the Army (and the man destined to replace
MacArthur as U.S. commander in the Far East), was on record as describing the Inchon Operation as a "5,000-to-one gamble," and other U.S. senior
officers agreed.

"If you came up with a litany of reasons why an amphibious operation
wouldn't work," said one high-ranking Navy officer, "Inchon would have
them all."

MacArthur countered that the very difficulties of an amphibious assault at Inchon were also the keys to its success. Because of them, he maintained, the North Koreans would never expect an invasion there and hence would be taken totally by surprise. "Inchon will succeed, and it will save 100,000 lives," he assured the Joint Chiefs with utter certainty in late August. "We shall land at Inchon, and I will crush them."

At the moment, no one anywhere could foresee whether the next few days would validate MacArthur's predictions or justify the "cold feet" approach of the JCS.

"Far away at the Pentagon," observed historian Bevin Alexander, "fears about the safety of Eighth Army had been magnified far beyond the reality that General Walker faced. For the Joint Chiefs, the threat that the North Koreans should throw the United Nations out of the [Pusan] perimeter seemed real, and Chairman [Omar] Bradley felt MacArthur's orders to release the Fifth Marines increased the danger."

Colonel Taplett, whose 3/5 would be the first Americans to test the merits of MacArthur's plan under enemy fire, classified the Joint Chiefs' support of the operation as "tepid" at best. "Several senior officers even called MacArthur's plan sheer madness and talked of excessive casualties," Taplett would write many years later. "Word had filtered down to the troops that . . . Bradley . . . considered amphibious operations obsolete in modern warfare."

On September 11, when MacArthur finally got around to replying to the Joint Chiefs' message of September 7, urging him to consider Kunsan as an alternative landing site to Inchon, his argument in favor of the latter was brilliantly phrased, powerfully presented, and utterly convincing. It also exaggerated the positives, minimized the negatives, and was significantly less than totally factual. MacArthur's reply stated,

There is no question in my mind as to the feasibility of the [Inchon] operation, and I regard its chance of success as excellent. I go further and believe that it represents the only hope of wresting the initiative from the enemy. . . . To do otherwise is to commit us to a war of indefinite duration, of gradual attrition, and of doubtful results. . . . There is no slightest possibility of our force being ejected from the Pusan beachhead. The envel-

opment from the north will instantly relieve the pressure on the south pe-
rimeter, and, indeed, is the only way that this can be accomplished. . . . The
seizure of the heart of the enemy distributing system in the Seoul area will
completely dislocate the logistical supply of his forces and . . . ultimately
result in their disintegration. . . . Caught between our northern and south-
ern forces . . . the enemy cannot fail to be ultimately shattered. . . . I and all
of my commanders and staff officers, without exception, are enthusiastic
and confident of the success of the enveloping operation.

Truth was, some Navy and Marine officers continued to have strong reservations about Inchon, even as MacArthur sent his message to the JCS. And the situation on the ground in the Pusan Perimeter wasn't nearly as rosy as MacArthur painted it.

By the time the Marine brigade was pulled off the front lines early on September 6, the back of the enemy offensive in the Naktong Bulge had been permanently broken. Indeed, the threat of an NKPA breakthrough had eased along three-fourths of the perimeter front. But the American defense of Taegu, anchored by the haggard, battle-torn remnants of the First Cavalry Division, who had withstood daily North Korean attacks for two weeks, appeared to be weakening by the hour. On September 5, most of the Eighth Army's irreplaceable headquarters and signal equipment was packed up and shipped south to Pusan, but General Walker—like General William Dean before him at Taejon—refused to leave and vowed to fight in the streets if necessary. Across the city and at the front, a terrible feeling of déjà vu was in the air.

Despite his bulldog tenacity, Walker knew he had to decide whether to order an Eighth Army retreat to the last-ditch defensive perimeter known as the Davidson Line or keep it where it was—and he had to make the decision now, while there was still a chance for an orderly withdrawal.

After meeting with his top officers, Walker went to bed on the evening of September 5 with the retreat order already drawn up and ready. It specified that the move to the Davidson Line would start at five o'clock the following morning. Walker wrestled with the dilemma during most of a fitful, sleepless night, and at some point he decided to keep his army where it was. The nail-biting was far from over, but the withdrawal order was never issued.

As of September 8, the enemy's First and 13th divisions were barely eight air miles from Taegu and still pounding away at the First Cav, whose 105-millimeter guns were so short of ammunition that their use had to be sharply curtailed. MacArthur was well aware of this situation, and he dispatched urgent orders to U.S. ammunition ships to resupply the division with all possible speed. But in the meantime, the shortage forced troops of the Seventh Cavalry Regiment to attack enemy-held high ground without effective artillery support, and they were thrown back with heavy losses.

By September 12, the NK 13th Division had gained control of a peak known as Hill 314, the dominating feature of a mile-long ridge overlooking the entire city of Taegu and commanding the terrain above the Taegu Valley. The hill was held by at least 700 well dug-in enemy troops, and the American unit assigned to attack it, Lieutenant Colonel James Lynch's Third Battalion, Seventh Cavalry, could muster only 535 effectives.

"As tough as it was, it was almost a relief to go on the attack," said Corporal Jack Brooks, one of Lynch's riflemen. "We'd made quite a few 'strategic withdrawals,' and we were getting pretty tired of it."

Again, there weren't enough shells available for advance artillery preparation, but after a U.S. air strike on Hill 314, Lynch massed his two rifle companies—Love and Item—so that maximum small-arms fire could be directed against enemy positions. At eleven o'clock that morning, he ordered an assault on the hill.

Almost immediately, enemy heavy mortars began blasting bloody holes in the ranks of the Americans as they charged up the steep slopes. Most of the two companies' officers and NCOs were cut down, but the rest of the men forged on, many ignoring wounds as they went. As they struggled toward the top, they were rallied by Captain Robert B. Walker of Madison, Wisconsin, commander of Love Company. When Walker reached the crest, he turned, ignoring the bullets whizzing around him, and waved his men forward, shouting,

"Come on up here! You can see them from here! There's lots of them, and you can kill them!"

His men took Walker at his word. Along the crest of the ridge, they met and overpowered the counterattacking North Koreans in vicious, hand-to-hand fighting. After two hours of savage combat in which the men of the Seventh Cavalry had to take Hill 314 three times before they finally held it, Walker reported the hill secure. He was the only living, unwounded officer left in the two companies.

When Hill 314 was captured, Love and Item companies had only about eighty combat-capable men remaining between them. On the hilltop, they found more than 200 enemy dead, all clad in U.S. Army uniforms and armed with American M-1s and carbines. Nearby lay the bound bodies of four GIs who had been shot and bayoneted and one American officer who had been doused with gasoline by the enemy and burned alive.

After that day, September 12, as author and former Army battalion commander T. R. Fehrenbach observed, heavy fighting continued in the perimeter, but the situation before Taegu and elsewhere never seemed quite so desperate again.

"There was no place left to go," Fehrenbach wrote, "and all along the thin perimeter line, American soldiers were stiffening. Hatred for the enemy was beginning to sear them, burning through their earlier indifference. . . .

"A man who has seen and smelled his first corpse on the battlefield soon loses his preconceived notions of what the soldier's trade is all about. He learns how it is in combat, and how it must always be. He becomes a soldier or he dies.

"The men of the First Cavalry, the Second, 24th, and 25th divisions were becoming soldiers. . . . [U]nderneath the misconceptions of their society, the softness and the mawkishness, the human material was hard and good."

When the North Koreans had gone for broke and come up empty, both their confidence and their physical stamina had sunk to new lows. The Americans' suffering, meanwhile, had taught them some hard lessons— and they had just begun to fight.

On September 13, the First Provisional Marine Brigade was officially disbanded, and its commander, General Craig, assumed the position of assistant commander of the First Marine Division. The Fifth Marines, still commanded by Lieutenant Colonel Raymond Murray, again became an integral part of the division as one of its three infantry regiments. The others were the First Marines, commanded by Colonel Lewis "Chesty" Puller and now embarking from Japan for the trip to Inchon, and the Seventh Marines, commanded by Colonel Homer Litzenberg and still en route from the Mediterranean by way of the Suez Canal and the Indian Ocean.

A native Californian who'd grown up in Harlingen, Texas, and graduated from Texas A&M College, where he starred on the college's football and basketball teams, Ray Murray was exceptionally young for a Marine regimental commander—only thirty-seven. But he was also exceptionally experienced on the battlefield. As a World War II battalion commander at Guadalcanal, Tarawa, and Saipan, Murray had been awarded two Silver Stars, a Navy Cross, and a Purple Heart. He was destined to add two more Silver Stars, a second Navy Cross, and the Army's Distinguished Service Cross for his valor and leadership in Korea.

Virginia native Chesty Puller, who'd dropped out of VMI in 1918 to enlist in the Marines, had missed seeing combat in France in World War I but had established himself as a living legend of the Corps during World War II. As a battalion commander at Guadalcanal, he'd won the first of four Navy Cross medals, then started his first stint as commander of the First Marines in February 1944 and continued to lead the regiment through the horrific fighting at Peleliu the following September and October. After filling a variety of other assignments, Puller resumed command of the First Marines in time for the Inchon landing. A fifth Navy Cross awaited him in Korea.

A Pennsylvania Dutchman known to his troops as "Litz the Blitz," Homer Litzenberg was one of few Marine officers to see duty in Europe and North Africa during World War II as a member of a U.S. planning staff. Later, he moved to the Pacific to command the Third Battalion, 24th Marines, in the newly formed Fourth Marine Division and served as regimental executive officer for the assault on Roi-Namur in the Marshall Islands. Before his retirement in 1959 as a lieutenant general, Litzenberg's combat awards would include three Silver Star medals, a Navy Cross, and a Distinguished Service Cross.

Also joining the First Marine Division for the Inchon operation was the 3,000-man First Korean Marine Regiment, commanded by Lieutenant Colonel Kim Sung Eun, with Lieutenant Colonel Charles W. Harrison, who had grown up in Korea as the son of American missionaries, serving as the unit's liaison officer.

On September 13, as the interservice Inchon planning team prepared for a countdown strategy session aboard the command ship *Mt. McKinley*, now lying off the Korean coast with the seven-nation, 260-ship invasion fleet, two of the team's most junior members could scarcely contain their excitement.

"These final meetings were supposed to be only for the top commanders involved," recalled then–Lieutenant Colonel Bryghte Godbold, G-1 personnel officer of the First Marine Division, "but a young Navy officer friend of mine and I thought we'd figured out a way to sit in on it. We'd prepared some charts showing the relative strengths of various Marine units, and we set them up early in the meeting room in hopes that, after we made our presentation, the big brass would let us stay around."

To the delight of Godbold and his friend, their little ruse worked like a charm, and they were allowed to remain in the room for the entire meeting.

"It was one of several times that I was face-to-face with General MacArthur, and I was surprised and pleased that he remembered my name," Godbold said, "but that wasn't the only reason that the meeting was an unforgettable experience."

After an opening statement by MacArthur, spiced with his usual flare for the dramatic, the architect of the Inchon "end run," now designated as Operation Chromite, called on other commanders seated around a large table for their comments and concerns.

"One by one, the men in charge of the Army, Navy, and Air Force segments of the operation stood up to say their piece," Godbold recalled. "The Navy admirals were extremely concerned about a typhoon brewing in the Sea of Japan. 'If it moves west,' they said, 'there's no way we can make a landing on the fifteenth. It could wreck everything.' And even without stormy conditions, they worried about getting ships and small boats through the narrow, tricky channel leading to the invasion beaches. They considered the problem nearly insurmountable.

"Then an Army general got up to complain about not having enough tanks and trucks for the drive on Kimpo Airfield and Seoul. Next, an Air Force general expressed fear that weather conditions might make effective air cover impossible, worried that he didn't have enough planes, and lamented the fact that his squadrons would have to fly out of Japan, rather than from bases in Korea.

"Finally, when all the others had had their say, General Smith, our division commander, stood up. He was a very soft-spoken, scholarly man who looked more like a college professor than a Marine general, and I knew that he had serious concerns about the safety of his men under the existing invasion plan, but he didn't say a word about them. His statement was a single sentence.

"'Gentlemen,' he said quietly, 'the First Marine Division will land at Inchon beginning at 0630 [6:30 AM] on September 15, as ordered.' Then he sat back down again."

In the words of Marine historian Edwin H. Simmons, "Oliver Prince Smith did not fit the traditional Marine Corps' 'warrior' image. He was deeply religious, did not drink, seldom raised his voice in anger, and almost never swore. . . . [B]ut when his mind was made up, he could be as resolute as a rock. He always commanded respect."

The tall, silver-haired, pipe-smoking Smith, who, as far as is known, was never called "Ollie" by any living human being, had been born in the dusty West Texas hamlet of Menard in 1893. A graduate of the University of California at Berkeley, he'd been a Marine officer since a week after the United States declared war on Germany in April 1917. Like General Craig, Smith had never seen combat in World War I, but he'd commanded the Fifth Marines at Cape Gloucester during World War II, then served as assistant commander of the First Marine Division at bloody Peleliu and as deputy chief of staff of the Tenth Army at Okinawa.

"There was no love lost between Smith and Army General Almond, overall commander of X Corps and the Inchon operation," said Godbold.

"Almond went out of his way to be high-handed, condescending, and inconsiderate toward Smith, perhaps because of his desire to shift credit away from the Marines. Smith was always outwardly civil to Almond, although some of us on the division staff wondered how he managed it."

Some observers said the trouble between the two started at their first meeting, in early September 1950, when fifty-eight-year-old Major General Almond persistently addressed fifty-seven-year-old Major General Smith as "son." Almond also went out of his way to exclude Smith and General Lemuel Shepherd, commander of the Fleet Marine Force in the Pacific, from some of the early high-level meetings because of their reservations about Inchon.

From there, the Almond-Smith relationship would deteriorate steadily as time went on. Reportedly, the two generals' mutual disdain peaked when Smith walked out of a lavish party hosted by Almond at Thanksgiving 1950. Smith couldn't hide his disgust at the fact that while Almond's staff feasted and made merry, hundreds of Marines and GIs were suffering frostbite in subzero cold and/or being slaughtered in massive attacks by Red Chinese troops who had secretly entered North Korea from Manchuria.

The Joint Chiefs of Staff and other officials in Washington might have felt far less anxious about Operation Chromite had they known the results of a commando-style reconnaissance mission to Inchon led by Navy Lieutenant Eugene Franklin Clark. Intelligence reports indicated that the vast majority of available enemy troops had been sent southward to join the drive on Pusan. But hard information on the disposition and strength of NKPA forces at Inchon was sketchy at best, and even less was known about the geographical oddities of the harbor.

On August 26, Clark had been summoned to a meeting in Tokyo with Army General Holmes E. Dager and Navy Captain Edward Pearce and offered the uniquely dangerous job of unraveling the myriad riddles of Inchon. With a small team of South Koreans, Clark was asked to slip into the harbor two weeks before the invasion to obtain crucial information on tides, seawalls, the vast expanse of mudflats in the harbor, the tricky "Flying Fish Channel" leading to the beaches, locations of major gun emplacements, and the size of the enemy garrison.

As a member of General MacArthur's geographic staff, Clark had already devoted considerable time and effort to studying Inchon, but no American had ever examined the port's eccentricities at close range. "I already knew that the approach to Inchon was complicated by tides that rose and fell twenty-nine feet in a twenty-four-hour period," Clark would later write, "leaving miles of mudflats, some extending six thousand yards from the shoreline at low water."

Although rough estimates placed total NKPA troop strength in the Inchon area at 4,000 to 5,000 men, it took the work of Clark and his team to verify the actual numbers: about 2,500 mediocre, inexperienced troops were stationed in Inchon proper, with another 500 on Wolmi-do, and several hundred others scattered at points around the harbor. These findings made it obvious that (1) no major assault on Inchon by UN forces was anticipated by the North Koreans, and (2) more than 90 percent of NKPA forces, including all of its best remaining combat units, had been thrown into the offensive in the far south and could not possibly reach Inchon in time to counter an invasion.

On the small island of Yonghung-do in Inchon Harbor, where only a handful of enemy troops were present, Clark and his team recruited dozens of loyal South Koreans who were eager to help with covert reconnaissance missions aimed at pinpointing NKPA bases and fortifications. They did so under the very noses of about 400 enemy troops occupying the adjacent island of Taebu-do, which was within wading distance of Yonghung-do at low tide. At night, Clark dispatched teenage Korean civilians into the harbor in small boats to measure water depths and seawall heights. Remarkably, none of them betrayed either Clark or the invasion plan to the NKPA.

"Lieutenant Clark was a very brave man to undertake this assignment," recalled Eddie Ko, one of the young Koreans who assisted Clark, decades later. "He came to the island as the only American, with only two or three ROK soldiers as guides. He knew his risk of exposure to the enemy was very high, but he carried out his mission faithfully. We all admired him."

(Following the Inchon landings, the patriotic, fifteen-year-old Ko accompanied the Marines inland, serving as an interpreter and errand boy. After the war, his Marine buddies helped him immigrate to the States, where he settled in Florida and still lives there today.)

During the two weeks between September 1 and 14, at constant risk to Clark and his Korean accomplices, more than fifty of whom were killed by the Communists during this period, they would learn—and report—information about the secrets of Inchon that would never have been available otherwise.

Finally, at midnight on September 14, Clark switched on a major navigational beacon on a tiny harbor island to illuminate the treacherous Flying Fish Channel through which the troops of 3/5 would have to navigate in darkness en route to Wolmi-do. As a result of all this, the lives of countless Marines would be spared on D-day, and Clark would be awarded a Silver Star and the Legion of Merit for his "exceptionally meritorious conduct."

By any measure, the hotly argued, often altered landing force plan for Inchon—much of which was necessarily hammered out without benefit of Lieutenant Clark's reports—was heavily laden with risks and imponderables.

For Colonel Taplett's 3/5 to land on Wolmi-do's Green Beach at 6:30 AM on September 15, as the first Americans ashore, the landing force would have to make its approach in total darkness and board its boats no later than 6:00 AM for the trip through winding, mud-lined channels. The Navy eventually decided to move tanks and other heavy equipment aboard much larger, radar-equipped LSDs (landing ships, dock), then transfer their bulky cargo for the landings to LSTs (landing ships, tank), which were in short supply anyway. The first wave of infantry assault troops would travel aboard seven LCVPs (landing craft, vehicles and personnel). Once ashore, 3/5's first objective would be 350-foot-high Radio Hill in the center of the island, which offered a commanding view of the entire harbor. Serious opposition and moderate to heavy casualties were anticipated.

In the twelve hours following its landing on the morning tide over a narrow beach barely fifty yards wide near the northern tip of Wolmi-do, 3/5 was expected to secure Radio Hill, then eliminate any remaining pockets of enemy resistance in an industrial area on the island's east side and caves on the north end. In the meantime, the rest of the invasion force would have to wait aboard the attack transports offshore until 5:30 PM, when the evening tide came in, to begin their landings.

The other two battalions of the Fifth Marines, Colonel Newton's 1/5 and Colonel Roise's 2/5, were assigned to land abreast northeast of Wolmi-do on Red Beach at 5:30 PM, closely followed by the newly formed First ROK Marine Regiment. Simultaneously, three miles to the south, the three battalions of Colonel Chesty Puller's First Marines were to land across Blue Beach. The first U.S. Army combat units—the 17th and 32nd regiments of the Seventh Infantry Division—weren't scheduled to come ashore until September 18, three days after the Marine landings. The Seventh Marines was expected to land at about the same time to take a major role in the drive toward Seoul.

Blue Beach, south of the city, was much wider than Red Beach and much less heavily developed, but both were overlooked by points of high ground a few hundred yards inland, and both were mostly fronted by sixteen-foot seawalls. The "downtown" area facing Red Beach was by far the more heavily populated of the two landing sites.

"Two things scared me to death," said Colonel Roise after reviewing the landing plan. "One, we weren't landing on a beach; we were landing against a seawall. Each LCVP had two ladders, which would be used to climb up and over the wall. This was risky. . . . Two, [the time of] the landing . . . would give us only about two hours of daylight to clear the city and set up for the night."

Roise was far from alone in his fears. "Everyone was very apprehensive about this landing," said Captain Ike Fenton, commanding B/1/5. "It really looked dangerous, and the lack of security while down south had us worried. Everyone in Pusan knew the Marines were going on some kind of amphibious landing, and we were afraid the North Koreans had a pretty good idea that we were coming up their way. There was a finger pier and a causeway extending out from Red Beach that reminded us of Tarawa [one of the bloodiest Pacific landings of World War II], and if machine guns were on that pier and causeway, we were going to have a tough time making that last 200 yards to the beach. We also wondered what we'd do if we were met by 200,000 hostile civilians when we landed."

• • •

Worried as he was, Fenton had a fierce desire to lead his B Company ashore at Inchon and take it on the offensive against the NKPA. It was a desire that came within a hairbreadth of going unfulfilled because of a photograph that appeared on the cover of *Life* magazine about two weeks before D-day.

Life photographer Dave Duncan, who had spent many hours with Fenton during the two Battles of the Naktong, had developed a close friendship with the young officer. During the height of the fighting, Duncan had shot a picture of a haggard, unshaven Fenton that seemed to capture the mixture of exhaustion, fortitude, and grim determination that characterized the Marines he led. Back in the States, Duncan's editors agreed, and they gave the photo the most prominent possible display.

"Until Ike's parents saw that picture, they had no idea that he was leading a rifle company in front-line combat," recalled Fenton's friend and trusted platoon leader Lieutenant Nick Schryver. "As their only surviving son, after Ike's brother was killed in action at Okinawa, Ike wasn't supposed to be placed in direct danger, but, of course, he wanted to be exactly where he was."

Fenton's father, Marine Brigadier General Francis I. Fenton Sr., was understandably upset, and he lost no time in applying pressure through official channels to have his son removed from harm's way and sent back to the States. The resulting order reached Marine brigade commander General Craig just as the Fifth Marines was preparing to embark for Inchon.

"You've served with courage and distinction, Ike," Craig told him when Fenton reported to brigade headquarters. "You've done a fine job, and I appreciate it, but now it's time to let someone else take over."

"Please don't make me leave, General," Fenton pleaded. "I've got to be in on this next operation. I owe it to my men."

Craig frowned and shook his head. "I know how you feel, son," he said, "but I've got direct orders from the commandant of the Marine Corps to detach you and get you Stateside. I can't very well disobey those orders."

"Just give me another week or two, sir. I beg of you. I promise I'll be careful, but I want to be with Baker Company when we get to Seoul. I want it more than anything in the world."

Craig and Fenton stared at one another for a long, uncomfortable moment. Then the general sighed. "Okay, just this one last operation, and that's it," he said, his misgivings obvious in his voice. "Then you're going home, Captain, and there'll be no further argument. Understood?"

"Yes, sir. Thank you, sir. You won't regret this."

I hope neither of us regrets it, Craig thought. *I'll keep my fingers crossed that we don't. I wouldn't want to face the wrath of the commandant and your father, too!*

Craig knew that for the amphibious phase of the operation, at least, Fenton's B Company would be in battalion reserve, with A and C companies sharing the initial thrust onto Red Beach One. A Company would land first on the left side of the target area, and C Company would land moments later on the right side. Then B Company would follow in the comparative safety of A Company's tracks. The landings were being staggered that way only because the beach was too narrow to accommodate all three companies at once.

Going ashore, the odds would likely be in Fenton's favor, Craig conceded. But about 200 yards inland, the town itself began, and just beyond that point, the maps showed the first major terrain feature in the path of the advance: a sheer cliff called Cemetery Hill. Craig didn't like the name, or the visions it conjured up in his mind.

This, he knew, was the kind of place where things could get ugly in a hurry—for Ike Fenton and every other man on that beach.

CHAPTER 12

★ ★ ★

TURNING THE TIDE AT INCHON

I T WAS 3:00 AM on September 15, 1950, and the sky was pitch-black when First Lieutenant Robert "Dewey" Bohn heard the engines stop aboard his ship, the U.S. fast destroyer-transport *Diachenko*. Moments later, the lights flashed on in the troop compartment where Bohn's G Company, Third Battalion, Fifth Marines, was bedded down, and reveille squalled over the PA system.

"On your feet, you guys!" platoon sergeants shouted. "Time to saddle up for a beach party!"

The yelling was hardly necessary. Most of the men were already wide awake, their nerves raw from a short night of waiting that had seemed to last for days. They knew that in just over three hours, the Marines of G and H companies, followed within a minute or two by those of I Company, would be the first American troops to land on the smoldering island of Wolmi-do to launch the Inchon invasion.

"Hey, Sarge, we gonna get steak and eggs for breakfast?" inquired a PFC, referring to the traditional "warrior's meal" before an amphibious assault.

"Ask the Navy," the sergeant replied, "but don't count on it."

The sergeant's skepticism was well justified. Instead of the robust fare consumed by the World War II Marines who invaded such hellholes as Peleliu and Okinawa, the men of 3/5 were served an uninspiring breakfast of powdered scrambled eggs, dry toast, and canned apricots.

Meanwhile, on the dark seas beyond the chow lines, captains and navigators of the nineteen ships carrying the assault forces pushed back from their radar scopes after guiding their vessels through twisting, treacherous Flying Fish Channel.

"It was like threading a needle blindfolded," recalled Seaman First Class Jim Holdman of Roswell, New Mexico, who would guide his ship into and out of Inchon Harbor many times during a long tour of duty as coxswain of the Navy attack transport *AKA 104*. "One false move and you'd be stuck in the middle of miles of mudflats."

On D-day morning, frequent rain squalls had added to an uncertain, nail-biting atmosphere for the ships' crews, but now that the channel was cleared, they could relax a bit. Not so for the Marines. Shortly after they finished eating, a final Navy bombardment of Wolmi-do got under way. The island had already been pounded, unmercifully and almost continuously, for forty-eight hours, but that morning's pyrotechnics were the capper. The big guns of the U.S. cruisers *Toledo* and *Rochester* and the British cruisers *Kenya* and *Jamaica* seemed to shake the entire Yellow Sea.

The barrage was quickly joined by seven destroyers of Advance Attack Group 90.1, commanded by Navy Captain Norman W. Sears. As a crowning touch, three LSMRs, medium landing ships converted to rocket launchers, unleashed thousands of five-inch missiles. After working over the Wolmi-do beach one more time, one rocket ship veered south to plaster the crest and slopes of Radio Hill with salvo after salvo. In the words of a Marine historian, "The whole island seemed to explode under the impact."

At 5:45 AM, the cruisers turned their eight-inch guns on Inchon proper, giving targets within the city a vicious shellacking. By this time, the blistered, blackened seaward side of Radio Hill, 3/5's first major objective on Wolmi-do, was almost obscured by huge clouds of smoke raised by naval artillery and bombs from Marine and Navy planes. Corsair squadrons from the escort carriers *Sicily* and *Badoeng Strait*, which had provided air support for the Marines since early August in the Pusan Perimeter, were now augmented by swarms of attack aircraft from three of the Navy's "big boys"—the carriers *Boxer*, *Philippine Sea*, and *Valley Forge*.

"The skies were so full of our planes," said one observer, "that it was hard to see how they could find room for even one more."

At 5:50 AM, responding to Captain Sears's order to "Land the landing force," Colonel Robert "Tap" Taplett's three 3/5 infantry companies started to board seventeen LCVPs, and nine M-26 Pershing tanks began offloading from an LSD onto three smaller LSUs (landing ships, utility).

Once loaded, the landing craft moved in tight circles until about 6:15 AM, when they straightened into lines and started the 2,000-yard trip to Wolmi-do's Green Beach. As the boats plowed toward shore, the Corsairs swooped low and zoomed ahead of them, peppering the beach with rockets and machine-gun fire.

A mile away, aboard the command ship *Mt. McKinley*, the flag bridge was jammed with intently staring Army, Navy, and Marine Corps brass as the ship's loudspeaker blared, "Landing force crossing line of departure."

At that instant, General MacArthur strode outside into the damp morning, calmly raised his binoculars, and prepared to watch what he expected to be the crowning achievement of his military career.

As his own landing craft followed in the wake of the first wave of boats, Colonel Taplett was worried. The thirty-two-year-old battalion commander from South Dakota had been warned by division headquarters to expect stiff resistance and potentially heavy losses on Wolmi-do.

"Regardless of what happens," Taplett had been told, less than reassuringly, "your men will be totally on their own until the tide returns. No attempt can be made to reinforce you unless your casualties go above 80 percent."

Taplett had kept this grim information to himself, but it gnawed relentlessly at his mind as Green Beach rushed toward him.

"The heavy naval beach bombardment ended just at the moment the landing craft carrying George and How companies plowed through the surf

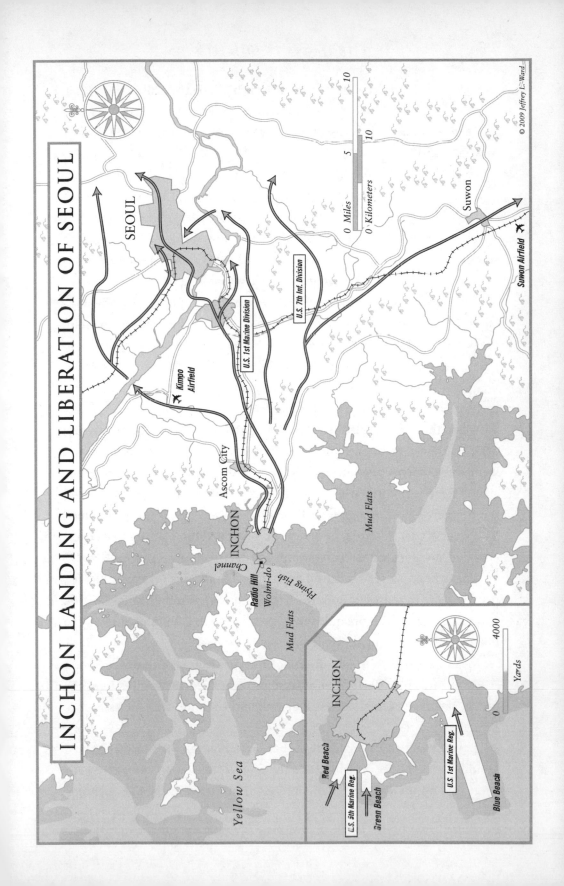

INCHON LANDING AND LIBERATION OF SEOUL

SEOUL

Kimpo Airfield

Ascom City

U.S. 1st Marine Division

U.S. 7th Inf. Division

INCHON

Radio Hill

Wolmi-do

Flying Fish Channel

Mud Flats

Mud Flats

Yellow Sea

Suwon

Suwon Airfield

0 Miles   5   10
0 Kilometers   5   10

© 2009 Jeffrey L. Ward

INCHON

Red Beach

Green Beach

Blue Beach

U.S. 5th Marine Reg.

U.S. 1st Marine Reg.

Yards
0   4000

and scraped their way onto the sandy beach," Taplett recalled more than half a century later. "For a moment, an eerie silence greeted the Marines just before the assault boats dropped their ramps and the naval gunfire moved inland."

To PFC Fred Davidson, a veteran rifleman in G Company, the silence was almost more unnerving than the constant roar of explosions, but it didn't last long. "It got quiet as hell," Davidson remembered. "The only sounds were the LCVPs' engines and the slapping sound of the surf. Then several flights of Corsairs roared in . . . only thirty feet over our heads, strafing the beach and their hot, empty shell casings falling on us."

As it turned out, the nearest thing to an injury during G Company's landing occurred an instant after Lieutenant Bohn yelled, "Okay, men, hit the beach!" and jumped from the ramp of his LCVP. Bohn promptly disappeared into a deep, submerged shell hole caused by the Navy bombardment, but he surfaced again a few seconds later and suffered nothing worse than wounded pride and a lost field pack.

When the first wave landed at 6:33 AM, followed by the second wave at 6:35, the Marines found themselves confronted by utter devastation and virtually no enemy resistance. Only a few scattered shots were fired at the assault force as it stormed ashore and punched inland. The main obstacle to the invaders—besides submerged shell holes—was the wreckage of small Korean craft that cluttered the beach and restricted the Marines to an overcrowded landing area barely fifty yards wide.

After a brief pause to shake off the salt water and wipe his eyes, Bohn led his company to the right, toward the northern approaches to Radio Hill, while H Company, commanded by Captain Patrick J. Wildman, swung to the left in an encircling movement.

Meanwhile, at 6:46 AM, the M-26s of Second Lieutenant Granville Sweet's A Company, First Marine Tank Battalion, squeezed themselves onto the beach, then rumbled a short distance inland to await calls for assistance from the infantry.

Taplett watched through a thick haze of smoke as the Marines moved rapidly up the slopes of Radio Hill. The few North Korean troops they encountered on the way were more interested in surrendering than fighting, and by 6:55 AM—twenty-two minutes after the first wave reached shore—Sergeant Alvin E. Smith, guide of Bohn's Third Platoon, clambered up a shell-torn tree on the crest of the hill with an American flag clutched in his fist. Seconds later, the Stars and Stripes fluttered from the tree trunk.

"It was no Iwo Jima flag-raising," said Taplett, "but it served its purpose."

On the flag bridge of the *Mt. McKinley*, General MacArthur smiled, lowered his binoculars, and stood up from his swivel chair. "That's it," he said. "Let's get a cup of coffee."

While MacArthur savored his coffee and the early triumph of 3/5, the Marines on Wolmi-do still had plenty of dirty, dangerous business to attend to. Ironically, it was Item Company, the battalion's reserve unit, which didn't land until Radio Hill was secure, that ran afoul of what Marine historians called "the angriest hornet's nest" on the island.

Led by Captain Robert A. McMullen, I Company was following a detachment from H Company through an area on the northern tip of Wolmi-do that had supposedly been cleared of NKPA troops, when it was surprised by a flurry of hand grenades. After scattering for cover, the Marines determined that the grenades were coming from a platoon-strength enemy force in a string of bypassed holes dug into a low cliff at the shoreline.

One large cave in particular seemed to be the major source of the trouble, and McMullen called up one of Lieutenant Sweet's M-26s to deal with it. After one blast from the tank's 90-millimeter cannon, about thirty dazed enemy troops staggered through the smoke to surrender. Another group of diehard North Korean holdouts was sealed in a second cave by a Sherman tank equipped with a bulldozer blade. After the Marines cleared the shambles of an industrial area facing Inchon on the east side of Wolmi-do and occupied the west side of Radio Hill, the fight for the island was basically over except for some mopping up.

"Captured forty-five prisoners," radioed Taplett to the *Mt. McKinley* at 7:45 AM. "Meeting light resistance."

Taplett credited the preinvasion shelling and air attacks for the relative ease with which Wolmi-do was seized. "The damage the island defenders sustained had cured their desire to fight," he said, "although they were well armed and had a well-planned defense system protecting Radio Hill." Apparently the heavy weapons emplacements facing Green Beach were never manned by the defenders. Neither was a seacoast battery facing the island from Inchon proper.

At 8:30 AM, less than three hours after the first Marines set foot on Wolmi-do, Taplett sent another terse message to the *Mt. McKinley*:

"Mission completed. Wolmi-do secured. Casualties 17 WIA, none dead."

Enemy losses, by Taplett's informal tally, included 118 dead counted by the Marines, 136 prisoners herded into an empty swimming pool at an abandoned resort, and an estimated 150 to 200 other North Koreans sealed into caves and revetments.

When news of 3/5's success blared over the loudspeakers of the venerable troopship *Henrico* ("Happy Hank"), the Marines aboard yelled their appreciation. "A cheer erupted that probably could've been heard in Inchon," recalled Corpsman Herb Pearce. "We'd been holding our breath and waiting for word about casualties, and now we all knew that our mission was doable."

Moments after General MacArthur received Taplett's report, he scribbled a congratulatory message of his own to Vice Admiral Arthur D. Struble, commander of the U.S. Seventh Fleet and boss of the Navy's Inchon amphibious force, aboard the cruiser *Rochester*.

"Never," the general wrote, "have the Navy and Marines shone more brightly than this morning."

The operation was off to an auspicious start, but Wolmi-do represented only the first small piece of the puzzle. Inchon itself was believed to be much more heavily defended, and many of the men scheduled to land on the Red and Blue beaches late on the afternoon of September 15 were more in the mood for prayer than celebration.

"When they announced that Protestant and Catholic services would be held on the fantail, I thought the ship might sink at the rear as the Marines rushed that way to make their peace with God," recalled Herb Pearce.

Since there were no chaplains aboard the LST carrying Blue Beach–bound H Company, Third Battalion, First Marines, Captain Clarence E.

Corley, the company CO, found himself pressed into an unfamiliar role as a stand-in.

"The men are requesting a devotional service, skipper," said Corley's orderly, First Sergeant Elwood Cabe, a World War II veteran of Tarawa and a steadying influence on the company's younger Marines.

"Sounds like a fine idea to me," Corley said, "but who's going to do it?"

"Uh, I guess you are, sir," Cabe replied.

A short time later, armed only with a pocket-size New Testament that he routinely carried in his dungarees, Corley faced an anxious crowd of some 400 Marines gathered on the bow of the ship. After asking the men to remain standing and lower their heads, the captain read a prayer from the book. Then he told them to have a seat on the deck and added uncomfortably,

"If you're a Protestant like me, I hope you'll accept my prayer, and if you're a Catholic, I also hope you'll find it acceptable. Now, for you Jewish fellows out there—and I know there are several—I guess you're pretty much on your own because I don't have a clue about how to pray for you."

The crowd laughed, and everyone seemed to relax a little as Corley finished up the service with a brief pep talk.

"Thanks, skipper," Sergeant Cabe told him later. "You did a heckuva fine job, and the men appreciated it."

At noon on September 15, the troops of 1/5 and 2/5 were fed a hearty lunch aboard the *Henrico* and the attack transport *Cavalier*, then given a single K ration apiece to carry ashore.

"Don't lose it," they were advised, "or you may get awful damn hungry. We can't be sure when we'll get resupplied with food and ammo."

Corpsman Herb Pearce helped fold up the cots on which the Marines had been sleeping and clear spaces for them to be used to accommodate an expected flood of casualties when the landing craft returned from the beach. Four Navy surgical teams, each composed of three doctors and ten corpsmen, would follow close behind the assault troops to provide medical treatment on the beach, but the seriously wounded would be evacuated to the ship as soon as possible.

At about 3:30 PM, the Marines stowed their watches, wallets, cigarettes, and other valuables in small plastic bags for protection and gave their gear a final check. Then they began congregating near the cargo nets hanging over the side of the "Happy Hank" and staring down at the landing craft bouncing in a choppy sea below. In the distance, explosions from naval ordnance and aerial bombing runs dotted the shoreline, and black smoke boiled up from target areas along the Inchon waterfront as the men began scrambling down the nets. The sky was studded with dark storm clouds, and occasional downpours of rain lashed the surrounding area.

"As you climb down that net into the LCVP, you're scared," recalled PFC Doug Koch, a rifleman in D/2/5. "What keeps you going is knowing this is what you have to do." The fact that some of the nets were liberally coated with dried vomit deposited there by seasick Marines during the ocean voyage didn't make the descent any more palatable.

In their landing craft, the assault troops found two different types of scaling ladders—two to each boat and measuring about eight feet long each—intended to help the Marines get over the high seawall on Red Beach. One type, produced by a factory in Japan, was of lightweight aluminum with a large hook at the top end to help keep it properly positioned. But there were only a few of these because the factory had been damaged by a typhoon that had struck Japan a short time earlier. The second, more prevalent type of ladder was a makeshift wooden version hastily hammered together by Navy carpenters aboard ship. These also had a metal ring at the top, but the Marines would soon find that the ring wasn't large enough to hook onto the seawall.

"A few boats in each wave would be able to locate holes in the seawall and not have to bother with the ladders," said Captain Ike Fenton, commanding B/1/5. "But using the scaling ladders meant that only two men could get out of the boats at a time, then climb up onto the wall. Equipment had to be lifted by lashing and lowering lines."

The men, none of whom had any previous experience scaling seawalls under fire, eyed the wooden ladders grimly, and many swore under their breath—especially the men of Able Company, who had the dubious honor of making up the first wave to reach Red Beach.

Captain Blackjack Stevens, A Company's commander, was worried not only about the ladders and the seawall but also about a network of enemy trenches and bunkers that showed up in aerial photographs only fifteen to twenty yards inland from the wall.

"We knew that air, artillery, and rockets were going to work that area over for two days before we went in there," said Stevens, who'd faced similar beach fortifications in the Pacific during World War II, "but we had to wonder how effective they'd be in clearing out those bunkers."

Since the primary goal of any amphibious operation was to get off the beach as quickly as possible, many of Stevens's men echoed his concerns. "From the looks of those ladders," said Sergeant Mackie Wheeler, "we figured this could turn out to be the slowest invasion on record!"

By 4:30 PM, all the landing craft were loaded and trailing along in the wake of the high-speed destroyer-transport *Horace A. Bass*, the Red Beach control vessel, "like a brood of ducklings," in the words of a Marine historian.

The assault troops watched in awe as the supporting rocket ships delivered a final outburst of 6,500 five-inch missiles. The *Bass* joined in with an ear-splitting salvo from her own five-inch guns, then dipped her signal flag, and the first wave of eight LCVPs crossed the line of departure and wallowed toward Red Beach, 2,200 yards away.

For some, it was a long, harrowing trip. "Our LST was a newer one brought in from Hawaii, and it was all gussied up, but it took a pretty hard beating that day," recalled Major Richard Elliott, a Guadalcanal veteran from Vernon, Texas, and executive officer of the First Engineer Battalion. "When we were still pretty far out, we started catching large-caliber machine-gun fire that tore holes in several barrels of diesel fuel and splashed the stuff all over us. None of my men were hit, but two sailors in our bow gun tubs were killed."

The skipper of Elliott's LST was under orders to lower his exit ramp halfway and ram the seawall hard enough to hold the craft onshore against the soon-to-recede tide while it disgorged its heavy equipment. "He stood there with tears in his eyes," Elliott recalled, "knowing his ship was going to be wrecked."

As the first wave reached the halfway point, two squadrons of Marine Corsairs streaked in low to strafe the beach, but the planes used up their ammo and departed too soon to please Captain Stevens, whose landing craft also was under fire.

Stevens immediately radioed air control for help. "We need further strikes on Beach Red," he said. "The more the better, but they'll have to be quick."

"You got it," said air control.

Moments later, four Navy A4D Skyraiders appeared and gave the beach another pounding. By the time they pulled up and wheeled away, A Company's first wave was barely thirty yards off the seawall and closing. Above them and to the left loomed Cemetery Hill, the company's first major objective. To the immediate front, an intact NKPA pillbox spouted machine-gun fire.

Stevens glanced behind him and saw one of his four landing craft—the one carrying half of his First Platoon—floundering in the surf with engine trouble. The other three LCVPs were about to bump the seawall, which, even at high tide, jutted four feet above the water.

Stevens's watch said 5:33 PM.

"Man those ladders!" he screamed.

A few miles to the south, the amphibian tractors carrying Colonel Chesty Puller's First Marines also had begun their ponderous journey toward Blue Beach. Owned and operated by the Army, the amtracks were as slow as turtles—top speed barely four knots—but it was presumed that they could crawl through the numerous breaks left in the seawall by U.S. shells and bombs and spare most of the troops from using scaling ladders.

To reach Blue Beach, the amtracks carrying assault troops of the First Marines had to cover 5,500 yards, more than twice the distance to be traveled by the LCVPs carrying 1/5 and 2/5 to Red Beach, and the trip would take three-quarters of an hour. During that time, the Marines crouching behind the amtracks' gunwales would be sitting ducks for enemy artillery or mortar rounds. A mixture of low clouds, drizzle, and smoke from the bombardment cut visibility to about 200 yards, so there was no way that enemy shore gunners could see the amtracks until they were practically on the beach—but that didn't keep them from firing.

"Jeez, this is just like a John Wayne movie," exclaimed PFC Jack Dedrick of H/3/1's Second Rifle Platoon, who was about to experience his first taste of combat, "but what's causing those little blips in the water?"

"Hell, they're shooting at you, you shit bird!" responded a veteran sergeant. "Keep your damn head down!"

Dedrick didn't have to be told twice. The warning jerked him back to reality, and his Hollywood fantasies evaporated.

To more seasoned hands, however, such as Sergeant Bill Finnegan, who had landed on Guadalcanal in August 1942, then on Cape Gloucester and bloody Peleliu, the Inchon landing was a piece of cake compared to what he'd encountered in the Pacific.

"We could hear small-arms rounds banging off our amtrack," recalled Finnegan, a Chicago-born machine-gun squad leader attached to Item Company, Third Battalion, First Marines, "but we found a hole in the seawall and rode a half-mile inland before we had to stop. Even then, the firing was light, and we only had a couple of casualties."

Finnegan saw nothing resembling the notorious slaughter he'd witnessed at the Tenuru River on Guadalcanal, scene of one of the largest banzai charges of World War II, in which he and other Marines slaughtered more than 1,000 Japanese in minutes.

"My first impression was that the gooks weren't nearly as fanatic as the Japs," Finnegan recalled, "but later on, they turned out to be pretty tough, after all."

Corporal Murdoch Ford peered at the indistinct Inchon skyline behind the narrow strip of Red Beach dead ahead. Ford was pumped with excitement but not nearly as nervous as he'd expected to be at this moment. He was in the driver's seat of an M-26 Pershing tank, and in two or three minutes he'd be guiding the forty-eight-ton steel monster ashore.

Ford and most of the other Marine tankers had trained at Camp Pendleton in M-4A3 Sherman tanks, only to find themselves suddenly equipped with the new M-26s, which were better than the Shermans in most respects but disturbingly unfamiliar. What little orientation they'd had to the new tanks had been shipboard instruction as they crossed the Pacific.

Ford didn't give it much thought at the time, but it would later dawn on him that he was probably the youngest tank driver in the First Marine Division—and quite possibly the youngest Marine in the entire Inchon invasion force. He was three months out of boot camp, and he'd just turned sixteen years old.

Had the Marine Corps known the truth about Ford's age, he'd still be back in the States, or possibly in Japan, but he definitely wouldn't be aboard an LST a few score yards from Red Beach. After an uproar was raised by concerned American parents, strict orders had been issued that no Marine under eighteen would be sent into combat in Korea. Somehow Ford had managed to slip around that rule.

"I looked older than I was," he explained, "maybe because I was the oldest of five kids raised by a single mom. In a situation like that, you grow up pretty fast. Everybody thought I was eighteen or nineteen, and I wasn't about to tell them any different."

Now the youngster from Bayonne, New Jersey, and his crewmates in the M-26—part of a free-ranging platoon of five tanks attached to the First Marine Tank Battalion—were going to be among the first American armor to hit Red Beach. The unit was an independent outfit whose primary job was to find, and destroy, enemy tanks rather than provide infantry support, and Ford and his mates knew they had to move fast and with little margin for error. Red Beach was narrow—only about 600 yards wide—and it would be heavily congested and chaotic. To make room for succeeding waves of Marines pouring in behind them, the tankers would have to get off the beach in a hurry and move several hundred yards inland.

"I had no idea what to expect," Ford said many years later, "but the adrenaline really flows when you're a kid like I was. I had lots of faith in my tank commander, Sergeant Joe Harris. He was in his thirties, and he'd seen it all in World War II, so that gave me confidence."

Ford glanced over at his gunner, Sergeant Wilfred "Woofie" Weaver, crouched behind the tank's 90-millimeter cannon, and the loader at his side, PFC Albert Metayer. Corporal Frank Gentile, the assistant gunner, was manning the .50-caliber machine gun. Their expressions told Ford that they were as tense as he was.

"I wasn't even old enough to drive a car legally when I joined the Marine Corps," Ford recalled, "but they decided I was a natural as a tank driver because I was so small. I was only five-foot-seven and weighed about 125 pounds."

Except for one small section at the north end of Red Beach, where a narrow open area allowed Marine tanks, trucks, and other heavy equipment to offload from their LSTs directly onto mud and sand as the tide fell, the rest was fronted by sixteen-foot stone seawalls. Although the walls had been gapped in numerous spots by bombs and shellfire, most of the infantrymen would have to scale them with ladders.

"I'd always been proud to be a tanker," Ford recalled, "but that day, I was especially glad I wasn't in the infantry. We knew the best those Russian-built T-34s could do was put some dents in us. I had the feeling we'd be okay."

Some 150 yards to the left of where Ford's tank rumbled down the ramp of its LST and onto Red Beach, A Company infantrymen were taking heavy fire from an enemy bunker facing them and another on their left flank. As Sergeant Charles D. Allen led his half of the First Platoon over the wall, several Marines fell, and the rest were quickly pinned down and unable to advance.

Coming in hard on the heels of Allen and his men was the second wave—the other half of the First Platoon, led by Tech Sergeant Orval F. McMullen, whose boat had developed engine trouble, and the Third Platoon, led by First Lieutenant Baldomero Lopez. At the seawall was a logjam of too many Marines crowded into too small a space, all under murderous fire and with no place to go. The crest of high tide lasted only about fifteen minutes. After that, the water would start to recede, and everything would get more difficult.

"Up and over!" yelled Lopez. "You gotta get up and over!"

"But the damn ladder won't fit!" someone yelled back above the whine of enemy tracers.

"Give it here," the young lieutenant said, "and follow me!"

Handsome, dark-haired "Lobo" Lopez was assumed by most of his men to be of Mexican descent, but he was actually the American-born son of an immigrant from the Asturias region of Spain who had settled in Tampa, Florida, in the 1920s. Lopez had joined the Navy in 1943 at age seventeen, and the following year he'd won an appointment to the Naval Academy, where he graduated in 1948.

Grabbing the ladder himself, Lopez jammed it against the wall and scrambled over the top. "Come on!" he shouted over his shoulder as he charged the nearest enemy bunker alone, clutching a hand grenade, then hurling it with deadly accuracy and silencing the bunker.

Lopez whirled toward the other bunker, pulling the pin from a second grenade as he stumbled forward. But just as he lifted his arm to throw the grenade, he was hit in the chest and right shoulder by a burst of automatic weapons fire.

As he fell backward, Lopez lost his grip on the live grenade, and it bounced away. Although bleeding profusely from his wounds, the stricken officer dragged himself toward the missile, trying desperately to retrieve and throw it. But when he was unable to grip the grenade in his bloody hand, he pulled it toward him in a sweeping motion and fell on top of it a split second before it exploded, smothering the blast with his body.

Lopez died instantly, but his protective act of self-sacrifice undoubtedly spared at least a dozen closely packed Marines nearby from death or serious injury. Two other Marines also were fatally wounded when they tried to attack the same bunker with flamethrowers, but it was finally silenced by a volley of grenades.

"I think I was the first BAR man to get off a ladder and onto the beach, and I was only about thirty yards from Lopez when he was hit," said PFC Ray Walker, who'd been shifted from A/1/5's 60-millimeter mortar section to Lopez's Third Platoon a few days before the landing.

"I was just to the right of the bunker that was causing all the trouble, and I didn't know what the hell to do," Walker recalled. "Then I heard a sergeant yell, 'Get off your dead asses and move!' So I did. It was a maelstrom of confusion, and I didn't know until later that we'd lost a fine officer and a great guy that everybody liked."

• • •

Meanwhile, the boat carrying Second Lieutenant Francis W. Muetzel and part of his Second Platoon managed to find a breach in the seawall, although it was directly under the muzzle of a machine gun in an enemy pillbox. Miraculously, the gun failed to fire as Muetzel and his men scrambled onto the beach and jumped into a deep ditch. From there, they pelted the silent pillbox with grenades until six blood-spattered North Koreans staggered out and surrendered. After leaving the prisoners under guard, the platoon advanced without further problems toward the Asahi Brewery, one of the major landmarks en route to Cemetery Hill.

On the left side of A Company's zone, however, the situation was at crisis stage when Captain Stevens reached shore at H plus five minutes. When Stevens learned that Lieutenant Lopez was dead and was unable to reach Sergeant McMullen by radio, he turned to his executive officer, First Lieutenant Fred Eubanks Jr.

"Take over on the left side and get the men organized and moving," Stevens said. "We've got to get off this beach fast. Otherwise we'll have hundreds of men falling over each other right here in the shadow of that cliff." He pointed upward toward the imposing bulk of Cemetery Hill.

After Eubanks left, Stevens contacted Muetzel on the radio. "What's your position, Frank?" he asked.

"We just got to the brewery," Muetzel said. "We took some prisoners on the beach. Otherwise we haven't seen even one gook so far."

"Well, we've got plenty of 'em down here," Stevens said. "I need you to bring your platoon back to the beach and help us clear this area."

Quickly forming his men in column, Muetzel struck out for the waterfront to help Stevens. But en route, he noticed that the southern slope of Cemetery Hill offered an excellent route of approach to the top. Muetzel's thoughts flashed back to an earlier remark by Stevens that seemed to justify a change in plans.

"*If Cemetery Hill should prove too tough for the First Platoon alone,*" Stevens had said, "*your guys should do everything they can to seize that high ground. It's the key to the whole beachhead.*"

In what a Marine historian termed "a creditable display of judgment and initiative," Muetzel decided to launch an assault on Cemetery Hill before returning to the beach. His Marines pushed rapidly up the southern slope, encountering almost no resistance and flushing out a dozen NKPA soldiers who meekly surrendered. At the summit, members of an enemy mortar company, perfectly positioned to wreak havoc on the Marines but dazed and demoralized by hours of pounding by U.S. ships and planes, threw down their weapons and filed quietly out of their emplacements with hands held high.

In less than ten minutes—and still without a single casualty—Muetzel's platoon had captured Cemetery Hill.

Back on the beach, Corpsman Herb Pearce had managed to locate a rent in the seawall and was able to get ashore without even getting his feet wet. But he and dozens of others were halted by relentless enemy fire and forced to hit the deck and hunker down.

While Pearce was lying there, he looked to his right and saw Marguerite "Maggie" Higgins, famed war correspondent for the *New York Herald Tribune*, hugging the sand beside him no more than a dozen feet away.

Lady, you must be crazy! he thought. *I've GOT to be here, but you don't!*

Soon, however, the First and Third platoons, led by Lieutenant Eubanks, were able to break the enemy grip on the area just beyond the seawall by outlasting NK defenders in a grenade duel. Then the Marines stormed out of the pocket where they were pinned down, driving inland to the edge of the city and hooking up with Muetzel's men.

"The gooks were throwing little percussion grenades that sounded like firecrackers compared to what we had," said Sergeant Mackie Wheeler. "Their stuff was really no match for ours."

At 5:55 PM, less than half an hour after A Company's landing, Stevens signaled the commanders offshore that Cemetery Hill and the north end of Red Beach were secure.

The firefight at the water's edge had cost the Marines eight killed and twenty-eight wounded. For his "exceptional courage, fortitude, and devotion to duty," Lieutenant Lopez would be posthumously awarded the Korean War's first Medal of Honor.

● ● ●

Despite A Company's early successes on Cemetery Hill, the larger strip of high ground designated as Observatory Hill remained a significant problem. The ridge, towering more than 200 feet above the Inchon waterfront and about 500 yards inland from Cemetery Hill, was still very much in enemy hands. It bristled with NKPA machine-gun and mortar emplacements, posing a serious threat to eight equipment-laden LSTs that crossed the line of departure at 6:30 PM and headed for shore.

C Company of 1/5 had been assigned to take the northern (left) half of Observatory Hill as "Objective A," and D Company of 2/5 was supposed to seize the southern (right) half as "Objective B," but when these troops arrived at the seawall in the third and fourth waves, logistical problems and mass confusion ashore played havoc with the plan. Both companies landed in the wrong area, and C's commander, Captain Paul Pedersen, was delayed for twelve minutes when the commander of his boat paused to tow a stalled LCVP.

From the congestion on the beachhead, the skippers of the LSTs concluded that the Marines were bottled up and unable to advance, and they alerted their gun crews for action. When *LST 859*, leading the pack, began taking enemy mortar and machine-gun fire, it promptly replied with its 20-millimeter and 40-millimeter cannons. The next two LSTs in the column, *975* and *857*, followed suit, unaware that they were targeting areas already occupied by the Marines—and doing far more harm than good. On the plus side, a chance round from one LST knocked out a Communist machine gun on Observatory Hill that had opened fire on Lieutenant Muetzel's platoon on the crest of Cemetery Hill. But this was only after fire from the landing ships had forced Muetzel's men to pull back from the hilltop and expose their position to the enemy gunner.

The most damaging "friendly fire" occurred when the LSTs showered Red Beach with shells just as the Weapons and Headquarters/Service companies of Colonel Harold Roise's 2/5 came ashore and started inland. One Marine was killed and twenty-three others wounded. Only the thick walls of the Nippon Flour Company, a major industrial building where Roise's men took cover, prevented worse casualties.

At about 7:00 PM, when the LSTs reached their berths at the north end of the beach, made contact with the infantry, and learned of their costly mistake, their guns finally fell silent.

At about dusk, although much of C Company was still stuck on the beach, Second Lieutenant Byron Magness's Second Platoon, reinforced by Second Lieutenant Max Merritt's 60-millimeter mortar section, managed to seize a saddle between the northern and southern peaks of Observatory Hill. Meanwhile, D Company had been held up by enemy gunfire but was positioned at the base of the ridge and prepared to assault its southern side.

With darkness closing in and C Company in no shape to continue the attack on the northern half of Observatory Hill, the task was handed to Lieutenant Ike Fenton's B Company, the First Battalion's reserve unit, which had landed by mistake in the Second Battalion's zone.

"There was confusion on Red Beach from H-hour until nightfall because the boat coxswains failed to land in their assigned areas," Fenton recalled. "All they were concerned with was getting everyone on the beach wherever they could find an opening. Units were intermingled, and unit commanders had difficulty organizing their commands. I received orders to pass through C Company and continue the attack."

Colonel George Newton, commanding 1/5, explained that part of C Company was holding the saddle on Observatory Hill, but the rest of the unit was stymied on the beach. "You've got to take over their mission and secure the northern half of the ridge," Newton told Fenton. "That means going through some of the main streets of Inchon in the dark, so be careful."

It was a daunting order, but the battle-savvy Fenton quickly discovered two reassuring facts: (1) the darkness was a greater asset to his Marines in achieving their objective than to the enemy trying to stop them, and (2) the abundant cover and concealment offered by the city's structures gave Fenton's well-prepared troops yet another important advantage.

"The men had been very thoroughly briefed," said Lieutenant Nick Schryver, commanding B Company's First Platoon. "They knew all the streets and where every house was. They knew the surroundings so well that even in the darkness they were able to make good speed and reach the objective with few problems."

By 8:00 PM on September 15, the Marines of B Company had reached the top of Observatory Hill against light resistance, and before midnight they were tied into a solid defensive perimeter, with A Company on their left and D Company of the Second Battalion on their right.

Despite the melee on the beach and a murderous volume of fire from Communist artillery, mortars, antitank weapons, and machine guns that ebbed away after dark, B Company's casualties for the day totaled only six wounded, none killed.

Atop the hill, Fenton's men found an abandoned NKPA battalion command post, numerous untended gun emplacements, and several dozen enemy corpses. The night around them was dead silent, and Marine patrols scouting the area up to 500 yards in front of their lines found no remaining evidence of hostile activity.

Colonel Chesty Puller's newly reconstituted First Marines bore little resemblance to the scarred, toughened World War II regiment that had stormed the nearly impregnable Japanese defenses at Peleliu and Okinawa and made up part of the core of the fabled "Old Breed."

The current version was an amalgamation of regulars and reserves—both units and individuals—drawn hurriedly from posts all over the United States. It had never operated tactically as a regiment and in fact had never been concentrated in one place as an organizational entity until it hit Blue Beach at 5:30 PM on September 15, 1950.

Small wonder then that the situation on Blue Beach became even more chaotic and confused that afternoon than the one several miles to the north, on Red Beach. Given the fact that visibility was less than 200 yards and rain squalls were pounding the sea, it was impossible to distinguish Blue Beach One from Blue Beach Two, much less locate the dividing line between them. According to intelligence reports, One and Two were separated by a road, but it actually turned out to be a drainage ditch.

With time running short and feelings of desperation growing, Major Edwin H. Simmons, commander of 3/1's Weapons Company, pulled up beside the Blue Beach control vessel, the destroyer-transport *Wantuck*, and asked the bridge for instructions.

"A naval officer with a bullhorn pointed out the direction of Blue Two,"

Simmons later recalled, "but nothing could be seen in that direction except mustard-colored haze and black smoke."

Proceeding as directed, Simmons was startled to discover that his LVT was crossing the path of another inbound wave of amtracks.

"Are you headed for Blue Two?" the major shouted.

"Hell, no," the wave commander yelled back. "We're the Second Battalion headed for Blue One!"

Simmons's amtrack veered to the right while the major broke out his maps, which weren't much help. "Do you have a compass?" he asked the driver.

The driver studied his instrument panel for a moment, then shrugged. "Beats me, sir," he said. "I don't know much about this tub. Six weeks ago, I was driving a bus in San Francisco."

Fortunately, the nine amtracks of the first wave for Blue One *were* equipped with compasses, so they made it to shore on schedule—only to find their advance blocked by a huge earthslide. The nine tractors bound for Blue Two were held up at the seawall by fire from scattered defenders in nearby buildings, plus their discovery that the "road" on which they'd hoped to move inland was actually a muck-filled ditch.

When the floundering tractors backed off and started to circle, they became intermingled with amtracks of the second and third incoming waves and, as the tide receded, some of them got hung up on a mudbank about 300 yards from shore. The resulting tangle of amphibious traffic didn't ease until several waves were diverted to the right to land on Blue Beach Three (which had earlier been ruled out as a landing site), and other amtracks slogged their way up the drainage ditch.

Landing with the third wave, Colonel Puller witnessed the melee at close range and helped straighten matters out. "There was a strong possibility of confusion and disorganization under the circumstances: namely, the unavoidable necessity of landing the regiment without a rehearsal," he later remembered. "The reorganization of the assault battalions was accomplished with remarkable speed and effectiveness. I recall, at the time, being extremely gratified."

Overall, enemy resistance on the Blue beaches was lighter than that faced by 1/5 and 2/5 on Red Beach. After landing across Blue Two and Three, Captain Clarence Corley's H/3/1 and its sister companies, I/3/1 and G/3/1, wheeled south toward a small fishhook-shaped cape dominated by a knob of high ground called Hill 94. I Company was held up briefly by an NKPA machine gun firing from a tower about 500 yards inland. But once the enemy gun was silenced, the company fanned out along a north–south road and made good progress. The problem was, the troops weren't sure where they were going.

Shortly after PFC John Corzan was sent out ahead of his unit in search of information on Hill 94's location, he came upon a stocky, middle-aged Marine squatting on the ground and consulting a map.

"Hey, Sarge," Corzan hollered, "where the hell is Hill 94?"

The figure raised his head and pointed to his right. "That way," he replied. "You can't miss it."

A dozen steps later, Corzan realized that the Marine with the map had been none other than Chesty Puller himself.

Damn! Corzan thought. *I just demoted the regimental CO to a sergeant!*

As full darkness descended, H Company's First Platoon, led by First Lieutenant William Swanson, reached Hill 94 and engaged a platoon-size enemy force dug in on the hilltop. In a brief but intense firefight, the Marines blasted the North Koreans out of their holes and captured the summit, but not before Swanson suffered a severe thigh wound and had to be evacuated.

Meanwhile, the rest of H Company moved into the gap between I and G, and at about midnight, its Second Platoon cautiously approached another piece of high ground, identified as Hill 233. The platoon encountered zero resistance, but halfway to its objective, it received permission to halt its advance and stay put for the remainder of the night.

Across the harbor, on Wolmi-do, General Eddie Craig, now assistant commander of the First Marine Division, arrived to set up an advance division command post, and Colonel Taplett's 3/5 crossed the Wolmi-do causeway to the mainland, rejoining the rest of the Fifth Marines on Red Beach.

Before dawn on September 16, the last of the estimated 2,000 NKPA troops defending Inchon proper—those who hadn't been killed or taken prisoner—had drifted away, leaving South Korea's largest port the undisputed property of the U.S. Marine Corps.

"The townspeople stayed in their houses and off the streets, which was a great help to us," said Captain Ike Fenton. "When daylight arrived, there was no sign of the enemy."

To make certain that the NKPA had withdrawn, a regiment of ROK Marines was sent into the city at dawn to deal with stragglers and mop up any isolated pockets of resistance. "This they accomplished with such a vengeance," wrote historian T. R. Fehrenbach, "that for a number of hours, no man, woman, or child of Inchon, friend or foe, was safe."

Total D-day Marine casualties stood at 21 dead, 1 missing, and 174 wounded. Despite all the missteps, screwups, and snafus, the invasion had been every bit as successful as General MacArthur had predicted it would be.

Now, with the conquest of Inchon complete, Seoul was only eighteen miles away.

"You'll be there in five days," a jubilant MacArthur told X Corps commander General Ned Almond.

This time, though, MacArthur was wrong.

CHAPTER 13

★ ★ ★

THE BLOODY ROAD TO SEOUL

IN THE VIEW of many military experts and historians, the Inchon invasion stands out as the most brilliant offensive military action of the Korean War—and possibly of the entire twentieth century. It was planned with incredible boldness and executed with striking determination and skill, although a sizable measure of luck was involved, too. No condemnation of General MacArthur's later conduct of the war, however justified, can alter that fact.

"Inchon remains a monument to 'can-do,' to improvisation and risk-taking on a magnificent scale," British historian Max Hastings would write more than three and a half decades later, "[and] above all, to the spirit of Douglas MacArthur. . . . The amphibious landings of September 15, 1950, were MacArthur's masterstroke."

Yet the stunning American victory at Inchon would have been impossible without the unwitting assistance of the enemy. Foremost of the key factors that helped the landings achieve such success at such a light cost in bloodshed was the arrogance of North Korea's political and military leaders. Because of the many hazards involved—the mudflats, the tides, the treacherous channel, the seawalls, the fact that the Americans had to land in the downtown area of a major city—they were convinced that UN forces had neither the resources nor the ability to seize Inchon by amphibious assault. Even in the face of overwhelming evidence to the contrary, NKPA commanders allowed themselves to be caught completely off guard.

During the first two weeks of September 1950, the Communist Chinese were well aware of both the buildup of American troops and equipment in Japan and the great massing of U.S. and UN ships and planes in the Yellow Sea. But Kim Il Sung, the North Korean dictator, seemed oblivious to the threat developing nearly 200 miles behind his army's sputtering offensive in the far South. Although he was warned specifically by Chinese leader Mao Zedong about the vulnerability of Inchon, Kim didn't even bother to have mines planted in the harbor, much less divert troops to the area.

On September 4, Kim brushed off a warning from a Chinese emissary by declaring, "We estimate that presently a U.S. counterattack is not possible; they do not possess sufficient troop support, and therefore a landing to our rear ports would be difficult." A week later, on September 11, when the same emissary returned to the North Korean capital of Pyongyang to urge a strategic withdrawal by NKPA forces in the South, Kim again turned a deaf ear. "I have never considered retreat," he said.

Now, a mere five days later, the whole complexion of the war had changed. In the space of twenty-four hours, Kim's army found itself mired in a situation as intractable as the mudflats in Inchon Harbor. Under the circumstances, there was no hope of the NKPA holding the key port city. Rather than leave its few surviving defenders to die there, Kim ordered them to fall back on Seoul while Communist forces already in the area were rushed forward to contest the American advance.

Victory at Inchon was, of course, only the first step. The ultimate goal for MacArthur and X Corps was the recapture of Seoul. If UN forces could reclaim the South Korean capital quickly and decisively, the feat would have a crushing psychological effect—and incalculable strategic impact—on the NKPA's ability to carry on the war. By gaining control of the city's rail and highway networks, X Corps could choke off the enemy's flow of supplies and reinforcements to his forces in the South, leaving them to wither and die.

This job wasn't going to be easy at best, but if Kim and his commanders had rushed even 10,000 or 15,000 battle-seasoned troops from the South to defend Seoul prior to the Inchon landing, the capture of the capital city could have taken weeks. In terms of miles, Seoul was enticingly close, but it was protected by an interlocking system of natural barriers, including the Han River and its tributaries, several sizable towns, and countless formidable, easily fortified ridgelines. (The removal of a significant number of NKPA troops from the Pusan Perimeter front might well have gone unnoticed by General Walker's Eighth Army at this time since, as would later be shown, U.S. intelligence had only the sketchiest idea of how many Communist soldiers Walker's men were facing.)

As it was, however, Kim had only about 16,000 troops available to counter the nearly 70,000 American personnel in the total Inchon-Seoul attack force, including the still-uncommitted Seventh Marines and the Army's Seventh Infantry Division. Yet for a while, Kim clung fiercely to the belief that Inchon could be recaptured. To that end, his commanders squandered many of the men and weapons that might otherwise have turned Seoul into a latter-day Stalingrad.

Kim's illogic may help explain why six enemy T-34 tanks were spotted rumbling toward Inchon in broad daylight early on September 16, as the First and Fifth Marine regiments prepared to link up and push eastward along the main highway toward Seoul. Although the tanks were unaccompanied by infantry escort or other visible support, their crews were obviously under orders to counterattack.

A flight of eight Corsairs from the carrier *Sicily* intercepted the NKPA armored column near the village of Kansong-ni, three miles east of Inchon, torching one tank with napalm and disabling two others on their first pass. On the Corsairs' second pass, bombs and rocket fire damaged two other T-34s and sent surviving crewmen scrambling for cover in the village. Several other enemy vehicles, some camouflaged and others standing in the open, also were hit. The pilots believed that all six tanks had been destroyed, but three of them survived the air attack, only to be finished off by Marine M-26s a short time later.

"It would soon become more apparent why Red leaders in Seoul had sacrificed precious armor in a clearly hopeless thrust against the swelling beachhead," noted the official Marine Corps history of the incident. "Communications were destroyed, so that NKPA defense forces fought or fled as isolated units. Adequate reserves were not at hand initially, with the result that stop-gap detachments were fed piecemeal into battle, only to be flattened by the Marine steamroller."

From their vantage point on a hilltop less than two miles away, men of the Second Battalion, First Marines, watched and cheered as the Corsairs tore into the T-34s. Their jubilation ended abruptly when one plane failed to pull out of its dive and crashed beside the highway. The pilot, Captain William F. Simpson, was the only American killed in the brief engagement, but the road into Seoul would be long and hard. Simpson's death would be the first of many.

At about midnight on D-day, Colonels Ray Murray and Chesty Puller had received their attack orders for D plus one from General O. P. Smith's First Marine Division headquarters. Murray was to have his Fifth Marines pull abreast of Puller's First Marines to begin the advance along the main Inchon–Seoul highway, one of the few fully paved roads the Marines had traveled in Korea. Puller's regiment would take the right (south) side of the highway, with Murray's men taking the left (north) side.

Before this junction could be made, however, the Fifth Marines, traveling in columns of battalions, would have to move directly through the shell-battered heart of Inchon. Colonel Harold Roise's Second Battalion was chosen to lead the march, followed by the First and Third battalions in that order.

The rain of the night before had given way to a clear morning and pleasantly cool temperatures, but the surroundings could hardly have been more grim or grotesque. In a numbed daze, Korean civilians ventured out into the sunlight, picking their way through huge mounds of debris, among blasted walls of brick and stone where fires still flickered, and past fallen power lines and splintered utility poles. They chattered and gestured nervously among themselves, and some wept. Occasionally they called out timidly to the passing Marines, repeating with bitter irony the only English phrase they knew:

"Sank you! Sank you!"

As Corpsman Herb Pearce and the 75-millimeter recoilless rifle platoon to which he was attached marched cautiously with 1/5 through the ravaged heart of Inchon that morning, there was no sign of organized enemy resistance. But a sniper's random round struck startlingly close to Pearce, and he ducked into the nearest building.

"I found it was the post office," the enterprising medic recalled decades later, "so while the war continued outside, I looked around and found some Korean stamps to mail home for my collection."

By early afternoon, the entire regiment was clear of the city, and the Marines were advancing rapidly along the highway and parallel railway line toward the Han River and Seoul. Many of them felt a pervasive sense of relief at the continuing absence of enemy activity, but others were itching for action and growing slightly bored.

"After going ashore and moving several hundred yards inland, we spent the rest of D-day just sitting there," recalled tank-driving, sixteen-year-old Corporal Murdoch Ford. "We encountered a little light resistance, but we didn't get a crack at a single enemy tank. We had a lot of competition for what few tanks there were, and it was the same story on D plus one. We were ready to go, but we were still waiting for somebody to call us."

Veterans such as Captain Ike Fenton of B/1/5, however, were elated at the Marines' progress and perfectly satisfied to accept whatever favors the North Koreans offered. "By nightfall, the regiment had traveled a good seven miles east of Inchon, where we tied in with the First Marines on the high ground just west of Ascom City," Fenton said, referring to a large supply center built by the Army after World War II on the site of a village called Taejong-ni.

All the day's objectives had been met, and the advance had now moved beyond the designated boundaries of the Inchon beachhead. The next morning, September 17, while Puller's First Marines pressed on toward the

Han River and Yongdungpo, a major industrial suburb of Seoul on the river's west bank, the Fifth Marines would veer sharply north. Their objective: Kimpo Airfield, the largest and most modern airport on the Korean peninsula.

Back in the Pusan Perimeter, where a breakout offensive by the U.S. Eighth Army was supposed to coincide with the Inchon operation and form the lower jaw of a massive hammer-and-anvil operation against the NKPA, things weren't going well. In fact, there *was* no breakout on September 15 or 16, only a continuation of the same impasse that had prevailed along the Naktong front for weeks. With air support hampered by heavy rains, General Walker's troops were initially unable to punch across the river.

Once the fall of Inchon was a fait accompli, the North Koreans tried desperately to react, but they no longer had the strength or the resources to fight for long on two fronts, especially under constant hammering by U.S. airpower. The NKPA command in the South, however, smartly withheld information from its rank-and-file troops about the landings in the rear of the Communist forces. The better part of a week would pass before they learned the truth, and during that period, as historian Bevin Alexander noted, "[They] were still looking forward, not over their shoulders. As a result, they resisted [U.S. efforts to advance] fiercely."

By this point, MacArthur's frustrations with the Eighth Army had reached the point of combustion, and he was openly threatening to replace Walker with a more forceful commander. Walker was equally frustrated with MacArthur and X Corps. On September 17, when he was first briefed on the Inchon landings and learned how lightly defended the invasion beaches had been, the Eighth Army commander unloaded his angst to a member of his staff.

"They expended more ammunition to kill a handful of green troops at Inchon than they gave me to defeat 90 percent of the North Korean Army!" he fumed.

Walker was particularly irritated that most of the engineering and bridging equipment needed by his troops to cross the Naktong in strength had been shipped to Inchon to help the Marines cross the Han.

"We've been bastard children here lately," Walker railed by phone to Major General Doyle Hickey, X Corps' acting chief of staff. "I don't want you to think I'm dragging my heels, but I've got a river across my whole front and only two bridges to cross it with."

With the Eighth Army bogged down in the Pusan Perimeter, the Seventh Infantry Division still aboard ship, and the Seventh Marines several days' voyage from Korea, Kim Il Sung glimpsed a brief window of opportunity to retake Inchon. But his belated attempts to bring a few thousand experienced combat troops from the South ran into severe problems. Forced to spend the daylight hours hiding from swarming UN aircraft, the troops were able to move only at night. As a result, a trip that normally would have taken only hours stretched into several days.

Meanwhile, the only nearby NKPA forces of consequence were the 18th Division, which, by chance, had been about to depart Seoul for the Naktong front at the time of the Inchon invasion, and the 70th Regiment, based at Suwon, about twenty miles south of Seoul. Both units consisted mainly of green, disorganized conscripts and other second-rate troops, but they were the best Kim had to challenge the Marines driving on Seoul. On their uncertain—often unwilling—shoulders he placed his remaining hope of reversing an epic military disaster. All told, they did a better job than Kim had any right to expect.

On the night of September 16–17, the troops of the First and Fifth Marine regiments were edgy and cautious, alert to the possibility of an after-dark attack. The Fifth Marines' Colonel Murray felt sure that the NKPA would fight hard to hold strategically vital Kimpo. Intelligence reports indicated that the former NKPA commander of the airport garrison had fled across the Han River in the face of the Marine advance. But behind him, he'd left a hodgepodge of about 400 enemy troops now commanded by Chinese-trained Brigadier General Wan Yong, and Murray didn't want any surprises.

As it turned out, the night passed quietly, except for one isolated incident. In the zone occupied by 1/5, members of Captain Fenton's B Company captured three North Korean sailors who were driving back toward

Inchon after a trip to Seoul to pick up medical supplies. The three were dumbfounded to find themselves surrounded by heavily armed U.S. Marines, and they surrendered without resistance.

"They had no idea that a landing had been made at Inchon," Fenton later said as he recalled the sailors' amazement. "No one had told them anything about it."

Colonel Roise's 2/5 launched the attack on Kimpo at 9:00 AM on September 17, with the veteran infantrymen of Captain Sam Jaskilka's Easy Company leading off. The column marched eastward on the Inchon–Seoul highway through the debris and carnage left by the defeat of another enemy tank thrust earlier that morning that had delayed the start of the U.S. attack for close to an hour and a half.

In a bizarre sequel to the previous morning's action, half a dozen T-34s—this time supported by about 250 infantry troops—had suddenly appeared, heading west on the main road a few miles east of Ascom City. Many of the infantrymen were perched atop the tanks, some casually eating breakfast and seemingly unaware that they were riding into grave danger.

Men of Second Lieutenant Lee Howard's Dog Company, manning an advanced highway outpost with machine guns and rocket launchers, had been the first to spot the tanks' approach. Howard promptly alerted Colonel Roise, who dispatched a platoon of M-26s and Lieutenant Charles M. C. Jones's recoilless gun platoon to intercept the enemy armor.

"The North Korean force was no match for all the weapons we had available," Jones recalled much later. "We reached the point where we were downright disdainful of NK armored counterattacks. If our Pershings and 75-millimeter rifles and 3.5 rockets didn't get them, our planes did. We turned the Russian T-34s into 'caviar cans' wherever we met them."

Jones's observations are borne out by the fact that of a total of fifty-three enemy tanks sighted by Marines on their drive from Inchon to Seoul, forty-eight were destroyed outright, and the other five were found abandoned.

Despite the ease with which the enemy tank attack was halted, its aftermath delayed the Marines' advance still further when General MacArthur and two jeeploads of American news correspondents arrived unexpectedly on the scene to inspect and photograph the wreckage.

"The remains were still burning when MacArthur and the correspondents drove up and stopped a few yards from me," said Corpsman Herb Pearce, attached to Lieutenant Jones's recoilless rifle platoon. "This was one of two times that I saw MacArthur close up in Korea, and his presence didn't make the Marine commanders happy at all. They worried that something might happen to him while he was in their area of responsibility and they'd catch hell for it."

Following the delays and distractions, 1/5, 2/5, and the ROK Marine Battalion closed in rapidly on the airfield, with scattered enemy troops falling back before them toward Kimpo and offering only light resistance. But another problem quickly surfaced.

Colonel Robert Taplett's 3/5 had deployed that morning in a reserve position west of Ascom City, but Taplett's men were unaware that the other two battalions had been held up and that the ROK Marines had failed to move into Ascom City as scheduled. Consequently, 3/5 had unwittingly advanced well beyond the front held by the other units.

"The [whole regimental] attack plan had gone awry," Taplett said. "Because of the lack of information . . . it appeared that 3/5 had thrust itself into a very precarious position."

When Taplett contacted the regimental command post to report his situation, Colonel Murray told him that 2/5 and the ROKs were meeting heavy resistance, and he ordered 3/5 to reverse course and relieve the pressure on 2/5 until the ROKs could mount their attack through Ascom City.

Taplett quickly complied, but after finding no evidence of either enemy activity or the ROK Marines among the bomb-blasted buildings of Ascom City, he decided to take a closer look, accompanied by Lieutenant Robert "Dewey" Bohn and a small reconnaissance party from Bohn's G Company.

At first the city seemed deserted, but as the Marines moved cautiously down a street on the southeast side of town, they detected sounds of activity on the reverse slope of a small hill directly to the east, in 2/5's zone and overlooking the main supply route toward Kimpo. Easing closer, Bohn and Taplett heard the low, chattering voices of a large number of North Korean troops. They froze in their tracks, realizing that they'd wandered into the rear of a major enemy force covertly preparing to attack 2/5.

Taplett nudged Bohn and pointed to the top floor of a damaged building nearby. "Let's climb up there," he whispered, "and see what we can see."

What they saw jolted them. More than 150 NKPA troops were setting up an ambush on the road ahead of 2/5's advancing troops. Among them, Taplett counted half a dozen heavy machine guns and several heavily loaded ammunition carts.

"Our group consisted of twelve Marines armed only with M-1 rifles and a single BAR," Taplett later recalled. Yet, given the height of their protected position and the capability of total surprise, Taplett could see that his little band—as badly outnumbered and outgunned as it was—was ideally situated to ambush the would-be ambushers.

"Let's set up a firing line along that wall," Bohn told his men quietly, gesturing toward a row of blown-out windows. "It's a perfect setup—just like a rifle range—so make every shot count!"

Seconds later, Bohn made a final check. "Ready on the right? Ready on the left? Fire!"

A sheet of lead and flame exploded from a dozen weapons in an unbroken roar. It lasted, by Taplett's later estimate, for "a good ten minutes." When it ended, the nearby hillside was strewn with North Korean bodies, and the surviving remnants of the enemy force were in frenzied flight.

Taplett reported the encounter to Murray, and since there was still no sign of the ROK battalion, he sent a platoon-size infantry/tank patrol, led by Lieutenant John Counselman, to scout the rest of Ascom City and the area to the north. The patrol flushed out and killed eighteen enemy soldiers and uncovered a large cache of ammunition and grenades in a small village north of the city. Counselman narrowly escaped death on the mission when a sniper's rifle bullet penetrated his helmet and ricocheted around inside, gouging abrasions in his scalp but not wounding him seriously.

While this action was playing out, two platoons of M-26 tanks located a remote road that led directly to Kimpo, and Roise's 2/5 advanced to a pair of high hills south of the airport. From there, Roise sent the riflemen of Dog and Easy companies on the assault. They moved swiftly through a cluster of villages on the fringes of Kimpo, encountering no more than sporadic small-arms fire. Then each company hooked up with one of the supporting tank platoons and moved on to the airport itself.

Beginning at about 6:00 PM on September 17, Roise's men were embroiled in a series of heavy firefights at the south end of Kimpo's main runway. After dusk, the firing tailed off, and Roise ordered D, E, and F companies to establish separate defensive perimeters for the night, each of them a tightly knit strongpoint that would be much harder to penetrate than the thinly stretched lines of the entire battalion. Second Lieutenant Edwin Deptula's First Platoon of E Company manned an outpost position in front of the rest of the battalion in the village of Soryu-li.

To stabilize the American lines, A and B companies of 1/5 moved up on the right of 2/5, with C Company in reserve. After its eventful afternoon, Taplett's 3/5 went back into regimental reserve two miles to the rear.

The men of the Fifth Marines had yet to secure Kimpo, but they were right there. In the distance, they could hear intermittent heavy-weapons fire from the First Marines' zone to their right rear, and they knew that another tense night lay ahead. Although the NKPA troops who had challenged them earlier had apparently withdrawn, no one believed that the fight for the vital airfield was over.

It wasn't.

To the south, the first significant enemy resistance to the First Marines' push toward Seoul also had developed on the morning of September 17 (D plus two) when its lead elements ran into a well-fortified enemy roadblock backed by tanks, machine guns, and infantry. An M-26 tank destroyed a camouflaged T-34 before the latter could get off a shot, allowing Marine riflemen to outflank the roadblock and kill twenty-one enemy soldiers.

This was only the beginning, however. Troops of the NKPA 18th Division attacked the Marine column from positions in the hills above the road west of the village of Sosa, about halfway between Inchon and Yongdungpo. More than a dozen clashes followed, costing the enemy four more tanks but bloodying the Marines and significantly slowing their advance.

Among the first units to come under heavy enemy fire was Lieutenant Colonel Allan Sutter's Second Battalion, which was attacking due east astride the main highway behind covering fire from artillery of the Eleventh Marines.

At the time, Colonel Thomas Ridge's Third Battalion was on a swing to the south to clear the Munhang peninsula of hostile troops. Ridge's men met negligible resistance, took several dozen prisoners, and seized large quantities of abandoned equipment and weapons. Among them were a battery of Soviet-made 120-millimeter mortars and four giant coastal guns pointed menacingly at American ships anchored offshore—sobering evidence of destructive enemy potential that had, fortunately, gone unused.

When the Second Battalion's advance stalled, Colonel Puller, the regimental commander, ordered Ridge's Third Battalion back to the north to cover Sutter's right flank. Puller also brought up a platoon of M-26s under Second Lieutenant Brian J. Cummings to help out. A group of North Koreans tried—and failed—to stop Cummings's tanks with grenades, and when Captain George C. Westover's G/3/1 managed to reach the high ground to the right of the road, the Marines broke the NKPA attack with a blazing crossfire.

By 4:00 PM on September 17, the village of Mahang-ri had been secured, and despite its difficulties, Puller's regiment had gained more than two miles during the day while suffering only 1 KIA and 27 wounded. Enemy casualties were estimated at 250 killed and wounded, and 70 enemy prisoners had been taken.

At that point, Sutter's and Ridge's battalions dug in for the night, still some three miles west of Sosa and now separated from the Fifth Marines by a gap of about five miles to the northeast.

As darkness closed in that evening and the recoilless gun company to which Corpsman Herb Pearce was assigned began scratching out shallow foxholes on the south edge of Kimpo Airfield, the young Mississippian was as bone-tired as he could remember ever being. His weariness led him to be uncharacteristically lax in making his usual defensive preparations.

"It was probably the only night in Korea that I didn't dig in or take some steps to protect myself," Pearce would recall much later. "It was a bad mistake—one I'd never repeat again, no matter how exhausted I was."

The first enemy counterattack came at about 3:00 AM on September 18, when Pearce jerked awake to find his position surrounded by charging enemy troops, all of them screaming *"Manzai! Manzai!"*

"They were all over us," he said. "I was sure I was dead. None of us ever expected to live to see the sun come up."

A couple of feet away, as Pearce grabbed for his carbine, he saw the dim figure of Corporal Russell "Moose" House, a burly former boxing champ of the U.S. Third Fleet, rise up in the darkness with a grenade gripped in his massive fist. House hurled the grenade toward the chatter of an enemy machine gun, then followed it with a second as the first explosion shook the ground.

"I need more grenades!" he yelled to Corporal Red Martin, a gunner on one of the 75s. "I'm out!"

Martin scrambled forward with a fresh supply, but before House could pull the pin on another grenade, a North Korean rifle bullet struck him squarely in the chest.

"He fell toward me, and I caught him in my arms," Pearce remembered. "But the bullet went straight through his heart, and he never knew what hit him. There was absolutely nothing I could do to help him. He died instantly."

After the attack was beaten off, House's grieving buddies in the recoilless gun company gathered around his body, staring silently and shaking their heads. "Moose was my gunner until Lieutenant Jones pulled him off for other duties," said Corporal Charlie Snow. "He was as rugged as they come, and it was hard to believe that such a big, almost indestructible guy was dead."

PFC George "Link" Waslinko, a youngster from the Bronx, whose prowess as a semipro baseball catcher had earned him a tryout with the New York Yankees (unfortunately during the same year that the team signed future Hall of Famer Yogi Berra to play that position), was especially shaken.

"Moose was the classic personification of a Marine," said Waslinko nearly six decades after House's death. "He'd been a bodyguard for the president of the Philippines, and he could pick up a 75-millimeter gun like a loaf of bread. He was the toughest guy I ever met. I still have guilt feelings about him. You know, like wondering why it wasn't me that got it instead of him."

With their once-successful strategy of nighttime shock attacks clearly fizzling out, the North Koreans regrouped sufficiently to stage three more small-scale assaults during the predawn hours of September 18, for the most part with weapons no larger than rifles and submachine guns.

Lieutenant Deptula's isolated forward outpost at a road junction in the village of Soryu-li was hit shortly before the attack on Lieutenant Jones's recoilless gun crew. In this case, however, the enemy approach was detected in time to react decisively. Deptula had his men hold their fire until the attackers were within a few feet of them. Then the Marines blazed away from the roadsides, cutting down a dozen Communist soldiers and scattering the rest.

None of these uncoordinated enemy attacks came close to dislodging the well-entrenched Fifth Marines but merely further diluted the flagging strength and morale of the airfield's defenders.

The grenades thrown by House permanently silenced the targeted enemy machine-gun emplacement. "When the sun came up, we saw that the ground around it was covered with dead North Koreans," recalled Corporal Martin. House was posthumously awarded the Navy Cross.

As the sun slipped above the horizon on September 18, Captain Ike Fenton noticed something that set his pulse to racing. In the distance, Fenton could see scores of enemy troops scurrying along the left flank of his B/1/5, moving into position to attack the Second Battalion. Instantly he grabbed his radio and contacted his own battalion command post.

"I don't think they know we're up here on the high ground," Fenton told First Battalion commander Colonel George Newton. "It looks like there's about 200 of them, and they seem totally unaware of our presence."

"Hold your fire till they get past you," Newton said. "Then we'll let them have it from both sides. I'll notify Colonel Roise and arrange for mortar and artillery support."

Fenton held his breath as the North Koreans moved past. "Tell your men to wait until they hear the Second Battalion open up," he told his senior platoon leader, Lieutenant Nick Schryver. "Then give it everything you've got. Pass the word."

Moments later, the harsh rattle of small-arms and machine-gun fire erupted in the Second Battalion's area, punctuated by the blasts of mortars and artillery.

"Go for it!" Fenton yelled. "Fire! Fire!"

For the next few minutes, the response of the B/1/5 riflemen was deafening. Caught in the crossfire between 2/5 and Fenton's company, the attacking North Koreans were wiped out almost to a man. Marine casualties were light, but they included two veteran NCOs who lost their lives almost simultaneously. Staff Sergeant Robert J. Kikta of F/2/5 fell mortally wounded as he moved among his men shouting encouragement, and Sergeant David R. DeArmond, normally a bulldozer operator with the engineers, was killed as he manned a machine gun.

While the slaughter was taking place, Colonel Newton moved his C Company around Fenton's left flank to cut off the escape of any enemy troops still in the area of the airfield.

Following the brief, bitter clash, NKPA survivors fled through the rice paddies and hills toward the Han River. For all practical purposes, the fight for the mile-long airport was over.

At 10:00 AM on September 18, Kimpo and the surrounding villages were declared secure. Moments later, while mopping-up operations continued, an HO3S-1 Marine helicopter, piloted by Captain Victor A. Armstrong, became the first U.S. aircraft to land at the airfield since the beginning of the war. Aboard was General Lemuel Shepherd, commander of Fleet Marine Force, Pacific, and his G-3 operations officer, Colonel Victor Krulak. Standing by to greet them was General Eddie Craig, assistant commander of the First Marine Division.

It's difficult to exaggerate the advantages gained by the First Marine Air Wing with the successful seizure of Kimpo. Now, instead of operating from carriers at sea, Kimpo's excellent facilities put the Corsairs' close air support almost literally at the fingertips of the ground troops. "Sometimes it was hard to keep all our planes in the air because of a shortage of parts," said Houston-born PFC Leo Dacus, a member of one of the first Marine ground crews to begin operations at Kimpo. "But being able to do all our fueling and mechanical work so close to the action was a big plus."

Meanwhile, plenty of other objectives remained for the one-two punch of Marine ground and air units. Barely half an hour after Kimpo was fully secured, 2/5's Colonel Roise sent his D Company, supported by planes, tanks, recoilless rifles, and heavy machine guns, to seize Hill 131, a piece of high ground dominating both banks of the Han north of the airfield. By 11:45 AM, the Marines had occupied the hilltop without opposition. In the misty distance to the south, they could see the area west of Yongdungpo, where the First Marines were still struggling. Faintly visible beyond the river to the east lay the outskirts of Seoul. They were only about five miles away as the crow flies, but for X Corps, the journey would seem much longer.

The First Marine Regiment, meanwhile, was still beset by difficulties. On the morning of the 18th, Colonel Puller's men had moved through and around Sosa, but east of the village they were stopped cold by NKPA artillery that neither aerial nor ground observers were able to locate. They stayed pinned down for most of the afternoon, suffering numerous casualties.

To make matters worse, the North Koreans also had planted mines in the highway, damaging two American Pershings and temporarily halting tank support for the infantry. Marine engineers were called in to take on the tedious, potentially deadly job of locating and removing the mines.

"I can tell you lifting mines is a lot harder on the nerves than filling potholes or making chalk marks on bridges," recalled Texas-born Corporal Bob Speights, a member of A Company, First Engineers, who still bore vivid scars a month later from snipers' bullets that had struck him on both cheeks in mid-August. "But somebody had to do it, so the engineers did. When the nastiest jobs were done, we'd trade an abandoned Russian jeep or truck for a couple cases of medical alcohol, and everybody'd get drunk as hell."

As the Marines slugged it out with the fragmented North Korean defenders of Kimpo and Yongdungpo on September 18, the Army's Seventh Infantry Division began disembarking at Inchon. The GIs' first assignment was to move quickly to the right (south) of the Marines and establish a blocking position on the main supply route between Seoul and Suwon in case the NKPA attempted to move troops north from the Pusan Perimeter.

The following day, D plus four, the battleship *Missouri*, having completed a diversionary bombardment on the east coast well south of Inchon, also arrived at Inchon Harbor to support the Seventh Division's advance with its 16-inch guns.

In the opinion of Lieutenant Fred Wilmot, executive officer of B Company, First Battalion, 17th Infantry Regiment—and one of the division's few combat-tested junior officers—the Seventh was going to need all the help it could get.

"Figuratively speaking, we were an infantry regiment in the U.S. Army," Wilmot later recalled, "but most of the troops in B Company were Korean conscripts with a total of about three weeks' training in Japan, and it was apparent that these young men had simply been knocked off bicycles in Pusan and pressed into service."

When the war began, the ROK Army had had about 98,000 combat troops in uniform, Wilmot pointed out, but by mid-September, 44,000 of these were either dead, missing, or captured. "Under the circumstances," he said, "it was no wonder we received the bottom of the barrel."

The Koreans were so small in stature that the Army was forced to issue them the lighter, and far less effective, M-1 carbine, rather than the powerful M-1 rifle, as their basic weapon. Since almost none of them spoke English, communication was a constant problem—one that the Korean NCOs attempted to solve by beating the recruits unmercifully when they failed to understand or carry out an order.

As the troops of the Seventh went ashore, they could hear the distant rumble of artillery to the east and the occasional freight-train sound of inbound shells passing overhead from American ships offshore. They boarded waiting trucks in an assembly area just off the beach, then rode a few miles, passing numerous enemy corpses along the roadsides, to a bombed-out factory, where they spent their first night in Korea.

"Our trigger-happy little Koreans opened fire at nothing several times during the night," said Wilmot, "earning the company officers and NCOs a royal ass-chewing the next morning from the battalion commander— whom I don't recall seeing a single time during our training."

On the morning of September 19, a couple of miles north of where the Seventh Infantry was moving up to bolster the First Marines, Colonel Murray's

Fifth Marines began driving southeast from Kimpo Airfield toward Yong-dungpo with all three companies of 1/5 on line. The plan of attack called for A Company to hold its position to protect the battalion's right flank while B and C companies attacked Hill 118, the dominant high ground overlook-ing Yongdungpo.

C Company's portion of the attack bogged down temporarily when it ran into a sizable force of NKPA troops who had slipped across the Han River and occupied the ground to C Company's immediate front. With the help of air support and artillery, the company was soon able to dislodge the North Koreans and force them to withdraw. As they did, the enemy soldiers blundered into deep trouble in the form of Captain Ike Fenton's B Company.

"They ran right into us," said Fenton, "and we were able to wipe out most of them and take a lot of prisoners."

The troops of 1/5 advanced later that day on Hill 118, their primary ob-jective, moving unopposed to the tops of two smaller knobs that lay in their path, designated as Hills 80 and 85. After finding no evidence of the enemy on either hill, the entire regiment was ordered back to Kimpo to prepare for crossing the Han River in LVTs (landing vehicles, tracked) at dawn the next morning, September 20. In obeying the order, 1/5 had no choice but to re-linquish the hills it had seized and held securely on the afternoon of the nineteenth, leaving them just as it had found them—vacant and unfortified.

It was a decision that would come back to haunt the First Marines—in spades—the following day.

While the Seventh Infantry Division punched inland on September 19, troops of the First Marines were taking heavy casualties from enemy mor-tars and artillery as they attempted to clear a rambling ridge complex facing Yongdungpo and dominated by a peak known as Lookout Hill. The ridge-line stretched for more than three miles and also included Hills 118 and 123, but Lookout was its dominant feature and the final objective for H and I companies of Colonel Thomas Ridge's Third Battalion. The previous day, the same two companies had taken Hill 123 with the help of a 300-round barrage by the British cruiser *Kenya*.

On the west bank of the Han and beyond the ridgeline lay Yongdungpo, one of the most formidable objectives yet faced by the Marines. Separated from Seoul proper by a huge sand spit, the big industrial suburb was surrounded by what amounted to a natural moat, formed by the Kalchon River (a narrow Han tributary) on the north and west, a wide rice paddy on the west, and high ridges on the southeast.

Intelligence reports indicated that a full regiment of enemy troops was defending Yongdungpo, and Colonel Puller knew that his First Marines' only route to the Han led directly through this morass. At about noon on September 19, Puller ordered Ridge's H and I companies to attack the town and the hills protecting it.

"Yongdungpo was a bitch because of the hills and a system of dikes surrounding it," said Sergeant Bill Finnegan, a squad leader in I/3/1's machine-gun section. "We started up the side of one of them—it was about fifteen or twenty feet high—without knowing there were a bunch of gooks waiting on the other side." As the Marines topped the dike, the North Koreans opened fire, and Finnegan saw his gunnery sergeant clutch his chest and stumble.

"I'm hit! I'm hit!" the gunny yelled. Then he fell and rolled helplessly down the side of the dike to the bottom.

As Item Company's CO, First Lieutenant Joseph R. "Bull" Fisher, ordered his rifle platoons to "open up on the bastards" concealed behind the dike, Finnegan's two gunners hustled to set up their .30-caliber weapon. Seconds later, with the help of their six ammo handlers, they laid down a blistering volley of fire that wiped out the North Koreans inside the dike, but the company suffered several other casualties in the process.

"Our gunny was shot through the lung, but we hauled him out, and he survived," Finnegan recalled.

Meanwhile, later that afternoon, the men of H/3/1 had just reached the crest of Lookout Hill but weren't yet dug in when they were hit with an intense barrage of 120-millimeter mortar fire, inflicting heavy casualties. At the height of the attack, Captain Clarence Corley, the company CO, radioed the battalion command post, asking permission to advance beyond the barrage, but Colonel Ridge vetoed the request and ordered Corley to hold his present position.

"Being as we're stuck here," Corley told his men, "we'd better make these foxholes as deep as we can. Get to digging!"

Ridge's decision to have H/3/1 stay put was justified minutes later when a squadron of Corsairs and Marine artillery combined to knock out the enemy mortars. Corley's troops, soon well entrenched, remained on the hilltop for the rest of the night while other units of the battalion consolidated their positions, but H Company had paid dearly for Lookout. Nearly a quarter of the total casualties suffered that day by the entire First Marine Division—seventeen of seventy-two—were in 3/1.

Ironically, the Third Battalion's seizure of Lookout Hill was almost too successful for the Marines' own good. The battalion now found itself out on a limb, with the nearest friendly forces several hundred yards to the north on Hill 118 and along the main Inchon–Seoul highway a mile or more to the south. The Second Battalion had moved to within two miles of Yongdungpo, covering the area to the south until the Army's Seventh Division could assume responsibility for the First Marines' right flank.

It was an ideal opportunity for another enemy surprise attack, and the North Koreans were quick to take advantage of it. At 4:00 AM on September 20, they struck in battalion strength, with a convoy of T-34 tanks leading the way. It was the NKPA's largest attack yet against the First Marines, and it might well have succeeded if not for a badly placed enemy ammunition truck, an alert Marine squad leader, and the deadly aim and steel nerves of a nineteen-year-old rocket gunner attached to F Company, Second Battalion.

PFC Walter C. Monegan Jr. had already distinguished himself against another group of enemy tanks on D plus two when he'd taken them under fire at point-blank range as they rounded a bend in the road near the village of Soryu-li. Concentrated volleys of 3.5-inch rockets and 75-millimeter recoilless rounds by Monegan and other gunners had left all five of the tanks shattered and burning.

Now, three days later, Monegan was awakened in the predawn darkness by a yell from his squad leader, Corporal William Cheek.

"Gook tanks headed this way!" Cheek shouted. "They're about 300 yards down the hill! Get your gun and come on!"

Monegan grabbed his rocket launcher, and the two men raced downhill as fast as they could go. When they were within about 100 yards of the T-34s, Monegan ducked behind a water storage tank and loaded his weapon. Then, at almost the precise second that a Marine grenade ignited an enemy ammunition truck packed with explosives—illuminating the tanks as if it were high noon—Monegan stepped from cover, ready to fire.

"I've got one of them right in the crosshairs," he told Cheek.

"Fire quick!" Cheek barked.

Monegan's first shot hit the third tank in the line and set it ablaze, but it also drew answering fire from enemy small arms at close range. At that moment, PFC Robert Perkins, Monegan's loader, ran up, carrying more ammunition. With Perkins's help, Monegan scored a direct hit on a second tank as a third T-34 tried to turn around to flee.

"Come on, load me up!" Monegan yelled to Perkins. "Let's make it three in a row!"

As Monegan stepped out into the open and raised his 3.5 to fire, he was cut down by a burst from an enemy machine gun. Cheek and Perkins dragged him back behind the water tank, and Cheek tried to stop the bleeding from Monegan's multiple wounds while Perkins ran for a corpsman, but it was no use. Within a few seconds, the gallant young gunner was dead. (In February 1952, Monegan's wife, Elizabeth, accepted her husband's posthumous Medal of Honor from Navy Secretary Dan Kimball as she held their year-old son, Walter III.)

The third enemy tank was captured intact, and by dawn, after fierce hand-to-hand fighting in which the Marines met the charging North Koreans with fixed bayonets, the NKPA attack had collapsed, leaving 300 enemy dead.

Half an hour later, Colonel Sutter's Second Battalion launched its own attack against Hills 80 and 85, the same two pieces of high ground guarding the approach to Yongdungpo that 1/5 had held but given up the day before. The two hills had been free for the taking twenty-four hours earlier, but now the enemy was well entrenched atop both.

Captain Robert P. Wray, commanding C/1/1, sent Second Lieutenant John Guild's Second Platoon to lead the attack against Hill 85 by clearing a small village at the foot of the peak with support from the mortars and machine guns of Major William L. Bates Jr.'s 1/1 Weapons Company. When Guild's platoon stalled under heavy fire, Wray quickly committed the rest of his troops to the battle, and in brutal fighting they were able to smash through the first line of North Korean defenses and get the Second Platoon moving again.

Late in the afternoon, Wray launched a double envelopment movement against Hill 80, with Second Lieutenant Henry A. Commiskey's Third Platoon moving to the right, and Second Lieutenant William A. Craven's First Platoon swinging to the left. Except for scattered sniper fire, they met little resistance in reaching the crest of 80 while it was still daylight. Then, with darkness closing in, Wray aimed another double envelopment at Hill 85, where remnants of an NKPA company made a determined stand.

Displaying exceptional courage and determination, Lieutenant Guild led his platoon's charge toward the slopes of Hill 85 across 500 yards of intervening low ground. In close combat, Guild killed two enemy soldiers with his pistol, and he had almost gained the summit when he was severely wounded. Despite his life-threatening injuries, Guild refused evacuation or medical treatment and continued to direct the attack until he lost consciousness from loss of blood.

"He stayed on his feet and turned toward where I was climbing twenty yards behind him," Wray later recalled. "He dropped at my feet and made every effort to remain conscious long enough to tell me how his squads were attacking and plead with me to keep them going."

Guild died a short time later, but his troops—inspired and galvanized by his example—clawed their way to the top of the hill and held it.

On the right, Lieutenant Commiskey also performed with "conspicuous valor and intrepidity," as the citation accompanying his Medal of Honor would read, in leading his platoon up the bitterly contested slopes. As his men neared the crest of 85, the young officer from Hattiesburg, Mississippi, bounded ahead of them and scrambled over the top, leaping into an enemy machine-gun nest and killing all five of its occupants by the time his lead skirmishers caught up with him. Commiskey then ran forward again to wipe out a second enemy emplacement single-handedly.

At this point, the Communist troops had had enough. Those who were still able fled in disarray down the north side of 85 toward the Kalchon River.

As night fell, the battle-weary men of the First Marines looked down from their hard-won heights on tomorrow's objective. Directly in front of them—at long last—lay Yongdungpo, the final major strategic obstacle before the Han River and Seoul itself.

There was no infantry action during the night of September 20–21 as the First Marines and the NKPA forces facing them at Yongdungpo steeled themselves for the ordeal ahead. But artillery of the 11th Marines thundered continuously in the darkness, touching off scores of fires throughout the city.

By contrast, the atmosphere at Kimpo Airfield was one of festive celebration. Numerous news correspondents crowded the briefing area where Fifth Marines commander Colonel Murray was to announce his plan for crossing the Han River the next morning.

The overall scheme of attack called for all three of Murray's battalions to cross the river in covered landing craft north of Yongdungpo, beginning at dawn on the 21st. Colonel Taplett's 3/5 was to lead off, followed by Colonel Roise's 2/5, then Colonel Newton's 1/5. Taplett himself was none too happy with the plan, much less with the environment in which it was announced.

He disliked the fact that many journalists, apparently well fueled with alcohol, were "celebrating a victory before it had been achieved." As Taplett later recalled, "My staff and I found the carefree confidence and the public relations bonanza troublesome."

The 3/5 commander was especially concerned to learn that Murray intended for the First Marine Division's small, lightly armed Reconnaissance Company to be the first unit to make the river crossing. An advance Recon detachment was supposed to swim the Han under cover of darkness, then secure the landing site and seize two inland objectives, including a 500-foot cliff identified as Hill 125—an assignment that Taplett considered far too ambitious for so few Marines. The remainder of the company was to follow in amtracks to seize two other key objectives. Only later, at 4:00 AM, would

Taplett's battalion start across in a single-file column of slow-moving amphibious tractors.

"Apparently, little credence was being given to intelligence reports of enemy strength built up on Hill 125 and [at] the crossing site," Taplett warned. His uneasiness as a battalion commander leading a major attack was understandable, and in the early going it seemed amply justified.

Although the swimmers made it across the Han without incident, the amtracks carrying the rest of the Recon Company were hit by devastating enemy fire from Hill 125 and forced to withdraw, leaving a Marine corporal stranded ashore and several amtracks stuck in the mud.

From midnight until 3/5's jump-off time, Taplett argued his case for changing the attack plan with various regimental staff members, and sparks briefly flew between Taplett and Murray. In the end, however, the crossing by 3/5 was carried out just as the Fifth Marines' commander had mapped it. Taplett's battalion came under intense small-arms and machine-gun fire, but because of the amtracks' protective covers and armor, the firing had little physical effect.

In fact, the only casualties suffered in the landing occurred when an NKPA antitank round scored a direct hit on the leading amtrack as it lowered its ramp to discharge its troops.

Once ashore on the east bank of the river, Captain Robert A. McMullen's I Company led the assault on Hill 125, supported by 3/5's Weapons Company and backed up by G and H companies. Despite heavy enemy small-arms fire, McMullen's rifle platoons dashed up the slope and quickly captured the topographical crest of 125. Taplett then sent G and H companies, using their amtracks as personnel carriers, on long inland sweeps to search out lurking defenders and seize other major objectives.

Although I/3/5 spent much of the morning clearing enemy resistance from a fortified high ridge running west from the peak of Hill 125, all objectives were in Marine hands by 10:30 AM on September 21, and most enemy resistance in the area had ceased. The stranded Marine corporal from the Recon Company was found alive and unhurt, hiding in some wreckage.

By nightfall, the rest of the Fifth Marines was safely across the Han—soon followed by the First Battalion of the Korean Marines—and Taplett's

3/5, after penetrating several miles inland, was camped unmolested on the road to Seoul.

Sometime after midnight, however, any further victory celebrations by the Fifth Marines were abruptly put on hold. An enemy shell crashed through the roof of the native house where Colonel Murray had established his regimental CP, severely wounding Murray's executive officer, Lieutenant Colonel Lawrence C. Hays Jr., and forcing his evacuation.

Murray himself escaped with minor cuts, and the CP was hurriedly relocated. But the NKPA had served dramatic notice that the battle for the northwest approaches to Seoul was far from finished.

To the south, meanwhile, Yongdungpo had finally fallen to the First Marines, now poised on the banks of the Han and preparing to cross in amtracks. But the victory by Colonel Puller's men had come only after an exhausting three-day fight in which the North Koreans had made their first strong stand instead of merely mounting another delaying action.

Fortunately, the Seventh Marines, commanded by Colonel Homer Litzenberg, would land at Inchon on September 22 after one of its three infantry battalions had sailed half the distance around the world from the Mediterranean by way of the Suez Canal. All three battalions would be committed to action on the 23rd as a backup force protecting the north flank and rear of the Fifth Marines—and their arrival in the war zone would come none too soon.

Thousands of fresh enemy troops of the NK 78th Independent Regiment and 25th Brigade were now manning defensive positions in a hill complex on the outskirts of Seoul that formed the enemy's main line of resistance. Topographically, the area was a vast natural network of interlocking heights and fields of fire with spurs and defiles leading from one ridge to another, allowing the enemy to move in concealment to launch counterattacks from the most unlikely locations. Well dug in within this fastness were eight North Korean infantry and heavy weapons battalions, armed with heavy and medium artillery and 120-millimeter mortars and supported by reconnaissance, engineer, medical, and motorcycle units.

Standing now on the very doorstep of Seoul, the Marines were about to receive a vicious welcome.

CHAPTER 14

★ ★ ★

A "TERRIBLE LIBERATION"

B Y SEPTEMBER 19, four days after the Inchon landings, reports and rumors about the successful opening of a second front by American forces
were running rampant through NKPA units still stationed along the Naktong River in the far South.

As word spread from soldier to soldier, the will to keep fighting against
the UN defenders of the Pusan Perimeter rapidly withered. With most of
their best and most experienced troops now lost, the North Koreans were
tired, hungry, unmotivated, short of weapons and ammunition, and generally ripe for despair.

Once the panic began, it swept relentlessly through enemy ranks. Within
hours, the conquering horde of three months earlier would disintegrate
into a desperate, dispirited rabble whose only goal was to get the hell out of
South Korea before it was too late.

Up to this point, General Walker's Eighth Army had been sufficiently slow
in taking the offensive to incur the rising wrath of General MacArthur. (On
arriving at Kimpo Airfield shortly after the liberation of Seoul, MacArthur
would show his disgust by striding past Walker without so much as a nod

to greet X Corps commander General Almond with a warm "Ned, my boy!") But Walker, his staff, and his field commanders had several legitimate excuses for not moving faster than they did after Inchon.

For one thing, spending weeks on the defensive had made defense an ingrained state of mind for many Eighth Army officers, making it difficult for them to shift mentally into offensive gear. For another, virtually all the front-line American troops along the Naktong had been in combat for many days, and they were far from fresh. For yet another, vastly inflated U.S. intelligence estimates fueled American reticence by placing the number of NKPA troops still facing Walker's forces at more than 100,000—probably close to twice as many as were actually there. And finally there was an ongoing shortage of ammunition, especially for 105-millimeter howitzers, and of boats and other equipment for crossing the river.

Nevertheless, after MacArthur repeatedly applied the heat, Walker did his best to get his forces revved up for their long-awaited effort to smash through NKPA lines and strike north and west. The newly formed I Corps—encompassing the First Cavalry Division, 24th Infantry Division, First ROK Division, Fifth Regimental Combat Team, and British 27th Infantry Brigade—was assigned to spearhead the breakout.

Originally, the UN counteroffensive was supposed to coincide with the Inchon landings on September 15. But Walker was granted a one-day delay on the theory that news of the Inchon landing might demoralize enemy troops and make the breakout less difficult. That advantage was, of course, nullified when NKPA commanders purposely concealed the truth from their troops, but the news *did* provide an enormous morale boost for the Americans.

As historian Clay Blair explained, "Every GI immediately perceived [the landing's] strategic significance. It was like a miracle. It would liberate them from the ghastly prison of the perimeter . . . and enable them to get out of Korea soon. And the sooner, the better."

The new H-hour for the breakout was set for 9:00 AM on September 16, but even then, there was virtually no change in the battlefront. With heavy rain falling from leaden skies and restricting air cover, the two sides remained locked in the same positions. At several points, in fact, the enemy was continuing to attack, and UN forces were still on the defensive.

A major problem for Walker's troops was that the NKPA occupied tunnel-connected, heavily fortified minifortresses gouged into solid rock in the high ground and reminiscent of the underground Japanese labyrinths in the Pacific. Before any large-scale breakout from the perimeter could occur, these bastions had to be seized, destroyed, or somehow bypassed.

The overall plan for the counteroffensive involved three key lines of assault:

1. The main thrust would come in the northwest sector around Taegu, site of Walker's headquarters, where the First Cav and 24th Infantry divisions were to cross the Naktong and attack north and west toward Taejon and beyond, with the goal of eventually linking up with X Corps at Suwon.

2. At the southern end of the front, the Second and 25th Infantry divisions were to advance west and slightly north across the Korean peninsula toward the west coast port of Kunsan on three roughly parallel roads.

3. In the north and northeast, six ROK divisions were to push north into the Taeback Mountains and up the east coast.

Basically, the attack of the First Cav and 24th Infantry divisions would take the Americans back along the same route—and through the same towns—where they'd been flanked and thrashed by the NKPA in July.

For veterans of the 24th, the strategic linkup with X Corps was strictly a secondary objective. Their principal focus was on punishing the foe who had humiliated them earlier. And the prospect of returning to Taejon, the scene of the 24th's worst disasters, gave rise to a clenched-fist marching ditty composed by a poetic machine gunner:

> *The last time that we saw Taejon, it was not bright or gay.*
> *Today we'll go back to Taejon and blow the goddamn place away!*

Despite the thirst for revenge, the period between September 16 and 18 produced few positive results for the Eighth Army. While Walker fretted at Taegu and MacArthur fumed in Tokyo, UN lines along the Naktong remained disappointingly static.

There were, however, isolated exceptions. Among the more notable was the performance of the Second Division's 38th Infantry Regiment, which had earned the nickname "Rock of the Marne" in France in World War I. Commanded by Colonel George B. "Pep" Peploe, a soft-spoken, forty-nine-year-old officer from Waterport, New York, the 38th had been given the impossible assignment of covering a 30,000-yard front along the river but had emerged from a nightmarish series of clashes remarkably unscathed.

Much of the regiment's latent offensive capability stemmed from Peploe's firm belief that peacetime soldiers should train as long and as hard as their wartime counterparts. When he'd assumed command of the 38th in the early summer of 1950, he'd given his men a rugged regimen of field exercises under an officer corps in which eight of every ten platoon, company, and battalion commanders were combat veterans of World War II. In late August, Peploe's unit had relieved the 24th Division's 34th Infantry on the northern edge of the Naktong Bulge, and Peploe had immediately put all three rifle battalions on line, holding only his tank company in reserve.

Thus, on September 16, when the regiment was ordered to drive west across the Naktong, Peploe's men were ready. While American units to its south showed little or no movement, the 38th unhesitatingly followed the close-order air support of a squadron of Australian P-51s to the east bank of the river. Once there, Peploe stared perplexed at the wide, twelve-foot-deep expanse of brown water and called division headquarters. "Where are the boats?" he demanded of the lieutenant colonel who answered.

"There aren't any boats," the lieutenant colonel replied.

Undeterred, Peploe asked for volunteers to swim the river, conduct patrols, and secure a bridgehead on the opposite bank. A dozen GIs stepped forward, including one who almost drowned on the way across because, in his eagerness, he forgot that he couldn't swim.

After crossing the muddy river, they found no immediate sign of enemy troops but came upon a veritable gold mine of abandoned NKPA equipment, including several two-man rubber boats and a much larger craft capable of carrying up to thirty men at a time.

After two rifle squads navigated the Naktong in the two-man boats, Peploe again contacted the division CP. "I've gotten some boats," he said. "Let me go across the river in force."

At noon on September 18, after a delay of several hours, Colonel Gerald Epley, the Second Division chief of staff, gave Peploe the go-ahead to send a battalion to the opposite bank.

Within three hours, E and F companies of Peploe's Second Battalion had completed the crossing and occupied high ground a mile west of the river. They took a disorganized group of North Koreans by surprise, capturing more than 100 enemy troops, including 8 officers, plus about 100 tons of ammunition and a large cache of weapons.

Back on the Naktong's east bank, Army engineers hurriedly constructed rafts to carry across heavy weapons and a bridge for the 38th's vehicles. Within hours, the rest of the battalion was across the river and solidifying its position.

After six cruel weeks of standoff along the Naktong, the Eighth Army—one small part of it, anyway—had finally battled its way out of the Pusan Perimeter. On the American side, it was the beginning of a northward victory stampede; on the North Korean side, it was the beginning of the end.

Except for Peploe's success, few other material gains were made by American or UN units for the next twelve hours. But on the night of September 18–19, as news of Inchon became common knowledge, the North Korean front started falling apart. In the far South, the NK Sixth and Seventh divisions began a massive "bug-out" under cover of darkness.

Meanwhile, the U.S. Fifth Regimental Combat Team attacked a crucial piece of high ground north of the Naktong Bulge known as Hill 268, held by the NK Third Division. After two days of savage fighting, the Americans overran the hill, captured the town of Waegwan, and sent the enemy reeling backward, leaving several hundred dead behind.

Beginning on the morning of the nineteenth, other U.S. and ROK forces also launched decisive offensive thrusts. The Third ROK Division retook the lost east coast port of Pohang-dong and chased the NK Fifth Division northward, and the First ROK Division exploited a gap in enemy lines to penetrate thirteen miles into the rear of the NK First and Thirteenth divisions.

That same day, the Fifth RCT continued its advance, slashing holes in NKPA lines west of Taegu and effectively relieving any remaining pressure on that key city. By September 20, a crossing site for the entire 24th Division had been secured on the Naktong, and enemy resistance in the area was melting like butter against a hot knife.

"Things down here are ripe for something to break," Brigadier General Frank A. Allen, the Eighth Army's chief of staff, informed MacArthur's headquarters.

One facet of that "breakage" took shape on the night of the twentieth, when Colonel James Lynch, commanding the Third Battalion, Seventh Cavalry Regiment, First Cavalry Division, was placed in charge of a newly formed force designated as Task Force Lynch. For days, the First Cav had fought as hard as any unit in the Eighth Army, and it had inflicted staggering losses on the North Koreans. But it had taken terrific punishment in return and had, as yet, been unable to budge the enemy forces facing it. Task Force Lynch was to become a key factor in changing all that.

The task force's first assignment was to seize the river crossing at Sonsan, some thirty miles north-northwest of Taegu, but it was destined to accomplish much, much more. Besides Lynch's own battalion, it included two tank platoons, a dozer-equipped engineer company, a 4.2 mortar platoon, and elements of the 77th Field Artillery. An Air Force squadron also was assigned to provide close air support for the group.

"I never knew why I was picked for the job," said Corporal Jack Brooks, who'd been fighting with Lynch's battalion since July, "but I ended up being Colonel Lynch's bodyguard and going everywhere with him. I really came to admire him. He was a super person."

Lynch launched his initial attack at 6:30 AM on September 21, and over the next six days, his task force advanced a total of 120 miles, knifing deep behind enemy lines and fighting off repeated desperate counterattacks by NKPA troops trying to flee north. Finally, on September 27, after breaking

up an assault by ten infantry-supported tanks, Lynch's group would link up
with elements of the Seventh Infantry Division at Osan, where Task Force
Smith had begun America's involvement in the Korean War almost three
months earlier.

"We killed or captured between 600 and 700 enemy troops and wiped
out at least thirteen tanks," recalled Brooks, who was awarded a Bronze Star
for his actions with the task force. "It was quite a ride."

"We were able to split the enemy down the middle," Lynch said later in
summing up the breakthrough, "and we effected a solid juncture between
the troops of I Corps and X Corps."

After skies cleared and American and UN planes returned to the skies in
droves, it was the same story all along the Naktong as napalm and high
explosives scorched and shattered the retreating enemy. Caught now in full
flight, entire units of the People's Army were slaughtered by American
planes on the roads leading north.

"The North Koreans began abandoning their equipment and running,"
wrote historian Joseph Goulden. "A few stayed and died in their foxholes in
futile rearguard actions; others fled so fast they left wet laundry hanging on
bushes and hot food in headquarters buildings. Uncountable thousands
simply shucked their uniforms and tried to meld into the general population."

On September 22, General Walker issued a five-word directive to his
troops. It was an order that many Eighth Army veterans had almost given
up hope of ever receiving, but it succinctly summed up the new situation
along what had been, ever so recently, the Naktong front:

"Pursue and destroy the enemy."

Some 150 miles north, on the western edge of Seoul, the picture on the 22nd
wasn't quite so rosy for the Americans. North Korean dictator Kim Il Sung
had pieced together a force of some 20,000 troops to defend the city. They'd
been made aware of how urgent it was—both militarily and psychologi-
cally—to maintain control of their enemy's capital, and they would fight
fiercely to do so. Failing that, their mission was to see Seoul reduced to brick
dust, ashes, and corpses as by-products of its own liberation.

In some instances, the tens of thousands of civilians who remained in the city—many of whom were eager to greet the Americans with outpourings of gratitude—appear to have been specifically targeted by the North Koreans. Marines advancing through the ruins told of coming across groups of as many as 250 dead men, women, and children who apparently had been gunned down execution-style.

Two newly activated NKPA units provided impressive muscle for the defenders. The 78th Independent Regiment, with about 2,500 men commanded by Colonel Pak Han Lin, included three infantry battalions supported by motorcycle, mortar, reconnaissance, medical, and weapons companies as well as a platoon of engineers. Another unit that quickly won the respect of the First Marine Division was the 5,000-man NK 25th Brigade under Major General Wol Ki Chan, with four heavy weapons battalions, an infantry battalion, two artillery battalions, a 120-millimeter mortar battalion, and other support units.

With their big guns lodged in strong positions in a string of ridges, and with deep caves packed with adequate supplies, these forces formed a formidable barrier at the western edge of Seoul that was impossible to flank. Only by breaching this main line of resistance could the Americans reach the heart of the capital city.

The struggle to gain a northwest entryway into downtown Seoul began in earnest at 7:00 AM on September 22 as two battalions of Colonel Murray's reinforced Fifth Marines (now designated as Regimental Combat Team Five following the recent addition of a battalion of ROK Marines) jumped off together. Colonel Taplett's 3/5, occupying a peak called Hill 296 overlooking the embattled city, anchored the left side of the advance, with the First Korean Marine Battalion in the center and Colonel Newton's 1/5 on the right. Colonel Roise's 2/5 was in reserve.

The bloodiest three days of Marine casualties in Korea lay ahead. When they were over, seventeen of eighteen of the Fifth Marines' original platoon leaders and five of six of its company commanders who'd landed with General Craig's brigade on August 2 would be dead or wounded.

As one of his regiment's last company COs still standing, Captain Ike Fenton of B/1/5 faced perhaps the thorniest objective of his career on the morning of September 22—an inconsequential-looking knob of rock designated as Hill 105-S (for south). To confuse matters for the Marines, there were actually three hills numbered 105, but 105-S was a greater obstacle than either 105-C (for center) or 105-N (for north) because the former was the southern terminus of a 6,000-yard system of high ground that the NKPA had made its main line of resistance.

Fenton's sister company, A/1/5, was able to get within 500 yards of 105-S before it was pinned down by withering fire from an enemy antitank gun and several heavy machine guns that were, in Fenton's words, "really raising Cain" on the hill.

At that point, C Company, which had been following A Company, tried to go around A's flank and move up the slope, but it, too, was pinned down with heavy casualties, including two A Company platoon leaders. First Lieutenant Nathaniel F. Mann Jr. was killed and First Lieutenant Joseph A. Schimmenti was severely wounded before the company gained a foothold near the base of 105-S.

Fenton figured that his B Company would be next in line to contest the entrenched enemy on the hill, and Colonel Newton, the battalion commander, soon confirmed that fact.

"I want you to pass through A Company, then coordinate your attack with C Company, and take that damned hill," Newton told Fenton. "I'll send you thirty minutes of artillery and a heavy air strike to soften things up."

It took Fenton's men more than two hours to complete this maneuver, but by about sunset on the twenty-second, the crest of 105-S was declared secure. B Company had managed the move at a cost of just one KIA and six wounded. C Company had suffered the heaviest losses—nine killed and seventeen wounded—and A Company reported two dead and eight wounded.

Now, having taken the hill as ordered, 1/5 faced the even more excruciating task of holding it. As his men hurriedly dug in to defend the summit for the night, Fenton's suspicions were aroused by the total lack of evidence of any earlier enemy presence atop 105-S.

"During the afternoon, we'd seen groups of ten to twenty NKs on the hill at four or five different times, and each time I'd called in air strikes on them," he recalled. "But now there weren't even any empty cartridges or things like that lying around. It looked like the North Koreans had dragged their dead and wounded and everything else down the eastern slope."

If so, Fenton reasoned, live enemy troops were almost certain to be hiding somewhere down that same slope and waiting to attack after dark. The hill was barren, with little cover on its flat, egg-shaped top, and it was already being swept by enemy antitank and machine-gun fire, both from the rest of the long ridgeline and from Seoul itself, which lay to Fenton's immediate front. It was a bad situation to be in.

"Tell your guys to stick close to their holes and keep a sharp eye out," Fenton warned his platoon leaders. "Watch that eastern slope. I think we may have company tonight."

At about midnight, the North Koreans stormed the Marine positions, overrunning a platoon of C Company, killing a machine-gun crew, and seizing its gun. Then they moved around the base of the hill, firing the captured weapon into Marine lines in an effort to draw return fire that would pinpoint B Company's position. But Fenton kept his men quiet, and hearing only silence from the Marines, the enemy troops grew bolder. When they started up the hill again, Fenton was determined to be ready for them.

"I want every man on the line to have a grenade in his hand and get set to throw it," he ordered. "When the NKs get close enough, everybody cut loose at once."

With held breath, the Marines waited . . . and waited . . .

"Now!" Fenton yelled. An instant later, the hill shook under the force of scores of simultaneous explosions. The counterattacking force was wiped out almost to a man.

Before dawn the next morning, September 23, the NKPA tried a second counterattack in the same spot, suffering the same result. By the time Fenton and his men were relieved by 2/5 the following day, B Company's losses totaled seven killed and seventeen wounded—miraculously low numbers, all things considered—but they'd held the crest of 105-S against everything the Communist force at the hill's base could throw at them.

Generals MacArthur and Almond were pushing the troops of X Corps relentlessly, hoping to be able to declare Seoul secure by day's end on September 25, the three-month anniversary of the North Korean invasion. This obsessive quest for speed would add immeasurably to the agony suffered by Seoul and its inhabitants. But as the hours passed with no letup in the fighting and only a small fraction of the city under American control, it became painfully obvious that the deadline was unrealistic—at least to the troops on the line.

"MacArthur dearly wanted the city recaptured by the anniversary," recalled Colonel Robert Taplett, commander of 3/5. "The constant harassment, based not on realistic military consideration but on political promises . . . grew increasingly irritating." As word of the deadline filtered down the chain of command, Taplett and other battalion-level officers also learned that MacArthur was intent on staging a triumphal return to the capital by himself and South Korean President Syngman Rhee.

For his part, Taplett was far more concerned about the loss of such trusted field commanders as Lieutenant Robert "Dewey" Bohn, CO of G/3/5, than about MacArthur's "well-orchestrated ceremony." After sustaining his second serious wound, Bohn had been evacuated on September 22 and replaced by his executive officer, First Lieutenant Charlie Mize, a Purple Heart veteran of Okinawa.

Left in the wake of the struggle to breach the NKPA's main line was what one observer described as "a ghastly killing ground," and the block-by-block, house-to-house battle for central Seoul was still ahead. But now three American regiments—two Marine and one Army—were inside the city and advancing over converging routes from the northwest, west, and southwest.

In addition to the First and Fifth Marines, the 32nd Infantry of the Army's Seventh Division and the 187th Airborne Regimental Combat Team had now joined the fight, along with the ROK Marines' First Battalion. Colonel Litzenberg's Seventh Marine Regiment, while still in reserve, also was deployed so it could be committed to the offensive on short notice.

Corpsman Herb Pearce's confident prediction on the eve of the Inchon landings that the Marines would be in Seoul within ten days had held true—in a manner of speaking. But despite a series of premature reports from Almond's headquarters that the city had been recaptured, Seoul was nowhere near secure as night fell on the twenty-fifth. Fortified barricades and hidden mines still blocked many intersections along major thorough-fares. Squads of NKPA snipers still fired at random from ruined buildings with rifles, machine guns, and mortars. Enemy tanks and self-propelled guns still roamed the streets.

"That street fighting in Seoul was the worst, bloodiest thing I saw in Korea," said Pearce's fellow medic Corpsman Cecil Carpenter, attached to Colonel Taplett's G/3/5. "We had one corpsman to every twelve-man squad, but the casualties kept me so swamped that they had to assign Sergeant Jack Mason, one of our fire team leaders, to help me."

Texas-born Carpenter's attempt to rescue one wounded Marine ended in a horrifying discovery. "I ran out and grabbed him and dragged him back behind a tank," he recalled. "I thought he might not be hurt too bad because there was just a small bullet hole in the front of his jacket. Then I discovered I had his blood all over me, and I turned him over. His whole back was blown open. There was a hole there I could've put both my fists in."

A short time later, Carpenter himself was hit by shrapnel but treated his own wounds and refused evacuation.

Before the last serious resistance was eliminated, the Americans would learn, much to their torment, that merely being *in* Seoul was a far cry from actually *owning* it.

The beginning of the end for the NKPA's main line of resistance had come on the morning of September 24, when the fresh troops of Colonel Chesty Puller's First and Second battalions were ordered into action just minutes after crossing the Han River. Within a few hours, they'd literally overrun the North Korean fortifications in the ridges on Seoul's western edge. Colonel Allan Sutter's 2/1 had led the assault, establishing contact with the Fifth Marines' right flank, then wheeling to the east to attack an objective desig-nated as Hill 79, from whose heights the men could look down on Seoul's railroad yards, electric generating plant, and gas works.

Sutter's battalion had moved smartly but not fast enough to satisfy Puller, who crossed the river on the heels of Lieutenant Colonel Jack

Hawkins's 1/1, only to find the battalion quietly standing by in an assembly area.

"What the hell are you doing, Hawkins?" Puller demanded.

"I'm in reserve, sir," Hawkins replied.

"Well, not for long you aren't," Puller said. "I want you to lead the attack—now!"

"But sir, we can't pass Sutter," Hawkins protested. "He's moving fast. Are you going to stop him so I can get out in front?"

"Hell no," Puller snapped. "I had trouble enough getting 'em started. You'll just have to advance a little faster than he does."

Puller's order made Hawkins's jaw drop. It meant that to pass through 2/1, the entire First Battalion would have to cover ground at double time and with weapons in hand—a maneuver almost unheard of in the annals of modern warfare. But somehow, Hawkins's men managed to pull it off. Captain Robert P. Wray, commanding C/1/1, later described the spectacle as "just knots of men driving across the landscape so fast that the enemy didn't have a chance to get organized."

As the two intermingling battalions rushed past Hill 105-S, they drew small-arms and automatic-weapons fire from the North Koreans clustered at its base and suffered a few casualties. But by 3:00 PM on the twenty-fourth, Hawkins's battalion was camped atop Hill 79, where Captain Robert H. Barrow's A/1/1—acting on Puller's orders—ran up the first American flag within the city limits of Seoul atop an abandoned schoolhouse.

In the words of Marine historian Robert D. Heinl Jr., the Fifth Marines were "outraged" at this affront by Puller's Johnny-come-lately regiment after 1/5 and 2/5 had absorbed two days of punishment while hammering at the main enemy line. Colonel Ray Murray's men were especially galled to learn that the flag-raising had been captured on film by *Life* photographer David Douglas Duncan.

From that point on, wrote Marine Major Andrew Geer in his book *The New Breed*, "Each unit obtained a supply of flags, and the race was on."

The final "liberation" of Hill 105-S wasn't completed until the morning of September 25, when a company of Pershing tanks, commanded by Captain Bruce F. Williams, arrived in the vicinity of the no-man's-land recently vacated by 1/5. The tanks were accompanied by a single rifle platoon, led by Staff Sergeant Arthur Farrington, and a small group of engineers under First Lieutenant George Babe.

Farrington spotted some enemy arms stacked beside one of several nearby huts at about the same moment that one of the engineers saw movement among the trees on the slope of the hill. As the Marines took cover, a shower of grenades flew from the direction of the huts, and bursts of small-arms fire came from the hillside.

Lieutenant Babe rallied his engineers as riflemen until an enemy round from a hut felled him with an arm wound, but three of his men rushed forward with a TNT charge and blew the hut to splinters. Meanwhile, Sergeant Farrington quickly set up a skirmish line facing 105-S while other engineers guided a flame tank forward to sear the hill with napalm. When the enemy fire slackened, a Korean interpreter began calling to the NKPA troops to surrender, and after a moment, the Marines joined in.

"Everything got quiet as we yelled," Farrington recalled. "The 'trees' on the hillside stopped moving. A Korean stood up halfway up the hill and held his rifle over his head. . . . That did it. They started coming out in numbers, all carrying their burp guns."

As the Marines made their captives strip, a group of about forty other North Koreans jumped up along a nearby railroad track and tried to run away. They didn't get far.

"We killed them with rifle, machine-gun, and 90-millimeter fire as they went across the paddies, into the villages, and across the railway," Farrington said. At the same time, several of Captain Williams's tanks moved in to blow away the rest of the huts and reveal a hidden cave behind them. With the flame tanks closing in to "cure" the cave, a stream of North Koreans stumbled out with their hands raised. The fight was over.

When the shooting stopped, 150 enemy dead were counted on the hillside and in a nearby draw, and 131 naked prisoners were lined up three abreast. Hill 105-S would never again be a problem, but few Marines who were there would ever forget it. The bitterly contested ridgeline between Hills 105-S and 296 was littered with the bodies of more than 1,200 enemy dead.

"That ridge was probably the most heavily defended enemy strongpoint we'd encountered in Korea," said Ike Fenton. "Casualties for the Second Battalion were horrendous. In one day's fighting, they lost 69 killed and 268 wounded. Two of their companies were reduced to less than 50 men apiece."

All day on September 25, the Marines' tenuous drive into the ravaged heart of Seoul continued on what Colonel Thomas Ridge, commanding 3/1, termed "a foot-by-foot basis." Ridge's battalion moved doggedly through the ruins along Ma-Po Boulevard, once a bustling, tree-lined thoroughfare of grocery stores and small shops but now a wasteland of wreckage studded with land mines, snipers' nests, and bristling NKPA barricades.

The barricades had been thrown up at every major cross street, many of the barricades up to eight feet tall and five feet thick and composed of any materials the defenders could lay hands on: broken carts and furniture; bags of sand, dirt, and even rice; streetcar rails and chunks of concrete; wooden beams and other rubble.

The American tanks had been delayed for hours getting into the city because almost all the bridges spanning the Han had been destroyed and the armored units were forced to take long detours to points where they could be ferried across the river. Once they arrived, however, they shoved and blasted their way through the barricades with utter ruthlessness.

"Our tank was beat to hell when we got to Seoul," recalled Corporal Murdoch Ford, the young driver of an M-26, "but miraculously we'd had no casualties. We were among the first tanks to get into the main city streets, and it took us three days to get all the way through town. At some of the barricades, the NKs had women and kids sitting in front of them. It took us forty-five minutes to an hour to clear a lot of them."

Another obstacle to Ford and his fellow tankers was enemy soldiers hiding atop lampposts and utility poles and dropping Molotov cocktails as the American armor passed.

"We noticed several tanks catching fire on their engine compartments, and we finally figured out what was happening," Ford recalled. "After that, we just started ramming and knocking down all the poles as we went along. Sometimes the fall was enough to kill the NK soldiers, but we always shot them anyway. We had to do that through the whole length of Seoul."

Reginald Thompson, an on-the-scene correspondent for London's *Daily Telegraph*, offered harsh criticism of the ferocity of American battle tactics. "The slightest resistance," he reported, "brought down a deluge of destruction, blotting out the area. Few people have suffered so terrible a liberation."

British historian Max Hastings, writing more than three decades after the fact, expanded on those observations: "The battle for Seoul became a source of lasting controversy—and deep revulsion to some of those who witnessed it. It provided an example of a form of carnage that would become wretchedly familiar in Indochina a generation later—allegedly essential destruction in the cause of liberation."

By nightfall on the twenty-fifth, roughly 40 percent of Seoul was occupied by American troops, although little of it could be classified as secure. Besides the First and Fifth Marines, a battalion of the Army's 32nd Infantry Regiment was dug in on strategic high ground on the south side of the city. Colonel Litzenberg's Seventh Marines had taken over a zone of action to the north to protect the flank of the Fifth Marines and cut the main highway—and principal NKPA escape route—between Seoul and the North Korean capital of Pyongyang.

As the daylight failed, the fighting ebbed. Sporadic mortar and small-arms fire still echoed among shattered buildings, and flames from countless fires set by UN bombs and shells stabbed the dark sky. Bone-tired Marines whose roadblocks weren't under attack hunkered down over their C rations and tried to catch their breath.

It had been a long, arduous day for Corporal Jack Dedrick of H/3/1, who had recently returned to duty after being hospitalized for three days with mortar wounds in his back. Before it was over, the young machine-gun squad leader would win a letter of commendation from General Smith himself. Despite wounds that weren't completely healed, Dedrick had repeatedly exposed himself to fire from two enemy machine guns in a barricade during a series of attacks through Seoul's main streets, using his own weapon to neutralize both. The commendation would credit Dedrick with "great skill, courage, and confidence" that helped his company flank the enemy position and destroy it.

Although Dedrick knew nothing as yet of the commendation, that action had been the high point of his day. The indisputable low point had been when he'd stumbled into a Korean "honey bucket," splattered its contents all over himself, and spent the next several hours smelling like a privy. "Nobody could stand to be near me, and there was no way I could get it off," Dedrick said.

"Such is the life of a Marine," a squadmate jibed, keeping his distance. "Covered with glory one minute, covered with shit the next. At least it's quiet around here for the moment."

Unfortunately, the quiet interlude would be short-lived. As tough as the day had been, an even tougher night lay ahead.

Shortly after 8:00 PM on the twenty-fifth, the First Marine Division received a message from General Almond's headquarters that strained the credulity of General Smith and his staff. According to Almond's dispatch, the bulk of NKPA defenders was withdrawing from Seoul and fleeing north under heavy U.S. air attacks. "You will push your attack *NOW* to the limit of your objectives," the X Corps commander directed, "in order to ensure maximum destruction of enemy forces."

Smith, who was finishing a C ration supper when the message arrived, almost choked on the last bite of it. In disbelief, he put in a call to Major General Clark Ruffner, Almond's chief of staff, asking for confirmation.

"The order went out exactly as General Almond personally dictated it, and it's to be executed without delay." Ruffner's tone was sympathetic but firm.

Colonel Al Bowser, Smith's G-3 operations officer, was stunned by the order and convinced that the "fleeing enemy" mentioned by Almond was actually civilians trying to escape the flaming city. Bowser knew that heavy street fighting had raged until nightfall, when 1/5 and 2/5 had suspended their advance, set up roadblocks, and tied their lines together defensively. He also knew that Colonel Taplett's 3/5 was still under counterattack and receiving fire from NKPA tanks. In Bowser's judgment, it was hard to imagine a worse time to launch an offensive.

When Smith relayed the order to Colonels Murray and Puller, they could hardly believe their ears. It seemed clear that Almond was determined to meet his own manufactured deadline for securing Seoul without regard for the risks or potential bloodletting it entailed. Why else would he order a night attack to a depth of more than three miles through the heart of the fifth-largest city in the Orient with neither artillery/air preparation nor advance reconnaissance? At best, such an operation was rife with peril and pitfalls; at worst, it was nothing short of suicidal.

A short time later, however, a personal phone call to Puller and Murray from General Smith mollified both regimental commanders somewhat. "I want you to coordinate your attack carefully," Smith said. "Don't try to advance too rapidly. Take it slow, and stay on main avenues that you can identify at night. I'm ordering a fifteen-minute artillery preparation before you jump off."

After Murray briefed his staff on the new orders, Lieutenant Colonel Joseph Stewart shook his head. "We may have to delay our pursuit of the 'fleeing enemy,'" he said wryly, "until we see if Tap [Colonel Taplett] can beat off that counterattack."

At the First Marines command post, Chesty Puller felt heavyhearted. Never one to pull punches or take the easy way to victory, he was one of his Corps' strongest proponents of the frontal assault. But Almond's order ran counter to everything Puller had learned about military logic and common sense in his thirty-two years as a Marine officer.

As his regiment stood poised to enter Seoul on September 24, Puller had expressed fear that savage NKPA resistance would lead to heavy damage in the city and many casualties among civilians remaining in harm's way. Now his prediction was being borne out—but not because of the NKPA. With countless blocks of buildings already lying in ruins and hundreds of fires blazing out of control, more indiscriminate pounding of the city by American heavy guns was just ahead.

As senior regimental commander, Puller was to coordinate the attack, and he set the jump-off time for 1:45 AM on September 26. He knew that orders were orders, and they had to be obeyed, but his first concern was the welfare of his men. When the first fifteen-minute artillery preparation was over, he reluctantly ordered a second one, delaying the jump-off until two o'clock.

In the meantime, both regiments sent out patrols, accompanied by native Korean guides, to range a few hundred yards to the front and check out the lay of the land.

The eight-man patrol from Taplett's 3/5 (which had by now managed to repel the enemy tank-infantry attack) was led by Corporal Charles Collins and accompanied by three guides. But before making contact with the patrol from the First Marines, Collins's men stumbled onto a battalion-strength tank and infantry force from the NK 25th Brigade preparing to attack a fortified roadblock manned by elements of Colonel Thomas Ridge's 3/1.

The North Korean riflemen immediately opened fire, and Collins ordered his men to fall back and report to Taplett while he covered their withdrawal. They obeyed, most of them never expecting to see Collins alive again.

Within minutes, an awesome firefight was raging. Soon joined by enemy tanks and Marine 155-millimeter howitzers, it quickly spread until it consumed several blocks along Ma-Po Boulevard. It continued with no significant lull until 5:30 AM, when Ridge's rifle companies ran dangerously low on ammunition, and Ridge put in an urgent call for ammo for machine guns, 3.5-inch rocket launchers, and 75-millimeter recoilless guns.

The rate of fire with which the NKPA attack was beaten off set records for the Korean War and the Marine Corps. Four artillery battalions of the 11th Marines expended all their available reserves as well as those in a nearby Army ammunition dump, burning out many of their howitzer barrels in the process. Almost 1,000 4.2-inch and 81-millimeter mortar rounds were fired, and the Marines' 30,000 heavy machine-gun rounds eclipsed a one-day Corps record of 26,000, set at Guadalcanal in 1942.

Sunrise revealed the grisly extent of the massacre in front of Puller's lines. Piles of enemy corpses lay everywhere; four tanks and two NK self-propelled guns had been reduced to blackened, twisted wreckage. The rest of the enemy troops had melted away.

Shortly after the shooting stopped, Corporal Collins made his way back to friendly lines dressed in the traditional white clothing of a Korean peasant. He'd found the clothing in an empty house and ridden out the battle there.

Three other assaults, including the one against Taplett's battalion, were mounted by Communist forces in Seoul that night. At 4:30 AM on September 26, F and G companies of the 32nd Infantry's Second Battalion were hit by a tank-led enemy force on a 900-foot hill called Nam-San, overlooking a network of major roadways. After a vicious two-and-a-half-hour fight in which the GIs were forced to give ground but then reclaimed it, the enemy withdrew, leaving nearly 400 dead behind.

When a news correspondent asked Puller that morning what he knew about Almond's reference to "fleeing enemy," he responded with typical curtness:

"All I know about a fleeing enemy is there's hundreds of 'em out there that won't be fleeing anywhere. They're dead."

Nevertheless, General Almond's headquarters had issued a press release the previous afternoon, which stated blithely, "Three months to the day after the North Koreans launched their surprise attack south of the 38th Parallel, the combat troops of X Corps recaptured the capital city of Seoul. . . . By 1400 hours [2:00 PM], 25 September, the military defenses of Seoul were broken. . . . The enemy is fleeing the city to the northeast."

Not everyone in the press corps swallowed Almond's fiction. At mid-morning on September 26, a Seoul-datelined Associated Press dispatch pointedly observed, "If the city had been liberated, the remaining North Koreans did not know it."

Another report, filed about the same time by *Time* reporter Dwight Martin, captured the gruesome scenes still unfolding along Ma-Po Boulevard:

"In the center of the street, six Pershing tanks wheeled into position to advance. Directly in front of the lead tank lay the body of a Red soldier who had been caught in the burst of a white phosphorus shell. The corpse was still burning as the tank's right tread passed over it, extinguishing the flame and grinding the body into a grisly compost. . . .

"Further along, behind a barricade just seized by the Marines, we saw another amazing sight. Less than 50 yards away, through dense smoke, came 40 to 50 North Korean soldiers. They dragged a light antitank gun. Apparently, they thought the barricade was held by their side. The Marines first stared in disbelief, then opened fire with every weapon available. The Reds screamed, buckled, pitched, and died on Ma-Po's pavement."

Colonel Bryghte Godbold learned through personal experience—one that he almost didn't live to tell about—that Seoul was still extremely *inse-*

cure on the afternoon of September 26. After visiting Chesty Puller's command post to make arrangements to have a Marine with "severe personal problems at home" transferred out of the combat zone, Godbold was traveling through the city by jeep when a sniper opened fire.

"The bullet hit the windshield squarely between the driver and me," Godbold recalled. "We both ducked, and the driver yelled, 'Goddamn!' I asked him if he was hit, and he said, 'No, but what the hell am I gonna do about my windshield?'"

It took the Americans two more days—until September 28—to reclaim Seoul in its entirety. Colonel Murray's regiment spent those forty-eight hours grinding slowly east against bitter, last-ditch resistance, finally linking up at the edge of Seoul with Puller's First Marines.

Meanwhile, tank-led elements of the Army's Seventh Cavalry also tied in with units of the Seventh Infantry Division near Suwon, sixteen miles south of Seoul. Other American armored units, driving north from the old Pusan Perimeter at speeds the fleeing North Koreans couldn't match, slaughtered hundreds of enemy troops along the network of good roads in central Korea. Scores of strafing runs by UN planes added to the carnage.

Near the village of Kochang, west of Taejon, Colonel Peploe's 38th Infantry Regiment, which had led the original breakout across the Naktong, again distinguished itself, knifing through thin lines of the NK Second Division, overrunning its rear areas, killing 200 enemy troops, and taking 450 prisoners. After capturing Kochang, Peploe's force drove south and west toward Chonju, a town near the west coast, advancing seventy-two miles in just over nine hours and killing or capturing 300 more enemy troops along the way.

As their units disintegrated around them, many North Koreans were bypassed by Eighth Army forces as they swept north, but few of these enemy soldiers had any stomach for continuing the fight. Most melted into the countryside in small groups without weapons, ammunition, or food. Among them was Marshal Choe Yong Gun, commanding what was left of the NKPA in South Korea, who ordered all his vehicles and heavy guns abandoned, then headed for the hills to conduct guerrilla operations.

Peploe's men were delayed for a day at Chonju by a shortage of gasoline for their trucks, but by September 29 they were on the south bank of the Han and looking across the river at Seoul. At that point the destruction of the North Korean People's Army was virtually complete.

In the words of U.S battalion commander/historian T. R. Fehrenbach, "The hammer had fallen. It had met the anvil, and what had been in between was no more."

On September 28, after relieving its enemy-surrounded D Company following an all-night vigil on a steep pass at the Seoul city limits, the Seventh Marines advanced through high ground north of the capital, cutting a major highway to the north and blocking another potential enemy escape route.

On the same day, troops of the First and Fifth Marines engaged in a friendly race to raise various national flags above major landmarks in the capital city. Led by F Company, Second Battalion, Puller's regiment fought its way into the French and Soviet embassies as well as several U.S. diplomatic residences. At the abandoned Soviet compound, the Marines hauled down the Hammer and Sickle and replaced it with the Stars and Stripes.

"It's starting to look like the Fourth of July around here," said one grinning gunnery sergeant.

Meanwhile, Colonel Taplett's 3/5 headed toward the biggest prizes of all—Government House, the seat of South Korea's national government, and Chandok Palace, home of President Syngman Rhee, both still decked with red banners and smiling portraits of Kim Il Sung and Joseph Stalin.

After fighting off a brief but vicious attack by diehard North Koreans manning two self-propelled guns, the tank-infantry teams of 3/5 moved up Kwangwhamum Boulevard, and the men of G Company burst triumphantly into the Court of the Lions at a shell-singed and virtually windowless Government House. There they tore down the Communist banners, and Gunnery Sergeant Harold Beaver ran up the American and UN flags while two ROK Marines raised South Korea's colors at the National Palace.

By dusk on the twenty-eighth, organized enemy resistance had ended in

Seoul, but fighting continued in the ridges north of the city, and the blood-shed associated with securing the city wasn't yet over.

Among the last Americans to die in the battle for Seoul was PFC Stanley R. Christianson of E Company, Second Battalion, First Marines. A veteran of three Pacific campaigns during World War II and a Bronze Star recipient at Inchon, the twenty-five-year-old native of Mindore, Wisconsin, was manning a listening post covering the approaches to his platoon area before dawn on September 29 when his position was attacked.

After sending another Marine to alert the platoon, Christianson held his position and fired relentlessly at the approaching enemy, despite knowing that he had little chance of escape. He was credited with killing seven North Koreans and enabling the rest of his platoon to organize its defense before he was fatally struck down. The enemy attackers were subsequently wiped out, with forty-one killed and three taken prisoner. Three other Marines were killed in the firefight as well. Christianson was posthumously awarded the Medal of Honor.

Also killed on September 29 were PFC Robert Kinder of A Company, First Battalion, Seventh Marines, and Navy Corpsman Peter C. Frosley of Long Branch, New Jersey, who went to Kinder's aid when his unit was attacked by NKPA stragglers in the hills just north of Seoul.

"I was sitting on the floor of our truck when the gooks opened fire," recalled PFC Gerald Kraus, a twenty-year-old A/1/7 rifleman from Minneapolis, "but Kinder was leaning out of the cab a few feet from me. He was a risk-taker, and it cost him his life. Frosley was just trying to do his job when they got him."

All told, the Marines suffered 700 casualties in the final three days of the fighting for the South Korean capital. During two of those days, the city was supposedly secure.

In the fifty-eight days between their landing at Pusan on August 2 and the triumphal return to Seoul by the South Korean government on September 29, the Marines sustained a total of 3,938 casualties.

Apparently oblivious to the fact that Marine units in and above Seoul were still engaging scattered groups of enemy diehards, General Almond had ordered all concerned battalion commanders to report to X Corps headquarters at the old U.S. supply center of Ascom City for an after-dinner conference at 8:00 PM on September 28.

The purpose of the meeting was to make final—and rather grandiose—arrangements for the arrival at Kimpo Airport of General MacArthur and President Rhee the next morning and their subsequent reentry into Seoul. Engineers were hurriedly constructing a pontoon bridge across the Han to accommodate the dignitaries' motorcade. Almond had drafted orders, to be delivered at the conference, directing the Marines to form up two honor guards, one at Kimpo and one at the National Palace, and ordering the Marine Band to play. Because the band's instruments had been left behind in Japan, the Fifth Air Force would be directed to airlift them to Kimpo posthaste.

When General Smith learned of Almond's plan to require Marine battalion commanders to attend the conference, he had once more grabbed the phone to X Corps headquarters. "I called up General Ruffner," Smith noted in his log, "and pointed out to him that we still had a war on our hands and that we would not call in battalion commanders for night conferences. I told him we'd have a representative of the G-3 section present [at the September 28 meeting]."

Reason eventually prevailed when MacArthur canceled the conference order and all the rest of Almond's ostentatious arrangements. There would be no band, no airlift, no honor guards, and no ceremonial cordons of U.S. troops. American forces would be present in strength, but they would be kept discreetly behind the scene while ROK Marines and soldiers shared the limelight. "I will personally conduct the proceedings," MacArthur announced.

MacArthur's plane touched down at Kimpo promptly at 10:00 AM on September 29, and the general, accompanied by his wife, stepped out onto the tarmac. A study in casual aplomb, he wore an impeccably creased uniform and his famous gold-braided cap but no necktie. Five spotless Chevrolet staff cars were lined up and waiting, the lead sedan bearing a five-star plate, and a string of forty equally spotless jeeps trailed out behind them.

President and Mrs. Rhee arrived an hour later after a flight from Pusan aboard MacArthur's old personal plane, the *Bataan*. Other dignitaries in the entourage included U.S. Ambassador John Muccio; Generals Walker, Almond, Smith, and Craig; Admirals Arthur Struble and Turner Joy; and Air Force General George Stratemeyer.

Admiral Sohn Won Yil and his wife headed a large group of Korean military officers and civil officials. Also in attendance were dozens of selected U.S. Army unit commanders and U.S. Navy ship captains, as well as several British naval officers in starched whites. Other than Generals Smith and Craig, the only Marine officers present were Colonels Puller and Murray, the two regimental commanders whose troops had borne the brunt of the battle for Seoul.

Puller almost touched off a major interservice incident when an Army MP officer tried to turn away his jeep at an airport entrance restricted to staff cars. The officer relented only after Puller told his driver, "Drive over that SOB if he doesn't move."

As the motorcade began the ten-mile trip into the city, Colonel Taplett's 3/5 was positioned on a hill overlooking the palace, and Colonel Ridge's 3/1 was spread out all along the motorcade route, unseen but "loaded for bear," in the words of Marine historian Joseph Alexander.

The Marines knew that they were supposed to remain virtually invisible to the official celebrants, and they did so, but some took the enforced vanishing act as a slap in the face. Colonel Litzenberg's Seventh Marines was still in deadly combat north of Seoul, and elements of the First and Fifth Marines were manning a human shield across the north side of the city against any attempted enemy incursions. Consequently, many men in the ranks were embittered by the apparent slight.

"For a moment on the afternoon of the 27th, Seoul had seemed their dearly won city," wrote Alexander. "Two days later, they were being told to remain out of sight."

As MacArthur and Rhee entered the vaulted National Assembly chamber in Government House at high noon, the grisly smells of death and destruction wafted through the open windows. In the distance, the muffled sounds of small-arms fire were clearly audible, and the blast of occasional artillery rounds sent slight shudders through the building.

MacArthur moved solemnly to the lectern and turned toward Rhee. "Mr. President," he began, "by the grace of a merciful Providence, our forces fighting under the standard of that greatest hope and inspiration of mankind, the United Nations, have liberated this ancient capital city of Korea. . . . In behalf of the United Nations Command, I am happy to restore to you, Mr. President, the seat of your government, that from it you may better fulfill your constitutional responsibilities."

MacArthur then bowed his head and recited the Lord's Prayer in a steady, unwavering voice, even as tears streamed down his cheeks. It was vintage MacArthur in his greatest moment and at his legendary best, and Syngman Rhee was almost overcome with emotion.

"We love you as the savior of our race," the old president said, laying aside his prepared remarks. "How can I ever explain to you my own undying gratitude and that of the Korean people?"

Moments later, the ceremony was over, and the celebrants were en route back to Kimpo Airport. "Twenty minutes after they left," recalled Sergeant Charlie Snow with a wry grin many years later, "the Marines found two heavily armed North Koreans hiding in a culvert MacArthur had just passed over."

In the jubilation of the moment, it didn't really matter. Not even the "savior" of Korea could have asked for a more perfect or fitting ending to a war that had been all but lost three months earlier.

But, of course, it *wasn't* the end.

"In the best of all worlds," wrote historian Alexander, "the Korean War would have ended on this felicitous note. In reality, however, the blazing speed with which MacArthur had reversed the seeming disaster in South Korea contained the seeds of a greater disaster to come in the north."

On September 27, even before the *actual* fall of Seoul, the Joint Chiefs of Staff had authorized MacArthur, with President Truman's approval, to pursue operations north of the 38th Parallel. On October 1, ROK infantry units surged across the old dividing line near the east coast, and on October 7, troops of the U.S. First Cavalry Division sent patrols over the parallel on the west side of the peninsula.

Meeting with high-ranking U.S. military and political leaders over the next few weeks, as UN forces marched unimpeded through North Korea, MacArthur predicted repeatedly that the war would be over by Thanksgiving and American combat troops home by Christmas.

It was a comforting fantasy—but that's all it was.

CHAPTER 15

★ ★ ★

TAKING THE HARD
WAY HOME

O N OCTOBER 15, 1950, President Truman and General MacArthur met face-to-face for the first—and only—time in their lives. The site was Wake Island, a remote speck of sand and coral in the western Pacific where the first pitched battle between American and Japanese forces had been fought in December 1941. The purpose was to decide how best to consolidate the smashing American victory in Korea and bring the war to a swift, decisive end.

Truman hoped to get a clearer picture of MacArthur's intentions in North Korea and, if necessary, to establish limits as to how far the general— now a bigger hero at home than ever before—should go. For this reason, the personal meeting was entirely Truman's idea. He'd originally wanted it held in Hawaii, which was roughly halfway between Washington and Tokyo. But MacArthur had already declined two pointed presidential invitations to the nation's capital, and he protested that even a trip to Honolulu would keep him away from his command for too long, so Truman obligingly agreed to travel almost three times as far as his supreme Far East commander for their conference.

Nevertheless, it was MacArthur whom witnesses described as "grumpy" on the flight from Tokyo. He complained profusely to U.S. Ambassador to Korea John Muccio about being forced to waste his time on a pointless "political" trip. Possibly to emphasize his displeasure, the general didn't bother to salute his commander in chief when Truman greeted him on Wake, a slight that the president seemed—or pretended—not to notice.

Militarily, the Korean "police action," which had begun so ingloriously in early July, was now being hailed as one of the great triumphs in American history. The NKPA lay in shambles, and the salvation of South Korea was complete. At this precise moment, the First Marine Division was about to make a second amphibious landing, ninety-four miles north of the 38th Parallel at the port of Wonsan—this one uncontested except for scores of enemy mines in the harbor. But the event was strictly anticlimactic because the First ROK Corps had arrived earlier by land and was firmly in control and waiting, along with a squadron of Marine night fighters already operating out of the Wonsan airfield.

"It took us thirteen days of sailing back and forth aboard an old rust-bucket Japanese LST to get from Pusan to Wonsan," recalled Corporal Jack Dedrick of H/3/1. "I didn't think we'd ever get off that tub."

The landing was delayed so long that by the time the main body of Marines came ashore, a USO troupe, headed by Bob Hope and Marilyn Maxwell, had already staged a show there, an event that prompted Army troops attached to the ROKs to add a mocking stanza to the "Marine Hymn":

> *Those tough and fighting Gyrenes,*
> *Wherever they may go,*
> *Are always bringing up the rear,*
> *Behind Bob Hope and the USO!*

As October unfolded, the situation across the Korean peninsula could hardly have looked brighter for the United States and the other Allies. An outcome that Americans fighting there could scarcely have visualized a mere six weeks earlier was suddenly an awesome reality. Yet Truman felt

impelled—and was pressured by some members of his staff—to sit down
with MacArthur to resolve three nagging, unanswered questions:

1. How far and how fast should UN forces advance into an almost su-
   pine North Korea before calling a halt?
2. How soon could U.S. combat forces be withdrawn and brought
   home?
3. And, with increasingly ominous rumblings coming from Peking
   (now Beijing) via neutral diplomatic circles, how great was the risk
   that the Red Chinese—or even the Soviets—might intervene in
   Korea with armed force to save their ally from oblivion and/or keep
   the Americans a safe distance from the Chinese province of Manchuria?

MacArthur's response to the last question was more a dismissal than a
genuine answer. He readily acknowledged that the Chinese had an estimated 300,000 men in Manchuria, including up to 125,000 just across the
Yalu River from North Korea (actually, the numbers were considerably
higher, and many of those 300,000 Chinese troops were already hiding
south of the Yalu). Still, he classified the risk of China's intervention as "very
little."

"Had they intervened in the first or second month [of the war], it would
have been decisive, [but] we are no longer fearful of their intervention,"
MacArthur assured Truman. "We no longer stand hat in hand. . . . They
have no air force. Now that we have bases for our Air Force in Korea, if the
Chinese tried to get down to Pyongyang [the North Korean capital], it
would be the greatest slaughter in the history of mankind."

As to a timetable for American troop withdrawals, MacArthur fairly
oozed confidence. Pyongyang would fall in a week, he predicted, and all
North Korean resistance would be over by Thanksgiving. By Christmas, he
hoped to withdraw the entire Eighth Army—which still operated sepa-
rately from General Almond's X Corps—and he even held out the possibility that one Eighth Army division could be quickly reassigned to duty in
Europe.

The most crucial question on the list—the one concerning how far north to go and where to stop—was never answered at all. Indeed, it was never seriously addressed.

Both Truman and MacArthur share the blame for this glaring omission. Instead of dealing directly with the subject, they tiptoed around its edges as though they were walking on eggs. Truman and his aides never pressed MacArthur for specifics, and MacArthur never volunteered any. Despite his petulance en route to Wake, the general turned on the charm, praising Truman for his outstanding support of the military effort. And Truman sidestepped the toughest, most dangerous questions about limiting the war. Neither he nor any of the top officials accompanying him, including General Omar Bradley, chairman of the Joint Chiefs, mentioned an existing prohibition—approved by Truman and the JCS and tacitly agreed to earlier by MacArthur—against sending UN forces into North Korean provinces adjoining Manchuria.

MacArthur himself, however, told Truman that he planned to use only South Korean troops in a buffer zone between Manchuria and a line running from twenty miles north of Pyongyang to twenty miles north of the east coast port of Hamhung. "I want to take all non-Korean troops out of Korea as soon as possible," he insisted.

At one point, Assistant Secretary of State Dean Rusk passed Truman a note suggesting a slower pace to the meeting to keep the media from assuming that it was merely a public relations ploy.

"No," Truman replied in his own scribbled note, "I want to get out of here before we get in trouble." Truman's reply indicates that he was eager to avoid anything resembling a confrontation with MacArthur and that he accepted MacArthur's explanation of how the latter intended to set limits on the U.S. offensive.

In the end, both parties seemed to assume that they were in broad mutual agreement when nothing could have been further from the truth. As a result, hundreds of thousands of human beings would die, and the course of modern history would be forever changed. As Rusk himself eventually admitted: "The real failure of the Wake Island meeting was in our assessment of Chinese intentions and of our ability to handle Chinese forces."

"The news was so good that no one wanted to know more," wrote journalist-historian David Halberstam fifty-seven years later, after inter-

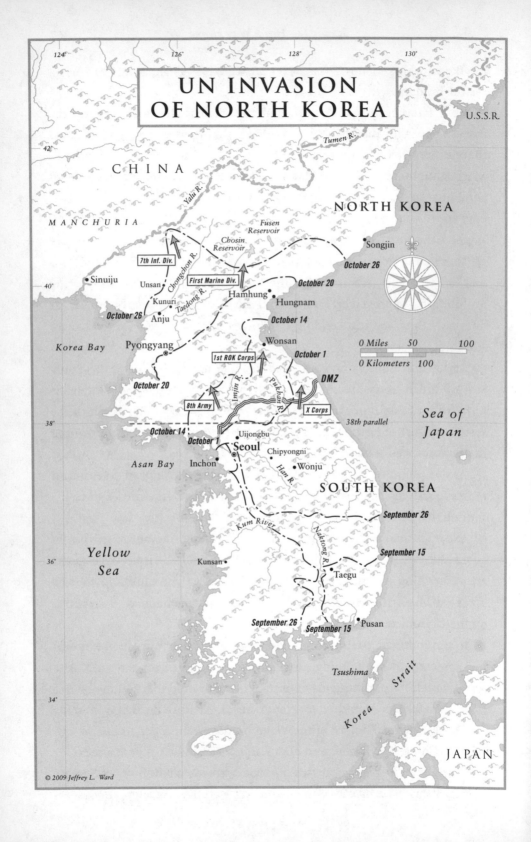

UN INVASION
OF NORTH KOREA

124°   126°   128°   130°

U.S.S.R.

Tumen R.

42°

CHINA

NORTH KOREA

MANCHURIA

Yalu R.

Fusen
Reservoir

Chosin
Reservoir

Songjin

October 26

7th Inf. Div.

Chongchon R.

40°   • Sinuiju

Unsan

First Marine Div.

Taedong R.

October 20

Kunuri   Hamhung   Hungnam

October 26   Anju

October 14

Pyongyang   Wonsan

Korea Bay   **October 1**

1st ROK Corps

October 20   DMZ

0 Miles   50   100

0 Kilometers   100

Imjin R.   *Pukhan R.*

8th Army   X Corps

38°   38th parallel

October 14   Uijongbu   *Sea of Japan*

October 1   Seoul   Chipyongni

Asan Bay   Inchon   • Wonju

Han R.   SOUTH KOREA

September 26

Kum River

36°   *Yellow*   **September 15**

Sea   Kunsan   *Naktong R.*

Taegu

September 26   **September 15** • Pusan

34°

Tsushima   *Korea Strait*

JAPAN

© 2009 Jeffrey L. Ward

views with several of those present at the meeting. "It was as if what they did not say or did not know would not hurt them. So what would happen if the Chinese *did* enter the war . . . was never discussed. Each of the principals, in the name of good manners and good politics, dodged the harder questions."

Tragically, the Americans who were marching in their lightweight summer uniforms steadily deeper into North Korea's autumn chill didn't have that option.

On the day of the Truman-MacArthur meeting, most Americans assumed that the Korean War was as good as over and that the good guys had won. And nothing that transpired between the president and the general appeared to dispute that assumption. But the real and growing danger of Chinese intervention had simply been swept under the rug. Later on, MacArthur defended himself by claiming, with some justification, that determining if the Chinese or the Soviets would intervene in Korea was Washington's responsibility, not his.

But the most amazing aspect of the two leaders' discussion of this crucial issue is that neither man allowed it to go farther. As MacArthur biographer D. Clayton James later wrote, "One question by Truman, a single response by MacArthur, and absolutely no follow-up questions, challenges, or further mention." James described this scenario in one word: "astonishing."

Even as Truman and MacArthur went their respective ways, tens of thousands of Chinese troops were slipping unnoticed across the Yalu River into North Korea. In late November, soon after American troops observed Thanksgiving in below-zero temperatures and their first units reached the Yalu, the Chinese struck with crushing power. Within days, the entire course of the war was again reversed.

Hence, no book—even one focusing on the first three months of the war, as this one does—could be complete without at least a brief examination of the battlefield factors and personalities involved in the monstrous debacle that followed those golden moments at Inchon and Seoul.

On September 27, before the last enemy resistance was stamped out in Seoul, President Truman and the Joint Chiefs of Staff authorized Mac-

Arthur's forces to go beyond the 38th Parallel in pursuit of the NKPA. How far beyond was never spelled out in detail, but MacArthur had made it clear as early as July that once the NKPA was finished, he intended to unify all of Korea under the control of the South Korean government. He obviously interpreted Washington's authorization to mean that he could go all the way to the Yalu to accomplish that goal, and the Joint Chiefs exerted little overt effort to restrain him.

Behind the scenes, however, there were numerous grumblings, some muffled and others more outspoken, by MacArthur's fellow generals, including members of the Joint Chiefs. General Matthew Ridgway, who, ironically, was destined to replace MacArthur as supreme Far East commander, was one of the harshest critics of MacArthur's conduct of the North Korean campaign. Ridgway called MacArthur's insistence on running the campaign from Tokyo "unsound and unwarranted" and described it as "largely responsible for the heavy casualties and near disaster that followed."

Ridgway also regarded the acquiescence that marked the JCS's relations with MacArthur as inexcusable. "[N]o one was willing to issue a flat order" to MacArthur, he later wrote, "to correct a state of affairs that was going rapidly from bad to worse."

After one meeting by the JCS with Defense Secretary Marshall and Secretary of State Acheson failed to produce any substantive action on the MacArthur issue, Ridgway approached Air Force Chief of Staff General Hoyt Vandenberg with some pressing questions:

"Why don't the Joint Chiefs send orders to MacArthur and tell him what to do?" Ridgway demanded.

"What good would that do?" Vandenberg responded. "He wouldn't obey the orders. What can we do?"

"You can relieve any commander who won't obey the orders, can't you?" Ridgway exploded.

Vandenberg stared in puzzlement at Ridgway for a moment, then walked away without a word.

The prevailing feeling on Capitol Hill and at the Pentagon immediately following Inchon was one of intense relief verging on euphoria—a feeling shared by Britain and other U.S. Allies. MacArthur's genius had delivered a miracle of such magnitude that Washington's power structure, up to and including the Joint Chiefs and Truman, jumped to the conclusion that the general could do no wrong, that his judgment was infallible. This was a key reason why Truman and JCS Chairman General Bradley had made no concerted effort to curb MacArthur's appetite for territorial conquest at the Wake Island meeting.

As British historian Max Hastings noted, "[H]owever unhappily, the administration in Washington muffled its own doubts and fears. The insuperable difficulty of containing or controlling MacArthur remained the same as ever: the general commanded in Tokyo upon his own terms, as he always had."

Without waiting for direction from MacArthur or anyone else, elements of the ROK Army stormed across the 38th Parallel into North Korea on September 28, intent on vengeance, while the Americans still struggled to secure Seoul. There seemed no reason to restrain the ROKs, since Peking's warnings focused entirely on the Americans, correctly assuming that the ROKs were incapable of posing any significant threat to Manchuria.

Except for a few exploratory probes by small patrols, it wasn't until October 9 that U.S. forces began crossing the border in strength. Even then, the Marines and the GIs weren't sure what their mission was, beyond hunting down North Korean troops. The idea of "reunifying" the two Koreas was probably the least of their concerns, although MacArthur had already embraced it, and South Korean President Rhee was pressing relentlessly toward that goal.

During this interval, after the fighting ceased around Seoul, the Americans had an excellent window of opportunity to cut off and obliterate what was left of the NKPA, now stumbling north in disarray, while it was still south of the parallel. If armored units of the Seventh Infantry Division, generally inactive at the time, had been rushed from the vicinity of Seoul to block eastern escape routes, most if not all the surviving North Koreans could have been captured or killed. For the most part, however, there was little offensive movement by U.S. forces as they solidified their positions north of Seoul and took a well-deserved break from combat.

At best, only 25,000 to 30,000 North Korean troops managed to escape back to their own country, most of them fleeing up the east coast, vigorously pursued by the ROK Third Division, which would penetrate nearly 100 miles beyond the parallel before the first U.S. units followed suit.

As it was, there were precious few obstacles standing in the Americans' way once they did start pushing north. The NKPA was utterly shattered, its remaining troops wandering disorganized, dispirited, and weaponless. In essence, the very ease and speed with which MacArthur's forces advanced through North Korea would become their greatest detriment. General Walker's Eighth Army was assigned to a westerly route through North Korea, while General Almond's X Corps moved north through the eastern portion of the country. But there was no clear-cut definition of their ultimate objective, much less any unanimous decision on when or where to stop. As they advanced, with orders only to proceed "with all possible speed" to the Yalu, major American units became widely dispersed and separated from one another in rough, almost roadless terrain by distances of many miles—a practice roundly condemned later as "reckless" by General Ridgway.

The U.S. command had ample opportunity at this time to order topographical studies to determine—and then fortify—a more physically advantageous and easily defensible line across the peninsula to replace the vulnerable 38th Parallel. A new boundary between the two Koreas could have been created 100 miles or more north of the parallel. It could have taken in Pyongyang and Wonsan if necessary to gain maximum advantage from favorable terrain. And there was no rule that such a boundary had to follow a parallel line; at this juncture, UN forces could do pretty much whatever they wanted.

"Even after UN troops moved northward," wrote historian Bevin Alexander, "there is a possibility that the Chinese might have been satisfied with a judicious halt of UN forces at the narrow waist of Korea above Pyongyang, thus leaving them with a modest buffer in front of the Yalu. This was not what Beijing was broadcasting to the world . . . [but] the Chinese acceptance of ROK invaders north of the parallel and their waiting until UN and ROK forces were virtually on Manchuria's doorstep before finally responding argues strongly that the United States could have achieved more by negotiation with Beijing after Inchon than . . . by two and a half years more of bloody war."

However, if anyone in high U.S. political, diplomatic, or military circles seriously suggested such a possibility at the time, neither Truman nor Mac-Arthur was listening.

Meanwhile, the closer the Americans came to the Manchurian border, the nearer the swarms of Chinese troops massed along the frontier came to jumping into the war.

Like those of Napoleon, Alexander the Great, and Adolf Hitler, the eccentric, ego-driven career of Douglas MacArthur will likely be studied and scrutinized as long as historians, military tacticians, and psychologists walk the earth. Indeed, the Korean War itself might be even more ignored than it is by latter-day historians if not for the fact that it and MacArthur are as inseparably bound together as a set of Siamese twins.

If the Inchon-Seoul campaign represents the height of MacArthur's daring brilliance as a commander, then his headlong rush into North Korea, and the dire consequences it produced, surely must represent the depth of his imperceptive witlessness. Blinded by his own arrogance, he was doomed to repeat, almost methodically, the same two key mistakes that had so recently spelled disaster for Kim Il Sung and the North Koreans: he stretched his supply lines to the breaking point through hostile country, and he ignored the possibility of massive intervention by outside forces.

As David Halberstam observed, "The same general who had argued for Inchon because of the vulnerability of the North Korean supply lines now allowed his own supply lines to grow dangerously long in territory over which he had no control. The same general who had wanted to land at Inchon because it might end the war quickly and spare his troops from fighting in the cruel Korean winter was now ready to send them further north just as the Manchurian winter arrived."

Many of MacArthur's subordinates in X Corps recognized the strategic fallacies and grave risks entailed in their commander's decision to cross the 38th Parallel and rush deep into North Korea, and they viewed the move with bitter misgivings.

"My first reaction when I heard we were crossing the parallel was 'We've got a problem,'" recalled then Colonel Bryghte Godbold, assigned as the G-1 personnel officer of the First Marine Division. "I had bad feelings about it from the get-go, and it was clear to me that [division commander] General Smith was also concerned. He moved the Fifth and Seventh Marines north very slowly and with great caution, despite constant prodding by [X Corps commander] General Almond. Later, he sent me up to Hungnam to expedite reinforcements and get our wounded out in a hurry. I think he sensed that we were heading into a trap."

Colonel Robert Taplett, the outspoken commander of 3/5, stated his and his staff's objections to the northward drive with characteristic bluntness: "Most of us in the Fifth Marines couldn't understand the reasons for a 'mad dash' to get to the Yalu. We figured that the UN forces already controlled the critical military objectives in North Korea with the seizure of Pyongyang, Wonsan, and Hungnam-Hamhung. . . . We felt that going to the Yalu made no sense, as it had no military importance and would only irritate the Chinese."

Taplett and other field commanders had already received intelligence reports about Chinese troops crossing into North Korea and taking up positions in the snow-covered high ground south of the Yalu, and he'd ordered his company COs to "keep a keen eye out" for any sign of the Chinese.

For the moment, however, Peng De Huai, commander of all Chinese units in Korea, was content to play a waiting game. He used the time at his disposal to fortify networks of mountain caves and stock them with supplies against the hour when the Americans marched into what one senior Chinese officer called "our selected killing zones."

The seeds of disaster were being irrevocably sown in the barren, icy hills of North Korea, and the time of harvest was fast approaching. Taplett's battalion and other units of the Fifth Marines would be among the first Americans to feel its fury.

Six decades after the fact, Washington's inability to recognize or react to the strident warning signals emanating from China in the late summer and autumn of 1950 remains as mystifying and illogical as it was then. For weeks, Peking had been delivering broad hints that the presence of U.S.

troops in northern North Korea wouldn't be tolerated, and beginning in mid-September, when Inchon changed the whole complexion of the war, Mao Zedong's regime had quit mincing words on the subject.

Chinese reinforcements had begun moving into Manchuria in mid-August, and the total troop strength there had swelled to 450,000 by September 21—half again as many as MacArthur would identify as being in Manchuria nearly a month later. Almost daily, U.S. intelligence sources began picking up reports that intervention by China's People's Liberation Army was imminent and that relatively small PLA groups were already conducting probing missions into North Korea.

On September 25, General Nie Yen-rung, chief of staff of the PLA, told Kavalam Madhava Panikkar, India's ambassador to Peking, that China wouldn't "sit back with folded hands" while American forces approached its borders. A week later, British sources reported that Chinese Premier Zhou Enlai had repeated the same warning to the Indian envoy.

But President Truman, who distrusted Panikkar, discounted the threats as mere propaganda, and General Bradley and the JCS also failed to take them seriously because the British sources who had relayed Panikkar's message described him as "a volatile and unreliable reporter." The U.S. Central Intelligence Agency, meanwhile, downplayed Peking's saber-rattling, saying there were "no convincing indications" that China would "resort to full-scale intervention in Korea." And in Tokyo, MacArthur's G-2 intelligence chief, Major General Charles Willoughby, acknowledged the presence of thirty-eight Chinese divisions in Manchuria, including twenty-four along the Yalu River, but he characterized threats to send them into North Korea as nothing more than "diplomatic blackmail."

On October 2, after Kim Il Sung had described the NKPA's situation as "most grave" and urged China to come to its aid, Chairman Mao met with leaders of China's Politburo to discuss military intervention. By this time, as far as Mao was concerned, jumping into the war was no longer a question of "if" but merely "when" and "how."

Some Politburo members voiced strong opposition, citing the vast superiority of U.S. weapons and China's economic exhaustion after its long civil war. But Mao left no doubt that he was emotionally in favor of intervention, regardless of the cost in Chinese lives. "China has millions of people," he told Indian Premier Jawaharlal Nehru. "They cannot be bombed out of existence. The death of ten or twenty million people is nothing to be afraid of."

On October 7, the UN General Assembly adopted a resolution, strongly backed by the United States, that further fueled MacArthur's ambitions. It urged "all appropriate steps" to ensure stability "throughout Korea" and called for a single government for both North and South elected under UN auspices and observation.

No American troops were yet north of the 38th Parallel at this point, but MacArthur read the resolution as full authorization for an all-out push into North Korea, and he wasted no time pondering what historian Max Hastings called "diplomatic niceties, political sensitivities," or the "fundamental constitutional limitations upon his own powers." Instead, he issued a direct ultimatum to the North Koreans: either they laid down their arms or he would take "such military action as may be necessary to enforce the decrees of the United Nations."

In all likelihood, MacArthur was also emboldened by a delicate political situation back in the States, where midterm congressional elections were scheduled for early November and conservative Republican leaders were demanding a continuation of the U.S. offensive in Korea. The Truman administration was already under a right-wing attack for allegedly being "soft on communism," and the followers of radical Senator Joseph McCarthy were a rising national political force that was sure to condemn any halt in the offensive as appeasement of the Communists. For Truman and the Democrats, trying to restrain MacArthur now would have been akin to dumping gasoline on a smoldering fire.

The die was cast, and once again the administration did little except to bite its collective tongue in dismayed silence.

From October 9, when major U.S. forces crossed into North Korea, through the third week of November, the Americans marched steadily north into bone-chilling weather, encountering only intermittent cursory resistance from the NKPA. By October 14, they were north and west of the Imjin River and twenty miles north of Wonsan. By October 20, they were in Pyongyang and had taken the east coast towns of Hungnam and Hamhung. By early November, Army troops of the Seventh Infantry Division were driving toward the Yalu, and elements of the First Marine Division were just south of the Chosin Reservoir, near the towns of Yudam-ni and Hagaru-ri. But even at this pace, the advance was too slow to please X Corps commander General Almond.

Almost two weeks earlier, on the night of October 19, Chinese "volunteers"—Chairman Mao's term—of the People's Liberation Army had begun crossing the Yalu in massive numbers, but Almond remained blissfully unaware of this development. In his zeal to see his X Corps (a mixture of Marine, Army, and ROK units) beat General Walker's Eighth Army (primarily U.S. Army units) to the Manchurian border, Almond continued to push his troops without letup and to disregard the corps' faulty organization. His major units were separated by wide gaps and paying little attention to their defenses.

Meanwhile, UN intelligence, based on aerial reconnaissance and intercepts of enemy radio messages, failed for nearly three weeks after Chinese divisions slipped across the Yalu in October to detect convincing evidence that Mao's forces were in Korea in substantial numbers. This seems incomprehensible in light of what happened to the U.S. Eighth Cavalry Regiment and the ROK 15th Regiment on the night of November 1–2 at Unsan, a village near the Yellow Sea and about fifty miles from the Yalu.

Shortly after 10:00 PM on November 1, major elements of two Chinese divisions attacked in great force, surrounding the Americans and South Koreans and blocking all escape routes. During savage fighting that raged until November 4, the Eighth Cavalry was mauled, losing more than 600 men, and the ROK regiment virtually ceased to exist. The surviving Americans finally managed to withdraw, and General Walker was forced to order a general retreat by the Eighth Army to the south bank of the Chongchon River.

The onrushing masses of enemy troops defied description. "We threw everything we had at them, and I think I must've killed a thousand men in those first attacks without any exaggeration," recalled PFC Herb Holdman of Perryton, Texas, an Eighth Cavalry tank driver who fired the .50-caliber machine gun on his M-26 Pershing at point-blank range against the Chinese hordes.

"I killed them until they were stacked around me like piles of cordwood," Holdman would tell members of his family years later, still deeply shaken by the experience. "But we couldn't stop them all."

The Chinese attacks continued until November 6, with the Americans and the British 27th Brigade suffering hundreds of additional casualties. But then, with complete victory seemingly within their grasp, the attackers inexplicably disengaged and pulled out of the fight, marching north and disappearing back into the mountains in what historian Bevin Alexander called "one of the strangest events in the history of warfare."

Actually, though, it was a carefully calculated maneuver by the Chinese, according to recently declassified National Security Agency documents. Beijing was delivering a pointed warning to UN forces not to continue north, but it scarcely caused a raised eyebrow in Tokyo. General Almond blamed the Eighth Cavalry slaughter simply on the regiment's "failure to take precautions against a night attack." Meanwhile, X Corps G-2 General Willoughby estimated the attackers' strength at only a battalion or so, but intelligence reports later revealed that no fewer than four Chinese armies—130,000 men—had taken part.

Almond's unconcern was partly based on the growing strength of X Corps. Besides the Seventh Infantry and First Marine Divisions, he now had the Third and Capital ROK divisions at his disposal, and the Third Infantry Division, although heavily populated with raw recruits, was on the way, bringing Corps strength to 102,000 men. Compared to the Inchon force's 70,000, the numbers were impressive—but they wouldn't be nearly enough.

The overriding reason why Almond and his staff chose to ignore the Chinese incursions, however, was "complete insanity in the command," according to one of Almond's own staff officers, Colonel William McCaffrey.

"From the time we headed to the Yalu, it was like being in the nuthouse with the nuts in charge," McCaffrey recalled many years later. "You could only understand the totality of the madness if you were up there in the

North after the Chinese had entered in full force. . . . And what we were getting from Tokyo was absolute madness. The only real question was whether we could get any of our people out of there, and yet the orders were still to go forward."

Thus, a last opportunity to reconsider MacArthur's "insane plan"—as General Clark Ruffner, Almond's chief of staff, later described it—to drive all the way to the Manchurian border was steadfastly ignored.

There would be no further warnings from the Chinese—and no further backing away, either. The next time they struck, it would be for keeps.

Colonel Ray Murray's Fifth Marines, chosen to lead a westward attack that would spearhead Almond's "offensive to end the war," was the first large Marine unit to meet Chinese soldiers in combat. On November 9, the regiment was ordered to take up positions on the main supply route leading to the Chosin Reservoir. The next day, a patrol from Colonel George Newton's 1/5 was ambushed, and the entire battalion had to come to its rescue. Several Marines identified their assailants as Chinese.

Four days later, on the thirteenth, another 1/5 patrol ran afoul of a company-size Chinese force, suffering seven killed and three wounded in the ensuing firefight. That same day, as Colonel Harold Roise's 2/5 moved toward Koto-ri village, its Marines captured a dozen enemy soldiers. One of them was a talkative young Chinese "volunteer." He told the Marines that twenty-four Chinese divisions had already crossed into North Korea.

By now, even MacArthur could no longer deny that Chinese troops were present in significant numbers south of the Yalu, but he clung stubbornly to the belief that China wouldn't dare attempt a full-scale military intervention.

At this point, Colonel McCaffrey later charged, MacArthur had turned "nutty as a fruitcake." The stage was set for a disaster of epic proportions.

On November 10, General Smith observed the 125th birthday of the U.S. Marine Corps by slicing a modest cake with a Korean sword at First Marine Division headquarters in Hamhung. The division's three infantry regiments, still unaware that Chinese troops were pouring into North Korea, also had their own celebratory cake-cuttings, but the festivities were brief and subdued.

"We stood in snow up to our knees, eating birthday cake and singing the "Marine Hymn" loud enough to be heard in Peking," said PFC Ray Walker of A/1/5, recalling the anniversary observance. "I'm sure any Chinese within earshot were dumbfounded."

At the Wonsan command post of Colonel Puller's First Marines on the east coast, the ground was blanketed with snow, but temperatures were still relatively mild. To the north on the Chosin Plateau, however, Colonel Homer Litzenberg's Seventh Marines and Colonel Murray's Fifth Marines were already shivering in subzero weather. Warming tents were set up in the village of Koto-ri, but as one Marine historian put it, the cold seemed "to numb the spirit as well as the flesh." It would only get worse.

"We got to a place called Sasaru-ri about November 20, and jeez, it was cold!" said Ray Walker. "I heard the windchill was 100 below zero with gale-force winds and blowing snow. There was no further reason for us to keep going north, and we were more than ready to get the hell out of there. We hoped we'd make a few patrols, clean our weapons, and then we could go home. No such luck.

"All our weapons froze. Everything froze," Walker remembered. "It never occurred to me that keeping my BAR in my sleeping bag would disable the gun, but it did. It caused the weapon to collect moisture, which froze its firing action and made it useless."

On November 21, to General Almond's great delight, Army troops of the Seventh Division's 17th Infantry Regiment became the first Americans to reach the Yalu. They did so without encountering a single Chinese soldier, and Almond himself flew in to make a rare appearance at the front lines with General David Barr, the division commander.

"There was a great deal of competition among the officers to be the first to piss in the Yalu," recalled Lieutenant Fred Wilmot, executive officer of B Company, First Battalion, 17th Infantry, many years later. "I still think I hold that distinction but only because some of the senior officers deferred to me on account of my age."

Almond and his unit commanders also joined the ritual urination. It would be their last cause for celebration for many days to come.

• • •

On Thanksgiving Day, November 23, the turkey-and-trimmings dinners served to many Marines and GIs froze solid in their mess kits before they could be eaten.

The American troops who were about to be cut off and trapped by the Chinese near the Chosin Reservoir still talk of readings as low as minus forty degrees, and official recorded temperatures at Hagaru-ri would reach thirty-five below during that Thanksgiving period. "I'm from snow country," recalled Corporal Jack Dedrick of H/3/1, a Massachusetts native, "but, my God, I've never been so cold. I didn't think anyone *could* be so cold. The ground was frozen like rock, and there was no way to dig in it. It was the toughest time of my life."

Unlike the infantrymen, Corporal Murdoch Ford and the other four members of his Pershing tank crew at least had a place to hide from the biting thirty-mile-per-hour winds and blowing snow, and the tank's fiery exhaust provided a way to heat food or coffee. "We had to start the tank every fifteen minutes to keep the engine from freezing up," Ford recalled, "but we realized in a hurry how lucky we were to have it."

In the predawn darkness of November 25, troops of Colonel Taplett's 3/5 were attacked by Chinese at a roadblock north of the battalion's perimeter. In a brief firefight, the attackers were driven off, leaving three dead and trails of blood behind in the snow. When Taplett ordered a reinforced platoon to give chase, it ran into a larger Chinese force, apparently screening a major troop concentration, and a longer, more intense firefight broke out.

Taplett studied the situation from a helicopter, then ordered Lieutenant Blackie Cahill to withdraw his platoon and return to the battalion perimeter. "Both of us agreed that further advance would lead into an ambush in the threatening valley to the north by a superior force," Taplett recalled.

Cahill agreed to withdraw only with the greatest reluctance, however, said Corpsman Cecil Carpenter, who witnessed Cahill's reaction firsthand. "Blackie was my platoon leader, and I loved the guy," Carpenter recalled decades later. "When the Chinese hit us, he said, 'I'm not gonna let those bastards run me off this hill!' A Chinese concussion grenade rolled by him and he just kicked it out of his way. It blew his shoe off but didn't hurt him. He was the bravest man I ever saw."

As Taplett and his pilot swung north over the snow-covered country-side, they spotted numerous holes or depressions along both sides of the valley and faint vehicle tracks along the nearest road but failed to sight a single Chinese soldier.

"Don't be fooled by the serene landscape," the pilot said. "The Chinks are there in force, and I think we'd better head for home."

Taplett agreed and immediately rushed back to his CP to notify Colonel Murray, the regimental commander, of the enemy contact. Taplett's concerns were greatly eased when Murray told him that the Army's 32nd Infantry was on its way to take over 3/5's position.

"I had never felt such relief during my stay in Korea as I did in ridding ourselves of this perilous position and [being] on our way elsewhere," Taplett later recalled. His relief didn't last long, however. Within hours, he would realize that he and his men "were jumping from the frying pan into the fires of Yudam-ni"—a place that would soon rank with Peleliu's Bloody Nose Ridge and Okinawa's Sugar Loaf Hill on the Marines' all-time list of horrors.

The Fifth Marines set out for Yudam-ni early on November 26 on a roundabout route along narrow, winding roads, first to the north, then west around the icy shores of the Chosin Reservoir, then north again through rugged mountains, the highest of which rose to some 7,000 feet. By nightfall, the Marines were still three miles from Yudam-ni when their column was attacked by three Chinese divisions.

"The night of November 26–27 was when the Chinese sprang their trap to isolate, divide, and annihilate the First Marine Division," recalled Corpsman Herb Pearce, attached to a Fifth Marines recoilless rifle platoon. "No one who was there will ever forget that night."

The next morning, the disheveled Fifth Marines was ordered to consolidate its forces with the Seventh Marines at Yudam-ni, also besieged by three enemy divisions. Together, they would try to break out of the trap and reach Hagaru-ri, fourteen miles to the south and just below the tip of the Chosin Reservoir, where elements of the First Marines also were surrounded and fighting desperately to hold the town.

"Item Company's lines were the only ones in the whole regiment that the

Chinese didn't break through at Hagaru-ri," recalled Sergeant Bill Finnegan. "We blew holes in the frozen ground with TNT to make foxholes, then strung barbed wire and placed fuel barrels beyond it with grenades attached to them by trip wires. We had to break out every available machine gun and hit them with everything we had, but we held."

Colonel Murray, the Fifth's commander, who now shared command of the combined Marine force with Colonel Litzenberg of the Seventh, pulled no punches about the ordeal the two regiments faced. "We're coming out of this as Marines, not as stragglers," he told his men. "We're going to bring out all our wounded and equipment. We're coming out as Marines, or we're not coming out at all."

"By this time, the very magnitude of our problem was becoming apparent," said Corpsman Pearce, "and it was also apparent that we were going to have to fight our way back down the same road that we'd come up."

The Marines fought like fiends against a foe that contested them every foot of the way. Mortarmen and infantry of A/1/7 broke up one Chinese blocking attack with the help of a giant black Marine nicknamed "Ivan the Terrible," who charged the enemy, swinging a long-handled ax, crushing skulls, and severing limbs left and right until the Chinese fled in terror. As the attackers scrambled toward a wooded area, a Marine Corsair swooped low and dumped a canister of napalm in their midst, killing about forty enemy soldiers.

"The worst flying conditions we faced in Korea were around the Chosin Reservoir," recalled veteran Corsair pilot Captain Lyle Bradley. "We operated with a 300-foot ceiling and in blinding snowstorms against targets on winding mountain roads. The Chinese dressed in white to try to hide from us, but their uniforms were slightly yellowish against the pure white snow, and we mangled them. The Chinese corpses stacked up like cordwood."

It took fifty-nine hours for the leading point troops of the Marine advance to reach Hagaru-ri, and seventy-nine hours—until 2:00 PM on December 4—for the rear guard to complete the journey. The route they had to travel was barred by eleven Chinese roadblocks, and both regiments took a heavy beating from flanking small-arms, machine-gun, and mortar fire along the way. When the survivors finally made it into the First Marines' perimeter, General Smith, the division commander, was at the road-side to greet them personally.

Also awaiting them was the work of an anonymous amateur sign painter—one who obviously had retained his sense of humor—that greeted them with this Burma Shave–style message:

> *Have no worry;*
> *Have no fear.*
> *The mighty Fifth*
> *Marines are here!*

Men wept with relief, but there was no sense of victory. The First Marine Division had advanced as close to the Yalu River as it would ever get.

By the first days of December, the fortunes of war had shifted as drastically against UN and American forces as it had shifted against the NKPA in mid-September. An estimated 300,000 Chinese troops were on the attack in North Korea, but no one knows for sure to this day how many were actually there. Sergeant Mackie Wheeler and other members of A/1/5 heard persistent scuttlebutt to the effect that the actual number was closer to 800,000.

"However many it was, it was too damned many," Wheeler said. "We killed them as fast as we could, but it was impossible to kill them all. They just kept coming."

The cold was unrelenting, and virtually all the men withdrawing from "Frozen Chosin" had some degree of frostbite, severe in many cases and fatal in more than a few. "I watched guys freeze to death standing up while I was talking to them," recalled tank-driving Corporal Murdoch Ford. Dysentery also ran rampant through the ranks. Under normal circumstances, almost every Marine would have been in sick bay for one reason or another, but to have any hope of escaping to the South, they would have to fight harder—against sickness, the cold, and the enemy—than they'd ever fought before.

With most of their frozen weapons not functioning, the Marines in many instances had only grenades with which to stop the onrushing enemy.

On November 28, while the Fifth and Seventh Marines were still hanging on at Yudam-ni, PFCs Ray Walker and John Kelly of E/2/7 frantically ripped open cases of grenades with their K-Bar knives and tossed them downhill at charging Chinese troops for a solid hour before the enemy gave up the attack.

The encounter was destined to become a life-changing experience for Walker. When he stooped to pick up a Chinese grenade, mistakenly thinking it was one that he or Kelly had dropped, the percussion missile blew up in his face.

"I threw up my right arm for protection and caught some of the fragments," Walker recalled. "The arm was broken, although I didn't know it until later, but my main concern was my face. The force of the blast picked me up and tossed me about ten feet, and I landed on my back, screaming like a banshee: 'My face! My face!' I thought I was dying for sure."

A corpsman ran up and leaned over Walker's inert form. "Just lie still," he said calmly. "Your face is gonna be okay. You've got a nasty cut above your lip, but it's just enough to make you look like a big, bad Marine."

Later, as the column struggled south, Walker discovered that he also had a chest wound from the grenade fragments in addition to the facial damage. He was in agony from his wounds every inch of the trip, but he was better off than many of his comrades—well enough to "ride shotgun" in his jeep with a .45 automatic to hold the Chinese at bay.

He and the other wounded men around him tried to ignore their pain by singing popular songs during the fighting retreat. While the column inched along, their incongruous lyrics echoed among the icy, unforgiving ridges:

> *Last Saturday night I got married;*
> *Me and my wife settled down.*

En route, Walker suffered severe frostbite in both feet and was struck in the upper thigh by a random sniper's bullet. He was unaware he'd been shot until he felt warm blood trickling down his leg. At Hagaru-ri, a coveted green tag—signifying immediate evacuation—was placed on his litter.

"I had the so-called million-dollar wound," Walker recalled. "A few hours later, I was on a hospital ship bound for Japan."

Only a gallant stand by Captain William Barber's F Company, Seventh Marines, had kept the road between Yudam-ni and Hagaru-ri from being cut by the Chinese, allowing the Fifth Marines to reach the only functioning airstrip in the area. In recognition of their valor, Barber and two of his enlisted men were awarded the Medal of Honor.

But there is no greater example of superhuman courage and fortitude during that nightmare march than Lieutenant John Yancy of Little Rock, Arkansas, leader of the First Platoon of Easy Company, Seventh Marines.

As he led a counterattack against onrushing enemy troops threatening the Fifth and Seventh Marines' command posts on a ridge designated as Hill 1282, Yancy was struck in the cheek by a .45-caliber slug that popped his eye from its socket. After killing the Chinese soldier who shot him, Yancy pushed his eyeball back into place and rallied his platoon for a second counterattack. Again he was hit by a bullet, which entered his left cheek and exited his right cheek, taking half a dozen teeth and part of his jaw with it, but his wounds scarcely slowed him down.

Spitting out shattered teeth and leaning forward to keep from choking on his own blood, Yancy led yet a third charge against the enemy, only to be struck in the mouth and knocked down by a large piece of shrapnel. After the Chinese attackers were beaten off, corpsmen who rushed to the lieutenant's aid counted fifty-seven entry and exit bullet holes in Yancy's field jacket. Incredibly, he survived to receive the Navy Cross.

Thanks to Yancy, Barber, and others like them, 5,400 ill, frostbitten, and wounded Marines (roughly one-fifth of the surviving members of the First Marine Division), none of whom was capable of walking, reached Hagaru-ri alive and were soon airlifted to safety.

Meanwhile, near Korea's west coast, hordes of Chinese fell on stunned troops of the U.S. Second and 25th divisions on the afternoon of November 29, severely mauling the Americans and blocking their only route of escape through a craggy pass.

Panicked, General Laurence B. "Dutch" Keiser, commander of the Sec-

ond Division, first underestimated the size and strength of the Chinese attackers, then told his men, "We've got to get out of here before dark!"

They tried to head south, but it was too late. Between them and safety lay
a six-mile stretch of hell manned by tens of thousands of Chinese troops
and blocked by an incredible junkyard of wrecked and disabled American
jeeps and trucks. The division's Ninth Infantry Regiment, along with British
and Turkish units, was cut to pieces. One of the last vehicles to make it
through the pass was a jeep carrying the Ninth's commander, Colonel
George "Pep" Peploe, a hero of the Pusan breakout, and more than a dozen
wounded. Most of the rest of the Second was trapped and surrounded in a
storm of automatic weapons fire. Of the Ninth and 38th regiments, only
about 600 men in each unit lived through the ordeal.

"Our losses were devastating," recalled Captain Harris Pope, a company
commander in the Ninth Infantry, Third Battalion. "The next day, we could
find only thirty-seven men of our battalion. Some more straggled in later,
but not many."

Back in the States, when word of the debacle reached famed news commen-
tator Walter Winchell, he told his nationwide listening audience, "If you
have a son overseas, write to him. If you have a son in the Second Division,
pray for him."

Zombielike survivors of the Second eventually reached the town of Sunchon, then continued south to Pyongyang on their way out of North Korea.
They had suffered 4,940 casualties along the way.

On December 6, when General Smith ordered the First Marine Division to
evacuate Hagaru-ri, a British news correspondent, accompanying a group
of British Royal Marines who had linked up with their American counterparts, asked pointedly if the operation could be considered a retreat. "No,
we're not retreating," insisted the taciturn division commander, "we're just
advancing in a different direction."

Despite almost impossible flying conditions, Marine aviators flew more
than 1,300 sorties between December 1 and December 11 to hold Chinese
attackers at bay. Although they tried tirelessly to protect the ground troops,

American fliers' ability to inflict damage on Chinese troop concentrations fell far short of MacArthur's confident projections during his meeting with Truman two months earlier. The rugged terrain, bitter cold, blowing snow, and the PLA troops' ability at concealment largely nullified U.S. air superiority.

It took almost twenty-four agonizing hours for the Fifth and Seventh Marines to march the nine miles to the town of Koto-ri, suffering 600 additional casualties on the way. On December 8, after burying their dead in shallow graves gouged out in the frozen ground by bulldozers and sending their latest batch of wounded out by air, they moved south again. Their objective was the port of Hungnam, from which four decimated divisions of Army, Marine, and ROK troops were to be evacuated by sea to South Korea. Other UN forces would be evacuated in smaller numbers from Wonsan, farther south.

The general abandonment of North Korea by all units of X Corps and the Eighth Army began in earnest on December 6. The Eighth Army had already fled Pyongyang and was withdrawing by land toward the 38th Parallel. In the space of two dizzying weeks, the Korean War had entered an ominous new phase, and American commanders in Korea and Tokyo were again searching for somewhere to set up a sustainable line of defense below the parallel.

Day by day, the UN-held perimeter around Hungnam steadily shrank until still-firing American artillery was confined to the docks at water's edge, then hustled aboard ship. Finally, on Christmas Eve, after a convoy of troop-laden vessels put out to sea under the protective guns of U.S. warships, the port and surrounding city were destroyed by naval gunfire. Behind them, in mass graves near Hungnam and Koto-ri, the Marines left the bodies of 714 comrades killed during their flight from "Frozen Chosin."

"I believe we killed at least 35,000 Chinese between their first attacks at the reservoir and the time we were evacuated," said PFC Ray Walker, "and probably another 30,000 froze to death. We had 900 Marines killed, and 12,000 were either wounded or disabled by frostbite."

Only American dead and severely wounded made it home from Korea for Christmas in 1950. Thousands of the triumphant GIs and Marines of the

Inchon-Seoul campaign never returned to the States alive. The ones who eventually did—even those who came back with feet, fingers, and toes lost to frostbite or permanently scarred by crippling battle wounds—invariably considered their return a miracle.

MacArthur's forces, so flushed with victory after liberating Seoul and driving the wreckage of the NKPA out of South Korea, would spend their holiday season that year fighting for their lives against ten Chinese armies in the frozen hell around North Korea's Chosin Reservoir and along the west coast of the Korean peninsula.

Among the thousands of American fighting men who didn't live to see that Christmas was one of the major players in the pendulous back-and-forth drama of Korea. On the cold, misty morning of December 23, Eighth Army commander Lieutenant General Walton H. "Johnnie" Walker was killed in a jeep accident that may have been precipitated by his own desperate frustration.

Walker had a long-standing reputation for never slowing down, for being constantly in motion, and in times of turmoil, his urge to hurry was intensified. As historian Clay Blair noted, "remarks about his reckless speeding [and] the speculation that one day he would be killed in a car wreck, like his mentor [General] George Patton," had become commonplace.

On the morning of his death, as Chinese pressure built toward a major offensive to wipe out all the stymied and freezing units of his Eighth Army, Walker was on a whirlwind schedule as usual. He stopped at 24th Division headquarters to confer with General William Kean and paused to visit briefly with his son Captain Sam Walker, who had received a Silver Star just the day before. Then he sped off toward the British Commonwealth Brigade's command post to present an ROK presidential citation to the unit. Minutes later, and not quite three weeks after his sixty-first birthday, he was dead.

With siren screaming and the short-statured Walker standing and gripping a specially installed "grab bar," the jeep collided with an ROK weapons carrier on an icy road jammed with bumper-to-bumper southbound traffic. The general and his driver, Sergeant George Belton, along with two other passengers, were thrown into a ditch and severely injured. The others survived, but Walker was dead on arrival at a nearby mobile Army surgical hospital (MASH) unit.

General Matthew Ridgway was summoned from the States to assume command of the Eighth Army. Walker's body, escorted by his son, was shipped home to be buried in Arlington National Cemetery. He was posthumously promoted to four-star general.

By late January 1951, UN troops would be forced to give up Seoul, Inchon, and Kimpo Airfield, then continue their southward retreat with terrible feelings of déjà vu. The withdrawal would end only when they were able to establish a new defensive line in the South some fifty miles above the Naktong and Kum rivers. At this high-water mark of the Chinese offensive, American and other UN forces would control an area much larger and better defended than the original Pusan Perimeter. Yet most of the gains of the previous September, October, and November would be wiped out by the crushing defeat sustained in North Korea at the hands of the Chinese.

The conflict would drag on until July 27, 1953, when both sides grudgingly accepted a demilitarized zone (DMZ) as the boundary line between the two Koreas, replacing the 38th Parallel. The DMZ dips south of the parallel near the west coast. But then it climbs about thirty miles above the parallel near the bitterly contested point of high ground known as Pork Chop Hill, on the Imjin River. From there it runs in a jagged line all the way to the east coast, giving South Korea slightly more territory—and a far more defensible border—than it had in June 1950.

Before the war ended—in deadly stalemate and not by a peace treaty but a mere cease-fire—the United States would send more than 1.7 million young Americans to serve in Korea. Nearly 34,000 U.S. soldiers, Marines, and airmen would be killed in action there, and another 103,000 would suffer nonfatal battle wounds. U.S.-Chinese relations would be poisoned for decades, and North Korea would remain a "rogue" state, continuing to threaten its neighbors and the world to this very day.

In the fifty-six years since the Korean War cease-fire, no authority figure in Washington has ever again suggested eliminating the Marine Corps as the nation's premier fighting force.

EPILOGUE

★ ★ ★

THE REST OF THE STORY

NUMEROUS FACTORS UNDOUBTEDLY played a role in *Harry S. Truman's* decision not to run for a second full term as president in November 1952. Truman formally announced the decision at an annual Jackson–Jefferson Day dinner on March 29, more than seven months before election day, but he insisted that it had been reached much earlier.

As his chief motivation for retiring, Truman said he was weary of the demands imposed by the nation's highest office during almost eight tumultuous years in the White House. But the Korean conflict—which Truman still refused to call a war, and which was then deep into its second year with no end in sight—surely was a major reason for his desire to go home to the peace and quiet of Independence, Missouri. Like Lyndon Johnson sixteen years later and George W. Bush in 2008, Truman was inexorably tied to a war he had initiated or escalated and been unable to finish, and his public approval rating was abysmal when he left office.

In years to come, historians would deal kindly with Truman, awarding him at least an "A-minus" on his presidential report card. Today, most of his countrymen who remember him at all tend to identify him as an "ordinary guy" thrust suddenly into the most powerful, demanding job on earth; a leader with the guts to drop atomic bombs on Japan, confront worldwide communism head-to-head, and generally live up to the axiom he displayed on a desktop plaque in the Oval Office, "The buck stops here."

But in the spring of 1952, Truman was still being vilified as the "little man" who fired *Douglas MacArthur*, one of the greatest generals in America's history, and sent tens of thousands of her sons to suffer and die in an unwinnable war.

In a nation increasingly fed up with the bloody stalemate in Korea and ready for a change after twenty straight years of Democratic control of the White House, sacking MacArthur was a heavy cross for Truman to bear. But in true buck-stopping fashion, he never apologized for it—and he shouldn't have. In *Plain Speaking*, Merle Miller's best-selling Truman oral history, published twenty years after Truman left Washington, the former president pulled no punches about MacArthur's dismissal.

"I fired him because he wouldn't respect the authority of the president," Truman said simply. "I didn't fire him because he was a dumb son of a bitch, although he was, but that's not against the law for generals."

What much of the public failed—or refused—to understand at the time was that the only other option available to Truman was to allow his head-strong Far East commander to plunge the United States into an all-out shooting war with Communist China.

MacArthur spewed outrage at the "limited war" he was being forced to fight. He demanded authorization to bomb Chinese troop concentrations, airfields, and supply depots in Manchuria. He wanted to blockade the Chinese coast and bring Chinese Nationalist forces from Taiwan into the fighting. He wanted at least four more U.S. divisions sent to Japan and Korea at a time when only the Army's 82nd Airborne was in strategic reserve, and the newly formed North Atlantic Treaty Organization (NATO) was desperately shorthanded in Europe, requests that historian T. R. Fehrenbach called "impossible, short of [full U.S. military] mobilization." MacArthur even talked of arming and involving Japanese troops in Korea, knowing that Japan was prohibited, under terms of its unconditional surrender some five years earlier, from fielding an armed force capable of offensive action.

Furthermore, the general repeatedly issued dark predictions of impend-

ing doom in Korea unless Truman and the Joint Chiefs gave in to his demands. In February 1951, with the Eighth Army's confidence and spirits at
low ebb, MacArthur sent this message to Washington:

"Under the extraordinary limitations and conditions imposed upon the
command in Korea . . . its military position is untenable, but it can hold, if
overriding political considerations so dictate, for any length of time up to
its complete destruction."

MacArthur challenged his government to recognize that a Chinese-
imposed "state of war" now existed and that the most effective means of
countering it was to drop up to fifty atomic bombs on Manchuria and China's major mainland cities.

Clearly, if Truman had allowed MacArthur to have his way, the result, at
best, would have made the existing Korean conflict look like a Sunday
school picnic. At worst, many in Washington feared, it would trigger World
War III with the Communist bloc.

For many months, MacArthur had made no secret of his desire for an
all-out military showdown with Communist China. In August 1950, during
a meeting with General Matthew Ridgway and top Washington diplomat
Averell Harriman, MacArthur had commented that he "prayed nightly" for
a Chinese attack on Taiwan to give the United States justification for war.
Ridgway would later speculate that MacArthur's desire to cast himself as
"the swordsman who would slay the Communist dragon" was a major motivation three months later for "his reckless drive to the borders of Manchuria."

By spring 1951, MacArthur had spun so totally out of control that many
Washington and Tokyo insiders seriously believed him to be mentally un-
balanced. He bombarded every reachable media outlet with his own pronouncements on the war, never bothering to clear them with anyone
beforehand.

The clincher came on March 24, when MacArthur committed what Secretary of State Acheson called "a major act of sabotage of a government
operation." At this point, UN and Chinese forces were locked in trench
warfare near the 38th Parallel, but most of South Korea was securely held
by American troops. Hoping for a cease-fire, Truman, Acheson, Defense

Secretary Marshall, and the Joint Chiefs worked feverishly to craft a Korean peace proposal that might pave the way for serious negotiations with Peking and Pyongyang.

Unfortunately, the planned overture was revealed to MacArthur in advance. Three days later, as the State Department consulted with other friendly governments about the content of the proposal, the general stunned Washington by issuing his own call for peace. But it came in the form of an ultimatum, not as a request for negotiations.

The proclamation, released to the international news media by MacArthur's headquarters in the form of a communiqué—without any notification to Truman or the Joint Chiefs—read in part,

> [Enemy] military weaknesses have been clearly and definitely revealed since Red China entered upon its undeclared war in Korea. Even under inhibitions which now restrict activities of the United Nations forces and the corresponding military advantages which accrue to Red China, it has been shown its complete inability to accomplish by force of arms the conquest of Korea.
>
> The enemy therefore must by now be painfully aware that a decision of the United Nations to depart from its tolerant effort to contain the war to the area of Korea through expansion of our military operations to his coastal areas and interior bases would doom Red China to the risk of imminent military collapse. . . .
>
> Within the area of my authority as military commander . . . I stand ready at any time to confer in the field with the commander in chief of the enemy forces in an earnest effort to find any military means whereby the realization of the political objectives of the United Nations in Korea . . . might be accomplished without further bloodshed.

Years later, General Omar Bradley would still wonder if the realization that the war MacArthur so desperately sought with Communist China was never going to happen had caused "his brilliant but brittle mind" to snap. Yet recent research into MacArthur's performance as a regimental commander in World War I suggests that abuse of authority and lust for the limelight were traits deeply ingrained in the general's character, not merely the result of some sudden aberration.

In his 2008 book *The Question of MacArthur's Reputation*, author Robert H. Ferrell cites an incident in the pivotal 1918 American offensive against Germany's Hindenburg Line, in which MacArthur misled his superiors and claimed credit belonging to other officers to gain personal recognition. The general's false accounts of his own bravery and leadership may have shaped his entire later military career, according to Ferrell. The claims brought MacArthur what may have been an unwarranted Distinguished Service Cross and laid the foundation for a legend of battlefield courage and infallibility that had swelled to superhuman proportions by 1951.

At any rate, Truman's fury when he first saw the MacArthur communiqué was summed up by the president in an outburst to his daughter, Margaret. "I was ready to kick him into the North China Sea. . . . I was never so put out in my life. It's the lousiest trick a commander in chief can have done to him by an underling. MacArthur thought he was proconsul for the government of the United States and could do anything he damn pleased."

In his diary that evening, Truman scribbled these words: "Gross insubordination! The Big General in the Far East has to be removed!"

And he was. On April 11, 1951, Truman relieved MacArthur of all his commands and ordered him home, naming General Matthew Ridgway as the new U.S. supreme commander in the Far East. Prominent Republicans howled for Truman's impeachment, and House Speaker Joseph Martin of Massachusetts demanded a full-dress congressional investigation of Truman's war policies.

On arriving in North America for the first time in more than fourteen years, MacArthur was hailed by millions as a hero during a triumphal tour of U.S. cities, and Republican leaders invited him to address Congress. New York longshoremen staged an impromptu strike to protest the firing. A Maryland women's group threatened to march on Washington. In several towns, Truman was burned or hanged in effigy, and the city council of the city of Truman, Texas, called a special session to vote the municipality out of existence.

MacArthur concluded his emotional speech on Capitol Hill, watched by a then-record 30 million on television, by quoting from an old Army barracks ditty,

"'Old soldiers never die; they just fade away.' And like the old soldier of the ballad, I now close my military career and just fade away—an old soldier who tried to do his duty as God gave him the light to see that duty. Good-bye."

Twenty years after leaving the White House, Truman dismissed MacArthur's speech in far more colorful terms than those he'd used to dismiss the man who made it. The general's dramatic oration before Congress, Truman told biographer Merle Miller, "was nothing but a bunch of damned bullshit."

Despite seven weeks of subsequent congressional hearings on MacArthur's dismissal, talk of making him the Republican vice presidential nominee in 1952, and an invitation for him to give a presidential nominating speech for Senator Robert Taft of Ohio at the GOP National Convention, MacArthur *did* fade away.

As his message became more and more vindictive and self-serving, the audiences he commanded grew steadily smaller until almost no one was listening anymore. In his last years, MacArthur lived reclusively in a Manhattan hotel, shying away from public comment on his clash with Truman, except to deny any insubordination on his part. But during a 1954 interview with Scripps-Howard News Service correspondent Jim Lucas, MacArthur showed a momentary flash of the deep bitterness he harbored toward his former commander in chief. "The little bastard actually thinks he's a patriot," the old general said of Truman.

In April 1964, almost thirteen years to the day after he'd been stripped of his command, and as another unwinnable war mushroomed in Vietnam, MacArthur did, in fact, die. By then, Truman claimed an increasing share of his countrymen's affections, as well as the admiration of many historians. In the decades since he departed this world on the day after Christmas 1972 at age eighty-eight, the thirty-third president has come to be regarded by scholars as one of the ten best American chief executives of all time.

In the final analysis, despite his brilliance at Inchon, MacArthur's overall performance in Korea is more tragic than heroic. But often obscured amid the rancor and confusion of this most-forgotten of American wars are thousands of more deserving—and far less celebrated—heroes. The following are but a few examples:

In the life-and-death struggle to maintain a UN toehold in Korea during the summer of 1950, the battlefield brilliance, tireless determination, and inspired leadership of *Edward A. "Eddie" Craig* spelled the difference between salvation and damnation for American forces in the Pusan Perimeter.

Without the toughness and skill of General Craig and his Marine brigade, it seems impossible that Pusan could have been held against the NKPA juggernaut. "Craig was a great leader, whose personal courage equaled that of any of the brave men who served under him," said *John A. Buck*, Craig's former aide-de-camp, who maintained a lasting friendship with his old boss after the war. "Regardless of how bad the situation was, he was always upbeat. I don't have the words to adequately express my admiration for him."

"General Craig was a very impressive figure, although he wasn't large," added legendary Marine hero *Raymond L. Murray*, former CO of the Fifth Marines, whose regiment formed the nucleus of Craig's brigade during the fight for Pusan. "His posture was very erect. He had steely blue eyes and an air about him that he knew what he was doing. He inspired confidence."

On January 24, 1951, Craig was promoted to major general and ordered back to the States to head the Marine Reserve. He left Korea in disappointment that soon turned to disgust when he reached Washington. "I felt my men had been let down," he said bitterly. Five months later, he decided to quit the Corps and resisted all efforts to talk him out of it.

Craig never publicly discussed the reasons for his anger at the U.S. military, but from all indications, they were substantial—and some of them deeply personal. Craig despised X Corps commander General Almond for ordering the First Marine Division's headlong charge into North Korea, which almost resulted in its annihilation, but he also never forgave Almond for ordering him back to Korea when Craig's father was on the verge of death in the States. At the time, Craig was on emergency leave to be with his father, and Almond's order bordered on capriciousness. Craig's father died two days after Craig left, and by the time Craig reached Korea, it was too late for him to participate in the division's withdrawal. Not coincidentally, during World War II, Craig's commanding officer had refused him leave when Craig's wife was dying at home.

After retiring as a lieutenant general, Craig settled in the San Diego area, where he was later joined in retirement by Buck. For many years, they got together regularly for lunch and to swap reminiscences, and Buck's voice still turns hoarse with emotion when he recalls their final meeting, shortly before Craig's death in December 1994 at age ninety-eight:

"After lunch, we were sitting in his room, looking through an old Japanese telescope, when General Craig remarked very calmly, 'I think my time is getting close, Jack. I'm just waiting for the bugler to call taps.' He died in his sleep three days later."

After surviving combat duty in three major wars—at Peleliu in the Pacific, in Korea from Pusan to Chosin, and finally in Vietnam—Buck retired from the Marine Corps as a major, then served a hitch with the CIA. The father of two grown sons and a frequent volunteer at the Marine Corps Recruit Depot Museum, Buck lives in San Diego with his wife, Litzie.

Ray Murray, a onetime football star at Texas A&M who went on to become a hero in the Battles of Guadalcanal, Tarawa, and Saipan in World War II, received both the Distinguished Service Cross and a Navy Cross (his second) for leading the X Corps breakout from the Chosin Reservoir. When he retired from the Marines in August 1968 as a major general, after thirty-three years of service, he held virtually every available valor-based decoration except the Medal of Honor.

Murray retired to Oceanside, California, near Camp Pendleton, where he had served as commanding general. He died there in November 2004 at age ninety-one.

Lewis B. "Chesty" Puller, another Marine Corps legend, led the First Marines into battle twice—first at bloody Peleliu in 1944, then at Inchon and Seoul in 1950. In January 1951 he was promoted from colonel to brigadier general and appointed assistant commander of the First Marine Division, succeeding General Craig. A few weeks earlier, Puller had won his fifth Navy Cross for his role in his regiment's agonizing escape from "Frozen Chosin."

He later commanded both the Second and Third Marine divisions before retiring for health reasons in November 1955 and moving back to his native Tidewater Virginia. He made his home there in the small town of Saluda until his death at age seventy-three in October 1971.

Before completing a year-long hitch in Korea, *Bryghte Godbold* left the staff of the First Marine Division and briefly assumed command of the Fifth Marines, following Colonel Murray's transfer to Washington. In 1958 Godbold retired from the Marine Corps as a brigadier general after a twenty-two-year career interrupted by forty-three months in Japanese prison camps during World War II. He later returned to South Korea several times on brief missions for the U.S. Defense Department.

During the more than five decades since he left military service, Godbold has served in numerous capacities in government, public education, and private business. In 1963 he moved to Dallas to take a position as vice president of the Southwest Center for Advanced Studies, now the University of Texas at Dallas.

As this is written, General Godbold is the only surviving member of the small interservice team of officers who planned the Inchon-Seoul operation and one of a handful of veterans of the Battle of Wake Island still living. He and his wife, Patricia, make their home in Dallas.

Despite his somewhat irascible personality and sharp tongue—or perhaps because of them—*Robert D. Taplett* was held in highest esteem by the men who served under him in the Third Battalion, Fifth Marines, and Colonel Taplett returned their feelings. Commissioned a Marine officer in 1940, the tall South Dakotan spent World War II aboard the heavy cruiser *Salt Lake City*, which narrowly escaped catastrophe at Pearl Harbor on December 7, 1941, then fought with distinction in the Aleutian Islands and at Iwo Jima and Okinawa.

When he took command of 3/5 in the summer of 1950, he demanded the best of his men, and they never disappointed him. From November 27 to December 10, 1950, the battalion was in constant combat as it fought its way out of the Chinese trap at the Chosin Reservoir.

"I don't think I slept two hours that whole time," Taplett later recalled. "You had to keep moving or you'd freeze. We left Yudam-ni with roughly 1,300 men and got to Hagaru-ri with 326 effective Marines. Over half our casualties were caused by the weather."

Taplett himself suffered such severe frostbite on that march that he had difficulty walking for the rest of his life.

"The members of 3/5, whether Marines or Navy men, youngsters fresh out of high school or college graduates, reinforced the Leatherneck code of toughness and discipline," Taplett wrote more than fifty years after their ordeals at Pusan and Chosin. "They stood proud and strong and laid their lives on the line to defend their Corps. . . . They were men of honor, valor, integrity, and loyalty. . . . When they lost their leaders, they *became* the leaders."

On February 20, 1951, much to his troops' consternation, Taplett told them good-bye. The lingering effects of his frostbite forced him to relinquish command of 3/5 and return to the States.

After earning a Navy Cross, two Silver Stars, a Bronze Star, and the Legion of Merit, Taplett retired from the Marine Corps in 1960, and he and his family settled in Arlington, Virginia. In his latter years, he devoted much of his time to writing and self-publishing a book on his Korean experiences titled *Dark Horse Six* (his radio code name). He died in December 2004 at age eighty-six.

In the savage summer action of 1950, no Marine infantrymen in Korea were handed a more daunting task than those of Able and Baker companies, First Battalion, Fifth Marines—and none carried out the job with greater courage, determination, or sacrifice.

A/1/5 and B/1/5 were part of the heart and soul of General Craig's "Fire Brigade" in the Pusan Perimeter and later the first American combat troops to go ashore in the city of Inchon. Had these two companies—totaling only about 500 officers and enlisted men between them—failed in either of these crucial roles, the Korean War might well have been lost. It's no exaggeration to say that every Marine in their ranks was a hero, but no man had a stronger claim to that distinction than *Francis I. "Ike" Fenton Jr.*, the young World War II veteran who commanded B/1/5.

On October 3, less than a week after Seoul was secured, Captain Fenton broke the distressing news to the men of B/1/5 that he was being ordered out of the combat zone. "I just got the word," he told *Hugh "Nick" Schryver*, the only other original officer of the unit that had landed at Pusan on August 2. "They're sending me home, and I've got to go."

One person who was overjoyed to see Fenton leave Korea, however, was his wife, Ellie, who was waiting at home with two small children and who had already been subjected to rumors that Ike had been killed in action—not once but three times.

"My sister had heard the rumors and tried to keep them from me," recalled Mrs. Fenton some fifty-eight years later, "but then I got four letters from Ike assuring me to ignore any letters of condolence I might be getting because he was still alive."

The man who succeeded Fenton as B/1/5's commander wasn't so fortunate. Weeks after taking over the company, First Lieutenant John Hancock was fatally wounded by a Chinese sniper.

In the late 1960s, after retiring from the Marine Corps as a colonel, Fenton and his family moved to Peachtree City, Georgia, where he took an executive position with National Cash Register Company and also worked with the Professional Golfers Association. He died in October 1998 and is buried in Arlington National Cemetery.

Carrying on a family tradition, Fenton's son, George, also retired from the Corps as a colonel, and as this is written, Ike's grandson, Lieutenant Patrick Fenton, is on active duty with the Marines in Afghanistan.

After twenty-eight years as a Marine, rising through the ranks from buck private to lieutenant colonel, and serving in three major wars, Nick Schryver retired in 1969. He and his wife, Louise, make their home in the remote hamlet of Vanderpool in the Texas hill country.

In experience and battle savvy, *Mackie L. Wheeler* was typical of the NCOs in 1/5's Able Company, ably commanded by *John "Blackjack" Stevens*. A native of tiny Colgate, Oklahoma, Sergeant Wheeler had joined the Marine Corps in June 1940 and, as a member of the First Marine Defense Battalion, was among the first U.S. troops to reach and fortify strategically valuable Wake Island in the summer of 1941.

Assigned to one of the five-inch batteries that repelled a Japanese invasion fleet during the sixteen-day battle for Wake the following December, Wheeler stayed at his gun until the American garrison—cursing or weeping to a man—was forced to surrender. Then he endured three and a half years of beatings, starvation, and forced labor in a Japanese POW camp in China.

Ironically, Captain Stevens almost ended up at Wake himself. After joining the Marines as a private in September 1939, the Montana-born Stevens also was assigned to the First Marine Defense Battalion but was sent to Midway and Palmyra islands instead of Wake. By the time war broke out on December 7, 1941, he had returned to Pearl Harbor and was stationed at a Marine compound about 1,000 yards from the docks, where he dodged repeated strafing runs by Japanese planes.

In early July 1950, as the First Provisional Marine Brigade was forming, Wheeler—by then a ten-year veteran—was assigned to A/1/5, where Stevens had assumed command a few months earlier. "I didn't know a soul in the outfit at the time," Wheeler recalled. "Lots of the other guys didn't either, but once we got to Korea, we really came together as a unit. A lot of us already knew how to fight, and those that didn't learned in a hurry."

"Every NCO in the company had seen combat in World War II," said Stevens. "They knew what to do and what to tell their men to do when we came under fire. That made a tremendous difference at places like the Naktong Bulge."

Among those who benefited and quickly developed into seasoned combat Marines was *Ray L. Walker*, whose wounds and frostbite qualified him for 100 percent disability when he returned to civilian life after his four-year hitch in the Corps with a rank of corporal. He worked for several years as an undercover police officer in Glendale, California, then married a girl from Little Rock, Arkansas, and moved east. He and his wife, Mary, the parents of a son and two daughters—and grandparents several times over—make their home in Franklin, Tennessee.

From Pusan and the two battles of the Naktong, to Inchon and Seoul, and finally to the icy horror of the Chosin Reservoir, A/1/5 was in almost constant combat for five months.

"For me," recalled Stevens, "the first Naktong battle rates as my worst experience in Korea. At Obong-ni Ridge, after the company was badly beaten up in firefights that lasted all afternoon, we had to endure a long night with the enemy above us continuously rolling grenades down the slope at us. Words can't describe how terrifying it was."

For Wheeler, the ghastly retreat from Chosin in December 1950, where he saw several buddies bayoneted in their sleeping bags during a night attack by the Chinese, took the "worst" prize. Wheeler was hit in the chin by a chunk of rock flung by a Chinese machine gun bullet, but "I just got a doc to put some Mercurochrome on it and went on." A few days later, however, two severely frostbitten feet, aggravated by wading through a freezing stream, caused his evacuation.

"Twenty-two of us in the company were hospitalized with frostbite at about that same time," Wheeler recalled. "At the aid station, I told them I could go back to the company in two or three days, and they said, 'The hell you can!' They were right. I almost got trenchfoot and came close to losing both feet. Man, I'll never forget how they burned—it was so bad I couldn't stand to cover them with a sheet."

"I don't think a man in the company made it out of Chosin without some degree of frostbite," Stevens recalled. "I don't see how anyone could possibly have escaped it. I know I didn't."

Stevens and Wheeler were luckier than many, since neither suffered any lasting disability. Both remained on active duty until they retired, and Wheeler served another hitch in Korea before retiring from the Corps in 1960, then spent ten more years in the Marine Reserve.

Over his protests, Stevens was replaced as A/1/5's commander at the end of November 1950 and sent home. By then he was the last of the Fifth Marines' original company commanders still standing and on duty in Korea. He retired as a colonel in 1962, settling with his wife, Joanne, and their four children in the San Francisco Bay Area, where he took a position with IBM and later founded several high-tech companies of his own. Stevens's oldest son, Mitchell, followed in his father's footsteps, serving as a Marine captain in Vietnam.

After returning to civilian life, Wheeler signed on as a police officer in Alaska, worked as a zookeeper in San Diego, and finally settled in Flagstaff, Arizona, in the late 1980s. Mackie, his wife, Juanita, and their two grown daughters recently celebrated the couple's sixty-first wedding anniversary.

After spending "the worst seventeen days of my life" at the Chosin Reservoir and hauling up to a dozen litter cases at once on the deck of his M-26 tank during the bitter retreat, underage tank driver *Murdoch Ford* underwent three surgeries on his legs to save his frozen feet. He also was struck in the chest by shrapnel from an enemy shell but was too cold to realize that he was wounded until another Marine yelled, "You're hit!"

"I took a pair of pliers and pulled the chunks of metal out of my chest," Ford recalled nearly sixty years later, "but unfortunately I missed one piece, and it penetrated my left lung." In addition, he was left permanently deaf in his right ear from continuous exposure to the blasts from the Pershing's 90-millimeter gun.

While Ford was convalescing back in the States, doctors discovered that he'd contracted tuberculosis in his wounded lung, and he was placed in isolation for a year. Eventually the diseased lung was removed in what was then highly experimental surgery.

"One positive thing came out of all this," Ford said. "I met my future wife, Lucille, in the VA hospital, where she was a 'candy-striper' nurse's aide." The Fords, who moved to Zephyrhills, Florida, near Tampa, in 1972, had three children and were married for forty-seven years before Lucille's death in 2003.

As a leader in the Tampa area chapter of Korean War Veterans, Ford helped generate interest and raise funds for a permanent monument to honor posthumous Medal of Honor recipient *Baldomero Lopez*, a local Marine hero killed on Red Beach at Inchon. The monument's base is made from a large stone brought to Tampa from Inchon by *Eddie Ko*, the Korean teenager who helped Navy Lieutenant Eugene Clark lay the groundwork for the Inchon landings in 1950, then fought with the Marines all the way to Chosin. After the war, a group of Ko's Marine buddies arranged to bring him to the States as a permanent resident. He settled in the Tampa area, where he now owns and operates a golf course and is an active member of Ford's chapter of Korean veterans.

Early on the morning of December 7, 1950, while the Fifth Marines was fighting its way south from Hagaru-ri to Koto-ri, a sudden outburst of enemy fire struck the half-frozen regimental column from the roadside, and *Herbert "Doc Rocket" Pearce* heard a shout from a sergeant a few yards away.

"Better get down, Doc! I just got hit!" Then, a couple of seconds later, the sergeant cried out a second time, "Hurry up! I just got hit again!"

As Corpsman Pearce rushed to the stricken sergeant's aid and cautioned other Marines around him to stay low, he was struck in midthigh by a large chunk of shrapnel that knocked him down and left him unable to move.

"I also got fragments in one arm and lost the M-1 I was carrying," Pearce recalled much later, "and this left me in a bad way if the Chinese overran our position."

Fortunately, two close friends, *Edward "Red" Martin* and *Frederick "Rusty" Russell*, along with several other members of the recoilless gun unit to which Pearce was attached, rushed to the rescue. Corporal Martin and Sergeant Russell loaded the wounded medic onto the floor of a communications trailer, where he was shielded from the cold, and another Marine gave Pearce a spare .45 automatic for protection.

When Pearce reached a hospital in Japan, he was reunited with another close friend, *Charlie Snow*, who had recently been reassigned from the recoilless gun unit to a machine-gun section, then wounded at about the same time as Pearce.

"A mortar round blew part of a hill out from under me, and I took a pretty hard fall," Sergeant Snow remembered. "I didn't have a scratch on me that I could see, and I didn't think at first I was even hurt, but then I discovered I was covered with blood."

The diagnosis was a ruptured colon and severe contusions to Snow's kidneys as a result of the fall. "I spent five months strapped down in a hospital bed with a tube in me," Snow said.

After being discharged from the hospital, Pearce and Snow didn't see each other for many years. Then one day Pearce showed up on Snow's door-step, and they've stayed in close contact ever since.

Drawing on his experiences as a corpsman, Pearce went on to earn his M.D. degree at the University of Mississippi and practice medicine for more than forty years, specializing in general surgery. He and his wife, Betty, live in Jacksonville, Florida.

After twenty-one years in the Marine Corps, Snow retired to a secluded lakeshore home in Alabama, but since the death of his wife several years ago, he spends much of his time traveling leisurely around the country in a camper-equipped pickup truck.

Discharged after a four-year hitch in the Marines, Red Martin attended North Dakota State University to study engineering, then settled in Las Cruces, New Mexico, where he retired from Honeywell in 1989. His death in early 2009 deeply saddened his old comrades.

Rusty Russell, who fought under Chesty Puller at Peleliu six years before landing in Korea, remained on active duty with the Marines for twenty-two years, then worked for the U.S. Postal Service as a mail carrier. As this is written, he is disabled by severe neuropathy of his hands and feet caused by frostbite at Chosin. Since the death of his wife, Ruthie, in 2006, he lives alone in Indio, California.

Did the United States lose the Korean War? Did the young Americans who fought, suffered, and died there waste their blood and bravery in the same sort of "lost cause" as their latter-day counterparts a quarter-century later in Vietnam? Was that longest, hottest, darkest summer of 1950 in Korea nothing more than a "shadow victory"—a futile postponement of eventual defeat? Have the months of agony that came later left an indelible stain on our national honor or permanently tarnished our military history?

Fifty-six years after the last wartime shots were traded in Korea in July 1953, many twenty-first-century American citizens might well answer "yes" to these questions, especially amid the backlash against costly, debili-tating wars in Iraq and Afghanistan. But the several dozen veterans of the grisly Korean "police action" who granted author interviews for this book would respond—if anyone bothered to ask them—with an almost unani-mous "No!"

"There's certainly no way we lost the war, in either a military or political sense," said General Godbold. "Our sacrifice was huge, but we achieved our primary objectives, which were rescuing South Korea from a Communist takeover and securing the country as a stable democracy. From several visits there in the years since, I can vouch that South Korea is now among the most prosperous, progressive countries in Asia—as well as one of our strongest allies. We also showed Red China that we'd stand firm against its aggression, probably the main reason that Taiwan remains a free, independent state today. In all the years since, we've never again faced an armed challenge from the Chinese."

As Colonel John Stevens, who had recently returned from Seoul at the time he was interviewed for this book, puts it, "I don't think any American who has traveled to South Korea and seen the country as it is today would ever say we lost the war. The United States not only saved South Korea but has also guaranteed its security ever since."

Many students of the war agree. "If the Korean War was a frustrating, profoundly unsatisfactory experience," wrote British historian Max Hastings more than thirty-five years after the cease-fire, ". . . it still seems a struggle that the West was utterly right to fight."

Simply being morally in the right isn't the same, of course, as being the winner in a political or military conflict. But the crisis in Korea, and the forceful U.S. reaction to it, produced a formidable list of positives that continue to affect our world today. For one thing, the war provided a crucial wake-up call for our government and the general public. It showed that superior wealth and technology alone can't guarantee success against our enemies and that, even for the world's foremost superpower, the way isn't always easy. In the final analysis, our intervention in the war preserved not only the freedom of South Korea and its people but—in a very real sense—of the United States as well. Had we smugly continued for another five or ten years along the path we were following in June 1950, the Cold War could well have been lost.

The heroes of the First Provisional Marine Brigade and the First Marine Division, along with those of the rest of the Eighth Army and X Corps, prevented that from happening. In the process, America's fighting men taught a complacent, self-indulgent nation a series of invaluable lessons.

They taught us that we could never again afford to let down our guard, regardless of how vast a nuclear arsenal we might possess. They made us realize that short of triggering global Armageddon, we could never hope to eliminate the world's tyrants and aggressors with push-button weapons of mass destruction alone. In that summer of 1950, they made us understand—again—that only courageous human beings who stand ready to bleed and die in mud and slime, heat and dust, snow and ice, and the unmitigated hell of hand-to-hand combat can ensure our safety and the survival of democracy on planet Earth.

These were the values that the Marines brought to South Korea in August 1950 and displayed with such grit and determination at Pusan, Inchon, and Seoul. These values saved South Korea—and the Marines themselves—from oblivion that summer. And this is why, even after another sixty years—or 600 years, for that matter—the Korean War should never be forgotten, much less written off as a defeat for the United States.

As long as we heed these lessons and recognize these values, Korea will always remain an American victory.

SOURCES AND NOTES

I. SUDDENLY, A NOT-SO-SUDDEN WAR

The scenes unfolding as North Korean forces launched a massive invasion of South Korea—particularly those in Seoul on the evening of June 25 and early morning of June 26, 1950—are re-created by author T. R. Fehrenbach in his 1963 book *This Kind of War: A Study in Unpreparedness*. The situation confronting the late Captain Joseph R. Darrigo, the lone American officer on duty at the 38th Parallel that night, is reconstructed from several published sources, including a June 2000 interview with Darrigo by David Lightman of the *Hartford (Conn.) Courant*. Other information is drawn from *The Forgotten War: America in Korea, 1950–1953* by Clay Blair; *The Korean War* by Max Hastings; and *Korea: The Untold Story of the War* by Joseph C. Goulden.

2. AN ARMY IN DISARRAY

The frenzied, behind-the-scenes action in Washington and Tokyo as the Truman administration and U.S. military leaders scrambled to formulate a response to North Korea's aggression are based on numerous published sources. These include President Harry S. Truman's *Memoirs, Vol. II: Years of Trial and Hope, 1946–1952*; David McCullough's *Truman*; David Halberstam's *The Coldest Winter*; Blair's *The Forgotten War*; and Hastings's *The Korean War*.

In *This Kind of War*, author Fehrenbach, himself a former Army battalion commander, presents a brutally frank assessment of the deplorable condition of America's military and the causes of its stunning deterioration following the end of World War II.

These sources are augmented by author interviews with numerous survivors of the small, ill-equipped Task Force Smith, commanded by Colonel Charles B. "Brad" Smith, which was the first U.S. Army unit to meet the North Korean invaders and their tanks in combat. Among the interviewees are General Miller Perry, who commanded Smith's artillery; Sergeant Phil Burke, an Army medic; Lieutenant John Doody, who led Smith's mortar section; PFC William Thornton, a rifle squad leader; the late Lieutenant Carl Bernard, a platoon leader who tried in vain to halt enemy tanks with an obsolete bazooka, then helped a seriously wounded GI escape capture; and others.

A graphic description of the Americans' ill-fated battle against overwhelming enemy odds comes from United Press correspondent Peter Kalischer, the only American journalist present that day. Kalischer narrowly escaped with his own life when Smith's force retreated in panic, and he managed to file the only eyewitness report of the fight to appear in major U.S. newspapers.

3. A PROUD CORPS IN PERIL

Multiple author interviews with Lieutenant Colonel (later Brigadier General) Bryghte D. Godbold, last surviving member of an interservice team of officers who worked with General Douglas MacArthur to plan the Inchon invasion, provide priceless insights into America's frenetic preparations for war. Godbold, who rushed from Washington to Camp Pendleton, then flew to Tokyo within the first few days after the invasion, also offers an insider's perspective on the precarious situation faced by the Marine Corps at its time of greatest peril. His personal acquaintance with MacArthur; General O. P. Smith, commander of the First Marine Division; and other military leaders gives him unique knowledge about one of the most critical periods in U.S. military history.

Goldbold's overview is enhanced by other author interviews with enlisted men and field officers caught up in the scramble to organize the First Provisional Marine Brigade and assemble the scattered units of the First Marine Division at Camp Pendleton. Among the interviewees are Corporal Wilbert Estabrook, Sergeant Bill Finnegan, Corpsmen Herb Pearce and Conraid Pope, Sergeant Frederick Russell, Sergeant Charles Sands, Sergeant Charlie Snow, and Captain John Stevens.

Published sources contributing vital information about the early war effort and the largely futile efforts to halt the North Korean onslaught include Andrew Geer's *The New Breed;* Orlando Ward's *Korea 1950,* an official Department of the Army publication; Volumes I and II of the official Marine Corps series *U.S. Marine Operations in Korea, 1950–1953* by Lynn Montross and Captain Nicholas Canzona; McCullough's *Truman;* Halberstam's *The Coldest Winter;* Hastings's *The Korean War;* Blair's *The Forgotten War;* and Fehrenbach's *This Kind of War.*

Notes

Page 45   *General of the Army Dwight D. Eisenhower:* Eisenhower's remarks, recorded in official Joint Chiefs of Staff documents, are quoted in James Warren's *American Spartans.*

Page 45   *Other major figures in the Army's power structure:* In *The Forgotten War,* author Clay Blair uses the term "curtail drastically" in reference to top Army brass's desires for the Marine Corps.

Page 45   *General Carl A. Spaatz, former commander in chief:* Warren's *American Spartans* cites specific top-secret Joint Chiefs of Staff documents (JCS 1478/10 and 11) that contain Spaatz's charges and recommendations where the Marines were concerned. Warren describes the documents as "shocking" in that they indicated a willingness on the part of high Navy brass "to compromise on protecting the combat power and missions of the Marines [in exchange] for guarantees that the Navy could keep its planes."

4. MISSIONS IMPOSSIBLE

The Americans' continuing defeats—and near despair of the U.S. Eighth Army—during July 1950 are captured through author interviews with Corporal Lacy Barnett, Corporal Jack Brooks, and Corporal Estabrook, all of whom were actually there.

Also helping to portray in vivid detail the attempted defense of the key city of Taejon, and its disastrous failure, is the autobiographical account by General William Dean, commander of the Army's 24th Infantry Division. Dean's account, published in book form a year after the war as *General Dean's Story*, describes how he personally fought enemy tanks in the streets of Taejon, was himself captured by the North Koreans as he attempted to flee the city, and served three years as a prisoner of war.

Important published sources providing important background information for this chapter include *Disaster in Korea: The Chinese Confront MacArthur* by the late Lieutenant Colonel Roy A. Appleman, perhaps the Army's most respected authority on the Korean War. Also contributing background on the Army's early struggles to establish and hold a defensive perimeter around the port of Pusan are Bevin Alexander's *Korea: The First War We Lost*, Blair's *The Forgotten War*, Fehrenbach's *This Kind of War*, Halberstam's *The Coldest Winter*, Hastings's *The Korean War*, and Goulden's *Korea: The Untold Story of the War*.

The issues surrounding the performance of all-black U.S. Army infantry units commanded by white officers during this period are examined in two books: *Black Soldier, White Army: The 24th Infantry Regiment in Korea* by William T. Bowers, William M. Hammond, and George L. MacGarrigle, and *Firefight at Yechon: Courage and Racism in the Korean War* by Charles M. Bussey.

5. ENTER THE "FIRE BRIGADE"

The most important single document describing the scenes and emotions as the First Provisional Marine Brigade disembarked at the embattled port of Pusan on August 2, 1950, is an official debriefing report given a few months later by Captain Francis I. "Ike" Fenton of B Company, First Battalion, Fifth Marines. Excerpts from this report—most of them published here for the first time—are used extensively in this chapter but also help form a framework for much of the subsequent narrative. This extraordinary document exposes the heart and soul of a Marine field commander under the most stressful imaginable circumstances. It reveals with foxhole-level candor what Fenton (who took command of the company when its previous commander was gravely wounded) and the men serving under him saw, thought, and experienced during the decisive battles that saved South Korea.

Another document of immense importance—again extensively utilized here for the first time in any book—is the handwritten daily journal of Brigadier General Edward Craig, who commanded the Marine "Fire Brigade" in the struggle to defend Pusan against overwhelming Communist forces. Titled "Incidents of Service," Craig's journal follows the brigade from its arrival at the panic-stricken port through its baptism of fire near the villages of Masan and Chindong-ni and the two crucial battles of the Naktong Bulge, then on to Inchon and Seoul.

These rare documents are augmented by author interviews with a number of Marines who served with or near Fenton's Baker Company. They include Lieutenant Hugh "Nick" Schryver, trusted leader of Fenton's First Platoon; Sergeant Mackie Wheeler, a rifle squad leader in Baker's sister company, A/1/5; Captain Stevens, A/1/5's commander; Corpsman Pearce, who treated wounded men in both units; and Sergeant Snow of the recoilless rifle platoon attached to B Company.

Another major—and extremely rare—printed source is Lieutenant Colonel Robert D. Taplett's self-published book *Dark Horse Six*, in which the commander of the Third Battalion, Fifth Marines, offers pithy, poignant, on-the-scene observations of his unit's early actions in Korea. Other published sources contributing to the narrative include the writings of *Life* magazine photographer-correspondent David Douglas Duncan, author of the postwar pictorial book *This Is War!*; the diary-style volume titled *Battleground Korea*, edited by Allan A. David, detailing the combat experiences of the 25th Infantry Division; Edwin P. Hoyt's *The Pusan Perimeter*; Fehrenbach's *This Kind of War*; Geer's *The New Breed*; and Blair's *The Forgotten War*.

Note

Page 134   *"Get outta the way, white boy"*: The exchange between Colonel Taplett and the black trooper is quoted verbatim from Taplett's *Dark Horse Six*.

6. A MELEE OF CONFUSION AND CHAOS

Drawing from Colonel Taplett's gripping eyewitness account in *Dark Horse Six*, the chapter details the first attempt by Eighth Army forces to launch an offensive on August 7, 1950, against the numerically superior North Vietnamese near the hamlet of Chindong-ni. Taplett, whose Third Battalion, Fifth Marines, led the U.S. assault, recounts in great detail how it dissolved into bloody chaos with the Marines suffering heavy losses because of confusion and poor coordination with participating Army units.

Taking up the narrative in his official debriefing transcript, Lieutenant Ike Fenton, then executive officer of B/1/5, explains how Army troops became stymied by an enemy roadblock at a key highway junction, causing the entire offensive to bog down and forcing the Marines to fall back to defensive positions. In his journal "Incidents of Service," General Craig describes the battle for Chindong-ni and a strip of high ground designated as Hill 342 as it raged in 114-degree heat and characterizes the situation as the "most confused" of his long career.

These sources are augmented by an in-depth author interview with Corpsman Pearce, who describes seeing a close friend blown to pieces by an enemy artillery shell and of narrowly escaping a similar fate, as well as information obtained through interviews with Lieutenant Schryver and Sergeant Wheeler.

Among published sources, Geer's *The New Breed* offers a notable account of the action at close range. Also providing significant background information and strategic overviews are John C. Chapin's Marine Corps–commissioned book *Fire Brigade: U.S. Marines in the Pusan Perimeter*; Dick Camp's *Leatherneck Legends*; James A. Warren's *American Spartans*; and Montross and Canzona's *U.S. Marine Operations in Korea, 1950–1953*, Vol. 1, *The Pusan Perimeter*.

7. TRIUMPH, TRAGEDY, TRAPS, AND TEARS

With major contributions from Captain Fenton's debriefing interviews, Colonel Taplett's memoir *Dark Horse Six*, and General Craig's journal, this chapter examines some of the darkest moments faced by Craig's First Provisional Marine Brigade—and B/1/5 in particular—during the entire Korean campaign.

The period from August 11 to 15, 1950, was marked by momentary triumphs as the "Fire Brigade" stopped the onrushing North Korean invaders in their tracks for the first time in the war. But it was also a time of intense tragedy—a time that cost the Fifth Marines their first heavy casualties, forced them to violate their time-honored rule of never abandoning dead or wounded men on the battlefield, and brought many of them to tears.

In the midst of this, they earned their "Fire Brigade" nickname when, after advancing a dozen miles toward the village of Sachon, they were ordered to withdraw immediately and rush to another hot spot. The combined recollections of Fenton, Taplett, and Craig drive home the pain, frustration, and anger of this period with wrenching clarity.

Adding to the drama are author eyewitness interviews with Lieutenant Schryver, Sergeant Wheeler, Corporal Bob Speights, and PFC Ben Wray. Among published sources, Geer's *The New Breed* offers an especially detailed look at Fenton's company's reaction to the sudden withdrawal order and the horror of leaving dead or wounded men behind. Chapin's *Fire Brigade*, Montross and Canzona's *U.S. Marine Operations in Korea, 1950–1953*, Vol. 1, Duncan's *This Is War!*, and Fehrenbach's *This Kind of War* provide additional background.

8. NIGHTMARE ON THE NAKTONG

In mid-August 1950, the Eighth Army's desperate struggle to hold the east and south banks of the Naktong River, the last major natural barrier between the North Koreans and the port of Pusan, triggered the first of two crucial battles for the so-called Naktong Bulge. If the enemy could cross the river in strength and overrun the American defenses near the town of Miryang, Pusan—and the war—would almost certainly be lost.

The First Battle of the Naktong, known in the American media as the "Battle of No-Name Ridge," is re-created here, as viewed through the eyes of Captain Fenton, Colonel Taplett, General Craig, and other Marines and GIs who were caught up in the thick of the fighting. Eyewitness accounts by Fenton and others of the Fifth Marines' first encounter with supposedly invulnerable enemy tanks—and how the Marines of a recoilless rifle platoon annihilated three of them—are especially gripping and noteworthy.

The intensity of the tank encounter is captured through numerous author interviews with victorious participants in the battle, including Sergeant Rusty Russell, Corporal Red Martin, Corporal Robert Whited, Lieutenant Charles M. C. Jones, Captain Stevens, Lieutenant Schryver, Corpsman Pearce, PFC Wray, and Sergeant Wheeler.

A published source of special note is James Bell's article "The Brave Men of No-Name Ridge" in the August 28, 1950, edition of *Life* magazine. Other sources contributing details and background include William Glenn Robertson's *Counterattack on the Naktong, 1950* (No. 13 in the *Leavenworth Papers* series published by the U.S. Army Command and General Staff College), Geer's *The New Breed*, Chapin's *Fire Brigade*, Duncan's *This Is War!*, and Montross and Canzona's *U.S. Marine Operations in Korea, 1950–1953*, Vol. 1.

9. COMMANDERS IN CONFLICT

Keen insights into the friction and disagreements that sometimes affected the relationships among U.S. military commanders in Washington, Tokyo, and Korea are obtained through author interviews with several retired Marine and Army officers. Of special assistance in this chapter were those conducted with General Godbold, whose remembrances are unmatched among living Korea veterans; and Major John Buck, who, as General Craig's longtime aide-de-camp, probably knew Craig as well as—or perhaps better than—anyone else in the Marine Corps.

Other major contributions were drawn from author interviews with retired Army Colonel Fred Wilmot and retired Marine Colonel Charles M. C. Jones. Captain Fenton's debriefing interview also reveals instances in which field officers clashed with their superiors, as do General Craig's "Incidents of Service" journal and Taplett's *Dark Horse Six*.

Such semiautobiographical volumes as General J. Lawton Collins's *War in Peacetime*, General Matthew Ridgway's *The Korean War*, and former Secretary of State Dean Acheson's *The Korean War* also make key contributions. Other published sources of note include Truman's and Eisenhower's memoirs, Fehrenbach's *This Kind of War*, Alexander's *The First War We Lost*, Blair's *The Forgotten War*, Halberstam's *The Coldest Winter*, McCullough's *Truman*, and Camp's *Leatherneck Legends*.

Note

Page 170   *According to observers, Collins leaped:* This scene, including General Collins's stunned exclamation, is recounted in Blair's *The Forgotten War*, where Collins is described as "flabbergasted and furious." Blair also alludes to the assumption by Collins that Marine General Lemuel Shepherd would be chosen to lead the Inchon invasion force. Thomas Marnane's caustic comments about Almond also are quoted in *The Forgotten War*.

10. THE ENEMY GOES FOR BROKE

Captain Fenton's debriefing interview provides an overall framework for this chapter as it re-creates the high-water mark of the North Korean invasion. Fenton's recollections are liberally supplemented by General Craig's journal and author interviews with Captain Stevens, Lieutenant Schryver, Corpsman Pearce, Major Buck, PFC Wray, Sergeant Wheeler, and PFC Walker.

Colonel Taplett's *Dark Horse Six* provides excellent on-the-scene descriptions of the Fifth Marines' second fierce struggle to prevent the NKPA from crossing the Naktong. Other published sources contributing important background include Fehrenbach's *This Kind of War*, Hoyt's *The Pusan Perimeter*, Addison Terry's *The Battle for Pusan*, Chapin's *Fire Brigade*, Montross and Canzona's *U.S. Marine Operations in Korea, 1950–1953*, Vol. I, Geer's *The New*

Breed, and William Glenn Robertson's *Leavenworth Papers No. 13: Counterattack on the Naktong, 1950.* General information also is obtained from Blair's *The Forgotten War,* Halberstam's *The Coldest Winter,* Hastings's *The Korean War,* and Alexander's *Korea: The First War We Lost.*

Note

Page 190   *"Stop, you yellow sons of bitches!* Walker's angry outburst at fleeing American troops, his subsequent confrontation with General Keiser, and General Bradley's removal from command of Colonel Hill are recounted in Halberstam's *The Coldest Winter.*

11. A 5,000-TO-ONE "SURE THING"

The events leading up to the Inchon landing, one of the most complex amphibious operations ever undertaken by America's armed forces, are re-created in detail through the eyes of author interviewees General Godbold, Lieutenant Schryver, Corporal Brooks, Corpsman Pearce, Corporal Martin, Sergeant Wheeler, and young Korean civilian Eddie Ko. Captain Fenton's debriefing interview, General Craig's journal, and Colonel Taplett's *Dark Horse Six* provide continuity and intriguing glimpses behind the scenes as the Marines prepare to storm ashore.

Navy Lieutenant Eugene Franklin Clark's book *The Secrets of Inchon* also supplies vital information on Clark's top-secret, one-man mission to Inchon prior to the landing, which produced vital data that helped make the American victory possible. Another important published source is Marine historian Robert Heinl's *Victory at High Tide: The Inchon-Seoul Campaign,* which offers numerous details on the enmity between X Corps commander General Almond and First Marine Division commander General Smith.

Other books contributing general information include Edwin H. Simmons's *Over the Seawall: U.S. Marines at Inchon,* Geer's *The New Breed,* Halberstam's *The Coldest Winter,* Blair's *The Forgotten War,* Fehrenbach's *This Kind of War,* Montross and Canzona's *U.S. Marine Operations in Korea, 1950–1953,* Vol. II, and Alexander's *Korea: The First War We Lost.*

12. TURNING THE TIDE AT INCHON

The eyewitness accounts drawn from numerous author interviews re-create a broad panorama of the three amphibious assaults by the First Marine Division at Inchon. Veterans of the actions at Green, Red, and Blue beaches who contributed to this scenario include Major Richard Elliott, Corporal Murdoch Ford, PFCs Jack Dedrick and Ray Walker, Seaman Jim Holdman, Sergeant Finnegan, Corpsman Pearce, Lieutenant Schryver, Captain Stevens, and Sergeant Wheeler.

An unpublished day-by-day history of H Company, Third Battalion, First Marines, written by PFC Paul Gulick, describes in detail the landing on Blue Beach by Colonel Chesty Puller's regiment, and Captain Fenton's debriefing interview provides similar close-up accounts of the Red Beach landing by the First and Second battalions of the Fifth Marines.

Colonel Taplett's *Dark Horse Six* graphically covers the Green Beach operation on Wolmi-do Island.

A video provided by Corporal Ford captures the heroism of Medal of Honor recipient Lieutenant Baldomero Lopez as he died crossing the seawall on Red Beach.

Other key published sources include Simmons's *Over the Seawall*, Geer's *The New Breed*, Fehrenbach's *This Kind of War*, Halberstam's *The Coldest Winter*, Blair's *The Forgotten War*, Heinl's *Victory at High Tide*, and Montross and Canzona's U.S. *Marine Operations in Korea, 1950–1953*, Vol. II.

13. THE BLOODY ROAD TO SEOUL

After their amazingly easy victory at Inchon, troops of the First Marine Division faced a much tougher task in their drive to take Seoul, as author interviews with Corpsman Pearce, Corporal Ford, Sergeant Finnegan, Lieutenant Jones, Corporal Bob Speights, Lieutenant Schryver, PFC George Waslinko, Corporal Snow, and Corporal Martin attest.

Captain Fenton's debriefing interview, Colonel Taplett's self-published book, and PFC Gulick's unpublished history of H/3/1 offer intense foxhole-level views of many portions of the action.

Previously published sources providing important details and background include Joseph H. Alexander's *Battle of the Barricades*, Simmons's *Over the Seawall*, Hastings's *The Korean War*, Blair's *The Forgotten War*, Halberstam's *The Coldest Winter*, Goulden's *Korea: The Untold Story of the War*, and Montross and Canzona's U.S. *Marine Operations in Korea, 1950–1953*, Vol. II.

Note

Page 257   *"We've been bastard children here lately"*: General Walker's caustic comments to
     General Hickey are quoted in Halberstam's *The Coldest Winter*.

14. A "TERRIBLE LIBERATION"

Author interviews with Corporal Brooks, Corpsman Pearce, Corpsman Cecil Carpenter, Corporal Murdoch Ford, PFC Gerald Kraus, Colonel Godbold, and Sergeant Snow help capture the scenes as the Marines fought their way doggedly toward Seoul against increasing resistance.

Captain Fenton's debriefing interview, Colonel Taplett's *Dark Horse Six*, Joseph H. Alexander's Marine Corps–commissioned commemorative *Battle of the Barricades: U.S. Marines in the Recapture of Seoul*, Colonel James Lynch's report on the actions of Task Force Lynch, and PFC Gulick's day-by-day history of H/3/1 also contribute numerous details and provide continuity for the narrative.

Other previously published books supplying vital information for this chapter include Heinl's *Victory at High Tide*, Geer's *The New Breed*, Fehrenbach's *This Kind of War*, Halberstam's *The Coldest Winter*, Blair's *The Forgotten War*, Goulden's *Korea: The Untold Story of the War*, and Alexander's *Korea: The First War We Lost*.

Note

Page 287   *"What the hell are you doing, Hawkins?"*: Several books allude to the unorthodox maneuver order delivered to Colonel Hawkins's First Battalion by Colonel Puller, but only Heinl's *Victory at High Tide* quotes the word-for-word exchange between the two commanders.

15. TAKING THE HARD WAY HOME

Numerous published accounts describe the historic meeting between President Truman and General MacArthur and offer opinions as to why the meeting failed to establish meaningful guidelines and limits on the American advance into North Korea. These include McCullough's *Truman,* the Truman *Memoirs,* Vol. II, D. Clayton James's *The Years of Mac-Arthur,* Vol. III, Halberstam's *The Coldest Winter,* Blair's *The Forgotten War,* Hastings's *The Korean War,* Matthew Ridgway's *The Korean War,* Dean Acheson's *The Korean War,* and Alexander's *Korea: The First War We Lost.*

Author interviews reveal the bitter realities and horrific suffering of the massive Chinese intervention and the disastrous Frozen Chosin campaign as experienced by such survivors as Corporal Dedrick, PFC Walker, Lieutenant Wilmot, Corporal Ford, Sergeant Finnegan, Sergeant Wheeler, Captain Bradley, and Corpsmen Carpenter and Pearce.

One of the best accounts of the Marines' plight in North Korea is Edwin H. Simmons's *Frozen Chosin: U.S. Marines at the Changin Reservoir;* and Colonel Taplett's *Dark Horse Six* adds unique first-person accounts of the Fifth Marines' desperate struggle to fight their way out of the giant trap sprung by the Chinese.

Notes

Page 305   *"The real failure of the Wake Island meeting"* Dean Rusk's admission is quoted in the declassified CIA document *Studies in Intelligence,* Vol. 45, No. 3, 2001.

Page 308   *Ridgway also regarded the acquiescence*: General Ridgway's remarks to General Vandenberg are quoted in Halberstam's *The Coldest Winter.*

Page 315   *The onrushing masses of enemy troops defied description*: The late PFC Herb Holdman's descriptions are based on the recollections of his younger brother, Navy Seaman Jim Holdman, during an author interview.

Page 315   *"From the time we headed to the Yalu"*: Colonel McCaffrey's caustic comments about Almond and MacArthur are quoted in Halberstam's book.

EPILOGUE: THE REST OF THE STORY

Published sources providing overviews of the historic showdown between President Truman and General MacArthur and its aftermath include McCullough's *Truman,* Miller's *Plain Speaking,* James's *The Years of MacArthur,* Vol. III, Truman's *Memoirs,* Halberstam's *The Coldest Winter,* Blair's *The Forgotten War,* Whitney's *MacArthur: His Rendezvous with History,* and Acheson's *The Korean War.*

Most of the details of the later lives of the officers and enlisted men featured in the epilogue's personal capsules are drawn from author interviews with Lieutenant Buck, Corpsman Pearce, General Godbold, Lieutenant Schryver, Captain Stevens, Corporal Ford, Korean civilian Ko, Sergeant Wheeler, PFC Walker, Corporal Martin, and Sergeant Russell. An author interview with Ellie Fenton, Captain Fenton's widow, is a key source of information about the intrepid commander of B/1/5 after his retirement from the Marines.

Also contributing information for the personal capsules were Camp's *Leatherneck Legends,* Simmons's *Frozen Chosin* and *Over the Seawall,* Taplett's *Dark Horse Six,* and Chapin's *Fire Brigade.*

Note

Page 334 　*As his message became more and more vindictive:* MacArthur's acerbic remark to reporter Lucas is quoted in Halberstam's *The Coldest Winter.*

BIBLIOGRAPHY

BOOKS

Acheson, Dean. *The Korean War.* New York: W. W. Norton, 1971.

Aid, Matthew. *The Secret Sentry: The Untold History of the National Security Agency.* New York: Bloomsbury Press, 2009.

Alexander, Bevin. *Korea: The First War We Lost.* New York: Hippocrene Books, 1986.

Alexander, Joseph H. *Battle of the Barricades: U.S. Marines in the Recapture of Seoul.* Washington, D.C.: U.S. Marine Corps Historical Division, 2000.

Appleman, Roy A. *United States in the Korean War: South to the Naktong, North to the Yalu.* Washington, D.C.: Department of the Army, 1961.

———. *Disaster in Korea: The Chinese Confront MacArthur.* College Station: Texas A&M University Press, 1989.

Blair, Clay. *The Forgotten War: America in Korea, 1950–1953.* New York: Times Books, 1987.

Bowers, William T.; William M. Hammond; and George L. MacGarrigle. *Black Soldier, White Army: The 24th Infantry Regiment in Korea.* Washington, D.C.: U.S. Army Center of Military History, 1996.

Bussey, Charles M. *Firefight at Yechon: Courage and Racism in the Korean War.* Washington, D.C.: Brassey's, 1991.

Camp, Dick. *Leatherneck Legends: Conversations with the Marine Corps' Old Breed.* St. Paul, Minn.: Zenith, 2006.

Chapin, John C. *Fire Brigade: U.S. Marines in the Pusan Perimeter.* Washington, D.C.: Marine Corps Historical Division, 2000.

Clark, Eugene Franklin. *The Secrets of Inchon: The Untold Story of the Most Daring Covert Mission of the Korean War.* New York: G. P. Putnam's Sons, 2002.

Collins, J. Lawton. *War in Peacetime.* Boston: Houghton Mifflin, 1968.

David, Allan A., ed. *Battleground Korea: The Story of the 25th Infantry Division.* Arlington, Va.: 25th Infantry Division Association, 1951.

Dean, William F. *General Dean's Story.* New York: Viking, 1954.

Duncan, David Douglas. *This Is War! A Photo-Narrative in Three Parts.* New York: Harper & Brothers, 1951.

Eisenhower, Dwight D. *The White House Years: Mandate for Change, 1953–1956.* Garden City, N.Y.: Doubleday, 1963.

Fehrenbach, T. R. *This Kind of War: A Study in Unpreparedness.* New York: Macmillan, 1963.

Ferrell, Robert H. *The Question of MacArthur's Reputation: Côte de Chatillon, October 14–16, 1918.* Columbia, Mo.: University of Missouri Press, 2008.

Geer, Andrew. *The New Breed: The Story of the U.S. Marines in Korea.* New York: Harper & Brothers, 1952.

Giangreco, D. M. *War in Korea, 1950–1953: A Pictorial History.* Novato, Calif.: Presidio, 1990.

Goulden, Joseph C. *Korea: The Untold Story of the War.* New York: Times Books, 1982.

Gugeler, Russell A. *Army Historical Series: Combat Actions in Korea.* Washington, D.C.: U.S. Army Office of Military History, 1970.

Halberstam, David. *The Coldest Winter: America and the Korean War.* New York: Hyperion, 2007.

Hammel, Eric. *Chosin: Heroic Ordeal of the Korean War.* Novato, Calif.: Presidio, 1981.

Hastings, Max. *The Korean War.* New York: Simon & Schuster, 1987.

Heinl, Robert Debs Jr. *Victory at High Tide: The Inchon-Seoul Campaign.* Baltimore: Nautical & Aviation Publishing Company of America, 1979.

Hoyt, Edwin P. *The Pusan Perimeter.* New York: Stein & Day, 1984.

James, D. Clayton. *The Years of MacArthur,* Vol. III: *Triumph and Disaster, 1945–1964.* Boston: Houghton Mifflin, 1970.

McCullough, David. *Truman.* New York: Simon & Schuster, 1992.

Miller, Merle. *Plain Speaking: An Oral Biography of Harry S. Truman.* New York: Berkley, 1973.

Montross, Lynn, and Nicholas A. Canzona. *U.S. Marine Operations in Korea, 1950–1953;* Vol. I, *The Pusan Perimeter.* Washington, D.C.: U.S. Marine Corps Historical Branch, 1954.

———. *U.S. Marine Operations in Korea, 1950–1953;* Vol. II, *The Inchon-Seoul Operation.* Washington, D.C.: U.S. Marine Corps Historical Branch, 1955.

Noble, Harold. *Embassy at War.* Seattle: University of Washington Press, 1975.

Ridgway, Matthew B. *The Korean War.* Garden City, N.Y.: Doubleday, 1967.

Robertson, William Glenn. *Leavenworth Papers No. 13: Counterattack on the Naktong, 1950.* Fort Leavenworth, Kan.: Combat Studies Institute, U.S. Army Command and General Staff College, 1985.

Schnabel, James. *U.S. Army in the Korean War: Policy and Direction, the First Year.* Washington, D.C.: Office of the Chief of Military History, 1972.

Seigle, David J. *Pusan: "Stand or Die."* Washington, D.C.: David J. Seigle, 1997.

Simmons, Edwin H. *Over the Seawall: U.S. Marines at Inchon.* Washington, D.C.: U.S. Marine Corps Historical Division, 2000.

———. *Frozen Chosin: U.S. Marines at the Changjin Reservoir.* Washington, D.C.: U.S. Marine Corps Historical Division, 2002.

Taplett, Robert D. *Dark Horse Six.* Williamstown, N.J.: Phillips Publications, 2002.

Terry, Addison. *The Battle for Pusan: A Korean War Memoir.* Novato, Calif.: Presidio, 2000.

Time Capsule/1950. New York: Time, 1967.

Truman, Harry S. *Memoirs,* Vol. II: *Years of Trial and Hope, 1946–1952.* Garden City, N.Y.: Doubleday, 1956.

Ward, Orlando. *Korea 1950.* Washington, D.C.: Department of the Army, 1952.

Warren, James A. *American Spartans: The U.S. Marines: A Combat History from Iwo Jima to Iraq.* New York: Free Press, 2005.

Whitney, Courtney. *MacArthur: His Rendezvous with History.* New York: Alfred A. Knopf, 1956.

PERIODICALS

Alsop, Joseph. "The Conquerors." *New York Herald Tribune,* September 27, 1950.

Bell, James. "The Brave Men of No-Name Ridge." *Life,* August 28, 1950.

———. "For God, for Country, but Not . . ." *Time,* September 25, 1950.

"Big Pipeline Arms Troops for Big Push." *Life,* September 4, 1950.

Brannon, Rob. "The Hero from Hillsborough High." *St. Petersburg Times,* July 22, 2003.

Chandler, James B. "Thank God I'm a Marine." *Leatherneck,* June 1951.

Cohen, Eliot A. "Military Misfortunes." *Military History Quarterly,* Summer 1990.

Davis, W. J. "Fire for Effect." *Marine Corps Gazette,* July 1954.

Duncan, David Douglas. "The First Five Days." *Life,* July 10, 1950.

———. "The Durable ROKs." *Life,* September 11, 1950.

"The Forgotten War: Three Long Years in Korea." *National Geographic,* July 2003.

"The Great Retreat Continues." *Life,* December 18, 1950.

"Hard-Hitting UN Forces Wind Up War." *Life,* October 30, 1950.

Holley, Joe. "Decorated Marine Robert Taplett Dies." *Washington Post,* January 8, 2005.

"The Invasion." *Life,* October 2, 1950.

Kalischer, Peter. "Reporter, Cut Off Behind Lines Two Days, Tells How Tank-Led Reds Mauled GIs." *St. Louis Post-Dispatch,* July 7, 1950,

Keighley, Larry. "Four Dead—Three Wounded." *Saturday Evening Post,* October 21, 1950.

"Korean War Incidents of Service." *Traditions: Military History Journal of the Pacific,* Winter 1997–1998.

Lightman, David. "A Good Soldier." *Hartford Courant,* June 26, 2000.

"The Marine Landing . . . and a GI Battle." *Life,* August 14, 1950.

"Marine Muscle Heads for War." *Life,* July 24, 1950.

Martin, Harold H. "The Epic of Bloody Hill." *Saturday Evening Post,* October 14, 1950.

———. "The Ordeal of Marine Squad 2," *Saturday Evening Post,* November 11, 1950.

Messenger, Robert. "The Search for a Hero." *Wall Street Journal,* November 24, 2008.

"The Mysterious Voyage." *Life,* October 30, 1950.

"Once More, 'We Got a Hell of a Beating.' " *Life,* December 11, 1950.

Osborne, John. "U.S. Counters Mass with Mobility." *Life,* August 21, 1950.

"The Peripatetic 27th." *Life,* September 11, 1950.

"Planes Pave Way for the Landing." *Life,* September 25, 1950.

Sandoval, Stephanie. "Forgotten War Remembered." *Dallas Morning News,* July 23, 2007.

"Seoul and Victory." *Life*, October 9, 1950.
"There Was a Christmas." *Life*, December 25, 1950.
Tucker, Abigail. "One Man's Korean War." *Smithsonian*, November 2008.

AUTHOR INTERVIEWS

Lacy Barnett, November 2007
Carl Bernard, July 2007
Lyle Bradley, April 2009
Jack Brooks, March 2008
John A. Buck, August 2007
Phil Burke, January 2008
Cecil Carpenter, October 2008
Leo Dacus, October 2008
Jack Dedrick, September 2008
Gene Dixon, October 2008
Joe Dominy, October 2008
John Doody, January 2008
David Douglas Duncan, February 2009
Richard Elliott, November 2007
Glynn Ellis, April 2008
Wilbert Estabrook, June 2008
Ellie Fenton, September 2008
Bill Finnegan, December 2008
Murdoch Ford, April 2008
Wendell Ford, February 2008
Norman Fosness, March 2008
George Gentry, September 2008
Bryghte D. Godbold, June 2007, February 2008
Paul Gulick, October 2008
Charles Harrison, June 2007
Jim Holdman, September 2008
Doyle Humphreys, May 2008
Charles M. C. Jones, August 2007
Eddie Ko, September 2008
Gerald Kraus, August 2008
Delora Lewis, December 2008
Otto Lowrance, August 2008
Joe Maddox, October 2008
George Madlock, June 2008
Carl Mahakian, May 2008
Edward "Red" Martin, October 2007
Frank McDonald, July 2008

Herb Pearce, October 2007, February 2008
Miller Perry, March 2008
Conraid Pope, August 2007
Frederick "Rusty" Russell, August 2007
Charles Sands, November 2007
Hugh "Nick" Schryver, October 2007, April 2008
Emmett Shelton, December 2007
Charlie Snow, December 2007
Bob Speights, November 2007
Kenneth Stelzel, August 2008
John Stevens, October 2008
William "Pop" Thornton, March 2008
Ray Walker, November 2008
George Waslinko, September 2007
Mackie Wheeler, June 2007, September, 2007, July 2008
Robert Whited, September 2007
Fred Wilmot, May 2008
Ben Wray, November 2007
Terrell Zoch, October 2008

MISCELLANEOUS

Basic Report. Commanding General, First Provisional Marine Brigade, September 6, 1950, courtesy John Stevens.
Craig, General Edward. Excerpts from "Incidents of Service" personal journal, courtesy John Buck.
———. Interview conducted by Nicholas Canzona, May 12, 1985, courtesy John Stevens.
Fenton, Captain Francis I. "Ike" Jr. Debriefing by U.S. Marine Corps Historical Division, 1951, courtesy Hugh Schryver.
Finnegan, Sergeant William. Oral history, courtesy National Museum of the Pacific War.
"Murdoch Ford, Korea Veteran," documentary video, courtesy Murdoch Ford.
Guidon. Newsletter of B Company, First Battalion, Fifth Marines, selected issues, 1986–2006, courtesy Emmett Shelton and Hugh Schryver.
Gulick, PFC Paul. Unpublished day-to-day history of H Company, Third Battalion, First Marines, 1950–53, courtesy Paul Gulick.
"Lieutenant Baldomero Lopez, Congressional Medal of Honor," documentary video, courtesy Murdoch Ford.
Lynch, Colonel James. Unpublished report on actions of Task Force Lynch, courtesy Jack Brooks.
Pearce, Corpsman Herb. Collected letters, courtesy Herb Pearce.
———. Unpublished memoir, courtesy Herb Pearce.
Special Action Report, First Battalion, Fifth Marines, July 7–September 6, 1950, courtesy John Stevens.

Wilmot, Lieutenant Colonel Fred W. "One Soldier, Three Wars." Unpublished manuscript, courtesy Fred Wilmot.

INTERNET WEB SITES

Archives. CNN.com/local/northeast
The Chosin Few. chosenbob@bob@yahoo.com
Frozen Chosin. www.homeofheroes.com/brotherhood/chosin
Korean War Educator. www.koreanwar-educator.org
Korean War Project. www.koreanwar.org
Harry S. Truman Museum and Library. www.trumanlibrary.org
Wikipedia, the Free Encyclopedia. http://en.wikipedia.org

ACKNOWLEDGMENTS

A S HAS BEEN the case with each of the three previous military histories I've written, the dozens of veterans who graciously granted me interviews for *The Darkest Summer* are the people who truly made the book possible. Without their intimate recollections and countless courtesies, I could never have captured the full drama and desperation of those first three months of the Korean War. I owe every one of these interviewees a lasting debt of gratitude.

There are, however, several key contributors whom I would be remiss not to single out by name. Herbert Pearce, M.D., the former Navy corpsman who witnessed the blood and death of that terrible summer at agonizingly close range, was among the first Korea veterans I managed to contact. He sent or gave me stacks of materials, ranging from photographs to personal letters to old magazine articles to long personal interviews—and he also entertained my wife and me like royalty during a visit to his home in Jacksonville, Florida. Just as importantly, Herb put me in touch with a dozen or more of his old Korea buddies who also provided important information and insights. I traveled to the other side of the continent—to Southern California—to interview some of these veterans, including retired Major Jack Buck, former Corpsman Conraid Pope, and former Sergeant Frederick "Rusty" Russell, and each made unique contributions to my research. Former Sergeant Charlie Snow, another close friend of Herb's, was kind enough to come all the way from his home in Alabama to talk with me.

One of the principal figures in my narrative, Captain Ike Fenton, had been dead for several years when I began working on *The Darkest Summer*, but retired Lieutenant Colonel Hugh "Nick" Schryver, who had served as a platoon leader in Fenton's B Company, Fifth Marines, gave me more than a few personal glimpses into his CO's character and personality. Nick also loaned me a rare copy of a debriefing report made by Fenton after he was withdrawn from combat. It contained invaluable details of major battles, presented in Ike's own words, which, in effect, brought the young officer "back to life." Nick also provided contact information that made it possible for me to interview Ike's widow, Ellie Fenton, and gain additional background on her heroic husband.

I had first become acquainted with retired Marine Brigadier General Bryghte Godbold, a fellow Dallasite, in late 2001 while conducting research for *Given Up for Dead,* my book about the Battle of Wake Island, and I had learned at that time that Godbold also served in Korea. What I didn't know, until he told me in 2007, was that he had been a member of the interservice team of officers who planned the Inchon invasion and had worked personally with General Douglas MacArthur in that historic operation. The information that Bryghte provided in a series of face-to-face interviews couldn't have been obtained from any other living source, and I'm deeply appreciative—not only for the information but also for the friendship that developed between us.

Retired Marine Sergeant Mackie Wheeler, another Wake Island veteran whom I first talked with in 2002, also contributed priceless eyewitness information about his later experiences in Korea with A Company, Fifth Marines. So did Wheeler's company commander, retired Colonel John "Blackjack" Stevens, and former Sergeant Bill Finnegan, another A Company survivor.

I'm grateful to several Korean War veterans who shared vital information from unpublished manuscripts, memoirs, and obscure documents. Among them were former Army Lieutenant Colonel Fred Wilmot, former Marine PFC Paul Gulick, and former Marine Corporals Bob Speights, Murdoch Ford, and Emmett Shelton.

My heartfelt thanks also goes out to each of the more than forty other individuals who allowed me to interview them for *The Darkest Summer.* A few of these men aren't mentioned in the book simply because they weren't in Korea during the period covered by the narrative. Nevertheless, each of them added in his own way to my overall understanding of a complex and nearly forgotten war, and I'm most grateful.

Thanks, too, to my literary agent, Jim Donovan, for his wisdom and inspiration; to Roger Labrie, my editor at Simon & Schuster, for his expert guidance; and to my wife and primary copy editor, Lana Sloan, for catching innumerable typos and other mistakes in my rough drafts and putting up with me along the way.

Bill Sloan
Dallas, Texas

INDEX

ILLUSTRATION CREDITS

U.S. Army photo: 1, 5, 8, 9
National Archives: 2, 4, 6, 7, 22, 28, 31, 33, 34, 35, 37, 40
Courtesy Miller Perry: 3
Courtesy Bill Finnegan: 10
Courtesy Herb Pearce: 11, 12, 15, 16, 38
Marine Corps photo: 13, 14, 19, 20, 25, 26, 30, 36, 41
Courtesy Bryghte Godbold: 17
Courtesy Frederick "Rusty" Russell: 18, 27, 42
Courtesy Mackie Wheeler: 21
Photo © David Douglas Duncan: 23
Courtesy John Stevens: 24
U.S. Navy photo: 29
Courtesy Murdoch Ford: 32
Courtesy Hugh Schryver: 39

ABOUT THE AUTHOR

Bill Sloan is the author of more than a dozen books, the most recent being *The Ultimate Battle: Okinawa 1945—The Last Epic Struggle of World War II* and *Brotherhood of Heroes: The Marines at Peleliu, 1944—The Bloodiest Battle of the Pacific War.* During his ten years as an investigative reporter/feature writer for the *Dallas Times Herald,* he covered many of the major events and personalities of the second half of the twentieth century and was nominated for a Pulitzer Prize. He lives in Dallas, Texas.